Piercing the Veil

Other Books

by

Richard H. Jones

———

Science and Mysticism

Mysticism Examined

Reductionism

Mysticism and Morality

Curing the Philosopher's Disease

Time Travel and Harry Potter

Nagarjuna: Buddhism's Most Important Philosopher

*For The Glory of God: Christianity's Role
in the Rise and Development of Modern Science*

Indian Madhyamaka Buddhist Philosophy After Nagarjuna

One Nation Under God?

The Heart of Buddhist Wisdom

Analysis and the Fullness of Reality

Early Indian Philosophy

*Philosophy of Mysticism:
Raids on the Ineffable*

Piercing the Veil

*Comparing Science and Mysticism
As Ways of Knowing Reality*

(With 2014 Revisions)

Richard H. Jones

Jackson Square Books
New York

Distributed by www.createspace.com

Printed in the United States of America

Copyright © 2010, 2014 Richard H. Jones

All Rights Reserved

Library of Congress Cataloging-in-Publication Data

>Piercing the veil: comparing science and mysticism as ways
>   of knowing reality / Richard H. Jones
>Includes bibliographical references and index.
>ISBN: 1-4392-6682-4
>ISBN-13: 978-1-4392-6682-3
>1. Religion and science—1946- 2. Mysticism 3. Buddhism and Science
>BL 240.2.J59.2010

PREFACE

When I wrote *Science and Mysticism* (1986) more than twenty years ago about Theravada Buddhism, Advaita Vedanta, and western science as ways of knowing reality, I thought it would become part of a growing body of literature in academia on the philosophical relation of religion to science when we look at Asian religions rather than Christianity. I thought the topic of "science and mysticism" would develop as its own subdivision of the field of "science and religion." Well, that did not happen. One would be hard pressed to add even a dozen works to the section of my earlier work's bibliography on the philosophical issues of relating science and mysticism from the ensuing years. True, the *science-and-religion* field has exploded as never before, and *neuroscientific studies of meditation* have also blossomed. Outside of academia, works ignoring the philosophical issues—such as Fritjof Capra's *The Tao of Physics* (2000 [1975]) and Gary Zukav's *The Dancing Wu Li Masters* (2001 [1977])—remain popular. His Holiness the Dalai Lama has also become interested in the science (2005). Even a film—*What the BLEEP Do We Know!?*—centers on "quantum mysticism." In addition, Hindus and Buddhists continue to produce polemics showing how their religion is "scientific."

However, *philosophical works* on science and Asian religions have not been forthcoming. Alan Wallace's *Choosing Reality* (1989) deals with some of the issues in philosophy of science. (For a popular overview of philosophical implications of the scientific study of meditators, see Horgan 2003.) Outside of philosophy, there is also little scholarly interest in the relation of science and mysticism. Sal Restivo's articles on sociology of mysticism (1983) remain the only significant study in the social sciences on the subject. (For reviews of earlier comparative efforts, see Clarke, Parker-Rhodes, and Westphal 1978; Clarke 1981; Esbenshade 1982; Crease and Mann 1987, 1990; Scerri 1989; for a bibliographical review of the literature, see King 1983.)

Scholars of science-and-religion have not been very interested in Asian religions. Nor has the topic of science and Christian, Jewish, or Islamic *mysticism* been given scholarly attention beyond the occasional short (and thus not very informative) article. Mysticism is generally considered antiscientific, and so there is little reason to look at how mysticism and science might relate as ways of knowing reality or how they might interact in the history of science. Indeed, in religious studies today "religious experience" is generally explained away and mysticism is increasingly associated with irrationality, and so fewer and fewer scholars in this field would look at mystical experience as a way of knowing at all. Moreover, it is rare for any scholar to notice that "science and religion" involves more than "science and Christian theology." Scientists and philosophers in the past did show some interest in the relation of Buddhism and science. (For histories of Westerners' interest in the issue of Buddhism and science, see Verhoeven 2001, McMahan 2004 and 2008: 89-116, and Lopez 2008.) But today as Peter Harrison says, science-and-religion studies "cannot be conducted on the assumption that today the religion pole of the discussion is a kind of generic natural religion that is essentially neutral with regard to the more specific contents of various faiths" (2006: 104). Richard Payne rightly warns that the fundamental concerns of Buddhist thought differ substantially from those of Christianity and other theistic traditions and that this affects the nature of science-and-religion outside the theistic context (2002: 153-54): the difference in the "conceptual landscapes" between Buddhism and theism is not adequately recognized by a science-and-religion dialogue that is based solely on the theology of theistic traditions (ibid.: 161). This applies equally to science-and-mysticism: mysticism has been a part of all religious traditions, but the strand of religiosity that treats mystical experiences as cognitive of transcendental realities in any tradition raises issues that Christian theology in general does not cover. Certainly today the issue of "science and Buddhism" can no longer be ignored—Buddhist thought may be able to influence science, and in fact it may be influencing cognitive science today.

Scholars of Asian thought have also disregarded the issue. Scholars of Asian religions have hardly been interested in the topic of science-and-religion at all. Indeed, few scholars in Asian studies are interested in science at all, and few of the scholars who are interested in the sciences of different civilizations are interested in the issue of the possible influence of religion or mysticism on those sciences. Because modern science arose in the West and not in India and China, scholars of the latter civilizations naturally have less interest in the interaction of science and religion, especially when those cultures did not see things in terms of an interaction of "science" and "religion"—indeed, they did not even have concepts corresponding to those in the West that evolved into the modern senses of "science" and "religion." This is changing a little today. (On Hinduism and science from the perspective of "science and religion," see Gosling 2007, 2012; Dorman 2011; Edelmann 2012; Raman 2012; Brown 2012. These deal more with historical relations and reactions than with philosophical issues.)

And today there are signs of life in the neglected subfield of "science and mysticism." Under the influence of followers of the Dalai Lama, Western-trained scientists and Buddhists are entering into discussions. This is certainly encouraging—at least the field is not being handed over exclusively to New Age enthusiasts. However, while neuroscientists have become more interested in studying meditators, the *philosophical issues* surrounding the scientific results have still not gained much attention. Nor have the wider philosophical issues arising from comparing such disparate enterprises as science and mysticism received much attention. This book is an attempt to remedy the situation at least partially. (This work is not intended to replace my earlier book, which can be read for more on Buddhist and Advaita doctrines. Rather, this book, although it is not organized by the same topics, supplements that book with discussions of more recent works and the current situation. But while this book remains a follow-up to the earlier book and revises a few of the earlier book's points, it stands on its own and does not presuppose that the reader has read the first one.)

In Part I, the distinctions important to any science-and-mysticism study will be laid out. In Part II, the central points raised in the current crop of works comparing scientific and mystical theories will be examined. This section will focus on the basic doctrines of different mystical traditions, not collateral issues that may seem "unscientific." It will emphasize Buddhism since that tradition receives most of the attention in current discussions. New Age enthusiasts see science as supporting their worldview, but no attempt will be made here to cover all New Age teachings but only those matters touching on the matter of "science and mysticism." Other teachings of New Age prophets, shamans, psychics, astrologers, reincarnated seers and gurus, and alien beings from "astral planes" will be left for others to analyze (e.g., Price 2008). The starting point for Part III is the acceptance of science. There certain matters in the general philosophy of religion surrounding mysticism as a way of knowing reality will be addressed. Also a reconciliation will be set forth in which the scientifically-minded can accept mysticism as a way of knowing without limiting science, and thus the scientifically-minded may be able to have places for both science and mysticism in their lives.

Hopefully, this book will be a step toward both saving science from those who see it only through the prism of mysticism and making mysticism a little more palatable to those who value science.

* * *

The Kindle file of this book became corrupted, so I have taken the opportunity to update the text a little, although there have been only minor changes. (Chapters 1, 2, and 5 will be superseded by my forthcoming *Philosophy of Mysticism: Raids on the Ineffable*.)

Contents

Preface iii

Part I
A Prolegomenon to "Science and Mysticism" Studies

1 Mystical Experiences and Mystical Enlightenment 3
   Mysticism and Mystical Experiences
   Two Types of Mystical Experiences
   Mindfulness
   The Depth-Mystical Experience
   Mystical Enlightenment
   Differences in Metaphysics
   Notes

2 Mystical Knowledge and Religious Ways of Life 23
   Mystical Knowledge
   Perennial Philosophy and Comparisons to Science
   The Question of "Mystical Union"
   The Depth-Mystical Experience and Their Interpretations
   Weighing Mystical Experiences Against Other Religious Experiences
   Mystical Experiences and Mystical Ways of Life
   Notes

3 Mystical and Scientific Ways of Knowing 40
   Do Scientists and Mystics Approach the Same Reality?
   Being and Structures
   The Mutual Irrelevance of Science and Mysticism
   Mysticism's Possible Indirect Aid to Science
   Science's Possible Indirect Aid to Mysticism
   Science, Mysticism, and the Realm of Becoming
   Mystical Versus Scientific Attention
   Metaphysics in Mysticism
   The Divergence of Science and Mysticism
   Notes

viii Contents

4   Mysticism and the History of Science 63
    Mysticism and Pre-Modern Science
    Mysticism and the Rise of Modern Science
    Mysticism and Modern Science
    Mystical Metaphysics and Science
    Notes

5   Scientific Studies of Meditators 77
    The Openness of Mystical Experiences to Physiological Explanation
    Scientific Study Versus Mystical Practices
    Are New Theories of the Mind Needed?
    Can a New Science of the Mind be Developed?
    Can Consciousness be Studied Scientifically?
    Objective Versus Subjective Responses
    Notes

Part II
Errors in Comparing Scientific and Mystical Theories

6   Everyday Phenomena Versus Scientific Structures 95
    The Difference in Context
    The Fields of Mysticism
    The "Emptiness" of Reality
    Consciousness and the Phenomenal Realm
    The New Physics and the Old
    The Levels of Reality
    "Quantum Mysticism"
    Does the New Physics Have Implications for Society?
    Accepting the Reality of the Everyday Level
    Notes

7   Distorting Science and Mysticism 123
    Distorting Science
    Distorting Mysticism
    Was the Buddha a Scientist?
    Naturalizing Brahman
    Causation and Buddhist Dependence
    An Illustration: Fritjof Capra
    Caution and Criticism
    Notes

Contents   ix

8   What is the Alleged Relation of Scientific and Mystical Claims? 143
        Different Endeavors
        The Insubstantiality of Alleged Convergences
        Complementarity
        The Dangers of Claiming Convergence
        Notes

9   How Science and Mysticism May Intersect 156
        The Metaphysics of Mystical Systems
        Quantum Physics
        Consciousness
        Cosmology
        Biology
        Mystical Metaphysics and Science
        Can Mysticism Constrain Science?
        Science, Mystical Experiences, and Mystical Metaphysics
        Notes

10 Are Science and Mysticism Converging on One Worldview? 178
        The New Worldview
        Creating a Worldview
        Problems with the New Vision
        Notes

11 Where Do We Stand? 186

Part III
Reconciling Science and Mysticism

12 Can We Take Mystical Experiences Seriously Today? 191
        Naturalism
        "Modern Epistemic Standards"
        Science and Naturalism
        The Issue Survives
        Notes

13 Scientific Explanations of Mystical Experiences 203
        Explanations and Naturalistic Reductions
        Can Scientific Studies Confirm or Refute Mysticism?
        Science Versus the Philosophical Assessments of Mystical Claims
        Applying Occam's Razor
        The Principle of Credulity

Natural Explanations and the Question of Evidence
The Neutrality of Science
Notes

14 Constructivism and the Claim to Mystical Knowledge 226
Constructivism
Extreme Constructivism, Moderate Constructivism,
    and Nonconstructivism
Is Constructivism Applicable to the Depth-Mystical Experience
Can the Dispute be Resolved?
Notes

15 Does the Depth-Mystical Experience Have Cognitive Value? 237
Is the Depth-Mystical Experience Evidence
The Problem of Religious Diversity
The Limitation of Any Mystical Knowledge
The Role of Doctrine in Mystical Knowledge
The Impossibility of a Neutral Resolution
"Properly Basic Beliefs"
The Analogy to Sense-Perception
Ultimate Decisions
Notes

16 A Reconciliation of Science and Mysticism 261
A Worldview Incorporating Science and Mysticism
Our Metaphysical Situation in the World
Science's Contribution
Mysticism's Contribution
A Balanced Life
A World of Two Dimensions
Notes

References 279

Index 293

Part I

A Prolegomenon to "Science and Mysticism" Studies

— 1 —

Mystical Experiences and Mystical Enlightenment

At first glance, science and mysticism make strange bedfellows. The former is the paradigm of objective knowledge while the latter seems both strictly subjective and totally irrelevant to the things scientists study; indeed, many doubt that mysticism is a form of knowing at all. Both as ways of knowing and in the resulting claims about what is real, science and mysticism seem to have little in common—in fact, their claims seem to conflict. Thus, any mix would seem to be unstable. Philosophers and theologians interested in the interaction of science and religion seldom bother with the strand of religiosity giving mystical experiences central importance. Yet many popular writers, and today more and more sophisticated thinkers, are attracted to the idea that what Asian mystics have said in the past and what scientists are saying today show that the two endeavors are now converging on the same basic view of reality. However, to reach this conclusion some obviously very bright people—many practicing in the physical sciences—engage in some very sloppy reasoning and say some incredibly ridiculous things.

To see if indeed there is any substance to the alleged commonalities between science and mysticism and also to reveal both what is unique and what is not unique about science-and-mysticism within the broader field of science-and-religion, five distinctions regarding mysticism must be made. (1) *Distinctions between two types of mystical experiences and between mystics' unenlightened and enlightened states.* Most people writing on science and mysticism make broad generalizations about "mysticism" or "Eastern mysticism" and fail to make either of these key distinctions. (2) *Mystical experiences versus mystical knowledge-claims within different mystical ways of life.* Religious studies scholars can contribute to these first two topics by analyzing accounts of the differences between types of mystical experiences and between the unenlightened and enlightened states and by presenting the different mystical systems of beliefs and values within different religious traditions. (3) *The different aspects of reality that are the focus of mysticism and science.* Philosophers can analyze the different ways of knowing in science and in mysticism, the differences in mystics' and scientists' subject-matter and aims, and the relations between science and mysticism as ways of knowing reality. (4) *Any influence mysticism has had on the history of science versus the philosophical relation of the two endeavors.* Historians can analyze what role, if any, mystical traditions have played in the development of the sciences in traditional cultures and in the rise and development of modern science in the West. (5) *Scientific studies of mystical experiences and meditation versus mystics' claims of insight.* While scientists can empirically study the effects of meditation and mystical experiences on the brain and other parts of the body, philosophers can analyze the issue of whether what scientists discover in studying meditators has any bearing on the validity of the claims that mystics make about the nature of reality. Each of these five topics will be introduced in a separate chapter of Part I.

Mysticism and Mystical Experiences

"Mysticism" is more encompassing than simply practices for aiding in the generation of mystical experiences and attempts to formulate beliefs for understanding those experiences.[1] The strict sense of "mysticism" also must be distinguished from its popular sense, since it is only claims from classical Asian traditions emphasizing the former that are used in comparisons with science. (The term "mysticism" comes up in science only as an insult to dismiss some claim as irrational or not really science at all.) Traditionally, mysticism is tied to comprehensive religious ways of life and is a form of religiosity that has been a shaping force in all religious traditions. The modern reduction of mysticism to only a matter of personal experiences was solidified by William James (1958). Mysticism is more comprehensive than these experiences, although it is its experiential nature that distinguishes mysticism. Nevertheless, only certain types of experiences are central to mysticism. Nor is mysticism the "essence" or "core" of all religion—there are other ways of being religious and other types of religious experiences. Indeed, some Christian traditions today exclude mystical experiences as a way of knowing God. Nor is "mysticism" simply the name for the experiential component of all religious ways of life or for the inner life of the intensely pious or scrupulously observant followers of any strand of religiosity. One can be an ascetic or rigorous in fulfilling the demands of a religion without having the experiences that distinguish mystics. Conversely, not all people who have mystical experiences today are religious. And it is also important to note that mystical experiences need not be given any transcendental explanations: they can be given naturalistic explanations and still be accepted by naturalists as something other than a brain malfunction.

Not all "ecstatic" experiences are mystical, nor is a mystical experience a vague sense or feeling that there is more to reality than the material universe. Mysticism in the strict sense is tied to two specific types of experiences involving certain altered states of consciousness. At the center of mystical ways of life is an internal quest to still the conceptual and emotional apparatuses of the mind; in "extrovertive" mystical experiences such as "nature mysticism" and "cosmic consciousness," the mind retains sensory or non-sensory differentiations; and in "introvertive" mystical experiences, the quest culminates in a consciousness void of all sense-experiences, mental images, or any other differentiable mental content (the "depth-mystical experience"). "Mindfulness" will be the most important type of "extrovertive" experiences for this book.[2] Either way, an awareness of a fundamental component of reality is allegedly given. Mystical experiences can occur spontaneously without any cultivation or meditative preparation, and the impact of such isolated experiences may transform the experiencer. But classical mysticism was never about isolated mystical experiences.[3] Nor is this to deny that mystics may also have revelations, visions, auditions, or other numinous experiences or alleged paranormal abilities—indeed, meditation may open the mind to them.[4] But classical mystics typically downplay paranormal powers as a distraction, and visions are often considered false, merely the manifestations of various states of consciousness that fill the mind when it is being emptied or when a mystic is returning to a "dualistic" state of mind. In Zen, visions, sounds, and sensations occurring during meditation are dismissed as hallucinatory "demon states (*makyo*)." So too, other altered states of consciousness may lead to other information about reality—e.g., if paranormal powers are in fact genuine, they might have to be explained in terms of interconnections binding the universe together that are not given in ordinary experiences. Nevertheless, in making comparisons between science and the central tenets of such religious traditions as Buddhism and Advaita Vedanta, the comparisons do not involve ecstatic experiences or occult phenomena, but claims connected to mystical experiences in this sense of *emptying the mind of conceptualizations, emotions, and other differentiated content*. If nothing else, this suggests separating off these "contemplative" states of consciousness from other experiences into a separate category of "mystical experiences" for these comparative purposes.

But the objective of a mystical way of life is not to attain exotic experiences: it is to correct the way we live by overcoming our basic misconception of what is in fact real and thereby experiencing reality as it really is as best as is humanly possible—i.e., experiencing the impermanent and interconnected world independently from our conceptualizations and manipulations in mindfulness states, or experiencing the source of the self or all of the natural realm free of mediation in depth-mystical experiences. By correcting our knowledge (and in the case of mindfulness, our vision), we can align our lives with what is actually real and not suffer from trying to force reality to conform to our misguided desires; this in turn leads to ending the emotional attachments caused by the misconceptions. Of particular importance is the misconception involved in the "I-Me-Mine" complex (Austin 1998, 2006): we normally think we are an independent, self-existent entity, but in fact this "self-consciousness" is just another function of the analytic mind—one that observes the rest of our mental life. By identifying with this function, we reify a separate entity—the "self" or "ego"—and set it off against the rest of what is real. We see ourselves as separated from the rest of the universe—only one entity in a sea of distinct entities—and our ego then runs our life without any deep connection to the source of its own being. This error (called "*avidya*" in Buddhism and Advaita Vedanta) is not merely the absence of correct knowledge but an active error inhibiting our seeing reality as it is: there is no separate self-existing "ego" within the field of everyday experience but only an ever-changing web of mental and physical processes. There is no need to "kill the ego" because there is no ego to destroy to begin with—what is needed is only to free our experience from a sense of self and see what is really there.

More generally, the error is that our attention is constricted by conceptualization. The inner quest necessary for overcoming this falsification involves a process characterized in different traditions as "forgetting" or "fasting of the mind" of all conceptual and emotional content and in the case of the depth-mystical experience the elimination of all sensory input and other differentiated mental content. The Christian depth-mystic Meister Eckhart spoke of an "inner poverty," a state free from of any created will and free of wanting, knowing, or having anything; such a state leads to an identity with the being of the Godhead that is beyond God (McGinn 2006: 438-43). This involves a calming or stilling of the mind's activity—a "withdrawal" of all powers of the mind from all objects. It is a process of "unknowing" all mental content, including all prior knowledge.[5] (See, e.g., *Dao de jing*, chap. 19, 48, 64, and 81; also see Jones 1993: 47-55 on "unknowing" in the *Isha Upanishad*.[6]) For Eckhart, nothing hinders the soul from knowing God so much as time and space, for time and space fractions and God is one—God is neither this nor that, as manifold things are, and so for the soul to know God, she must not regard anythng in time (2009: 354).

Sometimes theists characterize God as "nothing" to emphasize that he is not a thing among the things in the universe. Such negative terminology emphasizes that mystics are getting away from the world of differentiation, but they do not deny that something real is involved in mystical experiences. Nor does "forgetting oneself" mean desiring to cease to exist: in the words of the medieval English author of the *Cloud of Unknowing* in his "Letter of Private Counsel," this would be "madness and contempt of God"—rather, mystical forgetting means "to be rid of the knowledge and feeling" of independent self-being. Through this emptying, mystics claim they become directly aware of a power and reality, unmediated by conceptualizations, not merely conceive a new idea or interpretation of the world.

Cultivating such awareness is central to mystical ways of life, but it should be noted that classical mystics actually discuss *mystical experiences* very little. Only in the modern era has mysticism become seen as primarily a matter of experiences, rather than an encompassing way of life. Traditionally mysticism is not about isolated "mystical experiences" or "states of consciousness," but about *aligning one's life with the nature of reality* (e.g., aligning one's will with God's). The mystical quest is not completed with any particular experience. Rather, the knowledge allegedly gained in mystical experiences is utilized in a continuing way of life. The reality supposedly experienced remains more central than any inner state of mind. Mystics discuss such things as reality, knowledge, ethics, how to cultivate mystical experiences, how to live, and the path to enlightenment. Most mystical texts are not meditation manuals but discussions of doctrines, and to read all mystical texts as works about psychology is to misread them badly in light of modern thought. Even when discussing inner mental states, mystics refer more to a transformation of character or the enduring state of enlightenment than to types of "mystical experiences," including any transitional "enlightenment experiences." This does not mean that cultivating the special mystical experiences is not the defining characteristic of mysticism or that one could attain the enlightened state without any mystical states of consciousness. Nor does the need to understand what has been experienced eliminate the need for the experiences. It only means that what mystics value most is the long-lasting *transformed state of a person* in the world and not any *momentary experiences*, no matter how insightful.

In sum, mystics claim that they realize the reality present when all the conceptual and emotional content of the mind is removed. New messages from a transcendental reality are not revealed as in visions, but mystics allegedly have a direct awareness of the bare "is-ness" of the natural realm or direct contact with a transcendental reality (the source either of the true self or of all the universe, depending on the interpretation), and thereby they gain a new knowledge of reality. Both their knowledge and their will are corrected (since the will is based on the sense of an independent ego within the everyday world that is now seen to be baseless); and, free of self-will, mystics can now align their life with the way reality truly is and thereby end the mental suffering that results from constantly trying to manipulate reality to fit our own artificial images and desires.

Two Types of Mystical Experiences

Not all meditation is the same: there are many different techniques (concentration techniques, relaxation techniques, mindfulness techniques, ecstatic dance or other rituals that overload the senses), and different aspects of the inner life can be the subject of practice (attention, feelings, bodily awareness, and so forth). (See Shear 2006.) Nor can meditation in a religious tradition be reduced simply to breathing exercises. (E.g., see Lopez 2008: 197-207 on the full ritual of a Tibetan monk's complex visualization meditation.) Mystical traditions also have analytical exercises less directly related to emptying the mind. Overall, the inward mystical process has two different tracks. Thus, there is not one "mystical experience," but different experiences of two significantly different types: of importance here are the *mindfulness state of consciousness* and the *depth-mystical experience*. The quest may lead to sensing a connectedness or unity to the flux of experienced phenomena that can be seen when our mind is free of our normal conceptual and emotional apparatuses (the mindfulness state) or to an awareness of a transcendental reality underlying at least all of the experiencer's subjective phenomena or in fact all objective phenomena (the depth-mystical experience). Both types are allegedly cognitive.

Thus, both experiences are about the "is-ness" of things apart from the conceptual divisions we impose on it—the being of the world or an alleged transcendental source. Bare consciousness is experienced in the depth-mystical experience, from which mystics may conclude that everything is grounded in consciousness or in fact is consciousness. But it may only be that they are aware of beingness as conscious in such experiences. That is, through an inner experiences free of differentiable content (sensory input, mental images, and so forth), depth-mystics would consider beingness to be consciousness since consciousness is what is directly experienced. Thus, a characterization is that more neutral to any ontological questions is that mystics are aware of beingness in such experiences as consciousness.

The natural world must also be distinguished from the transcendental reality involved in the depth-mystical experience: mindfulness remains within the dynamic realm of becoming, while the depth-mystical experience delves into the changeless source underlying subjectivity or the entire natural realm. Mindfulness thus is not simply a low-level, failed, or partial experience of the depth-mystical reality: it is a distinct type of mystical experience in which the mind still has differentiated content, while the content of the depth-mystical experience is undifferentiatable consciousness or the ground of being alone. Mindfulness involves an alleged insight into the ultimate construction of the world of change, and depth-mysticism involves an alleged insight into depth of the experiencer or the source of the world of change. The depth-mystical experience, unlike mindfulness, traditionally is alleged to involve a reality transcending the natural realm. Thus, these experiences cannot be put on one continuum. If there is a transcendent source to the world that is experienced in the depth-mystical experience, there may be more to that reality than is experienced. Thus, the "transcendent" reality is also the ground of this world and so is also "immanent." It is also experiencable, and what is retained from the experience is a sense of fundamental beingness and oneness.

The meditative techniques differ for the two tracks: one for stabilizing consciousness, and one for observing what is experienced free of mental interference. The resulting physiological effects also differ. (See Hood 1997 and Dunn, Hartigan, and Mikulas 1999 for empirical evidence of the differences.) Mindfulness involves a passive receptivity free of any urge to manipulate and an attentiveness to what is presented free of conceptualization in the sensory or other events occurring in our mind (as with Buddhist *vipashyana* techniques). The depth-mystical experience involves a concentrative, "one-pointed" focusing of attention, leading ultimately to emptying our mind of all differentiated content (as with Buddhist *shamatha* techniques). The Transcendental Meditation mantra technique falls in the latter category. Meditators may practice different techniques on both tracks at different times, since each track can aid the other in calming and focusing the mind. That there are also other types of meditations in mystical traditions that involve the analytical mind (e.g., the *koan* practices of Zen Buddhism) should also be noted. (It should also be noted that meditating rigidly through a set technique for years may itself lead simply to a new habitual way of seeing the world and not to freedom from the conceptualizing process.)

Meditators, however, cannot *force* the mind to become still by following any technique or any series of steps. Mystical training techniques can lessen a sense of self and thus facilitate mystical experiences, but they cannot force the complete end to a sense of self—as long as we are trying to "get enlightened," we are still in an acquisitive state of mind and cannot succeed in becoming selfless. No act of self-will nor any preparatory activity can force mystical experiences to occur: we must surrender, simply let go. In short, no regiment of actions can force us to become selfless. But once meditators stop trying to force the mind to change, the mind calms itself and the mystical experiences occur automatically. To mystics, it seems that they are being acted upon: in the depth-mystical experience, the transcendent ground appears active and the meditator passive; in mindfulness, natural phenomena shine forth unmediated by our mental meddling.

Mindfulness

It is language that enables us to crystalize conceptualizations of what we want and what we think should be, thus leading to frustration, uncertainty, anxiety, and anger when reality turns out not to be as we wish. Such conceptualizations come to stand between us and what is real, interfering with our view of what is actually real. Thus, language-guided perception is the opposite of mystical mindfulness: through language, we see things as they were or might be or how we want them to be rather than how they are, and we act accordingly.[7] Through habituation, our everyday perceptions, and indeed the rest of our consciousness, become reduced to no more than seeing the very categories that our mind has itself created as being present in external the world—consciousness, in the words of the very nonmystical Willard van Orman Quine, becomes only the reaction of our mind to our own prior reactions. Mindfulness counters this: it loosens this grip that the concepts we ourselves create have on our sense-experiences, inner experiences, and actions. Even concepts of time and a separate ego vanish. Mindfulness results in seeing the flow of sensory input and the inner activity of the mind as it is free of memories, anticipations, emotional reactions, and the normal process of reifying the content into distinct objects based on our conceptualizations. Thus, mindfulness states of consciousness still have sensory or non-sensory mental content, but some or all the structuring normally associated with such content has been removed. Such mindfulness may be a transient experience, but it also may become an enduring state of transformed consciousness.

Thus, mindfulness exercises in working, walking, or just sitting destructure the conceptual frameworks structuring our perceptions. The resulting focus of attention produces an inner calm and clarity of awareness. This is not so much a change in the input of our sensory consciousness and inner awareness as a change in our relation to that content. Our usual thinking and experiencing both fade away. Normally, we abstract discrete, apparently permanent objects from experience and react to these creations. But mindfulness dissolves the conceptual boundaries we have imposed on reality. We normally see rugs and hear trucks—with pure mindfulness we would see patches of color and texture free of rugness and hear sourceless noises. This is a "bare attention" to what is presented to our senses, with no accompanying intellectual expectations or emotional reactions. It is not a trance-like state or self-hypnosis or a state of unconsciousness—the meditator remains fully awake—but it does involve a complete focus on what is being experienced.[8]

Through mindfulness our awareness becomes focused on the bare beingness of the natural realm and the impermanence and interconnectedness of it all. In the resulting state, an experience of a uniformity and interconnectedness to all we experience in the realm of perpetual change comes through—the simplicity of the "that-ness" or "such-ness" of phenomenal reality presented to the senses—accompanied by more intensity to the sensory input that is now freed from being routinely catalogued by our preformed characterizations.[9] In particular, a sense of a distinct ego within the natural world vanishes. The conceptual border separating us from the rest of the natural world has been broken, with the resulting sense of an intimate connectedness to everything. This sense of beingness can lead to the sensory glow in a transfigured sensory realm associated with "nature mysticism" or to a sense of the living presence of a timeless reality of light and love that is immanent to the natural world associated with "cosmic consciousness." This can come in various levels of intensity, but it always involves a profound sense of connectedness with the natural world, of knowledge, and of contact with reality (Marshall 2005).[10] One can have the joy of ecstasy or the abiding peace of well-being.[11] Theists may feel universal love or deep gratitude for existing or that a transcendental god is immanent to his creation. (It should be noted that mystics during mystical experiences do not experience the "trembling in the presence of God" involved in revelations, although mystics may feel the fear and distress of abandonment if they are not making spiritual progress. Any negative states during meditation are attributed to something demonic or the meditator's own mind, not projected onto a transcendental reality.[12]) One can be aware that there is content in your mind without dropping out of the experience, unlike in a depth-mystical experience. But if an experience involves a sense of the presence of a transcendental reality or the "mind of the world," then the mind is still not emptied of all differentiated content as with the depth-mystical experience and so will remain a mindfulness state focused on the inner or outer realm of becoming.

With mindfulness, we see what is presented to our mind as it is, free of our purposes, feelings, desires, and attempts at control. We do not pick and choose, setting one thing against another. We are living fully in the present, witnessing whatever arises in our consciousness without judging and without a sense of possession, and we respond spontaneously. (This spontaneity does not necessarily mean that mystics are acting free of values and beliefs; in their enlightened state, mystics may instead have internalized values and beliefs from their religious tradition or another source.) To most of us, the present is only the intersection of the past and the future; it is fully structured by our past categories and our future intentions and expectations. To mystics, as long as we have this intentional mind, we have no access to reality: only with a mindful mind do we no longer identify with our thoughts and emotions but simply observe things free of a sense of self, as if seeing events from a third-person point of view. There is a shift in consciousness from mental categorizations to the sheer beingness of things. Awareness is freed from the dominance of our habitual categorizations and anticipations, and our mind becomes tranquil and lucid. Awareness is no longer tied to the images we manufacture—i.e., in Buddhist terms, it no longer "abides" anywhere or "grasps" anything. In the words of the Dalai Lama, "nondual perception" is "the direct perception of an object without the intermediary of a mental image." Note that he is not denying that there is something there to be perceived—only now we see it as it really is, free of conceptualizations. The false world we create of distinct, self-contained entities is seen through, and phenomenal reality appears as it actually is. The mind mirrors only what is there, without adding or distorting whatever is presented. Mental categories no longer fix our mind, and our attention shifts to the such-ness of things, although some conceptual structuring (supplied in part by the metaphysics of the mystic's religious tradition) will remain present in all but a pure mindful state in which we have sensations but no structured perceptions. Thus, except in the case of pure mindfulness, mindful states will differ both in their content and in the structuring from different conceptual frameworks.

We like to think we normally see the external world "as it really is," but neuroscientists have found otherwise. There is evidence that our conscious and unconscious mind *creates* an image of the world, not merely *filters or structures* sensory data. (See Peters 1998: 13-15.) Experiments show that our mind "corrects" and constructs things (e.g., filling in visual blind spots). More generally, apparently our brain automatically creates a coherent, continuous narrative out of all the sensory input it receives. We see a reconstruction of the world, and this leads to the question of whether our visual world is only a "grand illusion." Overall, the brain seems to have difficulty separating fantasies from facts—it sees things that are not there and does not see some things that are (Newberg and Waldman 2009: 5). It does not even try to create a fully detailed map of the external world; instead, it selects a handful of cues and then fills in the rest with conjecture, fantasy, and belief (ibid.). Our brain constructs a subconscious map that relates to our survival and another map that reflects our conscious awareness of the world (ibid.: 7). Mindfulness interferes with the fabrication, making us more alert and attentive, and thus lets in more of the world "as it really is."

But it is another sense of "illusion" that is the central concern of mindfulness mystics: conceptualizing off "real entities" from the flow of events. To convey the sense of what is real and what is "illusory", the *Chandogya Upanishad* gives the analogy of a clay pot (VI.1.3-4). The clay represents what is real (i.e., the permanent beingness lasting before and after whatever shape it is in) and the pot what is "illusory" (i.e., the temporary, dependent, impermanent, and changing form the clay is in at the moment). If we smash the pot, the "thing-ness" is destroyed, but what is real in the pot (the clay) continues unaffected. Mindfulness mystics do not dismiss the world as "unreal" or "illusory" in any stronger sense. (Even for the depth-mystic Shankara the world cannot be dismissed as a complete illusion—the world is neither the same as the transcendental Brahman nor distinct from it, and so its ontological status is indescribable [*anirvacaniya*].[13]) That is, mindfulness still involves a realism about the experienced realm, but it is a realism not grounded in an awareness of differentiations or linguistic distinctions.

Since language refers to the differentiations in the realm of becoming and is itself a matter of differentiations, mystics always have trouble with applicability of language to undifferentiated beingness—in particular, language makes beingness into a thing among things when it is not. Moreover, apparently a nonlinguistic aspect of the mind is attuned to beingness, and thus conceptualizations remove us from the proper state of mind to experience beingness. Mindfulness mystics can be called "linguistic antirealists" since they do not think that reality is mirrored in any conceptualizations: words and concepts denote distinct entities, and reality is not so constructed. But this cannot be equated with antirealism in philosophy of science, i.e., the denial of unobservable entities—an issue mystics can take no stand on from their experiences alone (as discussed in Chapter 6). But mindfulness mystics are generally realists in the metaphysical sense of "realism": the world's beingness is affirmed, even if it may be dependent upon a god or impersonal transcendental source. Even though mystics uniformly reject the idea of ontologically distinct and self-contained entities within the everyday world, enlightened Buddhists are still said to see the phenomenal realm "as it really is" (*yathabhutam*). In short, the world is not a subjective illusion. There is a non-subjective world, and minds now are also part of the real world, if perhaps dependent on the body. The Indic metaphysical belief that minds or karma may have produced the entire natural realm complicates the picture, but this still does not warrant solipsism of an individual consciousness. Such common-sense realism does not have a built-in correspondence theory of epistemology or any views on materialism, determinism, reductionism, or naturalism, although many people who see parallels between mysticism and science try to read the latter philosophical positions into metaphysical realism in order to conclude from the latter's problems that realism is refuted. For example, realism cannot be equated with the belief in solid objects (contra Ricard and Thuan 2001: 113).

Misled by the appearance of permanence and our categorization of what is experienced, the unenlightened "create" distinct objects by imposing ideas onto the what is real—i.e., reifying our conceptualizations into a world of multiple, distinct entities. Nevertheless, what is actually there independent of our conceptualizations is real. In short, we take the conceptual and perceptual distinctions we ourselves create as capturing what is "real" in the world. This includes the idea of a distinct self—a "skin-enclosed ego." Buddhists affirm that there is thinking and other mental events, but no thinker: if we think of the "person" as a string of beads, there is a succession of beads (momentary mental events) but no string. The discrete "objects" of sense-experience and introspection are "unreal" only in this limited sense: what is behind the conceptual differentiations remains real. While on the path to enlightenment, a mindfulness mystic sees individual "objects," but it is their beingness that is the focus of attention, and once enlightened any self-contained individuality in the experiencer or the experienced world is seen as illusory.

In sum, we misread sensory experience and construct an illusory world of multiple realities out of what is real in the phenomenal world. What we conceptually separate as "entities" are only eddies in a constantly flowing and integrated field of events. The world of multiple "real" (permanent, self-contained) entities is an illusion but not what is really there—the eddies in the flow of events are not unreal, but are simply not isolated entities, unconnected to the rest of the flow. The alleged discrete entities are the "discriminations" that Buddhists deny are real. Nevertheless, there is a reality behind the conceptions, and the realm of becoming is not a featureless mass that we must treat as one indistinct whole. Rather, it is a collection of interconnected and impermanent parts. For example, a tree is not identical to the earth, water, and sun light that it is dependent upon for its life, but neither is it an entity totally distinct from the rest of reality; its configuration of elements remains a unique and identifiable part contributing to the interconnected whole of reality. Theorists in the Buddhist Hinayana Abhidharma schools (such as the Theravadins and Sarvastivadins) set forth in elaborate detail the elements constituting the experienced world (the *dharmas*); these elements are never denied as existing, even though they are empty of anything that establishes a permanent, independent nature and thus are "unreal" in that sense. In mindfulness mysticism in general, the interconnectedness of everything becomes prominent (and Buddhists set forth a theory of the arising and falling of conditioned things), but this does not deny the reality of what is interconnected.[14] Only the permanence and the independence of apparently distinct entities are rejected.

Thus, with mindfulness we see the mundane with fresh perceptions. It removes habituation from our perceptions. It renews attention to all that is presented and ends the role of concepts guiding our attention. All attention is "purified" regardless of what is observed. Mindfulness is thus not about attaining a higher state of consciousness unconnected to observations, or seeing something special about the world, or anything more (or less) profound than seeing the flow of the world as it is free of the constraints of our conceptualizations and emotions.

The Depth-Mystical Experience

With the depth-experience, attention shifts from the realm of constant change to an inner wellspring of beingness lying outside the realm of time and change. The inward turn is not a matter of changing the content of our mind (e.g., acquiring new scientific knowledge), nor of replacing the content with an image of nothingness (e.g., a big, black, silent, empty space), but of emptying the mind of all conceptual, emotional, sensory, and any other internal distinguishable content. The concentration of attention leads to an inward stillness and silence. This state of conscious awareness is separated from the flow of sensory and conceptual content, leading to a state of lucid awareness supposedly having ontological significance. (That there also are *unconscious* processes operating in ordinary states of mind—called "*samskaras*" in Buddhism—should not be overlooked [Peters 1998: 2]. According to Indic mystical schools, these are ended in enlightenment.)

The experiencer is free of all mental differentiations yet is still awake—in fact, mystics assert that only then are we conscious to the fullest extent possible for a human being. In ordinary states of mind, it is not uncommon to be so caught up in an experience that we have no sense of self or time and if we stop to reflect on those ideas we drop out of the experience. But when mystics look back on their depth-mystical experiences they have no memories of any differentiated content at all—the state is filled with consciousness, but there is no sense of a flow of time or any distinguishable content. It cannot even be called "self-awareness" since the experiencer is not aware of a subject experiencing anything—there seems to be no subject or object and no sense of ownership. That is, there is no sense of personal possession of this awareness since it is devoid of all personal psychological characteristics. Indeed, it does not seem to be an *individual's* consciousness at all but something transcending all observers: it is an event of "pure consciousness." Unlike mindfulness, such a state of consciousness can only be transitory, not a permanent state of a person, and so can be called an "experience."

When the mind is stilled completely, an awareness bursts forth allegedly of a dimension or aspect of reality that is not known through ordinary sense-experience and self-awareness: an unmediated implosion of reality, with a resulting sense of fundamental reality, certitude, and typically finality. The reality can be called "transcendental" since, if it exists, it exists outside the natural realm and is not open to ordinary experience—yet it is open to being experienced directly by beings within the natural realm. It is a depth-dimension to the experiencer or to the entire natural world, depending on the interpretation adopted. It can be characterized as an awareness of beingness, i.e., a sense of existence as such with no distinctions without any subject of the event or any other content.

The experience involves a modification of our consciousness, but there is no experience *of* any object (including consciousness) since there can be no object present that is set off from the experiencer when the mind is truly empty of all objectifiable content. There is not even an awareness of the experiencer. What is experienced becomes a mental object for the experiencer's understanding only after the experience is over—then, the mind makes an image of the reality, and so what was experienced becomes mentally another object among objects. What occurs is not "objective" in the sense of an awareness of something existing independently of the experiencer, nor "subjective" in the sense of experiencing something the experiencers themselves create. Rather, there is a sense of simply being rather than experiencing something. Self-awareness is the closest analogy since this cognitive awareness too does not involve sense-experience or any experience of a object distinct from the experiencer. But it too becomes an object of consciousness.

Is the depth-mystical experience truly free of differentiated features? Even in the Abrahamic traditions, there are mystics who affirm a "Godhead beyond God" free of all features. If the reality experienced were truly ineffable, we could label it but not know anything more about it; thus, we could not deduce beliefs and values from it. Do theists then simply read in features of a god into a neutral experience? Prior to the experience, they were already committed to a reality that is personal in nature, has knowledge, and is endowed with moral goodness. They want to see the power of love innate in everything—the universe is not dead matter, but is driven by love as its self-emptying energy. Theists may believe they need a personal god to make the transcendent religiously available to us. But do theists *experience* such properties in the moments of the depth-mystical experience, or do they return from an experience that conveyed reality and certitude and merely transfer their previous beliefs to this, thus producing an afterglow of a loving god? The beliefs of nontheistic mystics and theists such as Meister Eckhart suggest the latter—i.e., that what is experienced is devoid of any features that can be liken to anything in the natural world, including personhood. Consider Advaita. According to Shankara, Brahman is beyond all our characterizations. In our ordinary state of consciousness, we can see Brahman as a theistic god (*saguna brahman*) or as the opposite of all features (*nirguna brahman*), but both are our conceptions—Brahman-in-itself is beyond all attempts at conception, including Advaita's standard characterizations of reality (*sat*), consciousness (*citta*), and bliss (*ananda*) (*Brihadaranyaka Upanishad-bhashya* II.3.1; *Brahma-sutra-bhashya* III.2.22). Traditions that give more specifics to the transcendent do not necessarily do so in theistic terms. For example, in Daoism the Way (*dao*) is the constant but dynamic source of both being and the order underlying change in the natural world, with the emphasis on the ordering aspect. There is no suggestion of a theistic god who intervenes to help certain parts of his creation; rather the Way is a nonpersonal, law-governed guiding force—a self-giving source that benefits all equally.

It should also be noted that there is a *transitional state* from the depth-mystical experience back to more ordinary states of consciousness. During this transition, images, prior beliefs, and other dualistic phenomena flood back into the mind. This state is not part of the depth-mystical experience itself, but it may well be seen as part of the "total package" between the departure from dualistic consciousness to the depth-mystical state and the return to dualistic consciousness (see Sullivan 1995: 56-57), and thus mystics may well mistake its content for being what is experienced in the depth-mystical experience itself. The transition is an unconscious process and does not seem to be coming from the experiencer and so it seems objectively real. Any theistic content may come from this state.

In sum, the depth-mystical state of consciousness itself is free of any object of attention and hence is not intentional. It can be called a "contentless awareness"—a light not illuminating any object. Normally, we see only the objects and not the light, but in a depth-mystical experience the light is all there is. (This does not change the experiencer's ontological status since the light was already always there.) This "light" is the content of the depth-mystical experience, even though mystics are not aware that this is the case until the experience is over—there is no space in the experience itself to make labeling the content possible. Thus, the mind is not truly *empty*: it has a positive content—a "pure" consciousness or the ground of reality is now fully occupying it—even though the experiencer is not aware of the new content while the experience is occurring. But the mind is empty of all the differentiated content that normally occupies it—any object of awareness (sensory input, ideas, sense of self, memories, feeling, and so forth) or even an awareness of awareness itself. If the mind were in fact truly empty, mystics would have nothing to remember after the experience, and it would be hard to see how the event could be seen as an "experience" or "awareness" or as even being *conscious* at all. In that case, it could not have any impact on the experiencer. However, mystics are not unconscious nor do they suffer from amnesia for the period they undergo a depth-mystical experience: a sense of the new content, and an accompanying sense of profundity and bliss, is retained after the experience.

Mystical Enlightenment

Mystical experiences may be partial and not involve the complete emptying of a sense of self. So too, different types of mystical and nonmystical experiences may occur at different stages on a path that leads to a permanent ending of the sense of self. "Mystical enlightenment" can be defined as an enduring state of consciousness in which a sense of an individual ego in the natural world has been completely ended by means of the mystical cultivation discussed above. It involves knowledge of the fundamental nature of reality (as defined by each religious tradition) and subsequently living in accordance with it (typically by following the ethics of the mystic's tradition). Emotionally, fear, anger, and anxiety melt away as one realizes the true state of things. For depth-mysticism, enlightenment involves an insight into the underlying self or source of the natural realm. For mindfulness mysticism, enlightenment is different: its insight involves seeing the lack of any separate, independent ego cut off from the rest of the natural realm, and also seeing all of this realm as it truly is—interconnected and constantly changing. Buddhist nirvana is an example: it is the state of a person in which the "fires" of hatred, greed, and the root delusion concerning permanence have gone out. It is not merely accepting the proposition that "all is impermanent"—the unenlightened may well agree with that—but uprooting the most persistent sense of permanence ("I-Me-Mine") and actually seeing that it world is impermanent. In a Buddhist analogy, it is a case of not merely knowing the fact that water quenches thirst but actually drinking water.

Mystical enlightenment may be the result of a gradual spiritual development in which the sense of selflessness is finally completed with no special "enlightenment experience." But there may also be a sudden peak enlightenment experience—a flash of insight, accompanied by joy and the surprise of being hit by the unexpected. ("Sudden enlightenment" is not necessarily a spontaneous mystical experience—it too may have been preceded by arduous training for a long period of time.) However, the enlightened state of mind is constituted by an abiding sense of fundamental reality. The mystic's state of consciousness is transformed. Even repeated depth-mystical experiences do not guarantee this transformation. Conversely, falling out of enlightenment involves not simply forgetting some knowledge-claims—it is a change in consciousness.

Mystical experiences, however, cannot resolve the problem of the "meaning of life." In themselves, these experiences do not answer why we are here, how we fit into the scheme of things, or what the meaning of the world is. They may give an overwhelming sense of reality and convey a sense that everything is all right as is. But these experiences focus attention on living totally in the present, not on the time-framework of one's whole life or on the question of whether things fit into a big picture. The experiences may convey a trust in reality, even though no future-oriented hope is involved. No sense of a plan or purpose to the natural realm is given in the empty depth-mystical experience. Nor is a sense of any teleological causes at work in nature. Rather than feeling self-centered and isolated from the rest of reality, mystics may feel fully integrated into the natural world or more connected to a cosmic source, and any fear of death may be removed. They may feel complete and at home in the universe. Mystics might previously have thought life was meaningless and then after having a mystical experience think everything in the world is as it should be or is even inevitable as it is. In fact, the acceptance of life as "meaningful as is" may paradoxically end our mind's search for any specific meaning or purpose or any other explanation of reality.[15] Thus, the sense of connectedness may end the existential quest to see one's life as meaningful, even though no new facts or a statement of a meaning is given. Resulting claims on the meaning of life may sound mundane and trite since no new information is given, and the mystics may be content with the world as it is. In any case, mystical experiences do not provide a specific or complete answer to the meaning of the universe. Each particular religious tradition's ideas of the purpose of life, like the understanding of the significance of mystical experiences themselves, come from considerations outside of these experiences, although the experience would be one such factor. The mystic can, to use Meister Eckhart's phrase, "live without asking why" within the way of life defined by his or her tradition.

In depth-mysticism, our everyday sense of a distinct self—the linguistically- and socially-constructed ego—is replaced by the continuous inflowing of what is deemed the ground of either the true self or all of reality (depending on the particular mystic's beliefs). The result is a continuous mystical awareness. The enlightened state in depth-mysticism can be seen as a continual state of mindfulness, but it is one in contact with an alleged transcendental reality. It is a continuing state of consciousness with a permanent interior stillness even while the person is engaged in thought and activity—i.e., one remains aware of the center of one's being while still remaining fully conscious of thoughts and sensations. Because mindfulness states differ, there is no one "enlightened state"—the knowledge each mystic brings to enlightenment will structure his or her awareness differently.

Different enlightened mystics also make different knowledge-claims (and then take their experiences as experiential confirmation of those claims). But in all cases, the sense of a separate self in the everyday world is replaced by a continuing inflowing of the ground of the true self or of all of reality. More depth-mystical experiences and other types of experiences (e.g., paranormal and numinous experiences) may also occur, but the sense of a separately existing self has been eradicated.

With enlightenment, the experiences and actions we have in the natural world still remain. Even under classical Advaita, the enlightened cannot help but see diversity. From Shankara on, Advaitins have had trouble reconciling their metaphysics with this persistence of a perception of diversity after enlightenment. Shankara admitted that the "dream" world of multiplicity does not disappear for the enlightened, comparing the situation to a person with an eye disease seeing two moons even though he knows there is really only one (*Brahma-sutra-bhashya* IV.1.15).[16] Thus, the enlightened *know* that reality is actually one, but they still *see* the diversified phenomenal world. They overcome the perception of duality only during periods of introvertive one-pointed concentration (*samadhi*) (Nelson 1996: 45). This also means that the enlightened have not escaped the world into a trance, nor are they otherwise incapacitated. That the enlightened, despite their new awareness and the inner stillness at the core of their being, still live in a world of distinctions is evidenced by the fact that many teach others and leave writings. Many have also been active in the world socially and as administrators of religious orders. Indeed, the mere fact that they *speak* is evidence enough: any language necessarily makes distinctions, and while the enlightened's ability to use language may be in abeyance during certain mystical experiences, their ability to use language in the enlightened state shows that they do in fact make and understand distinctions. But unlike the unenlightened, the enlightened do not project these conceptual distinctions onto reality, thereby avoiding the creation of a false worldview of multiple discrete, "real" objects. That is, they can draw linguistic distinctions about phenomena without seeing ontological distinctions as the result. Thereby, they can use language to navigate in the world of diversity.

Thus, with enlightenment the world of diversity returns. But the enlightened remain in touch with the insight they have gained, and they now engage the world with a new mental clarity and calm. They greet all circumstances without distractions. They now live in the world in a state of freedom from the attachments and concerns generated by a false sense of an individual self—they act literally selflessly, i.e., free of a sense of self.

Differences in Metaphysics

Before closing, it is also important to note that the basic difference between depth-mysticism and mindfulness mysticism results in different types of metaphysics. The former involves a depth to reality that transcends the natural universe, while the latter involves the contents of our surface-world. Both types of mysticism involve beingness: depth-mysticism involves a *source* of being that transcends the world, while mindfulness mystics are concerned with the *phenomena of the experienced world* of diversity. Thus, depth-mysticism involves a "vertical" dimension to reality that is timeless, permanent, and changeless, while mindfulness metaphysics involve the constantly changing "horizontal" world of becoming.

This difference in dimensions also affects other concepts. First, there are two types of "nonduality" corresponding to the two types of metaphysics. There is the depth-type (the nonduality of the being of the source of reality and the experienced "dream" realm) and the mindfulness type (the absence of a plurality of independently existing, "real" entities within our experienced world). Both are referred to as "nonduality," and this may lead to confusions since they do not involve the same level of reality: the former involves the depth-dimension of the source of beingness, and the latter the surface-dimension of the realm of becoming. In short, there is a difference between "vertical" and "horizontal" nonduality. So too, there are corresponding different senses of "oneness": realizing the one simple, undivided reality of the depth-experience (interpreted as either our true self or the source of being common to everything) versus realizing that you are not an isolated entity but part of one interconnected, impermanent whole that is the natural realm. Thus, there are two classes of "enlightenment" corresponding to a depth oneness in depth-mysticism or a horizontal oneness in mindfulness mysticism, with the actual enlightening knowledge differing between traditions. There are also corresponding vertical/horizontal differences in the idea of "illusion": in depth-mysticism, it refers to the whole natural universe being less than fully real when compared to the transcendental source; in mindfulness, it refers to conceptualizing "illusory" discrete entities from the flow of things.

Notes

1. The term "mystical" entered the Christian lexicon in reference to mystical *theology* and the mystical *meaning* of the Bible, not a special class of *experiences*. (For histories of the term, see Bouyer 1980 and Schmidt 2003.) The term derives from the Latin word "*mysticus*" and ultimately from the Greek "*mustikos.*" The root is the Greek "*muo,*" meaning "closed" (as in "closed eyes" or "closed mouth") and hence "hidden." It came to mean silence or secret, i.e., what should not be revealed to other people. The word "mystics" and the abstract noun "mysticism" are only modern inventions of the seventeenth century, but the adjective "mystical" goes back to the second century, when it was adapted by early Christian theologians to refer, not to an inexpressible experience, but to the mystery of "the divine" in certain liturgical matters such as the invisible God being present in sacraments and to the hidden meaning of scriptural passages, i.e., how Christ was actually being referred to in Old Testament passages ostensibly about something else. Only in the modern era, when spirituality was separated from general theology, did the term come to refer exclusively to certain types of inner religious experiences and states of consciousness. This is not to deny that there were mystics in the modern sense in early Christianity, but they were called

"contemplatives." (That "contemplation" in medieval Europe also involved *philosophical reflection* should be remembered—there was no hard and fast line between mystics and philosophers when philosophy, following the Greeks, was considered a way of life leading to an inner transformation. Both philosophizing and meditating were "contemplative" activities.) Dionysius the Pseudo-Areopagite first used "mystical theology" to refer to a direct experience of God, and by the Middle Ages, when Christians contemplatives were expounding the mystical allegorical and symbolic meaning of biblical passages beyond its literal meaning, the meanings they saw were ultimately based on the idea of direct experiences of God. "Mystical theology" then meant the *direct awareness of God*, not a discipline of theology in the modern sense; and the "mystical meaning" of the Bible meant *the hidden message for attaining God directly*.

2. "Extrovertive" mystical experiences and states should not be designated "surface-mysticism" since that makes them sound superficial. So too, "dualistic mysticism" may be taken as claiming that this mystical experience entails a dualistic metaphysics; and the terms "deconstructing mysticism," "differentiated-content mysticism," "differentiated mystical consciousness," and "unstructured-content mysticism" are all too inelegant. Nor is mindfulness necessarily "extrovertive" since it may also involve internal mental differentiations and not only sensory input; thus, it can be introvertive. The distinction between mystical experiences with differentiable content, whether they are introvertive or extrovertive, and those without any such content seems more important since they may involve different mental states. Perhaps the terms *"nomenal mysticism"* and *"phenomenal mysticism"* capture the distinction better.

3. Spontaneous mystical experiences raise a definitional problem. Does having one or more such experience make the experiencer a "mystic"? Must a spontaneous mystical experience transform the experiencer for the label to apply? Or must one undertake mystical practices or even a full mystical way of life with a path to enlightenment? On the other hand, what if one is on a path but has not had any mystical experiences yet?

4. *Visions* are excluded from this definition, not out of a sexist animus (most women called "mystics" are more properly classified as "visionaries"), but because most people who have made comparisons between science and Asian mysticism have relied on traditions that downplay visions and revelations. (However, some scholars still see no distinction in making parallels [e.g., Raman 2008].) But the distinction is not absolute since people may have more than one type of experience and also may interact with others within their religious tradition who have had other types of experiences when developing doctrines.

5. The analytical mind does not give up control without a fight. It can reassert itself during meditation in the form of anxiety and fear; there may also be visions and other alternative states of consciousness. And it returns quickly after a depth-mystical experience.

6. "Unknowing" is also used in another sense in the work of Eckhart and other Christians: not as a process of emptying the mind, but as a positive knowledge of God that so contrasts with ordinary knowledge that we cannot even call it "knowing" at all.

7. Mystical mindfulness should be distinguished from *everyday mindfulness*. Both involve attention, but mystical mindfulness involves an "unknowing"—emptying one's mind of all conceptual and emotional content. Everyday mindfulness involves keeping some idea in mind—e.g., being mindful of others or of our rights or of our status in society. For a study of the latter type of mindfulness, see Langer 1989.

8. The alternative is that the state of "pure consciousness" is a state of *unconsciousness*—i.e., the meditator is awake but not conscious (Pyysiäinen 2001). But if mystics retain any sense of reality or of anything else, how can the state be classified as "unconscious"?

And how could it seem to be so profound or, indeed, have any emotional impact on the experiencer at all? But some scholars do think that. Alan Wallace quotes a Christian scholar who thinks that mystics undergo a "profound cataleptic trance" manifested by some psychotics and long-term coma patients (2003: 7). But Wallace rightly asks why Buddhist contemplatives would undergo long years of training to achieve a state that could readily be achieved through a swift blow to the head with a heavy, blunt object (ibid.)?

9. The classical Chinese idea that nature is "self-so (*ziran*)" should not be added to this list since it has nothing to do with these other concepts; rather, it is the idea that nature operates *autonomously* and has no external cause or agent operating on it. The unnameable Way is self-so (*Daodejing* 4, 11, 25, and 40). But the idea that the natural universe is "self-organizing" through an imminent Way was led people to see parallels to the "spontaneous order" of contemporary complexity theory. The two ideas do have in common the general idea of "naturalness"—a natural order operating without interference from any transcendental realities—but nothing more specific. The Chinese idea also has the antireductive dimension of each thing in nature operating with its own way (i.e., multiple ways [*dao's*] within the one Way), but complexity theory is not necessarily antireductive.

10. Paul Marshall describes the extrovertive "noumenal experience" as perfectly clear, luminous, highly noetic, fully detailed, and temporally inclusive, unlike ordinary sense-experience (2005: 267). He concludes that in the simplest extrovertive mystical experiences, the noumenal background is not felt strongly: the stream of phenomenal experience becomes nondual through a relaxation of sharp self/other distinctions, so that the everyday self and the body are felt to be an integral part of the stream; this brings a sense of unity, perceptual clarity, living in the "now," peace, and joy, but no dramatic transformations of phenomena (ibid.). In the more developed cases, the phenomenal stream begins to reveal its noumenal bedrock, bringing luminous transfigurations of the phenomenal content, more advanced feelings of unity, a growing sense of meaning and knowledge, and a significantly altered sense of time (ibid.). In the most developed cases, the noumenal background comes to the fore, blotting out phenomenal experience altogether, and the mystics experience an all-encompassing unity, knowledge, cosmic vision, eternity, and love, having accessed the depths of their own minds (ibid.). But Marshall's approach gives the depth-mystical experience differentiated content, places it in the same track as the mindfulness states, and removes any transcendental reality from being involved.

11. In his *Critique of Practical Reason*, Immanuel Kant said that "Happiness is the state of a rational being in the world for whom in the whole of his existence everything proceeds according to his wish and will." That would be the *opposite* of the selfless joy of a mystic for whom there is no longer an individual's "wish and will."

12. Meditative "purification" of the senses and mind can also have "dark nights," as John of the Cross made famous, leading to distress and suffering. The possible *negative effects of meditation* does not receive the attention they deserve. (See Garden 2007.) Meditation may aggravate the conditions of some people with mental disorders—indeed, it may be opening the same territory trod by schizophrenics and psychotics. Some training in a psychological framework and a set of beliefs to handle what is experienced may be valuable before any serious mystical training is undertaken. Otherwise, detachment from normal emotions can lead to depression or much worse.

13. The nondualist Shankara had trouble explaining verses in the Upanishads such as this. He argued that the world is not a creation or emanation of Brahman, but only an appearance (*vivarta*) that our root ignorance (*avidya*) imposes on Brahman. Thus, Brahman is not a *cause* of the phenomenal realm since phenomenal appearances are unreal, and what is real

cannot cause something unreal. But just as the clay is real and the form unreal, so too the being (*sat*) of this realm that is Brahman is real (*Brahma-sutra-bhashya* II.1.14). The natural realm thus is neither real nor unreal—not the same as Brahman nor distinct from Brahman—and its ontological status is thus ultimately indescribable (*anirvacaniya*). But, as noted in the text and note 16 below, even for the enlightened who know better the appearance of multiplicity remains (*Brahma-sutra-bhashya* IV.1.15)—i.e., their *perception of multiplicity* does not change with enlightenment.

14. In terms of the Buddhist "two truths" doctrine, the entities we experience are conventionally real—they are not totally *nonexistent* like the horns of a rabbit—but ontologically they are ultimately *unreal* because they are not independent or permanent. Buddhists here are using Advaita's criteria of "real" for the higher truth of ontological status. Buddhists do not discuss the nature of being but leave the subject with discussions of the "such-ness" (impermanence, dependency, interconnectedness) of what we sense.

15. Mystics often have a sense that there is a fundamental rightness to things at the deepest level. But this may lead even some theistic mystic who have an overwhelming sense of a loving source to deny that evil is real—everything is actually benign or even perfect as is. Thus, seeing God in everything can lead mystics to moral indifference or antinomianism: everything shares the same being or presence of God; so everything is fine the way things are, and there is no need or right to change anything; or everything is innately good, and so we can do whatever our body desires, since our body too is just part of nature. Suffering and death do not matter, if they are considered real at all, since they do not affect what is real (i.e., what is eternal and unchanging). The eons of sentient beings suffering during evolution are irrelevant because events in time are irrelevant to the timeless. Does this mean that any *sense of love* that accompanies some instances of selflessness is no more than simply feeling connected to all that exists rather than an indication of the nature of the source of things? In any case, an experience of underlying love only deepens the mystery of natural suffering.

16. Even explaining the appearance of the universe—the relation of "being" to a realm of "becoming"—is a problem for Advaitins since they reject any sort of emanation from a source. But under Advaita, the phenomenal world and the body are the products of ignorance (*avidya*)—they should *vanish* when ignorance is replaced with knowledge of Brahman (*vidya*) because according to Shankara this knowledge destroys ignorance and cannot coexist with it. From the highest point of view (*paramarthika*), the phenomenal world is simply not there (Nelson 1996: 47). So why does it not disappear? Even if the world appears only as a dream to the enlightened, why does the dream persist? Why can't they wake up? The Advaitins' answer is that karma that has begun to bear fruit (*prarabdha-karma*) must continue to bear fruit even after enlightenment. That is, once karma has become productive, nothing can stop it. But this would mean that karma can *overpower vidya*—i.e., karma has some *reality* with power even over the enlightening knowledge of Brahman. That is hard to reconcile with Advaita's absolute nonduality and Advaita's "deep metaphysical bias against the world" (ibid.: 24-31, 47). So too, why the realm of *maya* exists in the first place—why there is a root ignorance at all that creates this realm of multiplicity—is unexplained.

— 2 —

Mystical Knowledge and Religious Ways of Life

Mystics claim that their experiences give a knowledge of a fundamental reality. But it is important to note that the claims to knowledge in classical mystical traditions are not the result of isolated mystical experiences: the claims are always made in the context of encompassing ways of life having spiritual exercises, a path with codes of conduct, and a specified goal, all grounded in beliefs about the nature of a human being and the world.[1] Thus, mystical experiences are central to mysticism, but *mysticism* cannot be reduced to a series of *isolated experiences*—for classical mystics, mysticism involves total ways of life and their beliefs. Even depth-mystical experiences need not affect the experiencer's "ultimate concern," but when they do they become part of one's religious way of life. The depth-mystical experience involves an awareness of a root beingness, but the metaphysics of a given mystic's religious tradition determines what he or she takes as the actual *knowledge* given by the mystical experience. That is, what insight the experience is taken as providing will depend on beliefs and values outside the experience itself—the doctrines and values of the mystic's way of life. That the mystics' experiences in turn apparently shape the religious tradition complicates the picture (constructivists deny this, as will be discussed in Chapter 14), but the fact remains that experiences alone never are the final word on the question of knowledge.

Mystical Knowledge

Today many people argue on many different fronts that mysticism is not in fact about knowledge at all. Mystical experiences are considered valuable or interesting ends in themselves, but having no cognitive significance at all. Mysticism is only about producing changes in our personality or about attaining inner peace or becoming more compassionate. Meditation is only about purported physiological benefits; it only develops the centers of the brain connected to pleasure and the state of happiness. Mystical experiences increase our interest in knowing fundamental things about reality, but they do not provide any knowledge of such things. Or the fact that the Buddha taught one doctrine to beginners on the path to enlightenment and another doctrine to more advanced followers (e.g., *Anguttara Nikaya* I.10) shows that mystics are not really interested in doctrines but only in attaining the experiences—their doctrines do not ultimately matter at all, but are merely a raft to be jettisoned once we have had the experiences. More generally, theory in yoga or any spiritual discipline is seen as only in service to attaining an experience, and thus ultimately it does not matter what theory one has—theory is just a device, a trick to quiet the mind (Ravindra 1991: 284-85). Mystical teachings become no more than a pragmatic matter of "whatever works" in inducing an experience of selflessness, not claims about what is real; indeed, the doctrines in the end are irrelevant.

However, in the classical traditions, mystical contemplation is cultivated to gain alleged insights into the fundamental nature of reality so that we can live in accord with what is actually real, not for any possible psychological or physiological benefits. That is, even mystical knowledge is not an end in itself—aligning one's life with the fundamental nature of reality is. The objective is *to change our lives in order to live in accord with reality*, not anything about either knowledge or "developing our consciousness" per se. Still, mystical experiences allegedly do give knowledge about some fundamental reality. All classical mystical traditions contain explicit claims about the ultimate nature of the world and persons. They also have implicit knowledge-claims entailed by the doctrines and practices of their ways of life that are meant to depict the way the world truly is. For example, the Buddha accepted rebirth, even though it did not need an explicit defense at that time and even though the mechanics of how it works have remained an issue for Buddhists. In addition, mystics make claims about the nature of what is experienced in the depth-mystical experience, even when denying such claims are possible. Mystical experience is a matter, to quote the title of a Buddhist work, of "calming the mind and discerning the real"—finding the world "as it really is" (according to a particular mystic's belief-system). Thus, knowledge is not just central to philosophers studying mysticism, but is important to followers of mystical traditions: only with the proper knowledge can they see and live properly.

It is important to note that most mystical knowledge-claims are the same as some *nonmystical* religious and philosophical claims. Indeed, many mystical points are, from a metaphysical point of view, unexceptional. (The speculative and often elaborate metaphysics of *visionaries*—including mystically-minded visionaries like Jakob Boehme—are another matter.) For example, that all things share the same one beingness, or that the natural universe is one interconnected whole, or that the world is free of ontologically distinct entities (especially no "self") are all points that nonmystics, including naturalists, can easily accept and in fact find obvious. So too, most neuroscientists claim there is no "self" in our mental makeup. That this world is dependent on a transcendental reality is not a claim unique to mysticism, nor need we be mystics to follow the analogy of the dream and its dreamer to envision that there is a reality underlying this world and giving it being. The philosopher Milton Munitz can say things about "being-in-itself" that also sound very mystical, but his ideas are based on analytical philosophy alone (1965, 1986, 1990; also see Jones 2009: 24-27). And the problem of how language operates if there are in fact no permanent entities in the world to refer to is now prominent in postmodern philosophy. No special experiences, let alone mystical ones, are needed to understand any of these points.

However, mystics claim a new *experiential* awareness of our situation that *changes* their understanding of such claims. In Buddhist terms, with mindfulness the "such-ness" (*tathata*) of things is brought into awareness—it is the direct (i.e., nonconceptually-structured) perception of the impermanence and dependency of things that brings to light their beingness. The mystics' metaphysical claims about the world may have been adopted from their religious tradition, but traditional mystics allege that they now have had direct experience of the realities involved in these religious and philosophical claims. It is the distinction between intellectual, representational knowledge-that (*jñana*) and a participatory knowledge (*prajña*) surpassing even "knowledge by acquaintance" in which the knower, the act of knowing, and the known are not distinguishable entities.[2] This leads to believing that the consciousness involved is not personal or subjective since no distinct knower who could own it is involved.

Thus, there is an experiential, not merely intellectual, change resulting from mystical experiences. No new knowledge-claims may be advanced, but the new experience affects the mystics' understanding of the tradition's claims that they adopt. For example, the enlightened may still use the analogy of the dreamer and dream, but once they have awakened they see the "dreamer" differently. Or there may be no change in the understanding of a claim, but a new awareness of how it applies—in the Buddhist analogy noted in the last chapter, it is the difference between an intellectual acceptance of the idea that water quenches thirst and actually drinking water. That is, mystical experiences are not a matter of finally understanding a claim or becoming certain that the claim is true, but a new experience. To emphasize the difference in the knowledge allegedly given in these experiences from that given in sense-experience and reasoning, mystics have used terms such as "spiritual gnosis" or even "unknowing" or "nonknowledge" (to distinguish this knowledge from all other types of knowledge) or "intellect" (to distinguish the mental function involved in the depth-mystical experience from both sense-experience and reasoned speculations about a transcendental reality).

But the change in states of consciousness from ordinary or mindful consciousness to the depth mystical-experience introduces a major problem for any claim of knowledge based on the latter experience. Even if we grant that depth-mystics are aware of a transcendental reality, nevertheless what cognitive significance they see in the experience arises only after the experience is over—i.e., *outside* the experience itself. Even if the depth-mystical experience is structured, all evaluations of the experience's status and cognitive import are made only outside the depth-mystical state of mind once a mystic has returned to a "dualistic" consciousness, i.e., an awareness of differentiations even if the state is a mindful one. This is a problem unique to altered states of consciousness: devising knowledge-claims takes the experiencers out of the state of consciousness of their experience and thereby changes their stance toward what they allegedly experienced. Depth-mystical experiences are the most extreme instance of this since they have no differentiated content. After mystics return from the depth-mystical experience to an ordinary or mindful state of consciousness, what they have experienced will also be an intentional object for the mystics themselves, as it is for others. Indeed, Dionysius the Pseudo-Areopagite said that God is *unknown* to the mystic except in the moment of mystical experience since God can only be known there, not in dualistic consciousness. In sum, only outside the depth-mystical mental state are mystics able to decide what sort of insight the experience is, and what is experienced is then one mental object among many even for the mystic.

But this means that mystics in the end are in the same epistemic situation as the rest of us, even though they have a larger experiential base from which to make their decisions about what is real. This problem occurs whether the mystic is enlightened or not and regardless of how mindful his or her consciousness is. It is also worth noting that many major mystics such as Shankara and Eckhart do not appeal to *their own mystical experiences* to justify their claims: they appeal to their tradition's *revelations* recorded in scripture as the source of authority—albeit highly interpreted to fit their own ideas. If mystics have to check their beliefs against the Vedas, the Bible, the Qur'an, or another revealed source to be sure they are valid, then they are in no better position than the rest of us in determining the actual nature of what was experienced since the depth-mystical experience cannot tell us which source we should accept as revealed. The decision to accept something as a revelation typically comes prior to mystical enlightenment, and it is hard to see mystical experiences validating the choice when mystics in different traditions make the same claim for their own scripture. That mystics appeal to scripture does not mean that mystical experiences are not *cognitive*, but it does mean that more factors are involved in determining what insight is actually involved than the experiences alone—the insight depends in part on prior beliefs.

Shankara said the appeal to revealed authority is necessary since philosophers constantly contradict each other (*Brahma-sutra-bhashya* II.1.10-11). He also noted the objection that this itself is an instance of reasoning, but he still asserted that the Vedas, being eternal, provide the necessary true knowledge. He relied on the testimony of the Vedic seers, but he also insisted that even the Vedas needed *interpretation*: where non-duality (*a-dvaita*) is not directly taught, he said the Vedas are only speaking indirectly to lead the listeners to the truth. In short, Shankara justified his system with the Vedas, but he interpreted the Vedas to fit his system. Thus, his system, not the Vedas, is the ultimate court of appeal in the justification process, and this system was informed by mystical experiences. (This ultimate circularity is an issue in all metaphysics; at a minimum, it complicates the process of justification.) Of course, Vedantins of the non-Advaita variety, such as Ramanuja and Madhva, interpret the same passages differently, and followers of other traditions of course accept other texts as revealed.

Perennial Philosophy and Comparisons to Science

All mystical traditions have variations of the Buddha's exhortation to his listeners not to accept anything he says on his authority but to examine and test what he says for themselves and to accept it only when they have experienced it (*Majjhima Nikaya* I.265). However, the comparative study of mystical claims exposes a problem: there is *no agreed-upon core of doctrines* common to all or most mystical traditions that is derivable from what was experienced in mystical experiences in a straight-forward, empiricist manner to compare with scientific theories. But today "perennial philosophers," such Seyyed Nasr (1993, 1999) and Huston Smith (2001), allege that there is an enduring skeleton of ideas present in all cultures except the modern West.[3] They claim to have found an esoteric core common to all religious traditions, and they use this alleged core in comparing mystical and scientific claims. But whether the alleged core of doctrines is a modern invention is a real issue. Certainly, Neo-Vedanta's claim that all religions are equal emerged only after the encounter with Western Enlightenment thought and is not based on traditional Advaita, and the same may be the case with perennial philosophy.

Perennial philosophers handle the mystics' apparently conflicting claims (e.g., that the transcendent is personal or nonpersonal, or is either morally neutral or a loving person) by accepting a pluralism of competing paths all leading to the same summit.[4] They argue that the transcendent itself is beyond all our categories and is experienced differently depending on the context of a particular mystic. But we cannot experience or know the transcendent-in-itself. To use an analogy from science (and this does not mean that science supports perennial philosophy): we never know an electron-in-itself—an electron appears only as a particle or as a wave depending upon which experimental set-up scientists employ. We never see an electron as it is in itself outside of our experiments. Whatever it is remains a mystery—it is not a particle or a wave, but something capable of manifesting these phenomena when we interact with it in different ways. Indeed, if the Kantian-influenced Copenhagen interpretation of particle physics is correct, we will never know the electron-in-itself. Similarly, here mystics experience the transcendent differently depending on their religious and philosophical beliefs, but the transcendent-in-itself remains a mystery. Thus, each mystic is *wrong* in believing that his or her view is better than others: all are imperfect and dependent upon our beliefs.

The root metaphor for this position goes back to the Middle Eastern and Indian parable of a group of blind men who feel different parts of an elephant and mistakenly conclude from their limited perspectives that they know what the elephant must be. In a common version of the story, one man touches the elephant's side and concludes it is a wall; a second man touches a tusk and says it must be a spear; the third feels the trunk and concludes it is a snake; the fourth touches a leg and concludes it must be a tree; a fifth man feels the elephant's ear and the breeze it makes and concludes it is a fan; and a sixth man grasps the tail and concludes it is a rope. The men then quarrel, each being confident that he alone is correct, and eventually fight. The moral of the parable is not that the transcendent has different parts that different mystics experience, but that mystics are wrong in drawing final conclusions about its nature from their own experiences. Thus, perennial philosophers require all religious believers to admit that their formulations are inaccurate in some sense because we do not know the transcendent-in-itself. All depictions are penultimate at best. Religious formulations may have some pragmatic value for attaining mystical experiences, but, like Kant's noumenon, the transcendent-in-itself is unknowable and we have to accept the limited value of any formulation. The modern pluralistic approaches rely on *this mystery* of the transcendent: we do not know its nature "in itself" but only in relation to us. Indeed, those who argue for a pluralism as the proper epistemic relation between religious claims usually stress an ineffability and mystery at the core of things (e.g., Samartha 1988).

However, it must be pointed out that classical mystics do not see things the way pluralists today do: they did not see all religions as having only one underlying worldview or only one set of fundamental "esoteric" doctrines. When writing about their "esoteric" doctrines they do not converge. The mystics see their own view as superior, even if there is more to the transcendent than they have experienced. Formal debates in India between schools included debates on mystical doctrines. Much of the writings of such major Advaitins and Buddhists as Shankara and Nagarjuna is *against* other schools—including some within their own tradition—as they try to show how their own views are better and how the others are wrong. Classical Zen masters such as Dogen rejected the irenic view that all religions teach the same thing in different forms; rather, Buddhist doctrines are the best or the least inadequate.

The idea that perennial philosophers find as most important for comparisons with science is that reality consists of a hierarchy of emanations from a transcendental source in the opposite direction of materialism: spirit appears first, then consciousness, then life, and lastly matter. In particular, perennial philosophers reject the notions that life is the product of inanimate matter and that evolution is the source of the diversity and complexity of life on this planet, although evolution may account for some changes within species. To Nasr, the "philosophy" of evolution is the main support for the modern secularist worldview, and there can be no convergence between the view that we descended from above and the view that we ascended from a "soup of molecules" (1999: 174-75). He also inveighs against those who are satisfied with "superficial comparisons" between the dance of Shiva and the movements of electrons or between electromagnetic polarity and an East Asian *yin-yang* cosmology (ibid.: 175)—their "facile convergence of science and spirituality . . . is based more on fervent desire than on reality" (ibid.: 173). What is needed is not their "pseudo-spirituality" that repeats the current findings of science and then distorts traditional teachings but a new spirituality rooted in revelation and traditional worldviews that will formulate a contemporary metaphysics of nature and a cosmology in the traditional sense (ibid.: 176-77).

Scientists do accept levels of organization to nature, from the quantum realm to the everyday (leaving aside the issue of a final reduction of apparent structures), but the idea in perennial philosophy is something different: the source of the universe emanates planes of reality, and thus there are different "degrees of reality."[5] The hierarchy of levels and degrees of reality is also reflected in the inner structures of human beings, again starting with the spirit being the highest. "All is one" in the sense that the transcendent, the universe, and a human being all reflect the same principles. Thus, these thinkers reject naturalism (that there is only one ontological level to reality and all of it is open, at least in principle, to scientific scrutiny) and scientism (that science is the exclusive source of knowledge about reality). They also question the exclusion of teleology from modern science. They readily accept that science reveals aspects of the lower emanations of reality, but in order to learn all there is to learn about our world they advocate a return to the pre-modern "traditional sciences" that see the cosmos as a theophany and the phenomena of the world as symbols of a world beyond.

That many of the specific mystical claims explicitly conflict with each other makes perennial philosophy hard to maintain. And even if perennial philosophers have discovered a common skeleton of esoteric beliefs to all the doctrines of traditional cultures (rather than created one that they then interpret different religious traditions' ideas to fit), the fact still remains that each mystical tradition fills out the skeleton differently. It is these *specific claims* of particular mystical traditions that must be the subject of comparisons to scientific theories if the comparisons are to be to genuine mystical traditions rather than any abstracted "esoteric" doctrines that the contemporary perennial philosophers may see. To change this situation, perennial philosophers would have to offer a philosophical or theological argument for what is in effect a new religious system of belief.

The new perennial philosophy has influenced some people seeing parallels between science and mysticism. But at least Nasr and Smith have studied the various religious traditions of the world—most of those who see a convergence between science and mysticism today have only the very flimsiest of understanding of the actual doctrines of the South and East Asian mystical traditions, often based only on reading second-hand popularizations. Moreover, most of the new writers are not dealing with what perennial philosophers see as the core of all mystical traditions. In the end, most of those who today employ the label "perennial philosophy" in arguing for a relation of mysticism to science do so only as an easy way to use different religious traditions' key concepts interchangeably and to avoid going into any depth on any tradition's actual teachings.

The Depth-Mystical Experience and Its Interpretations

Even if the mind during a depth-mystical experience is empty of differentiated content, depth-mystics in the classical mystical traditions do believe these experiences give a sense of fundamental reality and oneness and reveal the nonexistence of the empirical ego. Thus, something is retained after the experience is over. If these mystics are correct, they experience an immutable reality transcending our natural world. But the reality experienced is nonetheless open to very different *interpretations*. Mystics typically speak in terms of a personal god or the nonpersonal Brahman or some other more specific idea rather than remain only with the abstract concept of "the Real." But because of the competing conceptions seem equally well-supported—both experientially and in terms of reasoning—it is hard to conclude that these more specific beliefs come from the experience itself. Rather, beliefs and values from outside the depth-experience must fill out the significance given the experiences after it is over. And even if mystics did confine themselves to such abstract terms as "reality" or "oneness," these still have a conceptual element and are the result of seeing the experience from a distance and through a conceptual lens after the depth-mystical experience is over. Whether there is a conceptual element in the depth-mystical experience itself is a subject for Chapter 14, but in any case any claim to knowledge or truth will have a conceptual element. It is a statement that is true or false, not an experience.[6]

After their experiences, members of different religious traditions will interpret the depth-mystical experience differently. Thus, many theists would dispute the claim that the depth-mystical experience is an experience of a fundamental beingness rather than of a personal agent. The claim that all depth-mystical experiences are experiences of "beingness" or "the source of beingness" is not the claim that all experiences fall into an abstract category (like different religions' soteriological goals all have in common the abstract fact that they are all soteriologies). Nor is the claim meant to be an alternative interpretation to traditional claims. Rather, it is based on two assumptions: that the defining characteristic of this experience is the complete absence of any differentiatable content, and that all depth-mystics experience the same thing, not different realities. If so, a basic beingness is the minimum of what depth-mystics in different traditions in fact experience: mystics differ on their understanding of the *full nature* of what is experienced—their conflicting highly-ramified interpretations in terms of different conceptions of transcendental realities—but at least the source of this universe's beingness is what is experienced, even if there is more to the reality than beingness alone. And even if no transcendental reality is involved, and the depth-mystical experience is only an experience of a natural self or merely the sheer that-ness of the aware mind, the root beingness of the self or the world is still experienced.

Arguably, any depth-mystical experience must always be the same for all experiencers, regardless of one's culture or beliefs, since there is no differentiatable content during the experience itself that would distinguish one experience from another for different people. (Experiences in the *mindfulness states* will differ from experiencer to experiencer since, except in the possible case of a totally structureless state, the state of mindfulness involves structuring our sensations or internally generated mental content, including ways developed from the experiencers' religious traditions. And even without structuring, the sensory experiences would differ for different experiencers.) If the experience is in fact a genuine experience of a transcendental reality, it would also be hard to conclude that members of one religion experience one transcendental reality while members of other religions experience other realities or that all theists experience a loving reality while nontheists experience a second reality that is morally neutral. Certainly, it is hard to believe that there are multiple creators of the natural world or multiple sources of beingness—as if different personal gods of different theistic traditions created the parts of the world where each theistic tradition predominates and different nonpersonal sources created the nontheistic parts. Nor is there any other reason to conclude that more than one reality could be the subject of the experiences.[7]

One may argue that theists and nontheists experience different *aspects* of the same reality, as with the blind men and the elephant. But if the mind is truly *empty of differentiating content* during the depth-mystical experience, this would not be the case: there are no different aspects to experience. It is hard not to conclude that mystics in all traditions all experience the same transcendental reality but *interpret* the depth-mystical experience differently according to their tradition after they have returned to a dualistic consciousness. And as noted earlier, in the post-experiential dualistic state, what was experienced in the depth-mystical experience now must be seen even by the mystics themselves as an object of some sort—our mind makes what was experienced into one more mental object among other mental objects. Even if the experience actually involves only the root of the self, it would be only natural that theistic mystics after they have returned to dualistic states of consciousness would see the experience as involving an encounter with a transcendental self—hence a personal god—given their prior faith and the profoundness of the experience. The transitional state back to a dualistic consciousness will differ in content according to different mystics' beliefs, with theists having some theistic content. But there is no dualism within the depth-mystical experience itself, as would be the case with an encounter with a personal being or a loving presence. Thus, while "Christian mysticism" as a total way of life with its doctrines, values, paths, and goal is unique, this is no reason to conclude that there is a unique "Christian depth-mystical experience" of a loving, personal, triune transcendental reality and that non-Christians or at least nontheists experience something less.

Nevertheless, Christians often argue that Christians' depth-mystical experiences are phenomenologically unique. One argument is that mystical experiences cannot be forced or earned, but are the result of God's grace. The concept of "grace" in the Bible (e.g., Romans 3:20-26), however, is not related in any way to having mystical experiences. Equally important, mystics of all traditions, theistic and nontheistic, agree that these experiences are not the product of human effort but require passivity—the experience cannot be forced, but requires letting go of the sense of self. Some mystical experiences do occur spontaneously, but most mystics engage in training. And Christian contemplatives too engage in spiritual training and prepare the way with effort (unlike with grace). If mystical experiences were the result of effort in other traditions but always occurred spontaneously for Christians, an argument might be made on these grounds, but this is not the case. Nor does the fact that letting go of the sense of self is involved mean that the experience is more than a natural event involving only the brain. Another common argument is that the depth-mystical experience for Christians seems like an encounter with another person: some distinctive residual sense of a loving, powerful, and personal being is retained from the experience itself and is not simply a result of the transitional state back to more normal states of consciousness or a theological interpretation applied after the experience. But again, if the experience is truly empty and all intentionality is cut off, this is not possible—there cannot be a loving relationship while the mind is devoid of all differentiable content. As John of the Cross says, it is an "imageless" communion. Of course, if Christians on the path to enlightenment believe they are being carried upward by love, then they will naturally interpret the resulting experiences in terms of a loving reality.

The Question of "Mystical Union"

Many today writing on mysticism think that all mysticism results in the same one metaphysical belief—i.e., all mystics treat what they experience as the power underlying being and thus the source of the natural world. Advaita Vedanta's radical monism of consciousness (i.e., a non-duality of the consciousness constituting the subject and the consciousness that actually constitutes objective phenomena) is the classic instance of a metaphysical system based on overcoming even the duality of subject and object—indeed, in this interpretation, there is only one reality and thus no "degrees" of reality or "dependence" of one reality on another but only reality and illusion. However, not all mystical systems involve an all-encompassing nonduality in which all of the apparent diversity in the world is in the final analysis unreal. For Samkhya-Yogins, there is no underlying creator or common ground to both matter (*prakriti*) and consciousness; rather, there is a fundamental dualism of those substances and a plurality of distinct selves (*purushas*).[8] Nor, as is also commonly believed, has any classical mystical tradition adopted a pantheism equating the transcendental reality with the natural world (creator with creation, Brahman with *maya*), thereby making the natural realm fully real in the final analysis. Neoplatonism is often considered "pantheistic," but the material universe is an emanation of the One and not the One itself. Pantheism, in sum, is a concept that theists devised within their theistic mind-set to contrast ideas with classical theism and does not reflect classical mystical thought at all.

Also contrary to yet another popular opinion, classical mystics do not speak in terms of a *union* of two *substances*—making the experiencer and another reality into one reality. In none of the major mystical traditions are there two previously distinct substances that become united into one in a mystical experience. There is no ontological transformation or transubstantiation of an "essence" converting the person into the transcendental reality. In the new awareness resulting when any differentiations fade away or our conceptual boundaries are broken in a state of mindfulness, there may be a *sense* of union or a *sense* of individuality melting away, but there is no *ontological change* from what has already been the true situation all along—only the false conceptual boundaries that we ourselves had created soften or disappear. The experiencer's *awareness* may become united to the reality experienced in a way that sense-experience does not become united to its object: the experience is participatory rather than knowledge by acquaintance. With the lost of a sense of ego, the experiencer may feel for the first time the true connection we all always have had to the rest of reality, but our true situation has not changed: experiencers do not attain a new ontological state, but merely realize what was actually always the case. The only ontological change may at best be in the brain. For example, in the theory of William James, C. D. Broad, and Aldous Huxley the mind is a filter or "reducing valve": mystical experiences loosen this filter, thereby letting in more of reality or of the cosmic mind. If they are correct and the brain is necessary for consciousness, the brain's wiring may have changed.

Theists will normally maintain the idea of creaturehood and insist that we creatures cannot be united to God or his mind. In Christianity, there may be a union comparable to that of two lovers or fire heating an iron rod (to use medieval images), but there is no literal "merging" or "absorption" of one reality into another resulting in only one entity (Jantzen 1989). The term "mystical union" is employed sparingly by Christian mystics; it is only in the modern study of mysticism that *unio mystica* attained a central place (McGinn 2006: 427). Christian mystics struggled over what "becoming one with God" meant, but they usually meant it in terms of a loving union of wills with God's or even a fusion of the mind with God's (ibid.: 427-29), but again this is an alignment of spirit, not an ontological union. In one of Bernard of Clairvaux's images, it is like a drop of water in wine taking on the taste of wine, but he added that no doubt the *substance* of the person remained distinct, if now in a new form—the will is now melted with God's (ibid.: 436). For John of the Cross, the consummation of the spiritual marriage is the union of two "natures" in one spirit and love (ibid.: 462). God's will and the mystic's will are now simply in "unison"—becoming one in spirit (1 Cor. 6:17). In Islam, Sufis speak of "the annihilation of the self" (*fana*) and the replacement of the self with the divine presence of God (*baqa*). Under one interpretation, God is the only reality and thus is the true agent of all of "our" actions regardless of a mystical experience—i.e., not only is there only one god, there is nothing else but God, and so we have no reality. However, the more common interpretation among Sufi sects is that the world is not an illusion and neither is each individual self—rather, both the world and all the selves are mirrors reflecting God and thus are themselves separate and real. The self is a created entity and thus distinct from God. For a mystic to claim to be one with God or actually to be God is a heresy punishable by death (as al-Hallaj found out the hard way).

In Neoplatonism, the opposite of emanation—"absorption"—may be a union, but as adopted by the Western theistic traditions the reality of a separate self remains the orthodox position. For Abrahamic theists, our individual creaturehood always remains a distinct reality, even though all beingness is supplied by God. Thus, Meister Eckhart, for whom "God's is-ness is my is-ness" and "all creatures are one being," did not deny our creaturehood: we remain created and distinct entities, although we all have the same being from the Godhead—the sense of self is simply "idle" while God works in the inner, silent part of the soul. The experiencer is not *aware* of his or her self during a mystical experience, but nevertheless it is still there, just as the experiencer is not aware of time during the experience and so it seems timeless to the experiencer, but the experience's duration can still be measured. Things remain ontologically unchanged: the experiencer, by "forgetting" a sense of "I" and all other knowledge, now simply knows the transcendental reality that has always been present in us. The correction of our knowledge and the end of our "self-will" and all accompanying emotions are the only changes.

The situation is the same for South and East Asian traditions. For Advaita, only the transcendent is real, and thus there is nothing to unite with it. The Upanishads have an emanationist position, but Advaitins and Samkhya interpret the situation differently. The popular image of a drop of water merging into the ocean does not fit the metaphysics of these traditions. In fact, an image used in Advaita is the exact *opposite*: just as the entire sun is reflected in full in each ripple on a pond (e.g., Shankara's *Brahmasutrabhashya* III.2.11), so too all of reality (*brahman/atman*) is entirely contained in each part of the universe.[9] There is still the reflected and what does the reflecting, with the latter eventually disappearing when all sentient beings become enlightened, thereby ending the unreal realm of rebirth. Realizing that "thou art that" is realizing what has always been the case: there is nothing for the *atman* to unite with, nor can it be changed in any way—all we need is a change in our knowledge and awareness. Under Samkhya, each self is a distinct, silent witness that is to be *isolated* from matter and not united to anything. For Daoists, the Way is already "in" us—we simply need to align ourselves with it. For Buddhism, there are no "real" entities and thus no things to unite. Thus, the mindfulness state is not conceptualized as a "union" in Buddhism. For mindfulness more generally: with the loss of the sense of self, the unreal conceptual boundaries we have imposed on phenomena disappear, and we feel we are "merging" with the rest of the cosmos or feel that our being is the same as the being of everything else. But there is no new uniting with another reality that had previously been ontologically distinct or any other ontological change: we were already connected with everything else and are now only realizing what has always been the case by dissolving our conceptualizations.

In sum, there are less conceptual differentiations in the mindfulness states and no differentiations during the depth-mystical experience, and with the absence of differentiations in the mind there is a sense of unity to our being: we finally realize that we have been part of one encompassing whole or that all of reality shares one simple and partless source, or our true transcendental self is isolated from the rest of reality. But with a mystical experience we are not "united to God" in any ontological way that was not previously always occurring. With enlightenment, only our sense of individual existence and its accompanying self-will are abolished. The experiencer does not "obtain" or "become" anything new—all that changes are our knowledge, will, and emotions.

Weighing Mystical Experiences Against Other Religious Experiences

Also notice that the significance of the depth-mystical experience has been interpreted to fit into radically different ontological schemes. The dualism of substances and pluralism of persons within Samkhya's metaphysics was just noted. Theists in the Abrahamic traditions and some Indian *bhakti* traditions have incorporated the depth-experience in two different ways—unison with God's will or experiencing the ground of the self—while retaining the reality of persons and the distinction between creator and creation. Among classical mystics, early Buddhists dealt the least with the relation of the individual and the natural world to any purported transcendental reality; in their quest for a deathless state, they bypassed the entire issue of the relation of a transcendent source to the world (if there is a source) and dealt instead with only the impermanence of the components of our experienced world. Buddhists more generally weight the insights of mindfulness over those of the depth-mystical experience in how they lead others to the freedom from a sense of an individual self and give a pluralistic interpretation to the nature of our experienced reality.

Theists may or may not weight the depth-mystical experience as the most important ontological insight. For theistic mystics, there is an underlying, self-emptying source of the world's being—a personal god or a nonpersonal, silent, inactive ground like the Godhead of Eckhart's Neoplatonist-influenced system. Theistic mystics may interpret the depth-mystical experience as only a partial insight into a theistic transcendental reality—an experience of the nonpersonal dimension of a personal reality, comparable to a physical examination of a human being's body rather than studying the full person. Under this view, revelations and other numinous experiences offer deeper insights into the transcendental reality. Advaitins would disagree and place all "differentiated" experiences on a lower plane; thus, they would attribute the numinous experiences' alleged cognitive content to projections of the unenlightened mind. Theists may contend that numinous experiences are in fact a deeper form of the depth-mystical experience than that experienced by nontheists—the depth-mystical experiences, in effect, clears the mind for a further mystical infusion of love or other content from God. (See Stoeber 1994.) But if the depth-mystical experience is indeed *devoid of all differentiatable content*—"cleansed and emptied" of all "distinct ideas and images," to quote John of the Cross—the experience of a personal divine reality cannot be a form of the depth-mystical experience. Part of this issue is simply a definitional problem: many want to include numinous experiences in the category of "mystical experiences." But again, the depth-mystical experience in the strict used here is void of all differentiable content. At best, it clears the mind for nonmystical, numinous type of experience. But any disinterested cross-cultural consideration of mystical experiences reveals that theists take the actual depth-mystical experience itself to be theistic in nature only for theological reasons rather than experiential ones. As suggested above, since nothing within the experiences can distinguish them phenomenologically, theistic and nontheistic mystics apparently have identical depth-mystical experiences; theists simply tend to attach more significance to visions and revelations.[10]

In sum, mystics are open to other types of experiences, but that mystics might have numinous experiences does not make those experiences *mystical experiences*. Either before or after a depth-mystical experience or enlightenment, mystics may have numinous experiences that theists will see as the presence of a loving god; indeed, the process of emptying oneself of a sense of self may leave a greater space for numinous experiences to occur. And theistic mystics may well attach more cognitive significance to the numinous experiences. Theorists in every religious tradition will need to rank the different types of experiences, and ranking either revelatory experiences or mystical experiences as a greater insight into the transcendental reality will depend on factors outside mystical and numinous experiences themselves. Indeed, that the depth-mystical experience is taken to be an insight at all—rather than merely a powerful exotic mental state with interesting psychological or physiological effects—depends on factors outside the experience.

Mystical Experiences and Mystical Ways of Life

Depth-mystical experiences are not tied to any particular set of beliefs or a particular religion but occur in all traditions. Nevertheless, mystics must provide some interpretation in order to understand it themselves. That is, some post-experiential interpretation must be present for even the mystics themselves to understand the significance of depth-mystical experience. What is important to note is that the depth-mystical experience alone does not determine its own interpretation. The experience itself is only one consideration: the doctrines, ethics, and practices of a given mystic's tradition all play a role. Mystical experiences may well affect the mystic's worldview or ethos, but the process of seeing the significance of the experience occurs only outside of the depth-mystical experiences in a dualistic consciousness, whether mindful or not. The interpretation given the experience may in fact be ready-made for particular mystics by their own tradition. And that mystics are aware of their tradition's interpretation prior to their experiences raises the issue of what is more important in the final claim to mystical knowledge—the content of the mystical experiences themselves or the beliefs, values, and practices of the mystic's traditions? Is the depth-mystical experience noncognitive in the sense that, even if an awareness of a transcendental reality is involved, the knowledge-claims themselves come only from other sources? That mystical experiences may, as noted in the last chapter, adjust a mystic's understanding of his or her tradition's beliefs also complicates the situation.

All of this means that mystical experiences alone do not determine a mystic's knowledge-claims. Mystical knowledge will always have a conceptual element that mystics supply outside the experiences. That classical mysticism is a way of life with a factual component should be remembered: it is only mystical experiences in the context of the mystics' encompassing mystical ways of life that allegedly give knowledge. How the mindfulness state or the depth-mystical experience fits into a worldview depends on what mystics decide its significance is while outside the experience, and this depends on religious, philosophical, and other considerations that encompass more than the experiences themselves. Thus, religious and philosophical ideas from the mystic's tradition will always play a necessary role in how the mystical experience is seen and in what is taken to be mystical knowledge. Advaitins will have to offer reasons other than the depth-mystical experience itself to conclude that the world is "unreal" in any sense whatsoever, and theists will have to offer reasons for treating revelations as fundamental in interpreting the significance of the depth-mystical experience and also for any particular brand of theistic metaphysics. But in all cases, factors outside the mystical experiences themselves are a necessary part of the picture.

This aspect of mysticism makes science-and-mysticism studies a subdivision of the general field of science-and-religion: it is the doctrines and values of the *concrete religious traditions* that become the subject for comparisons, not abstract claims to "reality" and "oneness." (Of course, those who see parallels between science and mysticism may forego classical mystical systems altogether and construct their own new interpretation of the significance of mystical experiences and call it "perennial philosophy.") Mystical experiences do not change this situation—the depth-mystical experience remains constant, and it is the various understandings and valuations that becomes distinct to each religion. Nothing of the mystical systems of beliefs and values within a religious tradition is unique in this regard. Indeed, it is often hard to tell from their writings if religious thinkers (including such prominent figures as Shankara, Eckhart, and Plotinus) have undergone mystical experiences or are nonmystical philosophers or theologians whose systems are not informed by personal mystical experiences but are merely the working out of the logic of some mystical philosophical or religious ideas.

Moreover, because there are many diverse mystical ways of life with different concrete sets of beliefs—many of which explicitly conflict with those of other traditions—there is no one generic "mystical view of the universe" to compare with scientific theories. Even traditions such as Buddhism are not monolithic, but are made up of competing schools and subtraditions; some doctrines may be common to most schools and may be "official" to Buddhism, but the total configurations of all the beliefs of each school lead to significant differences. And the differences between even different Indian traditions involve genuine conflicts of doctrines. This conflict cannot be ignored in favor of only one particular interpretation for comparisons with science without an additional philosophical or theological argument.

Because of the diversity of conflicting claims, any generalizations about "Eastern mysticism and science," let alone "all mysticism and science" when it comes to *mystical claims* about nature of the world or of an alleged transcendent reality are going to be severely limited or out and out wrong. However, *mystical experiences* enter science-and-mysticism studies in another way: mystical experiences as a particular *way of knowing reality* as compared to science as a way of knowing reality. This is the subject of the next chapter.

Notes

1. Today many people speak of being "spiritual" rather than "religious." The former focuses on an individual's own experiences and personal development, rather than religious institutions or the traditional doctrines of a particular religious tradition. But whether they are members of a formal religion or not, the spiritual still must have some beliefs for understanding both their own experiences and the rest of the world; they must also have values to guide their actions. This is so even if these beliefs and values are an eclectic blend of only what the person likes from different religious and nonreligious traditions and are not the highly-ramified beliefs of a specific theology. That is, they too have a "way of life."

2. Some may argue (following Sidney Hook's position) that science is *a way of knowing* the world since it gains new information but that mysticism is merely *a way of experiencing* the world since it results in no new testable "knowledge-that" claims as in science. But the awareness of another aspect of reality (the beingness of things) than the one studied in science is a type of *cognition* even if mystical knowledge-claims are limited.

3. The phrase "perennial philosophy" comes from Leibniz; it arose out of a quest at that time to find a "natural religion" common to all mankind. But the phrase is now more associated with twentieth-century thinkers such as Aldous Huxley and Frithjof Schuon who were influenced by Neoplatonic, Islamic, and Hindu thought.

4. See, e.g., Hick 1989; Smith 2001: 220-23. There are two types of pluralism here: one that denies the validity of any specific doctrinal claims (since they are at best partial truths), and one that is agnostic about which, if any, of the competing claims is correct. The religious have difficulty accepting either type of pluralism since it means having to accept that their own religious claims are in some way incorrect or not well-founded. Also, how can the religious know what is an appropriate response to the transcendent if they cannot be confident that they know at least some aspects of it correctly? How could theists worship or pray to something unknown?

5. Three different concepts must be distinguished here: emanation, emergence, and evolution. *Emanation* is about the appearance of phenomena from the source of being. *Emergence* concerns the appearance of new levels of organization within nature. *Evolution* is about changes within the same level of organization. That is, emanation is about "vertical" changes in the manifestations of being, emergence is about "vertical" changes of structures within nature, and evolution is about "horizontal" changes within one level of nature. Situations may be hard to distinguish. For example, is the appearance of complex life-forms from simple ones a matter of emanation or evolution? But the important point is not to

conflate *emanation with evolution* and then see the biological science of evolution as evidence for emanation or vice versa.

6. This leads to the problems in contemporary philosophy concerning the difference between truth and justification, how truth-claims can be grounded in experiences, and the role of coherence with other accepted beliefs in the acceptance of truth-claims. These issues will not be discussed here. (See Jones 2009: chap. 3.)

7. We in America typically refer to spiritual experiences as "experiences of God" because we are raised from childhood with that concept—we call it "God" because that is the only term we know that seems appropriate. The brain must affix some name to anything it experiences in order to file it into memory (Newberg and Waldman 2009: 76). But there is a great variety of feelings in spiritual experiences, and most people have their own definition of "God" (ibid.: chap. 4).

8. It should be noted that Samkhya was the most prominent philosophy throughout most of India's history. Advaita Vedanta became prominent only with the advent of Neo-Vedanta, a product in part of the West. It should also be noted that Advaita is not the only school of Vedanta and thus cannot be equated with "Vedanta," let alone all of "Hinduism."

9. In the thirteenth century, the Christian Richard Fishacre made a similar claim to explain how God could be omnipresent without being spatial: God is a reality transcending the universe and so he transcends any sense of spatiality, just as he is timeless; being spaceless, God can exist entirely in every part of space. But this "whole in every part" doctrine never became a mainstream doctrine within Christianity.

10. While someone is still on the path to enlightenment, mystical experiences that occur in the concentrative track may retain content, including a sense of self. This could be the source of the idea that there are "theistic mystical experiences" that are different from nontheistic ones. That is, the sense of self is not yet eradicated in these mystical experiences along the path, and theists may naturally see this as an experience of a separate self; this then is not seen as the phenomenal ego, but as a transcendental person, i.e., God. So too, the almost palpable sense of love that many theistic mystics have may be the product of enculturation of a theistic society or of the mystical training in a theistic tradition and not the result of the contentless depth-mystical experience itself. However, the enlightened depth-mystical experience is devoid of all content, including any sense of a self or separate person.

— 3 —
Mystical and Scientific Ways of Knowing

Unlike with mysticism, probably few readers of this book need an introduction to science. But one basic point must be emphasized: science is about *how things work*—i.e., identifying the material causes of things and the efficient causes in nature responsible for the changes in phenomena we see. To achieve this, scientists use observation and the analytical mode of mind to discern and explain the hidden *order of structures* at work in nature—i.e., the entities, fields, forces, or other constituents at work behind appearances that are responsible for the stable invariances and patterns within the changes we observe in the everyday world. Mystics, on the other hand, use another mode of the mind to focus on the *beingness* of the natural world in mindfulness or a transcendental source in depth-mysticism and not on the structures operating within the natural realm.

In sum, scientists and mystics approach the world in distinctly different ways, and thus science and mysticism are different ways of knowing reality. Both endeavors are interested in what is fundamentally real but in different aspects of it—they do not merely approach the same subject-matter differently and do not intersect in their central concerns. Mystical experiences do not give us any scientific knowledge of reality, and no science gives us any mystical knowledge.[1]

Do Scientists and Mystics Approach the Same Reality?

Most comparers of science and mysticism completely disagree with this position. They only see that both mystics and scientists are approaching reality and are out for knowledge; thus, they assume that mystics and scientists are engaged in gaining the same type of knowledge through different techniques. This leads to seeing some type of convergence: both science and mysticism pierce the veil covering reality and so disclose the same thing. Comparers do not consider that there may be fundamentally different aspects of what is real that might require different functions of the mind and that would foreclose any substantive convergence of knowledge-claims.[2] This includes even physicists making comparisons to Asian thought (e.g., Victor Mansfield 1976, 1989, 2008).

A full characterization of science need not be provided here—those seeing parallels with mysticism usually go no further than noting that science involves empirical observations and claiming that Newtonian science was reductionistic. But what is most important for the issues at hand is that scientists try to find the efficient and material causes involved in how events in nature work and make claims that ultimately depend on observations checkable by others. Pushing and poking at reality through experimentation may not always be possible, but some observations (and hopefully exact empirical predictions) of what happens are. Scientists establish patterns in the observed world through observation and also through experiments utilizing physical instruments; second, they use reasoning to try to identify the elements in nature that may not be open to direct experience but are responsible for the changes on the everyday level of the world. Under realist interpretations, scientists identify, however approximately, real parts of the world to explain the observed events; under antirealist interpretations, scientific claims are only about the observed events and we have no claim to know what we cannot experience. Antirealist empiricists do not deny that there are structures at work in the world; they only claim that we cannot obtain knowledge of them if we cannot experience them; in short, the structures remain a mystery. Under empiricism, all theoretical realities are rejected; the unexperiencable, hidden dimensions of space-time of string theory are the paradigm of this problem today. Scientific theories and models are at most merely shorthand devices for connecting observations. But under realism science is not merely a matter of predictions, but of understanding, and theories are explanations of the mechanics of nature.

From this, it is hard to argue that mystics and scientists approach the same aspect of reality. ("Aspect" and "dimension" will both be used for the different subject-matters of science and mysticism. Mindfulness mystics and scientists look at different *aspects* of the realm of becoming: the beingness of things versus structural causes. Depth-mystics look at a different *dimension*: the source of the self or all phenomena that both underlies and transcends the everyday world and the realm of becoming in general.) Mindfulness mystics are making claims about the *impermanence of macro-objects* we directly experience, not anything about features of the submicroscopic world that they have not experienced that may be the causes of what is experienced. They make no claims about any reality that cannot be *directly experienced*, unlike physicists. In such circumstances, it is hard to see mystics as making claims about the underlying features of nature that scientists are revealing. Even if mathematics and any scientific laws have no material existence but are timeless and transcend nature in some way, they are still differentiated and thus are not given in mystical experiences.

On the other hand, scientists focus precisely on the *differentiations* that mystics bypass. Scientific experiences remain ordinary, everyday-type observations, even when scientists are studying extraordinary parts of nature through experimentation or technology-enhanced observation; mystics' experiences are extraordinary even when (in the case of mindfulness mystics) they are looking at the ordinary. It is hard to see scientists, including quantum physicists, as making claims about any *undifferentiated* aspect of reality. To determine how things work, they need to distinguish objects and see how they *interact* with each other, and for this differentiations among phenomena are necessary. That is, scientists study the interaction of things, not the common beingness of things or bits of matter in isolation. This includes fields and the smaller and smaller bits of matter being theorized—quantum physicists are not interested in what gives fields or bits of matter their being but only in what is measurable by the interaction of objects. Even "mass" is measured only by the interaction of objects. And since being is common to all particulars, it cannot be poked and prodded to see how it interacts but is uniform for all phenomena. There is no way to conduct tests on what is free of distinctions; hence, no hypotheses about its nature can be scientifically tested in any way. Thus, there can be no "science of being" in any natural scientific sense—the oneness of beingness simply precludes it from any scientific scrutiny. In sum, in terms of the *Chandogya Upanishad's* analogy, scientists must focus on the pots and not the clay.

This alone should be sufficient to conclude that mystics and scientists are not focusing on the same aspects of reality. But in addition, consider the types of experiences central to each endeavor: mystical experiences require the suspension of the very activity of the mind necessary for scientific observation and theorizing—*analytical functions of the mind*. This also strongly suggests that something other than the objects of scientific interest is the focus of interest in mysticism. Indeed, mystics around the world see our *conceptual constructs*—the very thing that constitutes scientific theories—as positive impediments to achieving mystical experiences. Were mystics interested in the same aspect of reality as scientists, what scientists find through language-guided observation and theorizing would be seen as aids to mysticism, not an obstacle. Indeed, how could mystics approach the same aspect of reality that scientists are interested in with a mind free of attention to differentiations? Concepts do not control what is seen in scientific observations, but such observations are concept-driven: scientists are making predictions about what will be observed, not unknowing all that is conceptual altogether. The different approaches of mysticism and science to reality are appropriate for different aspects of reality: "forgetting," "unknowing," and "emptying" the mind of distinctions in order to experience what is common to everything versus focusing on distinctions among objects in order to see how things work. And for this reason those who accept science as the only way of knowing reality are right to reject mysticism as a source of knowledge and vice versa.

Or look at the last point from another angle: scientific knowledge is necessarily concept-driven, while mystics try to experience reality in a way that transcends the conceptual—logically, how can the two types of knowing end up with the same knowledge-claims? Granted, knowledge in both mysticism and science has a conceptual element, but *scientific observations* always involve a mixture of the conceptual and the experiential, while *mystical experiences* are direct, unmediated experiences of reality. How can the resulting conceptual and unconceptualizable "truths" be the same? So too, how could scientific theories be about the same aspect of reality as a mystical experience if one aspect is conceptualizable? If these theories were about the same subject, then mystics are *wrong* when they say that what they experience cannot be *conceptualized*. Even trying to see the paradoxes of quantum physics as failures in attempts to conceptualize what mystics experience will not work since the quantum realm is still differentiated, while mystics deny differentiations to what they experience. Conversely, mystics cannot be gaining scientific knowledge if what they experience is undifferentiable.

From all of this, it is reasonable to conclude that mystical experiences reveal an aspect of the everyday world and a dimension of reality that is missed in scientific knowledge and vice versa: mystics apprehend something common to all of reality—"is-ness" unmediated by mental conceptions, or the source of beingness in themselves or in all of the world—while scientists work through the mediation of our concepts to find structures underlying the changes we experience in the everyday world. Scientists and mystics each see something different about reality, and their subjects are irrelevant to each other. Thus, their claims do not cross, let alone converge at any point. At best, there may be some parallels in structure between the two endeavors, but there is no possibility of the two combining.

This also neutralizes what people might see as a conflict between mindfulness and science. The basic cognitive claim for mindfulness is that phenomenal reality is impermanent, interconnected, and constantly changing. Thus, the natural world has no discrete, permanent objects—in particular, no self. Does this mean that there are no permanent *structures* to nature for scientists to find? No. Mindfulness mystics deny only that there are permanent *objects* in nature, not that they may be structured by permanent *laws*. As far as mindfulness is concerned, there may be natural joints to nature to be described and explained in science. The law of karma is, after all, permanent; it involves our actions and their repercussions in the body, and there may also be other permanent structures at work in the universe. Scientists, on the other hand, are not making any claim about the nature of the things structured by the laws and forces they discover. They certainly are not committed by the practice of science itself to a metaphysics of permanent, discrete objects. Mystics may feel that scientists are missing the point of reality or are even deluded by focusing on the differentiations, and scientists may feel that mystics are deluded because of the mindfulness approach to the beingness of nature. But as long as scientists can see nature itself as in flux, even though it may be structured with permanent realities, science and mindfulness need not conflict in principle.

Being and Structures

In short, scientists and mystics deal with different aspects of reality. Mystical knowledge concerns the beingness of reality, not the uniqueness of any phenomenon or the structures operating in nature responsible for changes. Beingness is not a different scientific level that scientists simply cannot reach externally—it is an aspect that is free of differentiations and thus is not open to scientific study. Hence, the critics' regular criticism of mysticism—that mystics have not discovered anything new about the world in a thousand years—does not apply: mystics are not trying to do what scientists do and failing; rather, they are looking at another aspect of reality that does not have any new elements to be discovered through research. It is not surprising that they are not gaining new knowledge about the world that can be checked against empirical predictions when the knowledge gained in mystical experiences is not scientific in nature but about an aspect of reality that is not open to scientific study because it has no interacting parts.

Beingness is not simply undifferentiated matter: it is what makes matter—and energy and mind and whatever else is part of the universe—exist. It is "existence in general," to use a not too helpful phrase. Even if there is something within the natural universe that gives particles their mass (e.g., the Higgs field), we still have to ask why that exists and what gives that reality its being. Any further characterization of the nature of the "is-ness" of reality—being-as-such—is difficult. The question "what is being?" has been a part of Western metaphysics since Parmenides but is still a mystery today. The philosopher Milton Munitz asks whether we can even *speak* of beingness—"boundless existence" in his terminology—since it is not an object or set of objects (1965, 1986, 1990). Beingness never presents itself as a phenomenon—beingness, Munitz notes, "shines through" the known universe but is not identical with it. Nor is it an entity of any type: it is not a thing or combination of things or the totality of things. Unlike an object, it is not "conceptually bound." It has no properties, qualities, or structures to discover—it has nothing to describe. It is utterly unique in that it is not an instance of any category whatsoever. Thus, "beingness in itself" is unintelligible, since intelligibility requires the applicability of descriptive or explanatory concepts (1986: 274). That is, intelligibility relates to *what* something is or *how* it is, not to the underlying *that-ness* of reality. We live in a world of differentiated objects and see and speak only of those objects. Beingness itself remains beneath any conceptual map we could apply to it to create order. Once we start speaking of beingness—or even just naming it—we make it one object among objects, which "it" is not. That is, we see trees and cars, not "being," and we cannot formulate propositions about "it." As with "the mystical" of Ludwig Wittgenstein's *Tractatus Logico-Philosophicus* (Prop. 6.522), beingness manifests itself and hence we are aware of it, but it is unutterable and incapable of being conveyed in language. Thus, the proper response to our awareness of beingness is silence (Munitz 1986: 278). That is, beingness cannot be expressed or "captured" by any language, and thus we are left with only mystery about the very beingness of the world. (Note that Munitz's point is based on *philosophical analysis alone*, not on *mystical or other experiences*.)

If Munitz's position on language is correct, any explanations or understanding of the beingness of our world would be foreclosed. But the important point for the issues at hand is only that beingness cannot be studied scientifically since it is common to everything: it may be structureless, but even if it has some structures, we cannot put it to any tests to see how it works. Even if the mind in a mystical state resonates with the energies of the universe, as New Age advocates say, still it is the "energy" of being—i.e., what makes anything exist in the universe—not electromagnetic energy or any other distinct and measurable type of natural energy. In mindfulness, there is a Gestalt-like switch in attention from focusing on the differentiations within the everyday realm to focusing on the beingness of things—a switch from the "what-ness" of things to the "that-ness" of things in the realm of becoming. Mindfulness can also focus on inner mental states as well as on external phenomena. In the depth-mystical experience, something is experienced that is traditionally interpreted as the transcendental ground of the self or the transcendental source of the universe's being (whether a personal god or a nonpersonal reality). But no new information about beingness is revealed in new mystical experiences because there is nothing new to reveal about this beingness—no new parts or elements or causes. There is no way to devise new depth-mystical experiences to test something about beingness—new mystical experiences are simply the same old mystical experiences repeated over again and again.

Nor can anything new about structures be revealed in the mystics' contemplative function of the mind. It is distinct from the analytical functions of the mind that scientists utilize in their observations and reasoning. Indeed, no type of information or anything else differentiated is involved in either type of mystical experience—in particular, the depth-mystical experience of being is free of all the differentiations necessary to communicate any information. Thus, these experiences are not like revelations from a personal transcendental entity that might contain predictions or other testable information. So too, mystical experiences are also not like such paranormal phenomena as clairvoyance or precognition that should produce testable claims. This means that mystics cannot supply new information confirming or refuting any scientific claims about structure—in both the depth-experience and mindfulness, the mind is focused on the being of things, not the differentiations of things that are needed for scientific information.

Conversely, since scientists do not reveal anything about the nature of the underlying beingness of things, they cannot supply any evidence confirming or refuting any mystical claim about the that-ness of things or a possible source. Scientific findings simply cannot contribute to the mystical understandings of being. Science is not about the nature of the underlying beingness of things, but about the causes at work in nature. There can be no experimental support for any of the mystics' assertions concerning being since there can be no experiments or any other types of scientific analysis that reveal the nature of this dimension of reality because of beingness' uniformity. Thus, nothing scientists can do can provide a reason for accepting or rejecting a mystical claim about being. Indeed, from a scientific point of view, beingness is featureless—it is just the medium in which structures are embodied. But again, scientists are interested in the structures governing changes in reality, not what is structured.

As an analogy, consider this book. The letters, numbers, punctuation, and spaces are the smallest elements of the work, and the rules of grammar for forming the words and sentences are a component distinct from the elements. Thus, the rules of the structure of language (the grammar) cannot be reduced to the elements structured (the letters and so forth). Whether a string of letters forms a word or a sentence or is just nonsense cannot be determined by examining the letters individually—an entirely different dimension of the text must be examined (the rules of structure). Scientists are like grammarians identifying the universe's structures (its "rules of grammar") and the fundamental building blocks (its "letters"). However, as grammarians, scientists are not interested in the nature of the substance embodying the parts—the "ink" that embodies the "letters." Also note that physicists and chemists are not interested in the narrative of the story—the history of the universe—but only in the grammar and letters utilized in the narrative. Cosmologists and evolutionary biologists do deal with this historical, narrative dimension, but they are no more interested in the "being" dimension than are physicists and chemists.

To bring mysticism into the analogy: mindfulness is a matter of experiencing *the ink* on this page apart from the formed letters and the message of the text—i.e., the experiences involve the beingness of the letters that is irrelevant to the information that the scientists study. (The analogy breaks down since obviously science in the real world can also study the ink. This shows how difficult it is to make any analogies from our "dualistic" world about something as basic as the beingness common to everything.) In sum, mystical experiences involve a different type of knowledge than does science: we cannot get information about the ink from the information contained in the words of the text or vice versa. Thus, no theory in science could rule out the possibility that the depth-mystical experience or the mindful state might be knowledge-giving of an aspect of reality that scientists *qua* scientists ignore, and conversely mystical experiences are equally irrelevant to scientific theories of the components and structures of nature.

In sum, scientists are interested in the "what-ness" of objects (what categories we put things into) and the "how-ness" of what makes things tick (how things work or came to be), but not in the sheer "that-ness" of things (being) that is the domain of mystics. Scientists learn things by observing and thinking about how things interact, while mystics still the analytical mind and focus on the unchanging beingness common to all things. This distinction between reality's *beingness* and its *structure*—between the stuff of the cosmos and the forces organizing this stuff—must be maintained in any study comparing science and mysticism. Scientific and mystical insights are not of the same type because structure and being, while both real, are different and cannot be reduced to only one type of reality. Thus, even though both scientists and mystics are interested in learning more about the fundamental nature of reality, they are not arriving at the same destination through different routes, but are working on different subjects that remain distinct.

The Mutual Irrelevance of Science and Mysticism

As discussed, the two types of mystical experiences relate to beingness differently: mindfulness relates to the beingness of the experienced world of becoming apart from concepts; the depth-mystical experience relates, depending on the interpretation, to the source of beingness underlying the experiencer or all of the natural world. For either type of experience to occur, an emptying of the mind is required. This involves an "unknowing" of all the knowledge that we normally accumulate in our everyday life through our senses and the analytical function of the mind, *including all scientific knowledge*. No insights into the structures of the world are possible in such a state since differentiations are forgotten, and so mystical experiences cannot provide evidence for any scientific theory. To Plotinus, the mystical intellect (*nous*), a mental faculty distinct from both sense-experience and reason (*ratio*), shares in and knows only beingness. This gives no knowledge that would be of help to scientists. Mindfulness-msytics and depth-mystics experience a timeless "now": it is not an experience of the past, present, and future all rolled into one; rather, it is an experience to which temporal categories do not apply at all. That is, mystics are not experiencing all of history but something outside of time. So too, we may know the beingness of all of reality by knowing the beingness of oneself or of a grain of sand or a blade of grass, but this does not give omniscience in the usual sense of knowing all occurrences throughout the history of the universe (e.g., who won the 1948 World Series) or all scientific knowledge of underlying structures (e.g., a Theory of Everything in physics). (However, in Jainism the enlightened are traditionally said to be literally omniscient.)

The word "science" does come from the Latin word for knowledge (*scientia*), but even though mystical experiences are experiential and mysticism allegedly involves knowledge, this does not make mysticism *scientific* in the sense it is used today. That is, mysticism is not like the *natural sciences*. Yoga is not "a science of the mind" or "a science of higher consciousness" or "a transcendental science" in the sense of "science" today.[3] Buddhism is not a "science of experience" (Du Pré 1984) but a way of life centered around ending the existential suffering inherent in simply living (*duhkha*). Buddhism is not a "science of the mind" in any sense connected to natural science (contra Cabezón 2003: 49-50). One of Buddhism's main tasks is not "to study the nature of reality" (contra Ricard and Thuan 2001: 9). Buddhism's central objective is simply not acquiring *disinterested knowledge about how something works*—it is *transforming the person*. It does not involve a systemic study of mental states out of an interest in learning more about how the mind works—it is focused on overcoming our fundamental suffering. This is not to say that scientists are not also interested in the consequences and practical applications of their research, but in Buddhism there is no fundamental interest in learning the how-ness of things just to learn how things work, as with basic research science. Nor, as discussed, are mystical experiences geared toward learning any knowledge of differentiated phenomena, including any such knowledge of the mind.

To many, mystics are more like scientists in temperament than practitioners of the more common religiosity of faith and hope, but this misses the religious nature of the Buddhist objective. The point of the Buddha's teaching is to end suffering. To substitute a disinterested focus on how the parts of nature work—including even the mental states involved in ending suffering—in order to learn more about the universe distorts the fundamental nature of classical Buddhism entirely. Today many Buddhists, including the Dalai Lama, find scientific discoveries in physics, cosmology, and biology fascinating, and scientific theories may affect doctrines in their way of life (as discussed in Chapter 9), but they must admit such discoveries in the final analysis are irrelevant to their central quest. As the respected Theravadin Buddhist scholar Walpola Rahula said, while some parallels and similarities between Buddhism and modern science may be intellectually interesting, they are "peripheral and do not touch the essential part, the center, the core, the heart of Buddhism" (quoted in Verhoeven 2003: 45).

Mysticism does involve a search for a type of *cause*, but it is not the same type of cause as in science—i.e., the cause of things' existence and not the efficient and material causes operating within the natural order that bring about changes that are of interest to scientists. To give a visual picture, the beingness of things is a "vertical" depth-cause underlying all phenomena equally and is neutral to all matters of the "horizontal" causes involved in nature's structures. Thus, it is a matter of a ontological cause—the beingness of things or a source of being—not one making a scientific difference. Mystics ultimately focus only on the "now" of the experience of being, while scientists ignore anything not involving reproducible efficient causes. Mystical experiences do not provide any information on the causal questions of science, but only bring into awareness an ontological depth common to all things and hence is neutral to all "horizontal" changes. Conversely, whatever scientists find about structures is irrelevant to the beingness of things. Indeed, even any scientific findings about impermanence on levels of causes below the observable, everyday level would not be evidence for a mystical theory since the mindfulness claims are about what is actually experienced.

This means that science does not need mysticism or vice versa. A scientist does not need to practice a mystical way of life to enhance his or her science, and a mystic does not need science to aid in becoming enlightened. At best, classical mystical ways of life need only a limited scientific knowledge, comparable to the Sufis' need to know enough science to calculate the direction of the Ka'ba in Mecca and the proper time for their daily prayers. Such knowledge is certainly part of mysticism, but mysticism does not increase our knowledge of differentiations and so does not add to scientific facts, nor can it challenge any scientific claims about structures. Shankara granted sense-experience and reasoning complete freedom within their proper sphere: the content of the "dream" realm of the world of becoming (*Brihadaranyaka Upanishad-bhashya* II.1.20, *Bhagavad-gita-bhashya* XVIII.66). And there is no reason that any other mystics should not do the same, unless theological considerations dictate otherwise.

A scientific interest in efficient causal structures is not a way to any type of mystical enlightenment or a way to end suffering in the Buddhist sense: focusing on identifying and explaining the structures of reality only increases attention to the differentiations in the world and will never lead to the calming of the mind involved in focusing on the beingness common to all things. Thus, the Buddha condemned astronomy/astrology as a wrong means of livelihood because it was unrelated to the religious concern (*Digha Nikaya* I.12). No doubt he would have equally condemned physics if it had existed in the Indian subcontinent at the time. The Buddha even condemned for monks a practice as valuable in our eyes as medicine (*Digha Nikaya* I.12, I.67-69) since it interfered with a practitioner's quest for selflessness. (Later Buddhist monks took up this practice.) To use the Buddhist analogy: when one is shot with a poisonous arrow, one does not ask about who made the arrow or what the arrow is made of (or any other scientific question related to the arrow)—we just want a cure for the poison (*Majjhima Nikaya* I.63). So too, what is vital here and now is finding a way to the deathless state, not wasting time on scientific questions about the construction of the universe. The objective is to end a false sense of permanence to the world and to the mental life, with its accompanying ungrounded emotions, not to learn the physical mechanisms at work causing this sense, let alone all the other causes in the world. All mystical traditions have such soteriological goals—none are a disinterested endeavor to learn more about natural causes.

Mysticism's Possible Indirect Aid to Science

Although science and mysticism remain distinct endeavors, the physicist Victor Mansfield believes that mysticism can be a direct aid to science. In an enthusiastic review of Fritjof Capra's *The Tao of Physics*, he suggests that "[t]he infusion of an Eastern view of nature into modern physics could provide the significant paradigm shift that many claim is needed in physics" (1976: 56). He asks whether Eastern thought can help quantum physicists with such standard puzzles as the collapse of the wave-function. He thinks there is a "nontrivial synergy" between the "two very different disciplines" of physics and Madhyamaka Buddhism that can help us appreciate some of the ideas in Buddhism and "could aid in the development of physics" (quoted in Cabezón 2003: 52). However, it is not clear whether Mansfield means only that physicists can get *ideas* from Eastern thought that can be reworked into scientific hypotheses, or whether he thinks that *mystical experiences* themselves can somehow directly influence physics, or whether Madhyamaka *metaphysics* directly solves problems in physics. Some see Madhyamaka Buddhism as perhaps being able to provide a metaphysical framework for new developments in physics (e.g., Bitbol 2003 and Finkelstein 2003). But the physicist Ravi Ravindra seeks to change the character of both science and mysticism: "the most important of all [tasks] that can be undertaken by contemporary intellectuals" is *integrating* "modern science and ancient spiritual traditions . . . in some higher synthesis" (1991: 146). Others too see the next step in science as the integration of the objective and subjective domains within the framework of a new science—in the future, our current focus on objective phenomena alone will be seen as a temporary "transitional aberration" (Malin 2001: 230, 241). However, probably more scientists today would agree with Stephen Hawking who, in responding to his colleague Brian Josephson's interest in Asian mysticism, thinks that the idea of mystical influence on science is "pure rubbish" and says that "[t]he universe of Eastern mysticism is an illusion. A physicist who attempts to link it with his own work has abandoned physics" (quoted in Boslough 1985: 127).

And if mysticism and science do indeed deal with different dimensions of reality, then obviously neither can offer direct aid to the other: neither can offer verification or any empirical support or disconfirmation for theories or beliefs in the other field. Nor could what mystics experience about reality be used as a "god of the gaps" to fill in holes in scientific theories since what is experienced in either type of mystical experience is not an explanation for why one certain state of affairs exists and not another. Theories in the two fields will always be about different aspects of reality, and thus any merging of the two endeavors into one new "science" is not possible. It is not like unifying electricity and magnetism since beingness has no apparent structures to unify. Mystical experiences may offer new data for science (as discussed in Chapter 5), but it is the *mental/brain states* that neuroscientists had not previously studied that would be the new data, not anything about what is allegedly experienced in those mental states or any alleged insights. Any paranormal powers gained by mystics would also add new data, if they can be tested and verified. Paranormal abilities may also expand the scope of scientific observation. For example, Rolf Sattler suggests that "auras" might be perceivable in some altered states of consciousness (1999: 156). Nevertheless, such powers are subsidiary to the mystics' goal and are not a matter of mystical experiences proper.

However, many advocates of meditation and various mystical traditions (such as Robert Thurman) see mysticism as providing another type of direct aid to science that would be an even more important contribution: it may cause neuroscientists to expand their science to include consciousness as a substantive reality. That is, it may end what these advocates see as the deadening effect of the reign of materialism as the framework for consciousness studies and replace it with a more humanizing view of the mind. It would also expand science to include a direct, first-hand approach to knowledge of meditation's effect on the mind. Such an expansion would cause major changes in neuroscience. This possibility will be discussed in Chapter 5.

But even if these changes in neuroscience do not occur, mysticism can offer some *indirect aid* to science. Scientists need to come up with new ideas when exploring and trying to understand and explain new realms of the natural world, and mystical belief-systems are one possible source of new ideas. (See Sharpe 1984.) But this does not make mysticism part of science: ideas for hypotheses can come from any cultural sources—the chemist Friedrich August Kekelé got the idea for the benzene ring from a hallucination of two whirling snakes each grabbing the other's tail and thus forming a circle that he had while gazing into a fire after a long day of work; the physicist Erwin Schrödinger claimed to have gotten some ideas for physics from sex. Nevertheless, scientists still must rework any ideas they derive from any source into actual scientific hypotheses and then must determine on empirical or other scientific grounds alone if any of these new hypotheses are valuable—the ideas themselves do not entail any scientific hypotheses and are not themselves scientific evidence, any more than Kekelé's dream is. Indeed, the intuition is not the dream or whatever itself but the scientist seeing that the idea may be applicable to a scientific problem he or she is working on (although the subconscious mind may be at work on both).

So too, just because scientists may rely on intuitions rather than the rational mind to come up with these initial ideas does not make mysticism part of science (contra Albin and Montagna 1977). Dichotomizing the mind into only the "rational" and the "mystical" is not helpful. Not all of the mind's functions are either one or the other. Mystical experiences do involve a function other than rational thought, but other nonrational functions also exist. In particular, *intuitions* cannot be labeled *mystical* simply because they do not utilize the rational mind. Nor are mystical experiences "intuitions" in response to our analytical mind's questions. Mystical experiences are another type of nonrational consciousness not involving the manipulation of ideas: they involve emptying the mind of concepts and are not the result of the subconscious manipulating concepts. Intuitions in science and mathematics are a mental process that skips reasoning in steps, but they remain matters of manipulating conceptualizations, not a sense of undifferentiated beingness. Often a great deal of study of scientific ideas and problems must occur before the subconscious takes over and produces a useful insight. Nor can intuitions be labeled "*revelations*" to make them sound religious—revelations require an active, personal agent to do the revealing, and most scientists and mathematicians do not see their insights that way. Intuitions, unlike revelations, can also be *wrong*—as such scientists and mathematicians as Michael Faraday, Albert Einstein, and Henri Poincaré have noted—and are subject to testing and revision.

Scientists may read the Upanishads or other mystical literature (although this may be outside both the text's cultural context and outside the context of mystical training) and thereby come up with some new ways of looking at things. But scientists must rework any ideas they develop from mystical sources into scientific hypotheses about differentiated phenomena and determine exclusively on scientific grounds if they are useful—mystical ideas themselves do not entail any scientific hypotheses or any other ideas about differentiated phenomena, and mystical experiences supply no scientific evidence. If a scientific hypothesis pans out, it will be embraced by all scientists for scientific reasons, regardless of its ultimate inspiration from mysticism. The origin of the idea is ultimately irrelevant. (To be more exact, mystical ideas directly about the mystical experiences themselves entail nothing about structures, but mysticism consists of more than that—ideas about the nature of the world and a person from their encompassing worldview—and these ideas may be worked into scientific hypotheses. And as discussed in Chapter 9, whether metaphysical ideas from a mystical tradition affect theory-choice is also an issue. If so, commitments to the metaphysical belief-claims of a mystical tradition may come into play and affect the content of science.)

More generally, familiarity with mystical thought may loosen scientists from thinking only along traditional lines of thought.[4] Niels Bohr had read the *Daodejing* in his youth well before his theorizing on complementarity. Werner Heisenberg thought that the parallels he saw between Asian metaphysics and new scientific theories may make studying the former helpful for adjusting our minds to the latter: "It may be easier to adapt oneself to the quantum-theoretical concept of reality when one has not gone through the naïve materialistic way of thinking that still prevailed in Europe" in the early twentieth century (1958: 173). He also thought his discussions of Indian philosophy with the Bengali mystic Rabindranath Tagore were important to his thinking on physics because they showed that his ideas were not crazy. (Einstein supposedly had a well-underlined copy of H. P. Blavatsky's *The Secret Doctrine* in his office.)

Loren Graham and Jean-Michel Kantor present a fascinating example from the history of mathematics of aid resulting from an interest in mystical metaphysics when some Russian mathematicians became interested in the Eastern Orthodox practice of the Jesus Prayer (2009). These mathematicians did not get mathematical intuitions in an altered state of consciousness resulting from chanting. Rather, their interest in "name worship" led to an interest in mystical *metaphysics* and a passionate *subjectivism in mathematics*, even though this led to such odd claims as seeing the "set of all sets" as a symbol of the undifferentiated and featureless One of Neoplatonism (ibid.: 95).

Scientists may also meditate and come up with new ideas based on their own experiences and practices. The experiences themselves are irrelevant to science since they relate to beingness, but they may change the scientists' perspective on things in general by exposing something of reality that is outside of science's conceptualizations. This may lead to exploring new ideas, and science is a matter of ideas. For example, scientists may become convinced that consciousness is causal, and this would affect which theories in neuroscience they are drawn to. Or they may come away from the depth-mystical experience with a sense of the unity of the universe and switch this sense to a search to unify scientific laws or to reduce the number of independent structures. Or mindfulness may lead to a greater interest in the impermanence and interconnectedness of things, and this in turn may lead to an interest in fields emphasizing those features, such as complexity theory. Meditation of both mystical tracks may also produce a calmer, more focused mind and this may well aid scientists in theorizing or doing research. It also lessens emotions and a sense of ego, and this may lead a scientist to become more disinterested (i.e., less personally attached) to any one in a set of competing theories and thus more "objective" in that sense. On the other hand, being zealously attached to a particular theory may be a good thing during at least the early stages of theorizing and research.

Meditation also has another effect related to scientific intuitions. Emptying the mind of differentiated content and a sense of self leaves a mental space where other experiences can occur. For example, numinous experiences may occur in the cleared mind. But meditation may also let the subconscious mind open itself into the conscious mind. Thus, it is common for the unenlightened to encounter mental "demonic" forces reasserting themselves. However, if a scientist had been working on a scientific problem, the subconscious mind may emerge and manifest the results in the conscious meditative mind. This cannot be seen as the *mystical objective* of meditation, nor does it make the intuitions and subconscious creativity mystical in nature, but it is a possible effect of meditation that may aid science.

However, and more importantly, while concentrative meditation may help focus the mind, mindfulness meditation *interferes* with the type of attention that is needed to execute experiments and make scientific observations and to manipulate concepts mentally in the development of new theories: the focus on distinctions and particulars. In "forgetting oneself," mindfulness does involve the objectivity of disinterest, and this is how scientists are supposed to approach their research and their findings, but the selflessness of the mindful state of consciousness goes beyond the mere lack of self-interest: it lacks the *attention to distinctions* that scientists need and thus interferes with science (contra Nisker 2002: viii). Even enlightened mystics still see differentiations among phenomena (even though they do not see them in terms of permanent, distinct entities), but to conduct scientific observations and theorizing they would have to change the focus of their attention back to the differentiations, not beingness.

Of course, scientists may well treat their scientific activity as a religious exercise—many early modern Christian scientists saw their work, in the words of Francis Bacon, as "for the glory of God and the relief of man's estate"—and hence as a type of "meditation" or even "spiritual path." But science cannot be a "spiritual path" in a *mystical* sense (contra Weber 1986: 13) since it cannot even in principle provide us with "spiritual awareness" of beingness but remains a matter of the differentiations of reality. Neither cosmology nor quantum physics is a "spiritual science" because of its broad scope or deep content—they are still about differentiated structures in the natural realm. And while any activity could be conducted selflessly or as a means to self-transcendence, science is particularly ill-suited to this task since the focus in science is on differentiations. Manual labor may work well as exercises in mindfulness, if it involves repetitions and does not require much from the analytical functions of the mind once it is learned, but scientific research and theorizing is not like that at all—science requires the creativity of the analytical mind. In short, science is not a type of mystical meditation since the analytical mind is principally active.[5]

A mystical interest in the beingness of the world may also inspire an interest in understanding the workings underlying the wonders of nature, causing someone to take up science—a thirst to know more about reality and what is fundamentally real may begin from either source. So too, the *ethics* of various mystical and religious traditions may affect what topics are chosen for research (e.g., topics related to well-being) and how scientific knowledge is applied. (See Mansfield 2008: 24-25 on moral guidance.) Only extreme followers of scientism, holding that science is the only way to truth, would think that science can solve our problems without consideration of ethical consequences—like the proverbial mad scientist who shouts "Damn the consequences! Science demands that we proceed!" Indeed, mysticism may help *scientists as human beings*, if not *science itself* (contra Ratanakul 2002: 117), by reminding them that there is more to reality than what is revealed by science and that science may not be the only way of knowing reality—in short, mysticism can help them see the limits of science and that science is not naturalism or scientism. Perhaps meditation may lead scientists to accept that there is a fundamental element of reality that is not open to the scientific approach. But this too is something extra-scientific and does not make mysticism part of science itself. So too, mystical doctrines may provide a framework to integrate science into one's religious way of life, but this is also extraneous to the theories of science itself.

Science's Possible Indirect Aid to Mysticism

The lack of new theories in classical mystical belief-systems since the Middle Ages points to the fact that the beingness of the realm of becoming and the source of beingness are not open to fresh mystical experiences or new analyses. Depth-mystical experiences simply remain the same. For this reason, any reconceptualizations in mystical religiosity in the future of what is allegedly experienced in the depth-mystical experience (e.g., new forms of Vedanta) will reflect input into mystical traditions from other cultural sources but not new experiential input. And here science may help indirectly: scientific theories may be one such source of new ideas for new conceptualizations or new analogies for understanding what was experienced. Indeed, there have been new mystical systems put forth in the twentieth century based on science: Pierre Teilhard de Chardin and Shri Aurobindo combined mysticism with biological evolution, although it is the evolution of *consciousness* that they were concerned with. (See King 1980.) This, once again, does not make science *mystical*, any more than any ideas modified into mystical theories from other sources thereby make those sources mystical.

Second, scientific theories may aid the understanding of the *metaphysical* theories that mystics put forth. For example, the Dalai Lama finds Einstein's theory of relativity as giving "an empirically tested texture" to Nagarjuna's theory of time (Dalai Lama 2005: 205-206). Or to Varadaraja Raman, mathematical constructs that are not direct depictions of anything physical but are only mathematical tools for handling data (such as Hilbert space or the wave-function in quantum physics) provide a way of understanding the different representations of the transcendent in different religious traditions (2008: 281-82). But again, such indirect aid does not make science a mystical endeavor—it only offers one possible nonmystical source of assistance for comprehending mystics' metaphysics. Moreover, there is also the danger that this practice can actually *inhibit* our understanding of mystical metaphysics if we remain thinking about scientific structures and not beingness or if we force mystical ideas to conform to our scientific understanding—in short, if we see mysticism through the prism of science. For example, as noted in Chapters 6 and 9, Nagarjuna's analysis of time has nothing to do with relativity theory.

Third, for those who want to modernize a mystical tradition, science can weed out factual claims from a traditional worldview that are now known to be inaccurate. Arguably, this is a requirement of rationality. As long as such claims are irrelevant to the mystical objectives of the tradition, this is no problem and a new form of Buddhism may result. But there is a danger that advocates of, for example, a "scientific Buddhism" may change the nature of Buddhism. And, as discussed in Chapter 9, if the process touches core doctrines of a tradition (e.g., rebirth or that consciousness does not arise from matter), there are limits as to how much accommodation to science is possible.

Fourth, as noted above science cannot be a "spiritual path." At best, science can indirectly aid mysticism by revealing more of the impermanence to the natural world. Of course, we do not need science to see impermanence on the everyday level—the field of mystical interest—but as of yet scientists have not found any permanent entities on subatomic levels either. So far, it looks as if there is nothing but the impermanence of objects in the continuously changing natural world. (Whether finding any permanent entities on a subatomic level would in fact refute a Buddhist way of life will be discussed in Chapter 9.) As already noted, that the *laws and forces* of nature may be unchanging (and hence *permanent*) presents no more of a problem for a mystical metaphysics than the claim that the *law of karma* is unchanging: the flux of the mental and physical *parts of the universe* is still impermanent. That is, even if scientists determine that the laws of nature are permanent or eternal or in some sense transcend time and space, this does not change the impermanence of phenomena that is the subject of mystical interest in the everyday world. But this interest in the beingness of the realm of becoming still remains distinct from the scientific interest in the ordering factors of this realm, and so scientific equations and theories give no information even indirectly relevant to the content of the alleged mystical knowledge of beingness.[6]

Science, Mysticism, and the Realm of Change

Nevertheless, science and mindfulness do share an attention to the realm of becoming, albeit different aspects of that realm. But it is important to realize that what the depth-mystical Advaitins consider the "realm of illusion (*maya*)" is not *unreal* in the way that a delusion involving something that is not there is—e.g., to use the Indian analogy, imaging a rabbit's horns. Rather, the illusion involves misreading what is really there: we are misled by appearances to focus on the *temporary configurations of things*, and thus we end up being confused about what is real. In the analogy in the *Chandogya Upanishad* of the clay pot noted in Chapter 1, the preexisting clay is real and the pot (i.e., the temporary form the clay is in) is not. This conveys the sense of what is real and what is "illusory" in mysticism more generally: the temporary, dependent, and impermanent configurations are dismissed as ultimately not real (i.e., not eternal, independent, and unchangeable) and hence "illusory," but the reality of the underlying beingness is affirmed. The Upanishads represent a depth-mystical tradition, but mindfulness traditions use similar analogies. For example, the Buddhist Perfection of Wisdom texts use the analogies of mirages, dreams, optical illusions, echoes, reflections, and magicians' tricks to explain the emptiness of phenomena of anything that would give permanence. No classical mystical tradition dismisses the world as "unreal" or an "illusion" in any stronger sense: the beingness manifested in the everyday world remains ultimately real, even though the impermanent configurations are not—the world's being is either supplied by a source (God or a nontheistic analog) or is the source's own being. Similarly, Indian mystical traditions routinely distinguish *consciousness* from *mind*—i.e., the unchanging, underlying, observing consciousness from the changing mental processes such as sense-experience, discursive reasoning, and self-awareness. Samkhya is not alone among Indian schools in treating these mental processes as subtle products of *matter*, not consciousness.

Thus, according to mindfulness mystics, we misread sense-experience and create illusions out of what is real. Moreover, mystics need not deny that the world has stable structures that are open to scientific study. Enlightened mystics experience the world by focusing on its being and without attention to the what-ness and how-ness of things, but this does not mean structures do not exist any more than focusing on the color of things means that we must deny that things have mass. In principle, mystics can treat being and structures as two separate but equally real aspects of the world. The distinctions that scientists draw in the differentiated realm of reality need not be deemed groundless, even though they are not a matter of being. To alter the Indian idea of two "levels" of truth: from a mystical point of view, science is a matter of the lower truth (explaining changes within the realm of becoming), while mysticism is a matter of the higher truth (the ontological status of the realm of becoming—in Buddhism, that the content of the realm of becoming is impermanent; in Advaita, that an underlying consciousness is alone real and the realm of becoming has the ontological status of a dream).[7] As already discussed, nothing scientists could do would confirm or refute the mystical claims, and nothing mystics experience is relevant to scientific matters, but each type of truth in its own context states something finally true of reality.

In short, the what-ness and how-ness of reality still remains intact even if they are absent during mystical experiences. In mindfulness mysticism, the interconnectedness of everything becomes prominent, but this does not deny the reality of what is interconnected—again, only the seeming permanence or independence of apparently distinct entities is denied. But based on their experiences alone, neither depth-mystics nor mindfulness mystics need to repudiate anything scientists say about the nature of structures (with a possible exception concerning consciousness discussed in Chapter 16). What is experienced seems timeless during the experience, but how long the experience occurred can nevertheless still be measured, and the same applies more generally to the other features of nature absent in the depth-mystical experience—nothing of reality's underlying, causal structures is ultimately negated by the experiences alone. (Metaphysical judgments such as Advaita's are another matter.) Nor do any underlying structures change the fact that the everyday realm is still empty of permanent, discrete entities. So too, no scientific law can negate the possibility that the everyday world is devoid of permanent entities, and this is all that mindfulness mystics claim.

Mystical Versus Scientific Attention

This affirmation of the reality of the structures scientists study is not to deny that classical mystics oppose the discursive type of knowledge of which science is the paradigm. Daoism is a good example of the rejection of such knowledge: their interest in nature remained mystical and did not lead to a scientific interest in how things in nature work. (See Jones 1993: 127-46.) We cannot simply equate the Daoist interest in nature—or any interest in nature, for that matter—with a scientific interest in *understanding the causal order behind things that explains how things work*. Even if Daoists can go beyond the senses and conceptualizations in such a way that it enables them to flow with patterns inherent in nature, this does not mean that they have any scientific interests in dissecting, understanding, and explaining the efficient causes of those patterns. In the Daoist "forgetting" state of mind (*xu*), our mind is not guided by specific objectives, but responds spontaneously to what is presented without any preconceptions—this cannot guide scientific observations or theorizing. Scientific observations and experiments do not control their outcomes, but they do involve predictions, control, and manipulation rather than a simple mindfulness of whatever occurs. Scientific theorizing is a matter of conceptions and of changing conceptions. Thus, science only increases the amount of differentiations in our mind by its analyzing, selecting, and theorizing.

In general, science cultivates the analytical mind and increases attention to the differentiated and thus diverts attention from what mystics consider the most important approach for aligning our lives with reality. To Advaita, science is concerned with only the content of a "dream." Buddhism in general shows, in Winston King's phrase, a "disenchantment with the world," including any scientific interest in it. What we need to do for mystical experiences to occur is to empty the mind of what is central to science. The focus is working on the mind, not exploring the workings of the world and discovering new facts even about the workings of the mind. Mysticism thus is an attempt to get away from the selecting, categorizing, measuring, and theorizing mind of a scientist. The aim is to achieve a knowledge inaccessible to the analytical mind. As a Sufi saying puts it, the mind is "the slayer of the Real" because it separates us from an awareness of God. Thus, science and mysticism pull in opposite directions, and most practitioners of either endeavor may very well dismiss the other as a waste of valuable time and energy.

Metaphysics in Mysticism

Since science and mysticism involve different ways of knowing and different aspects of reality, there should in principle be no conflicts between them. But, as will be discussed in Chapter 9, this irenic picture is complicated by the fact that mysticism involves more than just cultivating mystical experiences—it involves metaphysical attempts to understand the significance of these experiences, and to lay out the general nature of a person, the world, and transcendental realities. Of course, the conflict of classical mystics' metaphysics that accept the existence of *transcendental* realities with the metaphysics of naturalism in which science entails the rejection of transcendental realities still remains. However, this is not a conflict of mysticism and science, but a conflict of metaphysics. Nevertheless, the *factual claims* within mystical metaphysics and science still present an issue.[8]

While mystical experiences do not focus on structures but on the impermanence of the realm of becoming and the underlying changeless beingness of things, mystical traditions contain analyses and metaphysics that refer to alleged facts about the world, including its structures. These include metaphysics related to nonmystical topics and also analyses related to mystical views of impermanence. Some metaphysics encompass broad features. For example, Buddhists set forth a metaphysics of the arising and falling of conditioned things that reflects their central view of the impermanence and dependence within the realm of becoming. An example of a more technical analysis is the Buddhist Abhidharmists' analysis in elaborate detail of "the elements of the experienced world (the *dharmas*)." These elements are not denied as "real," even though Buddhists emphasize that everything in our experienced world is momentary and empty of anything that could establish a permanent, independent nature (the *anatman* doctrine)—we create the phenomenal world by giving it "name and form (*nama-rupa*)," but we do not solipsistically create the beingness of reality. (Theravadins exempt *space* [*akasha*] and *nirvana* from being compounded and conditioned by other elements [*Anguttara Nikaya* I.286].) Mystical traditions such as Buddhism that emphasize mindfulness will be more fertile grounds for comparisons with science than traditions such as Advaita that emphasize the depth-mystical experience since the former's systems of metaphysics emphasize analyzing the phenomenal world while the latter can ignore such "details" in discussing the ontological status of the entire natural realm.[9]

Most often mystical traditions also adopt ideas from the encompassing religious traditions and the culture of their country and era. For example, Hindu and Buddhist mystics adopted the traditional Hindu cosmology and also the idea of karma and rebirth. The Buddha and other adepts are said to have experienced past lives. Karma is just as much a structure of the world as the physical structures of electromagnetism or gravity even though it involves our actions and their consequences rather than the interactions of inanimate objects. Even in Advaita, the realm of illusion (*maya*) is stable and law-like, with the law of karma governing our unenlightened actions, and it remains so even for the enlightened. (However, the enlightened are said to be able to control the consequences of some karma and also to have paranormal powers that would suspend other natural forces.) Daoists similarly adopted the standard Chinese cosmology, with the Way ordering the constant flux of things.

In general, mystics may show interest in the structures of experiences, but they show little interest in the physical structures of the experienced world. In the detailed Abhidharmist analysis, the focus is on a phenomenology of consciousness to help clear the mind of obstacles in order to achieve the desireless state. There is little interest in the material world—in fact, all of matter (*rupa*, "form") is grouped into only one of eighty-two *dharmas* and then is analyzed into factors of experience. Even the name "form" relates only to our *experience* and not "*matter in itself*"—it is about the form of things that we directly experience and not any possible material substance behind them. By naming things, we give what is actually there form—hence, the common phrase for the physical world: "name and form (*nama-rupa*)." It does not relate to "matter" or "physical energy." Or, as in Daoism and Neoplatonism, mystics' metaphysics may emphasize the emanation of things to explain the relation of "being" to the realm of "becoming," but not the efficient causal connections of things within the natural world. Classical mystics simply do not express any disinterested, intellectual curiosity in understanding how karma or any other structure works or in devising explanations of them, unlike what one would expect from scientists. And this makes perfect sense in light the mystics' interest in an aspect of reality not amenable to scientific analysis. Buddhist theorists do discuss such matters extensively, but only in the context of how to end suffering, not out of an disinterested desire to know the efficient causation of things.

Belief-systems in mindfulness traditions that have specific ontological claims about the general nature of the natural world create the possibility of contact with physics. That is, with the presence of metaphysics in mystical ways of life, ideas from different mystical systems do enter the domain of science, and this creates the possibility that a particular scientific theory and the doctrines of a particular mystical tradition will agree or conflict. Different mystical traditions advance beliefs about the structures related to the mind and human beings (in particular, that something in us survives death), and these may agree or conflict with specific scientific theories in neuroscience. The historical sciences—cosmology, geology, evolution—may present specific problems for the creation myths of different religions, and mystical belief-systems will share any of these problems when these myths are adopted from their encompassing religions.

The Divergence of Science and Mysticism

However, the divergence of interests and subjects in science and mysticism means that, even though basic mystical metaphysical claims and scientific claims are in "harmony" (since they do not overlap and so cannot conflict in principle), it is still impossible to say that science and mysticism "converge" or that science "confirms" the *specifically mystical claims* of any tradition since they diverge in the substance of their claims. That mysticism is about the beingness of the world and science about the structures governing events within the world precludes any contact of their core claims.

As discussed in Chapter 6, mystics are interested in unity, but it is a matter of the oneness of being, not anything to do with unifying structures. Thus, we cannot transmute any mystical insight somehow into a scientific study of the possible unification of structures. Nor is any science necessary to mysticism. Mysticism thrived before Einstein and before modern science. It could also thrive perfectly well within a Newtonian worldview: the same mystical source supplies the being of the unconnected parts (depth-mysticism interpreted as the source of all beingness), and the world of everyday phenomena is still impermanent even if their smallest components are not (which is sufficient for mindfulness). Indeed, some Buddhists in fact adopted a theory of discrete, minuscule atoms, as will be discussed in Chapter 6. Neither quantum physics nor cosmology nor any other science is getting us closer to a possible depth-mystical source of beingness, and any unification of physical or other forces at work in the world of phenomena into one structure is equally irrelevant to either depth-mysticism or mindfulness. In sum, the "new physics" of the twentieth century is not any more mystical than the older one. From a mystical point of view, Einstein is no different than Newton.

So too, contrary to what those making comparisons of science and mysticism may think, the quantum realm offers no evidence for any spiritual entities or a transcendental realm, nor does it offer evidence against naturalism: the new outlook still involves only parts of the natural realm, even if they are not "rock solid" bits of matter. Quantum physics and relativity theory present no problems for reductive materialists: the new sciences are as "materialistic" as Newtonian physics and no more "spiritual," even though fields of energy rather than discrete, material objects have become the primary physical reality.[10] Energy is as much a feature of the natural universe as matter. Quantum physics does involve the impermanence of "material" objects and the conversion of matter to energy and vice versa, but this is only a problem for a simplistic equation of materialism with solid objects, not naturalism.

The bottom line is that mystics and scientists are not trying to accomplish the same thing. The mystic's mindful mind shifts attention to the beingness of the experienced world independent of the conceptualizations we impose, while the scientist's analytical mind focuses on the differentiations within the experienced world and their underlying explanatory structures. Science will always be a matter of the very differentiations that mystics are directing our attention away from. Mystical experiences as a way of knowing an aspect of reality will always remain distinct from science, and the necessity of a broader metaphysics within a mystical way of life does not change this.

Notes

1. This must be qualified by again noting that all mystical traditions involve more than just cultivating mystical experiences. Some practices involve developing paranormal powers, and these may relate to scientific knowledge. For example, the *siddhis* discussed in *Yoga-sutras* III include observational knowledge on astronomy and the Indian *kundalini* physiology. How central these practices are to Yoga is a matter of debate, but it should be noted that many mystics (including Shankara) condemned these powers as an unnecessary distraction.

2. People comparing science and mysticism are not the only thinkers who fail to distinguish being and structure. That what gives being to matter and what structures matter are two distinct aspects of what is real is not usually a topic for reflection. Most people do not analyze the concept "reality," but merely assume it is all "one and the same," and so obviously everyone who studies reality is studying the same thing—that there may be fundamentally different dimensions to it is not considered. Indeed, it is common simply to assume that matter free from structure is "beingness" itself and that the physical properties of nature's structures are identical to that beingness. (See Jones 2009: 25-28, 87-90.)

3. In India, yoga commonly became referred to as a "science" in the twentieth century. But the yoga referred to was not primarily the *raja yoga* of mystical cultivation, but the *hatha yoga* of health and fitness (although the two are not always totally separated). The father of modern body-building had a greater influence on the form and practice of modern yoga than did Neo-Vedanta or any other mystical thought (Alter 2004: 10, 28, 32-36). Hatha yoga's *kundalini* physiology is also difficult to reconcile with Western physiology—all they have in common is a denial of a mind/body dualism (Goldberg 2005). (That yogins may have treated the *kundalini* physiology merely as an *imaginary construct* for focusing the mind should also not be forgotten.)

4. Theologians who are aware of the metaphoric nature of their discussions of the transcendent may be able to teach scientists more about the metaphoric use of language and its limitations; this may help scientists with understanding the nature of their theories, but this would not be an instance of theological tenets influencing science.

5. One may see a "mystical" dimension to the physicist Michael Faraday's science when he spoke of "self-abnegation" and the need for "self-awareness" and "self-knowledge." But this is more likely simply an early attempt to articulate the disinterested "objectivity" of the scientific method (Gooding 1991: 397). But David Gooding concludes that science, although not a spiritual path in itself any more than spinning is (despite Gandhi's use of it), was for Faraday an expression of his spirituality (ibid.: 402).

6. To stretch the possible help to mysticism from science, it could be argued that if we accept that there is a chain of rebirths and that mystical liberation will take many lifetimes, then we should become interested in science in order to improve worldly conditions (e.g., improving the environment or health care) so that the conditions will be better for people, including ourselves, in future rebirths, thereby making liberation easier.

7. Following the Upanishads (*Mundaka Up.* I.1.4-6), Hindus routinely classify the sciences as "lower knowledge (*apara-vidya*)" and not the "higher knowledge (*para-vidya*)" of Brahman. But then again, the *Mundaka* consigns even *the Vedas* to lower knowledge (I.1.5). Thus, this in itself does not rule out transcendent realities being subject to science.

8. In discussing my point about science and mysticism being "distinct and separate," Ian Barbour criticized me for perhaps drawing "too sharp a line between science and religion" (2000: 86). However, I am arguing that it is science and mysticism as *ways of knowing* that are distinct and separate—i.e., what aspects of reality scientists and mystics focus on and how they approach them. But mystical traditions are total *ways of life* having metaphysics and religious ideas, and these may indeed not be completely separate from scientific theorizing (as discussed in Chapter 9).

9. Whether early Buddhists denied any transcendent realities or merely did not discuss them for soteriological reasons is a matter of debate. For example, some read the "no self" doctrine (*anatman*) as not denying that there is a transcendental self but as only denying that there is a self to be found in the world we experience (as Hume and Kant would agree). Edward Conze, for one, argued that the Buddha was saying "Others tell you what the self is; I tell you what the self is not (*anatman*)" in order to clear his listener's mind of any possible images so that the experience of the true self could occur.

10. Cosmology is not any more "spiritual" than any other science. In the nineteenth century, the idea of the "ether"—a medium for the transmission of energy—had religious support from the physicist Sir Oliver Lodge and others: since the ether was *non-material*, it suggested the reality of mind and spirit, and it offered a medium for effects not produced by the mechanical operation of matter. Thus, many Christians objected when the Michelson-Morley experiment raised doubts about the ether's existence: the demise of the ether would have meant the end of the "spiritual" nature of the material universe.

— 4 —

Mysticism and the History of Science

The physicist Werner Heisenberg once remarked that "[i]t is probably true quite generally that in the history of human thinking the most fruitful developments frequently take place at those points where two different lines of thought meet" (1958: 187). Is this true of science and mysticism? To determine whether mysticism played any role in shaping the content of science or in helping or hindering the development of science, historians will have to distinguish different aspects of mysticism: mystical experiences, mysticism as ways of life, and the religious and philosophical doctrines in particular mystical traditions.[1] Mysticism proper also must be distinguished from such occult practices as astrology, alchemy, magic, or Pythagorean "number mysticism" that are not related to the cultivation of mystical experiences in the strict sense, although mysticism and these other practices often share many of the same followers.[2]

Historians will also point out that there is no such thing as "mysticism" or "a mystical worldview" in the abstract.[3] Rather, there are only specific traditions, with specific doctrines about the nature of reality. No one is "religious" in the abstract but always has a concrete faith—to reverse a remark by the philosopher George Santayana, no one can be "religious" in the abstract any more than one can speak "language" in the abstract rather than a specific language. This applies equally to mystical religiosity. But the term "mysticism" still remains a useful umbrella term for classifying some phenomena.[4] And just as linguists can do cross-cultural studies of languages and speak of the nature of language in the abstract, so too scholars can discuss the nature of mysticism, even though each mystic practices in a particular tradition and has particular beliefs and values. Nevertheless, historians will have to look at specific traditions and specific thinkers to see if there was any mystical influence on science and not make generalizations without concrete support.

Some issues for doing history are worth noting. Geoffrey Redmond points out that historians of the sciences of other cultures typically define science by its *content*—i.e., the then-current theories—rather than its *methods* (2008: 16). An anachronistic approach is a real danger when the people making comparisons because science and mysticism only know the current state of sciences and not their

63

histories. This can also lead to seeing a culture's metaphysics as being scientific when it is not. Cultural beliefs are looked at through the lens of science regardless of how they arose and are justified. Thus, the Indic idea of ages (*kalpas*) becomes seen as scientific in nature because cosmologists today have found the universe to be very old and perhaps cyclical. David Gooding points out another issue: so far historians of science-and-religion have focused on the intellectual matter of doctrines and not addressed "spiritual awareness as something which may inform attitudes, shape practices, and inspire scientific activity" (1991: 391). Yung Sik Kim raises another important point: the way science and religion interacted in the West is not necessarily the only way the two can interact or influence each other (1985: 43). In traditional China, we also deal with a different kind of science, a different kind of religion, and a different kind of social and cultural context (ibid.: 44).

As previously discussed, mindfulness and the depth-mystical experiences themselves do not foster an interest in science. Depth-mysticism directs attention away from events in this world and thus could only impede any interest in science from taking root or flourishing in a culture. Mindfulness is more this-worldly, but it too does not foster a scientific interest in the natural realm. Thus, the focus on mystical experiences precluded mysticism as a social institution from having been a positive factor in the development of science in pre-modern classical societies. That is, mysticism's most direct effect would be to take attention away from a culture's interest in science. However, as also discussed in the last chapter, mystical traditions can aid science indirectly. For example, mystical metaphysical beliefs may be a source of ideas that can be worked into potential scientific hypotheses; if so, mystical ideas may have shaped the course of science. So too, it must be remembered that no mystical tradition is "pure"—all are mixed with religious and metaphysical ideas, and these ideas may affect science. Thus, historians will still have to study specific mystical traditions within specific cultures, even though the thrust of mysticism *per se* is anti-scientific.

Mathematics also raises an issue. Both mystical experiences and mathematics involve mental introspection, and this leads many scholars to see a connection between them (e.g., Josephson 1987). Hermann Weyl thought "mathematics... lifts the human mind into closer proximity with the divine than is attainable through any other medium" (1932: 8). This sentiment was also prominent among the Romantics such as Samuel Coleridge and William Wordsworth. Mathematicians are also open to nonordinary experiences. Some mathematicians (e.g., Kurt Gödel) have states of consciousness where they *see* mathematical objects. They also have moments of great clarity in their mathematical thinking, with a resulting sense of astonishment and elation from finding a solution. But there is still a fundamental difference: these moments of insight involve differentiated mental objects, while mystical experiences involve emptying the mind of all differentiations. Mathematical reflection always involves focusing on distinct items and manipulating them. Any unconscious mental processes giving rise to a mathematical intuitions would also have to involve differentiations. Thus, different functions of the mind are involved: an analytical focus on distinctions versus a contemplative approach that empties the mind of such phenomena and quiets the analytical functions of the mind. Still, the historical question remains: did mystical cultivation or mystical ideas affect mathematicians in the East or in the West from Pythagoras on?

To see the type of questions historians will have to address concerning the direct and indirect effects of mysticism in aiding or hindering science and mathematics, it can be helpful to distinguish four historical periods: the traditional sciences of pre-modern societies around the world, the rise of modern science in the West beginning in the late Middle Ages, the development of the modern sciences to date, and the possible future course of science.

Mysticism and Pre-Modern Science

Was mysticism proper part of the mix at the roots of the West that got pre-Socratic Greek philosophers on the road leading to science? How about in the traditional sciences of the early and medieval periods throughout the West and East? All of these cultures had pre-modern but still genuine forms of natural science, i.e., some activity showing an interest in the efficient causation of how things work, even though experimentation and mathematics were not yet fully integrated into this quest. The modern sense of a "scientist" did not develop until well after the rise of modern science in the West; but prior to that, there were "natural philosophers" and "natural historians" in the West who became interested in the causes at work in nature, and some thinkers in Asian cultures shared that interest. These thinkers did not separate "science" and "religion" the way we do today—indeed, "science" was not a separate category at all. Nevertheless, they did some work we would classify as "science" in the modern sense. Although neither Asian nor Western scholars have paid much attention to the relation between spirituality and the various cultures' traditional sciences (Nasr 1999: 168), one can still ask whether mysticism played a role in these endeavors.

The interest necessary for the sciences to thrive is wanting to understand how the natural universe works in terms of the material and efficient causes operating within it. However, medieval Christendom, Islam, and India all had a general *anti-worldly ethos* that made this interest a low priority at best. In Islam, as Sufism gained prominence, Muslim science declined. Sufism was not the only factor causing this decline, but it probably was one of them. The early Sufi Rabi'a represented its general attitude: when asked to step outdoors to observe something, she responded "Contemplation of the creator preoccupies me so much that I do not care to look upon his creation." Such an attitude could not lead to an interest in science. (On religion and science in Islam, India, and China more generally, see Huff 1993 and Redmond 2008.)

China had a more positive view of the world than these other cultures, but its mystics, including the philosophical Daoists, did not contribute to the development of science.[5] Daoists' interest in nature never led to a scientific interest in the causes at work in nature. (See Jones 1993: 127-46.) Nor, contra Joseph Needham, did Daoists somehow see modern science and were trying to give birth to it but just could not succeed in their aspirations because they lacked the necessary theories. Daoists were not "groping after an Einsteinian world-picture, without first having laid the foundations for a Newtonian one" (Needham 1956: 543). Daoism did not retain "unborn within itself, science in the fullest sense," nor was it oriented in a direction that would have ultimately led to modern science (ibid.: 47, 60). The Daoists' interest in a natural life had nothing to do with science, and to view them from this point of view can only distort their thought. Needham's case for Daoists being even proto-scientists is "unconvincing" (Sivin 1970: 872). Needham had to "bludgeon" the Daoist texts in "translations" that "can only be described as travesties" to make his case (Wright 1957: 919). Indeed, Needham's suggestion that Daoist authors adumbrated the idea of natural selection in passages that point out the advantages of being useless (1956: 250) is "surely talking nonsense" (McNeill 1970: 367). Needham's theory of universal progress that holds that all civilizations have been leading to the goal of modern science (Wright 1957: 918) may well have warped his view of Chinese thought.

China, like India, never developed the idea that Greeks devised of a "natural world" separate from human beings and culture; thus, they never developed the curiosity about how the world works that the Greeks did that led to Western science (Nisbett 2003). Scientific and proto-scientific activities were never fully integrated into the scholarly pursuits of the dominant intellectual class, but were marginalized both socially and intellectually (Kim 1985: 41). Technologically, China in the Middle Ages was superior to the West, as is well documented by Needham and his colleagues, but the work of craftsmen and artisans was never integrated with the work of the intellectual elite (Sivin 1971: 871). Thus, we cannot cite its technology as evidence of an interest in the explanations that science provides. Buddhists in general seemed indifferent to scientific interests.[6] In China, Buddhism had a "very largely inhibitory" effect on any scientific interests because of its "profound rejection of the world" (Needham 1956: 396, 430). (Needham qualifies this by arguing that two Indic ideas transported to China by Buddhists may have influenced Chinese science: the idea of a long past in the theory of ages [*kalpas*] "was probably responsible for the recognition of the true nature of fossils in China long before they were understood in Europe," and the theory of rebirth may have led Neo-Confucians to make "a real effort to observe, and to understand, the nature of biological transformations" [ibid.: 420, 422].) When modern science was imported into Asia, it was first seen as part of Western colonialization and imperialism and thus resisted; at best, this led to a lasting indifference to science. This was also the Buddhists' general response (Cabezón 2003: 41).

Advaita Vedanta is the classic case in which the world is treated as a "dream," thus rendering valueless any study of its structures. But medieval Christianity also carried on early Christianity's "contempt of all things worldly (*contemptus mundi*)." To the author of the *Theologia Germanica*, "the devil and nature are one" (McGinn 2006: 421). This too could not inspire a scientific interest. It would be too extreme to claim that mysticism was solely responsible for this ethos or for holding a culture in its thrall (religious concern with a transcendental salvation would be a more general cause), but mysticism certainly contributed to the ethos and did nothing to overthrow it. Western Christianity, while maintaining a strong mystical tradition, was less mystical than Eastern Christianity. This difference in atmosphere may have enabled Western Christendom to be the first classical society to break the hold of the world-rejecting ethos that stood in the way of science. Thereby, Western Christianity's institutions tolerated more interest in the world and thus let the worldly interest of science take root. Nevertheless, Western Christendom's unique contributions permitting the rise of modern science remained social in nature (institutional support for natural philosophy and a relative freedom of thought from theological control for natural philosophers in universities), not a matter of basic Christian theological doctrines. (See Jones 2011, 2012.)

Some scholars see an aid to the rise of modern science in the medieval Benedictines' interest in physical labor and in Francis of Assisi's love of nature. These, however, are very weak grounds for claiming an alliance between mysticism and the empirical observation and experimentation of natural science. An interest in nature does not necessarily lead to an interest in the efficient causes that explain how things work. Mindfulness in manual labor might have indirectly fostered an interest in nature by nonmystics by making physical effort acceptable to intellectuals, but mystical mindfulness still would have an anti-scientific effect: attention is focused on the beingness of things, not the differentiations of phenomena essential to making scientific observations and theories. As discussed, in science attention is focused on differentiations within the phenomenal world, highlighting some features and not others, and mysticism does not foster this. The discipline of the monastic orders would also discourage any free thought among monks and nuns in favor of deference to what their superiors taught; trying to introduce a new interest, such as science, would be difficult in such circumstances.

Mysticism and the Rise of Modern Science

Looking for mystical assistance in the emergence of modern science in Western Europe in the late medieval and early modern periods is also difficult. (On why modern science arose in Christendom and not in the Islamic world, India, or China, see Jones forthcoming: chap. 2.) Even though empirical study was a key to the rise of modern science, historians cannot make mysticism an influence simply by equating "mysticism" with all things "experiential." In fact, historians have been across the board in their treatment of mysticism, and not very accurate in their understanding of it. Many simply group mysticism with other occult practices (e.g., Goldstein 1980: 136-45) without noting possible differences in effects. Others equate mysticism with empiricism in general in the battle with scholastic rationalism (e.g., Needham 1956: 89-98). Others go the other way and place mysticism on the side of rationalism since it involves cultivating the mind and not empirical research—in the words of the theologian Paul Tillich, "modern rational autonomy is the child of the mystical doctrine of the autonomy of the inner light" (1951: 141).

Clarifying mysticism proper in this situation will be important. In particular, various occult practices including alchemy and magic may well have played a role in the rise of modern science in the Renaissance, but mysticism proper should not automatically be grouped with them. For example, Johannes Kepler's interest in number and sun symbolisms cannot be called "mystical" in the strict sense—it has nothing to do with the inner quest of stilling the mind and emptying it of differentiations. So too, the fact that Chinese thought (especially Confucianism) became popular in the Age of Enlightenment among European intellectuals questioning Christianity does mean that Chinese ideas were among the mix of ideas circulating in that period among natural philosophers, but it does not mean that Chinese mystical ideas necessarily influenced European scientific thinking.

Thus, the question remains: did mysticism proper influence the rise of modern science? For example, did Christians' Latin writings on medieval Jewish Kabbala emanationism influence Isaac Newton's view of space as "the sensorium of God"? Did the Kabbalist *Zohar* influence the idea that the Bible did not have to be taken literally (thereby loosening the control of biblical factual claims on science)? More generally, did a mystical sense of the oneness of being inspire a quest for unifying nature through laws governing all of creation, both terrestrial and celestial? However, the contrast between mysticism proper and the "new philosophy" once again seems more prominent. Neoplatonism may have had a positive role in the rise of modern science: its belief that the world is a reflection of the One may have led some thinkers to believe the world is worthy of study. But Neoplatonists themselves, such as Henry More, tended to dismiss science as an unworthy activity since it dealt with the impermanent world of imperfect matter rather than the permanent spiritual realm of eternal forms. Fortunately for science, the Cambridge Platonists' most famous student—Isaac Newton—did not respond that way.

Certainly scientific experimentation takes a more *aggressive stance* toward nature than the passive *receptivity* of mystical perception. Francis Bacon set modern science on its course to "dominate" nature. His writings such as the *Novum Organum* are replete with images of torture, rape, conquest, and making nature our slave—e.g., nature's "beautiful bosom laid bare; she must be held down and finally penetrated, pierced and vanquished." Often he explicitly contrasts his experimental approach with the contemplative approach of medieval Aristotelians. More generally, natural philosophers adopting the "new philosophy" spoke of "putting nature to the question," i.e., of interrogating her under torture, and putting nature on the rack to get answers from her. This does reflect, if in extremely violent terms, the assertive and aggressive stance of modern science toward nature and directly conflicts with the contemplative approach of mysticism. It was the mystical and philosophical contemplatives who looked upon the Bible, not as a book of scientific knowledge (*scientia*), but as a book to be interpreted nonliterally to give wisdom (*sapientia*), e.g., seeing the Gospel story of Mary and Martha (Luke 10:38-42) in terms of the relation of the "active" and "contemplative" lives in a Christian way of life. But in the early modern period contemplation switched from primarily an inner quest to primarily external observation of nature.

Indeed, mysticism proper appears to have continued its anti-scientific effect in this period. But under the influence of Renaissance humanism, the superiority of the contemplative life became doubted (Gruner 1975: 67). This period was also a time of change in mysticism (e.g., the rise of quietism), thus further complicating the issue of what caused what, if any causation between the endeavors was involved at all. But the "world as an enemy" attitude continued in mystical circles well after the rise of modern science. For example, the works of the Englishman William Law in the eighteenth century can be seen as a mystically-inspired reaction against the world of modernity created in part by science. But the overall effect of the rise of science was the end of mystical experience as a cognitive authority: mystical experience was replaced with observation and experimentation as the means of gaining insight into the nature of the world, and mystical "contemplation" was replaced completely with philosophical "contemplation." Empirical observation, which had previously been held to be the lowest means to knowledge, eventually became the only means of knowledge of nature.

Mysticism and Modern Science

In the nineteenth century, Hindu and especially Buddhist ideas were often cited to support science and to counter Christian metaphysical ideas. Mysticism seemed to support a general empirical approach to the world. That mystical doctrines were supposedly based directly on experiences, and not on dogma or received revelations, impressed many thinkers. That Indian mysticism was presented as not involving any god was also a plus. Mystics were also said to be tolerant and tentative in their claims and totally free of any metaphysical claims whatsoever. All in all, Indian mysticism seemed to provide forms of religion fit for the scientifically-minded. It also played into the long-standing Western fantasy of rescue by the "mysterious East" (McMahan 2008: 214). That Buddhist and Hindu monks and teachers traveling to the West were beginning to present a modernized version of their religions—i.e., one already shaped by Western Enlightenment and scientific thought—no doubt helped this reaction. Buddhism was portrayed as being in exact agreement with the science of the day (ibid.: 64). The Buddha became modeled on a proper Victorian gentleman (ibid.: 65). (On the nineteenth century's "rationalized" and "demythologized" revision of Buddhism into "scientific Buddhism" or "modernist Buddhism," see McMahan 2004 and 2008. Paul Carus's popular *The Gospel of Buddhism* is its classic.[7]) However, a more significant issue for this book is whether ideas from mystical traditions have affected the course of any of the sciences in the modern period by providing either ideas for new theories or even a criterion of theory-acceptance between competing theories.

Early in the twentieth century, a number of theoretical physicists were interested in mysticism.[8] Tony Rothman and George Sudarshan suggest its psychological appeal: "Physicists are often agnostic or atheistic . . . . Buddhism, with its lack of a supreme being, and Vedantic philosophy, with its emphasis on Reality, satisfy their deepest spiritual yearnings without overtly compromising them. The Eastern religions' emphasis of unity is also not foreign to the physicist" (1998: 185).[9] Many important physicists had mystical leanings. (See Wilber 1984.) But Ken Wilber rightly notes that mysticism and physics are *separate* (although he does not separate them in terms of the experience of being and the study of structure), and that modern physics offers no positive support, let alone proof, for a mystical worldview (ibid.: ix, 5).[10] Indeed, he concludes that all of the physicists whom he surveyed saw their science and their mysticism as distinct: their concern for spirituality arose because they recognized that the domain of physics was limited to mathematical representations of reality and did not involve a direct experience of it.

Consider the astrophysicist Arthur Eddington, probably the most mystical in the strict sense of these scientists. He was a deeply religious Quaker who saw spirituality as being able to put us in touch with an unseen reality that physics cannot in principle reach—science provides only "a shadow world of symbols beneath which those methods are unadapted for penetrating" (quoted in Wilber 1984: 8). Eddington's religiosity was mystical, and he did want to reconcile and perhaps even unite the two most important areas of his life (Batten 1995). In each realm he saw himself as a seeker led by an "Inner Light" (ibid.: 233). He did rely on intuitions in science as in religion, and this may have influenced his science. For example, his belief that God spoke by a small voice caused him to reject the Big Bang theory in cosmology (ibid.: 239-40). And even if the specific doctrinal content of his religion did not influence the content of his science any more, values learned from his Quakerism—related to avoiding dogmatism or any certitude, being open-minded, and continuously seeking truth—may have influenced *how* he did science (Stanley 2007: 46-49).

Erwin Schrödinger was probably the physicist most enthusiastic about any Asian mystical teachings. He studied Asian thought throughout his scientific career and even learned Sanskrit to read such Hindu texts as the *Bhagavad-gita* in the original. (However, he had broad philosophical interests—he also wrote on Greek philosophy.) Advaita Vedanta in particular became central to his general thinking about the world. Advaita's claim that the consciousness constituting the reality of the individual self (*atman*) constitutes the reality of all phenomena (*brahman*) influenced his thought on consciousness: he concluded that, although there are many egos, there is only one mind, one consciousness. This became part of his framework for thinking about life in general. However, identifying any specific influence of Hindu thought on Schrödinger's *physics* is harder to do. It has been suggested that his familiarity with paradoxes in mystical thought may have made it easier for him to consider paradoxes in quantum physics, such as his famous cat paradox (see Jammer 1999: 235). But Schrödinger did not see Advaitic monism as supported by modern physics or as a reason to remove a frontier between observer and the observed in quantum physics (Wilber 1984: 7).

Albert Einstein is often cited as a mystic, but it must be emphasized that his sense of a mysterious power underlying the lawfulness of reality is not an experience of *"the mystical"* of any traditional religion. (Einstein supposedly said that in the future religion will be a "cosmic religion" that will "transcend a personal God and avoid dogmas and theology" and will be based on a "religious sense arising from the experience of all things, natural and spiritual, as a meaningful unity," and that "if there is any religion that would cope with modern scientific needs, it would be Buddhism." He probably never said that—at least no source in his published works has been tracked down—but he did say that Buddhism, based on his reading of Arthur Schopenhauer's work on it, has a stronger element of the "cosmic religious feeling" than has the Old Testament.) Einstein had a sense of a mysterious depth to reality, but this depth was always part of the natural universe, and he approached that part of nature as an analytical scientist rather than as a contemplative mystic. His humility was before *the mysteriousness of nature*, not before a transcendental reality. This "cosmic religious feeling" may have driven his science, but it did not make him a mystic in anything like a traditional sense but simply someone awed by the orderliness of all of nature (1954: 38-39). Indeed, he scoffed at the idea that he was a mystic (Jammer 1999: 125-26).

More generally, it is important to ask whether these "mystically-minded physicists" were interested only in mystical *ideas* rather than in having actual mystical *experiences*. The former might be reworked into possibly helpful scientific ideas without engaging in cultivating the latter. Evidence of actual mystical experiences or practices would have to be found to affirm an interest in the latter. Otherwise, it may only be a case of analytical scientists coming across some new ideas. The interest may have been restricted to metaphysics and philosophy rather than in new types of experiences. If so, calling these physicists *mystics* because of an interest in mystical philosophical ideas, rather than in cultivating mystical experiences, would be a mistake.

And it is certainly possible that "for all the close historical connection between physics and philosophy, physicists tend to make terrible philosophers" (Rothman and Sudarshan 1998: 257). The astronomer Martin Rees reminds us that "scientists' incursions into theology and philosophy can be embarrassingly naive and dogmatic" (quoted in ibid.). The physicist Steven Weinberg refers to some of the "dreadful examples of Werner Heisenberg's philosophical wanderings" (1996). In the end, scientists' own pronouncements on the matter of science and mysticism may not carry much weight—certainly, just because it is physicists who see parallels does not mean that *physics* warrants it. We cannot attach the imprimatur of science merely because they are scientists. A different justification for the alleged parallels would still be needed.

Still, the basic issue for all scientists with an interest in either mystical metaphysics or mystical experiences is: did their interest in mysticism influence their science—i.e., the *content* of their theories—in any way? It is one thing to say that some *physicists* are intrigued by mysticism and end up rejecting a naturalism that denies there is more to the world than what can be studied by science or endorsing an idealism based on consciousness; it is another thing entirely to say that their mystical interests influenced their *physics* or that they claimed their physics *supports* mysticism or vice versa. Familiarity with texts from other cultures may have led some physicists to be willing to think outside the box when it came to theorizing, but did the religious ideas in those texts actually affect their theorizing? In sum, did the specific beliefs in the one field influence the beliefs in the other?

And what of today and the future? Even if mysticism as a whole had a negative effect on science in the past, are the circumstances today different? Can any mystical ideas be of help to scientists for theorizing by supplying possible ideas that could be worked into testable scientific hypotheses? Does the greater familiarity with, and acceptance of, non-Western religions lead to the possibility of Asian or other mystical ideas may be influencing physics or other sciences? Asian thought has not had the history of interaction with modern science that Christian theology has had, but some of the most important physicists in the first half of the twentieth century had interests in mystical ideas. Since then, however, those seeing a convergence of science and mysticism can only point to physicists who are outside the mainstream and are of a lesser stature in the current physics community. Of course, what is the "fringe of science" today may become "the cutting edge of science" tomorrow depending on how science develops. But as things stand now, it is only the "unorthodox fringes" of science that are becoming increasingly holistic (Sattler 1999: 156).

That modern science has thrived successfully in modern India alongside its traditional religions is also worth noting. Modern Indians contribute to physics, other modern sciences, and mathematics without giving up their traditional religions. Science appears universalizable in a way that, say, Western classical music is not, although the fact that some Asians can do world-class science does not in itself mean that science is not "Western" any more than the fact that there are a few outstanding examples of Western exponents of Bharat Natyam makes that art anything other than an Indian form of dance (Ravindra 1991: 16-17)—it only means that Asians too have been trained in modern science. (To see how some modern Japanese philosophers attempted to accept Western science without eroding the spiritual and ethical values traditional to East Asia, see Kasulis 1995.) Another issue in the relation of non-Western religions to science in general, if not of science to mysticism specifically, is that in India today Vedic fundamentalists have emerged who want to produce "Vedic physics," "Vedic mathematics," and a "Vedic creationism" (Nanda 2003), much like Christian conservatives in the United States and now elsewhere and Muslim conservatives (especially in Turkey) want a "theistic science," although obviously their beliefs about creation would shape science very differently (Brown 2002).[11]

Mystical Metaphysics and Science

Thus, the basic questions for historians are: have core mystical ideas that were developed by scientists either through an interest in metaphysics or an interest in cultivating mystical experiences influenced the course of science? Or have other metaphysical ideas from the encompassing mystical ways of life that are not directly related to mystical experiences done so? For example, in classical China did Daoist doctrines on the interconnection of things lead to a type of "field" theory that in turn led non-Daoists in China who were interested in science to become interested in subjects like magnetism?

We may think that metaphysical or other philosophical ideas have no part to play in science, but in devising ways both to explore and to understand a new area of study scientists do rely on such beliefs. Theorizing and interpreting data is a human activity, and philosophical ideas may guide science forward at the edge of research and also in theory-construction and selection. (See McMullin 1981a, 1981b; Trusted 1991.) Steven Weinberg argues that the time has past when philosophy can help physicists (1992). He states that no one since World War II who has participated actively in the advance of physics has been significantly helped by the work of philosophers (ibid.: 169). He also points to instances in which the metaphysics of mechanicalism and positivism have actually hindered the science of particular physicists (see ibid.: 166-90). But he also has to admit that physicists carry around a working philosophy and that without some guidance they could do nothing at all (ibid.: 167) and that all physicists need some sort of worldview to progress (ibid.: 170). Thus, we may not be able to rule out all influence from metaphysics just yet.

If metaphysics can still influence science, metaphysical ideas may legitimately include considerations of mystical ideas. Mysticism in this way may tangentially affect the course of science through new a metaphysical framework. In particular, might a commitment to a particular mystical tradition's doctrines provide either the motivation or the ultimate grounds for favoring a particular scientific theory over its competitors? As discussed in Chapter 7, is Frithjof Capra's continuing commitment to a "bootstrap" approach in physics, even though the particle approach of quark theory is currently well-established in the physics community, only the result of his interest in mysticism? In the past, has the course of science been so affected? For example, did Neo-Confucian thought indirectly influence modern science through an influence on Leibniz and his notion of a self-contained and self-regulating universe?[12] Or did Nicholas of Cusa's mystically-inspired metaphysics influence Copernicus, both in the content of his specific cosmology and in finding it metaphysically acceptable and also more generally in his decision to apply geometry to nature? (Nicholas also contributed work in mathematics and medicine.) Are Asian mystical ideas influencing modern sciences today?

There is also a danger here in seeing an influence of mystical ideas where there may well have been none. For example, some scholars looking at the history of

Chinese science think that the Chinese interest in astronomy can be explained by the Daoist belief in "the oneness of human beings with all of nature." But obviously such a belief cannot explain this choice of subjects: how would the Daoist belief explain the Chinese interest in celestial phenomena when we are at least as much connected to terrestrial phenomena? So too, Daoists did advocate the end of all self-centered striving against the Way (i.e., non-assertive action [*wu wei*]) and Chinese scientists did show interest in magnetism, with its explanation in terms of a "field" rather than the mechanical pushing and pulling of objects against each other—but this does not mean that the former caused the latter. Why would Daoist beliefs cause an interest only in magnetism? Why weren't all phenomena treated the same way? If magnetism was treated differently, it may only be because of the nature of the phenomenon rather than the influence of any mystical framework. Magnetism in the modern West was initially approached mechanically by William Gilbert, René Descartes, and others, and only subsequently did scientists come to know that a field approach was better; no one alleges this was the result of some mystical influence in the West.

All in all, it is one thing to notice *post facto* a surprising parallel between a new scientific position on some structure and a classical mystical metaphysical doctrine, but it is another thing altogether to argue that as a matter of historical fact the latter actually *caused* the former. The second finding would be historically significant; the first would not. If parallels are established, they cannot now affect science since science already had the ideas incorporated in it. But a nonhistorical question would arise: do such parallels (if they exist) reveal only historical curiosities, or something about the way human beings think? Are the mystical ideas the result of mystical experiences, mystical metaphysics, other cultural beliefs, or from something about human ways of thinking in general?

Notes

1. The reverse question—how science may have affected any changes in mysticism—may also be of interest to historians, e.g., the transformation of Buddhism in the nineteenth century from its encounter with Western philosophy and science. But the topic for this chapter is the possible influence of mysticism on science.

2. Mysticism may be classified as "occult" since it is out of the mainstream of modern Western culture, but it should not be classified as "esoteric" even though the word "mysticism" comes from a Greek word for "silence" and the traditional etymology of "Upanishads" is in terms of "sitting near" (as when telling a secret). Mysticism does involve specialized training from masters and not everyone may be adept at cultivating mystical experiences. But not all mystical traditions involve groups that initiate members into closely-guarded secrets and that consider their knowledge powerful and hence dangerous to the uninitiated. Not all mystics try to keep their teachings secret and hidden from the uninitiated public. Mysticism *per se* cannot be contrasted with science here.

3. Today many scholars who emphasize the historical context of each mystic do not like the abstract term "mysticism" and think that looking at phenomena as "mystical" distorts them. Some would limit the use of "mysticism" to only Christians since the term arose in Christianity. Others would abolish the term altogether and look only at specific people or traditions. But then again, "Buddhism," "Hinduism," and "Christianity" are just as much abstractions too, since they each consist only of subtraditions. And by the same logic, there is no "science," only physics, astronomy, chemistry, biology, and so forth, and then only subcategories of these disciplines—there is no "physics" but only "optics," "quantum mechanics," and so forth. Indeed, all nouns are abstractions: there are no "dogs" but only German shepherds, collies, and so forth. But using abstract terms does not change the character of the phenomena covered or mean that we are looking for some "essentialist" core that makes them all the same—looking at letters, postcards, magazines, and packages in one abstract category of "pieces of mails" does not mean that we think of them as all really just the same thing but only that the different items fall into one abstract category. And the same holds when looking at phenomena from different cultures that are all labeled "mystical." "Mysticism" may be an abstract term, but it can highlight aspects of phenomena for analysis.

4. "Mysticism" existed before the modern concept was invented and existed in cultures that had no such concept. The same is true for "science." Postmodernists not withstanding, the invention of a *concept* does not invent the *phenomenon* in the world that the concept covers. Richard Owen invented the term "dinosaur" in the 1830's to classify some fossils. But to say "dinosaurs did not exist before 1830" would only be a confusing way of saying merely that this way of classifying fossils did not exist before then—dinosaurs existed much earlier, and their existence does not depend on our concepts. And the same applies to our concepts about human phenomena such as mysticism and science.

5. Mystical *philosophical Daoists* (*daojia*) must be distinguished from *religious Daoists* (*daojiao*). The latter, with their stories of immortals with shamanistic and magical power, did make contributions to alchemy and medicine. But the two groups remained distinct, sharing little more than a common name and the acceptance of the general features of traditional Chinese cosmology. (See Sivin 1978 and 1995 for the distinction of various groups in Chinese history designated "Daoist" and their relation to science.)

6. The Buddhist scholar Robert Thurman proposes the "radical idea" that "the Buddha and company in India might have foreseen the dangerous crisis that humans could get into if they did not make self-understanding a higher priority than environmental domination" and so *intentionally decided* not to develop the "outer sciences"—it was not a "failure of the intellect" not to develop modern science, but "a great success of the intellect" to decide to develop only "inner science" instead (Goleman and Thurman 1991: 57). However, he must admit that there is absolutely no historical evidence of any debate over the issue of "external" versus "internal" science or any evidence of a conscious choice to develop only the latter.

7. The emphasis on mystical experiences in Buddhism (and also in Hinduism) might, ironically, be the result of its modern encounter with *science*. By the modern period (and probably earlier), the emphasis in most Buddhist monasteries was on learning doctrines and the performance of rituals. In Asia today, few Buddhist monks or nuns actually meditate, and "path (*marga*) texts" are more revered than followed (Pyysiäinen 2006). Some have argued that meditation in Asian Zen monasteries is less a matter of internal investigation than a ritual re-creation of the Buddha's enlightenment (McMahan 2008: 209). This is not to say that Buddhism is not experientially grounded in mystical experiences—that Buddhaghosa and other authors of path texts were not relying on their own experiences in setting forth

stages of a path does not mean that others had not had these experiences or that these experiences were not central in devising Buddhist doctrines. It only means that the emphasis in Buddhism as practiced is not on mystical experiences or attaining enlightenment. Only under the influence of the Western idea of mysticism as a matter of privatized experiences has enlightenment become a meditative goal, especially among the laity.

    8.   When a given scientist uses the word "mysticism" or "mystical," we must be aware that what he or she means by the term may not be *mysticism* in the strict sense. They may think any unusual experience or an experience of elation, astonishment, beauty, or clarity is "mystical." On the other hand, a scientist may well consider his or her scientific discovery to be *religious*, i.e., of being in touch with a reality transcending the sum of nature's forces and the mundane events that routinely shape our lives—only that person can decide that (Brooke 2008: 159). When scientists with religious convictions claim to have had "something akin to religious experience in their work, their own interpretation cannot simply be brushed aside" (ibid.: 160). But, John Hedley Brooke adds, "[f]eelings of the numinous, of being overpowered by a majestic holiness, seem not to chime with the scientist's own quest for *power over* nature"—there is "a fundamental disanalogy between the incomprehensibility at the heart of religious experience and the rational quest for comprehensibility epitomized by the sciences" (ibid.: 161-62). What is the truth for science and for religion may be fundamentally different (ibid.: 162).

    9.   When the Nobel Prize winning particle physicist Abdus Salam was asked if his Muslim religious beliefs guided his research, he responded that nothing did consciously, but in the back of his mind the *unity* emphasized by Islamic thought perhaps played a role in his thought. This is not necessarily a mystical influence on science, but it is one of religious metaphysics: it is a case of applying, albeit unconsciously, a religion's general belief in unity to the study of scientific topics (although mysticism may have influenced the metaphysics).

    10.   Fritjof Capra calls scientists "mystics," but he admits that he is using the term in a "broad" sense, not in a strict sense. For example, he considers Niels Bohr a mystic, but "his work was his meditation"—"Bohr's science was his mysticism" (Wilber 1982: 247-48). In the strict sense of "mysticism," this claim is simply wrong. Of course, any activity, including science, can be performed selflessly and with a concentrated mind, but the analytical stance of science toward reality limits it as a type of *meditation* in the *mystical* sense or *as a path* cultivating mystical experiences and leading to mystical enlightenment.

    11.   "Vedic physics" is based on the sections of the Vedas that were produced prior to the mystical Upanishads, but it too relies on alleged meditative experiences. That is, the defenders of the idea that the Vedas are really science books claim that the Vedic rishis "intuited" or "experientially realized" or "directly perceived in a flash" the laws of quantum physics by altering their consciousness through yogic meditation: by knowing their own minds they came to know the world because a human being is a microcosm of the entire macrocosm (Nanda 2003: 115).

    12.   Joseph Needham and others see Neo-Confucianism as having influenced Western science through Leibniz. But David Mungello concludes from his detailed study of Leibniz and Confucianism that in the eyes of Leibniz Neo-Confucianism only corroborated ideas he had already formed (1977).

— 5 —

Scientific Studies of Meditators

Currently, most cognitive scientists in neuroscience, psychology, artificial intelligence, and philosophy of mind dismiss mystical experiences as simply the product of either speculative wishful thinking or some pathology that is already being studied. But today more and more neuroscientists studying the brain are accepting that mystical experiences are distinct "genuine, neurobiological events" worthy of study (Newberg, d'Aquili, and Rause 2002: 7). Meditative practices may induce long-term neural changes (Lutz et al. 2004). The experiences apparently have reproducible and measurable physiological effects. With advancements in technology, the last few decades have seen a marked increase in studies of the effect of meditation and other spiritual exercises (e.g., fasting, contemplative prayer, and liturgical practices) on brain activity and on other parts of the body. Meditators' responses to stimuli can be studied like any other physical event, since such activity is subject to the same laws of physics and chemistry as any other activity. The effect of meditation on various functions can be studied (e.g., changes in blood flow or in metabolic or respiratory activity), as can changes in the autonomic nervous system and neurochemical changes in the brain. Meditation's effect on such mental activity as attention, perceptual sensitivity, responses to stimuli, and the regulation of emotional states can also be studied (McMahan 2008: 204). There has also been a marked refinement in the precision in such studies, helped especially by neuroimaging technology. Drug studies with hallucinogens have also been revived (Griffiths et al. 2006).

Scientists are attempting to find a set of biological or chemical conditions such that anyone under those conditions would likely have a certain type of religious experience. The one-to-one correlation of conscious states with the neurological or biochemical states of the brain or with specific physiological states of other parts of the body would permit the stimulation of the bodily mechanisms at work in the religious experiences. Attempts have been made not only to identify the neurological bases for these experiences, but to explain how they occur. Different bases have been purposed. (See Cahn and Polich 1999 and Wulff 2000 for overviews; see

Horgan 2003 for a popular account; see Newberg and Lee 2005 for methodological issues in the neuroscientific study of religion.) Scientists are also asking whether there is a genetic base to religious experiences, or at least a genetic propensity to having religious experiences, and also whether there is some evolutionary basis for the continuing presence of religious faith or these experiences in human history.

These are "hard science" approaches to mysticism, not psychotherapy, and they present six points to discuss. Those points in turn lead to philosophical issues discussed in Chapter 13.

The Openness of Mystical Experiences to Physiological Explanation

First, whether mystical experiences are delusional (because of a malfunctioning brain or because experiencers misinterpret their significance) or involve a genuine insight into the nature of reality, it is now accepted that they do occur and are not a matter simply of new ideas. On the other side, no advocate of mysticism can seriously doubt that there must be a physiological basis enabling these experiences to occur. Even though the experience may feel ineffable and not amenable to any worldly categories, the experience's experiential feel and its physiological causes are two different issues. Mystics themselves have no reason to deny the possibility that there are physiological correlates of their experiences since mystical states of consciousness must somehow be mediated by neurological processes in human body—even if mystics are in contact with a transcendent consciousness, they would still need some basis in the brain for this to occur. So too, even if mystical experiences involve genuine insights, they are, after all, human experiences and so must somehow be grounded in the human body. In particular, all experiences apparently have neural substrates, and so there should be a biochemical basis in our brain for any experience. These experiences do not differ from any other experience in this regard. As professor of behavioral medicine Richard Sloan says, "there is nothing at all remarkable about reporting that ecstatic religious experiences are associated with a neurological substrate" since "all human conscious activity, religious or otherwise, has an underlying counterpart in the brain" (2006: 247-49). And, as discussed in Chapter 13, simply finding the neurological bases of the depth-mystical experience does not mean it cannot be an experience of a transcendental reality but must be only a brain event—i.e., identifying such effects or bases does not entail *reducing* the mind to the body for any experience.

Thus, there is no conflict of mysticism and the scientific study of mystical experiences per se. This applies to meditation: because of the interconnection or at least interaction of the mind and body, any calming of the mind during meditation will probably have effects on the body, i.e., at least calming and stabilizing various functions. Such effects may be measurable. Nor is there any reason to doubt that neuroscientists may eventually identify the exact parts of the brain that are active in such experiences. The picture in neuroscience at present is of an exciting field of study with different competing explanations of different types of religious experiences, both in terms of the mechanisms involved and in the alleged locale in the brain associated with the experiences. And there is no reason to doubt that eventually scientists may end up with a consensus about the mechanics of mystical experiences. Nevertheless, scientists should be cautious in jumping too quickly to a conclusion about the material basis of mystical experiences. To begin with, there are two different types of mystical experiences, and how the brain is functioning during them may differ. (See Hood 1997; Dunn, Hartigan, and Mikulas 1999.) If, for example, some drug could stimulate depth-mystical experiences, this does not mean that it can stimulate mindfulness. So too, different areas of the brain may be involved in the different experiences. In addition, within the two basic meditative tracks, there are a plethora of techniques and meditative sequences (see Andresen 2000); these may well involve different physiological states.

Broader talk of a "God gene" to explain spirituality in general will only be that much more risky. Apparently even simple human traits may involve hundreds of different genes (see Beauregard and O'Leary 2007: 47-55), and experiences may involve more than one area of the brain simultaneously. V. S. Ramachandran's identification of microseizures in the left temporal-lobe as the neurological basis of religious experiences reveals another problem: not everyone who has this type of epileptic seizures have religious experiences (1998: 186)—most just have epileptic seizures. (The reactions in this type of epilepsy are not the muscular seizures of the more familiar type of epilepsy.) Any explanation in terms of epileptic activity in the temporal lobe would have to explain why some people have religious experiences and others do not, and why the former experiences are positive in tone while the seizure state is not. Something in an individual's *personality* may be a factor in whether he or she has a religious experience or not. Moreover, this type of epilepsy involves areas of the brain associated with speech; at most, it is associated with triggering numinous *visions and auditions*, not the *silent, inner experiences* of mysticism. For example, the meditating Buddhist monks and Carmelite nuns studied by Eugene d'Aquili and Andrew Newberg exhibited no signs of this or any other pathology, and one cannot merely assume that they must have had this epilepsy because that is what causes these experiences without arguing in a very tight circle.

Indeed, mystical and spiritual experiences may not be associated with only one spot in the brain (Beauregard and O'Leary 2007: 255-88). Ramachandran realizes that scientists are still a long way from showing that there is a "God module" in the brain that might be genetically specified—scientists are currently in a "twilight zone" of neurology (1998: 188). Thus, any simple explanations in terms of, for example, temporal lobe activity may not be detailed enough to explain the physiological base of both types of mystical experiences, let alone all types of religious experiences. (See Albright 2000.) Arguably, it should be easier to find physiological bases for each type of mystical experience than for numinous experiences such as revelations since the latter experiences seem to be more complex events: they involve sensory-like activity (visions, auditions, tactile sensations, or a combination of these), memory, emotions, and motor activity. Mystical experiences seem simpler in this regard, but even they may be complex. (See Beauregard and O'Leary 2007.) Mindfulness combines calming with sense-experience, internal mental operations, and emotions. The depth-mystical experience may also involve many different parts of the brain, in which case it too would have no simple explanation. And considering the different physiological effects that the same type of meditation often produces, the picture may be a good deal more complex than could be handled by any simple explanation. Indeed, some critics today dismiss the entire enterprise of trying to locate a locus in the brain of any behavior or complex mental event as "the new phrenology."

Scientific Study Versus Mystical Practices

It must be remembered that these scientists are doing science, not engaging in a mystical practice. This may sound obvious, but those comparing science and mysticism often miss this. Getting readings on Tibetan monks during meditation does not make this science "mystical." Nor do mystics "observe" their consciousness for scientific purposes: they are trying to calm their mind to end a sense of self and are not making a catalog of different "altered states of consciousness" out of a scientific interest in the nature of the mind. They are simply letting scientists take readings while they conduct their meditative exercises. It is not as if they are trying to refine their observation in meditation because they want to develop a new neuroscientific theory. They witness events in their own mind as if from a third-person point of view, but not out of a disinterested desire to learn how the brain works: they are not interested in acquiring an altered state of consciousness, but in attaining the knowledge necessary to align their lives with reality. Buddhists have not been studying the problem of the relation of mind to matter for ages and have not been developing new hypotheses on the issue (contra Wallace and Hodel 2008: xviii)—they have been focusing on ending their suffering and not studying the relation of the mind to the brain at all. And putting the word "experiments" in quotation marks when discussing meditation (e.g., ibid.: 142) does not make the meditators' observation of their mental states, as they attempt to calm their mind, into scientific experiments. Buddhists have not been pursuing the "scientific study of consciousness" for two and a half millennia (contra Beauregard and O'Leary 2007: 256).[1] Not all introspection is for a scientific purpose—the Buddhist objective, again, is a spiritual enlightenment regardless of the findings of how the brain works. Buddhist meditators may have discovered states of mind or other things about the mind that are not known to modern neuroscientists, but this was not their objective. So too, mystics may let scientists study them while they meditate, but observing the brain at work and explaining how it works is not why Buddhists are engaged in meditation: they are trying to calm the mind and discern the real to live in accordance with reality and thus to end suffering. Of course, mystics may step off of their spiritual path and observe their states of mind for the benefit of scientists, but they would then be changing what they had been doing.

This divergence of purposes severely limits claims that science and Buddhism are "similar in spirit" (Dalai Lama 2005: 23-29), even though mystical practices do involve both observations of mental states and rigorous arguments about the nature of what is experienced. Scientists and mystics may share the goal of disinterested observation, but the divergence in their purposes and in how those observations are utilized in their respective pursuits precludes any substantial convergence. According to José Cabezón, there is "widespread skepticism" among meditating monks regarding the value of neuroscientific studies of meditative states and the long-term effects of meditative practice (2003: 42).[2] From a mystical point of view, such skepticism is justified. Meditation is part of an encompassing mystical way of life leading toward enlightenment, and any physiological mechanisms enabling mystical experiences to occur are simply irrelevant to those participating in these ways of life. It is the permanent transformation of a person that is central to mysticism, not any temporary or even permanent change in brain events that may or may not be accompanying such a transformation.

In sum, any scientific study measuring the brain activity accompanying mystical experiences is not a spiritual exercise, and any mystical exercise performed for scientists is not an instance of practicing science. Science may aid mysticism here: the scientific study of meditation might inform meditative practices by showing how practices could be more efficient in calming the analytical mind. Conversely, mysticism may aid science by providing new data to study. But Buddhism or another meditative tradition could be *incorporated* into cognitive science only by significantly altering that tradition's nature, and mysticism's contemplative approach precludes this possibility. But advocates of the new approach to cognitive science do seem to want each endeavor to "reshape" the other (e.g., Thompson 2006: 233).

Are New Theories of the Mind Needed?

To date, meditation has only been a source of new data about the functions of the mind for neuroscientists.[3] That is, scientists studying meditators at present are still primarily in the fact-gathering stage. Neuroimaging is beginning to demonstrate the areas of the brain affected by meditation. But it is one thing to study previously unstudied states of consciousness or mental functions; it is another to come up with a *new theory* of the mind or for how the brain works. Efforts at theorizing are also beginning. But to date there is no consensus on the underlying neurophysiological changes induced by meditation (Cahn and Polich 1999: 200) or on theories about how the brain or mind is affected. Investigators such as Andrew Newberg are modifying their own theories as their research continues. Nevertheless, these studies do lead to a broader question: do mystical experiences force a revision in the current framework of neuroscientific theories?

In studying meditation, Western scientists are looking at aspects of how the brain functions in certain unusual experiences, but it is not at all obvious that they must revise any accepted theory of how the brain works in light of these studies. (See Harrington and Zajonc 2006.) They may be able to explain the workings quite conventionally. However, meditation may reveal aspects of consciousness or types of mental functioning that cannot be explained by existing theories. Perhaps, as many classical mystics claimed, there is a unique mental functioning in mystical experiences distinct from reasoning and other experiences (e.g., the "intellect" of medieval Christian mysticism). Or there is the possibility that the depth-mystical experience is a matter of consciousness occurring without an object of attention—a "pure" lucid state free of any differentiated and objectifiable content or functional purpose (Forman 1990).[4] Meditation may aid in understanding consciousness itself by clearing away the noise in most conscious states, thereby leaving a "pure awareness," free of other activity (Forman 1998). Some evidence exists for such a state of awareness free of sensory and conceptual content. (See Peters 1998: 13-16; Sullivan 1995.) The depth-mystical experience may be presenting consciousness in its simplest form. Such a state would make it harder to see consciousness as merely a product of sensory or other bodily activity. The contemplative traditions can also be seen as enhancing and extending the faculty of mental perception through the cultivation of extraordinary states of meditative concentration and techniques for cultivating insight (Wallace 2003: 23). And just as high-energy physics caused physicists to rethink aspects of Newtonian theory, so too developing "high-energy states of consciousness" or new mental capacities may open neuroscientists to the need for new explanations (Wallace 2007: 167). Or maybe not: materialists may still argue that no new theory is needed since depth-mystical experiences only involve a malfunctioning brain when all sensory and other differentiated content is removed. And there is also the danger in engaging science that mystical traditions will be coopted: instead of expanding science, mystical traditions may end within a materialistic framework, thereby changing their character (McMahan 2008: 210).

But it is possible that neuroscientists may come to question the metaphysical framework of their science as currently practiced and treat the mind as a nonmaterial cause acting on the brain.[5] Currently the framework for most neuroscientists is materialist: consciousness is simply an activity or product of matter, and thus the focus in studying any experiences can be exclusively on the material bases producing our consciousness.[6] There is nothing more to a brain than there is to a rock except the intricacy of its organization, and consciousness, if it is treated as real at all, is at most "secreted" by the brain the way the stomach secretes digestive acids. Some neuroscientists recognize that materialism is a philosophical assumption and accept it only tentatively, but many think it is an empirical finding of science itself and do not qualify their claims—they go from establishing neural correlates to a reduction of mental events. (See Hick 2006: 92-103.) To their minds, there could be no correlation of conscious and material events unless the latter somehow constitutes or at least causes the former. However, others disagree: the causation could be the other way around or there may be some other explanation for the correlation. Consciousness may become accepted as an intrinsic part of the universe having its own causal powers, even though it is dependent upon material bases for its appearance. If so, neuroscience will have to change. But just because meditation may, for example, lower stress-levels in the body, does not mean that the mind necessarily is not a product of matter (Flanagan 2007: 92).[7] So too, "pure consciousness" events may be explainable in a materialistic framework, even if this requires dismissing these experiences as malfunctions due to sensory deprivation or some other interference with the brain's activity. Thus, a dualistic mind/body framework may not be needed to explain the effects of meditation.

But scientists arguably cannot develop an adequate understanding of consciousness using only the "instrumental/analytical" functions of the mind and any non-analytical functions currently recognized by scientists. That is, unless mystical experiences can be shown to be the result of mental malfunctioning, scientists cannot ignore mystical experiences but must account for the "receptive/contemplative" mode of both mystical tracks. But it would be the *experiences themselves* that are the new data on states of consciousness that scientists then accept—the alleged mystical *insights* would not be influencing science. It is not a "dialog" between mysticism and science: scientists are studying the brain, not engaging mystical claims. Scientists are not looking at any aspects of actual mystical traditions. If, however, the scientists revise their theories in light of Buddhist or other mystical beliefs, then this will be an instance of mysticism contributing to science. (See Goleman and Thurman 1991; Austin 1998; Wallace's response to Smith-Churchland's materialism in Houshmand, Livingston, and Wallace 1999: 33-36.)

Can a New Science of the Mind be Developed?

Over the centuries Buddhists have developed precise descriptions and a classification of the mental states relevant to their practices and goal of selflessness. But neuroscientists to date are using standard Western scientific techniques to study meditators, not adapting Buddhist or other theories to develop new approaches to the mind. In short, they have not come up with a new science, one that may have to be significantly different from current neuroscience. Only facts discerned by the analytical mind and current scientific methods are accepted into the body of knowledge. Currently, scientific explanations are mechanistic, i.e., trying to explain the mind in terms of material forces acting on the brain's constituent parts (DeCharms 1997). Any first-person approach emphasizing the test-subject's actual, immediate awareness or a second-person approach through trained interviewers have not been fully incorporated. First-person experience is simply not quantifiable or measurable in any exact way but is something different in character. Instead, only the third-person approach, with its repeatable results testable by others, is seen as leading to scientific knowledge in consciousness studies. Indeed, the "bedrock of scientific methodology is objective corroboration" by others (Shear and Jevning 1999: 189). Thus, the focus remains on the physical processes accompanying subjective experiences since these can be measured the same as any other processes in physics and chemistry. Even when a neuroscientist who is a nonreductionist and who has had mystical experiences—Mario Beauregard—speaks of a "new scientific frame of reference" that goes beyond materialism, he still ends up speaking only of the scientific investigation of the neural, physiological, psychological, and social conditions favoring the occurrence of mystical experiences (2007: 294-95), not a new type of *science*.

In sum, current neuroscience is a matter of the neural "hardware" of the brain. But others argue that we also need "soft sciences" to deal with the "software" of the mind (Goleman and Thurman 1991: 57-58). In current science, scientists need to specify and test theories in the ordinary state of consciousness. Charles Tart and Roger Walsh see this as problematic for the scientific study of any altered states of consciousness. They think that the nature of mystical experiences cannot be judged by the unenlightened in ordinary consciousness and thus a new type of science is needed. They propose that "state-specific sciences" be developed to understand the phenomena of the altered states. Since all sciences depend on methods appropriate to their subject-matter and replication depends on properly trained observers, scientists would need to be trained to be participant-observers of altered states of consciousness, both to report on the experiences and to test theories of their nature. (Walsh 1991; see also Wallace 1989, 2007. For a classic treatise on the general need for first-person experiences to study mysticism, see Staal 1975). This would separate the study of mystical experiences from the objective approach of physics, which remains the current paradigm for neuroscience.[8]

Such a "contemplative science," however, would not be a substitute or replacement for neuroscience as currently practiced, with its mechanistic approach that operates in the ordinary state of consciousness and studies physiological correlates of mystical experiences. Rather, all the first-person approaches would fulfill aims that the methods of the current natural sciences were never designed to achieve (Wallace 2003: 260; see also Ricard 2003). Thus, it would be part of a new expanded science of consciousness embracing both neuroscience and personal experience—a collaboration of first-person and third-person approaches. (See Shear and Jevning 1999; Cabezón 2003: 52-55; Lancaster 2004; Dalai Lama 2005: 133-37; Thompson 2006.) In fact, the basic idea of a research strategy linking the phenomenological approach with a neural approach is already in place; the study of mystical experiences did not introduce the idea (Flanagan 2007: 84).

While most of these thinkers view the first-person approach and current neuroscience as *complements* that should both be utilized together by scientists to produce a more complete picture of human consciousness, some are advocating a *synthesis* of the two into one new science that would change the character of current neuroscience. Some argue both that the first-person approach should not replace current neuroscience but only supplement it and that there is something fundamentally wrong with the current neuroscientific approach since it does not include consciousness as a cause (e.g., Wallace 2003: 144). In any case, little has been done on this front with regard to mystical states of consciousness. In addition, a first-person, introspective approach to studying mystical experiences may require studying meditation under the guidance of an expert meditation master. It would also be subject to all the problems of first-person reports for any science. Such reports are notoriously unreliable: how do we know mystics are not in the same category as the epileptic who says that "the table seems wavy" or a patient suffering a pathology who mistakes his wife for a hat (Forman 1998: 188-89)? How is science to accept any introspective account given after the fact as incorrigible evidence of any claim? Indeed, whether the "pure consciousness" of a depth-mystical experience is amenable even to any first-person introspection is an issue: "awareness itself" cannot become a phenomenal object—it is inherently subjective. When we "observe consciousness" (i.e., when we are aware that we are aware), what is observed is an object, and that by definition is not the subjectivity of consciousness. We become aware that we were aware only after the experience is over. While actually in the depth-mystical state, it seems contentless; it only becomes an object for inspection when outside the experience. But if consciousness constitutes a level of reality that is not reducible to material bases, then insights into certain aspects of what is real in the universe could only be achieved in a first-person manner and not by a third-person approach.

If consciousness is accepted as causally real, this raises another issue: whether during neuroscientific research scientists can actually bracket the metaphysical dispute over whether consciousness can be reduced to merely physical processes (Dalai Lama 2005: 136-37; Flanagan 2007: 93) or whether a new metaphysical framework is needed for neuroscience. That is, the question is not only whether a new type of science incorporating both first-person accounts of experiences and neuroscientific accounts of mechanisms is needed, but also whether third-person neuroscience as currently practiced is fundamentally misguided.

Can Consciousness be Studied Scientifically?

There is also a very real issue of whether the *subjectivity* inherent in consciousness can be scientifically studied at all. It is one thing to identify the neurophysiological correlates of an experience and another thing to study the "lived" experience itself. In consciousness studies in general, there is the problem of the "felt" aspects of such states as sense-experience and pains—"qualia"—versus the physical activity in the brain occurring during those experiences. (See Jones 2000: 88-94.) Because qualia remain experientially distinct, they are not explained away merely by discovering the base in the brain permitting them to occur. The first-person sensation of seeing the greenness of grass is not reducible to the sum of the physical events occurring when we look at grass. That the nature of consciousness is itself a mystery is revealed by the fact that the scientists and philosophers cannot even agree on what exactly they are studying or come up with a common definition. When scientists speak of a "science of consciousness" today, they are referring to identifying neural correlates of conscious events or other physiological bases that they believe consciousness is dependent upon, not the subjective side of these events. Reductive materialists think that the objective, physical bases are all that has to be studied. But for others, there is a difference between neurological or physiological evidence of conscious events and studying the events themselves. Identifying the material correlates of particular conscious events (e.g., identifying the areas of the brain activated when moral judgments are being made) or explaining how they arose is not getting into the conscious events themselves.

Both why consciousness exists at all in a material universe—why there is any subjectivity at all attached to material events—and how it fits into the material world are at present mysteries. Scientists prefer to study specific conscious activity (e.g., perception) and not grapple with the broad issue of how consciousness arises. Still, a global explanation of consciousness itself cannot be found by studying only its different various activities. Even how to study consciousness (as opposed to the brain) is a puzzle. Neuroscientists study the mechanisms of neural events, and they have been able to correlate certain experiences with certain brain activity. This approach is based on the materialistic assumptions that any "subjective" state of mind must be associated with some "objective" brain state and that any changes in that mental state must be associated with changes in that physical state. However, simply identifying the neural correlates of a conscious event tells us nothing about what consciousness is. Nor does correlation explain how or why the brain *produces* consciousness (if that is in fact what occurs) or whether the mind is *identical* to the states of the brain—indeed, correlation is not an *explanation* of anything but only something new to explain. Nor is studying the effects of consciousness. If, for example, intercessory prayer proved to be causally effective in helping patients, scientists could study its effects. But how could they study the conscious events themselves?

Most basically, there does not appear to be any way to study the subjectivity of a person's consciousness itself by objective, third-person means—i.e., no scientific examination of the subjective side seems possible at all. Neuroscience requires studying the mind from the "outside," i.e., by third-person observations of what is going on in someone's brain. (See Wallace 2000.) But putting electrodes on a person's scalp to discover what is occurring in human consciousness seems a little like putting electrodes on a television set to try to discover what program is on (West 1987: 194). No doubt scientists could conduct brain-imaging studies to demonstrate the differences in the activity of cerebral structures occurring while someone is listening to Beethoven or listening to white noise—but would this mean that this experience is explained by the activity of a specific brain region and that this is all there is to it (Sloan 2006: 253)? There simply is no way to present the subjectivity itself for inspection by others.

An unbridgeable gap apparently exists between the material basis and the experience. How is consciousness realized in the brain? Neurons produce electrical signals—how are these transformed into perceptions, thoughts, emotions, and the other things that make up our consciousness? Science to date may show how brain cells produce the signals associated with consciousness, but it has not taken any steps toward showing how the signals could produce another level of reality—the subjectivity of consciousness. As the philosopher David Chalmers puts the problem: how could something as immaterial as consciousness arise from something as unconscious as matter? He believes it will always be impossible to explain consciousness purely in terms of its neural correlates since for any physical process we can always ask why that process should give rise to experience. (He believes consciousness is another irreducible property like mass or charge.) Indeed, it is not al all clear how science could show even in principle how anything material could be conscious, or even how to address the issue scientifically. Despite the Turing test, making a computer that mimics our reactions perfectly still leaves the question of whether it is conscious. Nor does science touch the philosophical issue of materialism: it is unquestioned that every conscious event has a neural correlate, but even if this is so, mere correlation does not address the fundamental issues of how consciousness emerged or whether changes in consciousness can cause changes in the neural base or why conscious events are correlated with material events. Scientists can show that our conscious states are affected by changes in brain states, but this does not mean that consciousness is necessarily a product of matter—the brain states still may be only the material bases needed to allow a separately existing consciousness to appear.

With their success in the study of brain activity, it is easy to see why neuroscientists may simply ignore (or even be unaware of) the philosophical issues and claim to be producing a "theory of consciousness." But as things stand, neuroscientists only study something closely associated with consciousness—its biological underpinnings—and not consciousness itself. Only something that can be measured can be studied scientifically (Sloan 2006: 242), and it is only the correlates of conscious events in the brain that can be measured. Subjectivity is not phenomenal, i.e., it is not an object that can be presented for study. As noted earlier, pure awareness is not an object of consciousness even to ourselves: we can be aware that we are aware, but this does not make the subjectivity of self-consciousness an object for examination. Even if the mind and brain are identical, there is an "inside" to experiences that cannot be studied from the "outside" by examining the brain. It is not simply a matter of different perspectives on the same event—its inside and outside—there is an experiential difference. Any third-person experience of brains does not give us knowledge of anything but an object, and subjectivity cannot be made into an object. EEG's, functional MRI's, and PET and SPECT scans can only reveal the correlates of experience—the observable bodily responses, not the consciousness itself. Even the emerging technology that "reads minds" actually only reads brain states, not subjective experience. No scientific account of the mechanisms active during sense-experience or self-awareness can make us understand what it is like actually to experience those states. Indeed, even detecting the presence or absence of consciousness on the basis of neurological indices is a major problem at present (Peters 1998: 16). As Alan Wallace says, strictly speaking, at present there is no objective, scientific evidence even for the existence of subjective experience (2007: 39). No accounts of phenomena in purely third-person terms would ever even suggest the existence of, much less explain, the subjective qualities that constitute the bulk of our conscious life (Shear and Jevning 1999: 189).

In sum, experience is manifested to us as a level of reality separate from its material bases, and the matter/experience gap makes attempts at explaining experience in terms of any neurophysiological bases alone hard to conceive. The essential feature of consciousness can in no way be made into an object for study by others, and so there is no way to test it and establish explanations of it by objective phenomena alone. The experiencer's first-hand reports remain an uneliminatable part of any complete study of consciousness even if they never become part of an expanded science. And in studying consciousness, unlike in scientific observation, it is the *experience itself*, not an object or event that is observable by others, that is the subject of interest. The "easy problem" is studying third-person data connected to consciousness; the "hard problem" is explaining the first-person data; each set of data is not reducible to the other, and a science would have to build an explanatory connection between them (Chalmers 2004). In sum, any science of consciousness seems to require first-person reporting, leaving consciousness itself unexaminable by objective, third-party means. (For the prospects of an actual "science of consciousness," see Hameroff, Kaszniak, and Scott 1996; Chalmers 2004.)

This general inability of one person to witness what another one experiences applies equally to meditation. Even if what meditators experience can be reproduced by the meditators themselves during scientific experiments, the inability of others to see what is going on will always limit a "science of meditation." Moreover, even if others can in fact duplicate the physiological state of the brain of an enlightened mystic through meditation, how do we know the subjective state of consciousness is also being duplicated? Most materialists who claim that the mind is a product of the body do concede that at least there is a level of phenomena to be explained. And even a convinced materialist can see limitations on the scientists' ability to identify such correlates since the states of felt experience can vary and cannot be studied third-hand (e.g., Papineau 2002). Similarly here: identifying what is going on in the brain when meditation occurs is one thing; what meditators actually *experience*—the felt sense of selflessness, unity, timelessness, or whatever—is another. A "science of meditation" is not accomplished by a "science of a meditator's brain." (Again, reductive materialists would disagree.) And it must be admitted that as of yet the physiological studies of meditation have not produced anything dramatic about the nature of the consciousness occurring during meditation (West 1987: 196-97). Indeed, scientific studies to date, as Richard Sloan says, reveal the "entirely unremarkable findings" that during meditation the areas of the brain associated with concentration and attention show increased activity compared to other regions (2006: 247-49).[9]

Objective Versus Subjective Reactions

A problem related to the first and last points is that not everyone who meditates undergoes a change in consciousness even if they do have physiological changes. There is a great variety of "subjective" (i.e., experiential) responses accompanying the same physiological changes caused by relaxation techniques, including no changes of consciousness at all (Benson 1975: 115).[10] Practitioners well along the path to enlightenment may have the same physiological reactions as beginners, but they still may have very different subjective experiences. Conversely, it may be that enlightened states produce only very subtle differences or no differences at all in physiological reactions than do unenlightened ones in advanced meditators. In sum, meditators, including those within the same religious tradition, may be undergoing different experiences even when their physiology registers the same state. The reverse of this problem also cannot be ruled out in advance of actual study: meditators may undergo similar subjective reactions while having different physiological reactions. That different meditative techniques can lead to the same effect should also be noted, e.g., sensory overload and sensory deprivation apparently both lead to hyperactivity in the limbic system.

In the end, scientists may be able to trigger changes in brain states or other physiological changes, but it is not obvious that they can produce a given experience or subjective state. So too, meditation may work on the brain's wiring, but mystical experiences may be a different type of effect. Whether a given person has a mystical experience or not may be a matter of his or her personality (e.g., being open to new experiences). This also raises the related issue of whether all of the experiences induced by *artificial stimulation* by means of drugs or something else are in fact the same as those cultivated by *meditation* alone. The artificial stimulation of a mystical experience may duplicate the chemical reactions of a mystical experience but not the "subjective" experience. Drug-induced experiences may have less of a long-term impact on a person's physiology than do experiences resulting from cultivation on a path. May at least some of the experiences differ in nature too? It may be that experiences stimulated by drugs or electricity do not duplicate all the features of spontaneous or meditation-cultivated mystical experiences but only a shell of their physiological features—i.e., the stimulation may indeed activate the areas of the brain involved in "genuine" mystical experiences, but there may still be more to the subjective side of these experiences than is enabled by the laboratory procedures. Or it may be that some people who have the artificial stimulation administered to them do indeed have genuine mystical experiences and other people do not.

However, some religious believers express skepticism of any alleged stimulation of genuine religious experiences on these grounds. Whether technology is able to produce a genuine mystical experience or activate all the subjective aspects of such experiences is a real question. For example, Michael Persinger's "God helmet" generates a weak magnetic field that triggers a small burst of electrical activity in the temporal lobes; this causes some people to experience a sensed presence of a separate spectral entity; this entity is interpreted by the religious as a religious figure (1987). But Mario Beauregard dismisses such "religious experiences" as merely the products of suggestibility and not genuine religious experiences at all (2007: 96-99). John Hick, in criticizing neuroscientific studies of mystics in general, wants to define "religious experience" more broadly in terms of the transformed state of an experiencer rather than any momentary event that a scientist might study—the "sense of being in the presence of God" is much richer and more diffuse than the naturalistic understanding of religious experiences as unusual neurological episodes that scientists study (2006: 80). He wants to dismiss epileptic seizures or stimulated experiences as anything like true religious experiences except in the formal sense that these experiencers see their experiences in terms of religious concepts (ibid.: 71). Nevertheless, the study of the momentary episodes is certainly legitimate—even Hick concedes that there may be momentary glimpses of a spiritual dimension to nature (ibid.: 77)—and such studies may tell us something about how the brain works, although whether stimulated experiences ever duplicate all of a mystical experience is still an issue.

Notes

1. In the West, there has never been a "mystical science." At the dawn of modern science in the late sixteenth and seventeenth centuries, some Christian theologians (especially in France) spoke of a "mystical science." But this "science of the saints" was not an empirical science with mystics examining various inner mental states and theologians advancing testable theories. Rather, it was simply a field of theology differing from scholastic theology. And even this field of theology soon died out. (See Certeau 1992: 101-112.)

2. According to Thupten Jinpa, modern Tibetan scholars are divided on the issue of science. One group views modern science as a rival to Buddhist philosophy (2003; Wallace 2003: 69). A second group views science as an ally and is eager to see science validate Buddhist principles. A third group regards science and Buddhism as equal partners and advocates a model of complementarity in which there is no attempt to reduce one to the other; rather, both science and Buddhism will expand the horizon of human knowledge and thus will give rise to a more comprehensive understanding both of human nature and of the world we inhabit. He places the Dalai Lama in the third group. But, as discussed in Chapter 9, not everything the Dalai Lama and his followers say in discussions with scientists supports the idea of a totally independent science. Jinpa also expresses other concerns about the impact of science on Buddhism (2012).

3. Possible persisting effects of these experiences or long-term changes in experiences outside of meditation, as would be the case with mindfulness or as a possible after-effect of the depth-experience, have also been the subject of follow-up studies. But measuring any lasting, life-changing, transformative effects of practicing entire mystical ways of life may be difficult. Studying sitting meditation, whether the meditators are novices or experienced, and its aftermath is easier.

4. Most naturalists would need convincing that there is a state of "pure consciousness" devoid of any intentional object. Most think there can be no consciousness without an object being present: consciousness is inherently intentional—when there is no object, consciousness is not "on." At best, trying to remain conscious without an object produces a feedback effect that explains the properties of a mystical experience and thus explains away its alleged cognitivity.

5. A contentless consciousness would present problems for functionalism or any information-processing theories of the mind (Sullivan 1995). But mystical experiences do not present the challenge to materialism that *near-death experiences* do. If the latter are genuine, then conscious experiences occur when a patient is clinically dead and the brain is not functioning at all. If so, there would be no correlation of brain states with certain experiences—indeed, it would then be hard to argue that there must be a physiological basis for all conscious experiences. Thus, if genuine, they would suggest that the mind is independent of the brain. Mystical experiences may present new states of mind to study, but in themselves they do not suggest that the mind is not attached somehow to the brain—even if mystical experiences are cognitive, the mind may still simply be the product of the brain.

6. "Identity theorists" claim mental events and brain states are *identical*—when we talk about the mind, we are really talking about physical events in the brain from a different perspective. This approach has not yet been successful. Moreover, there may not always be the same type of physical cause for a given type of mental event. However, all materialists insist that the mind is simply a physical process, or at least that there are only physical causes for each mental state and for each change in a mental state.

7. It is often alleged that individuals' mystical experiences and meditation also have *social* effects—not merely mystics' *social actions* but a direct, paranormal effect on society from the *experiences themselves*. (For Transcendental Meditation's claims in this regard, see Shear 2006: 45. Maharishi Mahesh Yogi's Transcendental Meditation school follows Vivekananda's efforts to form a synthesis of science and spirituality, now by using quantum physics [Nanda 2003: 108].) If such effects are demonstrated, the most obvious explanation would be in terms of the meditator's minds paranormally affecting other minds, thus further complicating explanations of the nature of the human mind.

8. Alan Wallace defines "*objectivity*" only in terms of being "*unbiased*" in an attempt to make the first-person approach *objective* (Wallace and Hodel 2006: 142-44). That is certainly one sense of the term "objectivity" in discussions of the nature of science, but it is not what is meant when critics use the term here: they want something that is *presentable to others to experience*. He also uses the former sense of "objectivity" to loosen up the meaning of "empiricism" (ibid.: 144-47). However, the conflict of knowledge-claims from different mystical traditions makes it hard to speak of mystical states of consciousness confirming or disconfirming any claim in a straight-forward *empiricist* manner. And it is a mischaracterization of contemplative traditions to see them as advancing "hypotheses" for confirmation or disconfirmation (ibid.: 145) rather than engaging in a way of life with other aims and accepted belief-claims. Perhaps he means by "empiricism" simply "empirical" by which he means "experiential" (ibid.: 146). However, empiricism is a philosophical position that

involves more than simply having experiences—it is a matter of the limits of what we can know and of how the truth of empirical statements is established. In empiricism, in contrast to rationalism and realism, knowledge is limited to what we can directly experience. Moreover, whether meditation might establish even a phenomenology of mental states is questionable since meditators of different traditions see the states in terms of different typologies, e.g., the Samkhya versus Buddhist delineation of the constituents of the mind and whether there is a self—their reports may well be emotionally *unbiased*, but there appears to be no *objective* or *empirical* way to determine whose typology is best. Nor is it at all clear how such contemplation can present any information that would shed light on the relationship of the nonphysical mind to physical phenomena (contra ibid.: 147)—whether mindfulness and the depth-mystical experience are products of the brain alone as materialists say or involve something more, they would still have the same phenomenal character.

9. Richard Sloan is especially critical of Newberg and d'Aquili's studies (1999, 2002): he thinks they speculate too broadly based on two small studies with a total of eleven subjects (2006: 247). This may well be true, but he also is under the impression that in describing mystical experiences as "real" Newberg and d'Aquili mean that these experiences are genuine encounters with a transcendental reality and not delusions (ibid.: 249-50). However, all they actually mean by "real" is that mystical experiences are *genuine neurological events* and not merely wishful thinking (e.g., Newberg, d'Aquili, and Rause 2002: 7). They are remaining neutral on whether these experiences are authentic encounters with a transcendental reality or are delusions (e.g., ibid.: 143, 178-79). They do accept the transcendental "Absolute Unity Being" as real (based on it seeming "vividly real" and even more real than the ordinary world after the experience is over and the experiencer has returned to a baseline "dualistic" consciousness), but they realize that this is only their *theory* and is a separate claim from the experiences being *genuine*. (Indeed, the word "genuine" can be very ambiguous here: it can mean a real neurological event rather than wishful thinking, that the brain is not malfunctioning during the experience, or that a transcendental interpretation is veridical.) Sloan's general position that scientific studies of religion reduce religion to something other than what it is or "trivialize the transcendent" is hard to support: merely looking at the measurable physiological effects of religion (if possible) does not make the effects a substitute for religion or otherwise reduce religion to something it is not. (Also see Harrison 2006: 103.) Letting themselves be studied does not reduce meditators to objects or otherwise dehumanize them. Meditators can also acknowledge the physiological effects while still maintaining that their objective is far more than anything scientists measure, just as they can agree that the depth-mystical experience lasted only a certain amount of time while it seemed timeless to them. More generally, religion for the faithful would still remain more than any such effects. Nor would scientific study trivialize the transcendental aspects of religion, although the religious, as Sloan says, may object to "putting God to the test."

10. There may be physiological similarities between meditative states and sleep states (see Cahn and Polich 1999), but meditators remain aware. So too, concentrative meditation and mindfulness meditation differ significantly from each other in their EEG effects and also apparently differ from ordinary states of relaxation (Dunn, Hartigan, and Mikulas 1999).

Part II

Errors in Comparing Scientific and Mystical Theories

— 6 —
Everyday Phenomena Versus Scientific Structures

The distinctions discussed in Part I help expose the basic errors that persist today in science-and-mysticism studies when science as an endeavor or specific scientific theories are compared with mysticism. All center around the one fundamental error: the failure to recognize that scientists deal with how things in nature work in terms of material and efficient causes while mystics try to experience the beingness of the world unmediated by conceptual or emotional framing or experience a transcendental source of beingness. The reason scientists use the analytical functions of the mind is that they focus on distinctions within the realm of structures; mindfulness mystics, on the other hand, utilize a nonconceptual, contemplative function because they focus on something common to everything in the everyday realm that has no distinctions and thus has no elements for the analytical mind to grasp.

The basic problems when trying to establish parallels between the endeavors are these: (1) *Not distinguishing the phenomena of the everyday world from the underlying causal structures.* (2) *Distorting the basic nature of both science and mysticism.* (3) *Not being specific on exactly what is the supposed relation between scientific and mystical claims.* (4) *Not distinguishing mystical metaphysical ideas from claims about mystical experiences.* (5) *Failing to see the difficulties in establishing science and mysticism as converging upon one worldview.* Each of these problems will be discussed in separate chapters of Part II.

The Difference in Content

Many commentators note that scientists and mystics both make a distinction between *appearance* and *reality*. However, the distinction they are actually making is different. For scientists, the reality behind appearances is the underlying *structural causes* responsible for what we experience on the everyday. They need not deny the reality of the everyday world, although reductionists tend to. They are concerned only with the underlying structures that cause the physical phenomena of the everyday world, not beingness. Mystics, on the other hand, are concerned with the real *beingness* underlying our false creations in what we experience. Examining the physical causes of what we experience is simply irrelevant to this, and so mystics advance no claims on the underlying physical causes. For mindfulness mystics, it is the beingness underlying the apparent permanence of the objects we experience on the everyday level—as discussed, "illusions" in the mystical sense (i.e., our conceptualizations of reality into discrete entities) are unreal but not the being we impose the illusions upon. For depth-mystics, it is the distinction between this world and its real source. But not all depth-mystics dismiss the natural world as unreal in favor of a transcendental source—the source may be "more real" because the natural world depends on it, but this does not mean the natural world is totally unreal.

In sum, scientists and mystics are indeed interested in the reality behind appearances, but different aspects of it: scientists are interested in underlying structures, and mystics in underlying beingness. Scientists and mystics do converge on *abstract claims* related to this—e.g., "There is reality behind appearances," or "Everyday objects are constructs"—but focusing on the abstract claims misses the fact that they are dealing with substantively different aspects of reality and approaching the world differently, and hence the senses in which they reject appearances are totally distinct. Thus, contrary to what Victor Mansfield thinks, quantum physics and Madhyamaka Buddhism do not have "many deep links" and "remarkable and detailed connections" (2008: 6)—at most, they converge on an abstract metaphysical claim of impermanence, not on the substance of their claims.

This contrast in content must always be kept clear. However, most comparers of science and mysticism who see some type of convergence—the "parallelists"—see the same terms being used in mysticism and in discussions of science but miss the differences in context and thus believe that mystics and scientists are discussing the same thing.[1] Both scientists and mystics do discuss the "fundamental nature of reality," but this does not mean they are discussing the *same aspect of reality*: the distinction between being and structure still exists, even though both are real. Science and mysticism are not different approaches to the same aspect of reality or different experiences of the same aspect, but distinct endeavors devoted to different dimensions of reality. Science does not explain the mystery that mystics experience, and mystics do not experience what scientists conceptualize.

Parallelists misconstrue the "search for unity" by not distinguishing the unity of being in depth-mysticism from the unity of structures in the sciences.[2] Under the reductionists' approach in philosophy of science, scientists do search for a unity in reality, but it is a unified structure, not the oneness of being (contra Lorimer 1999).[3] These two concepts cannot be conflated: mysticism is neutral to the question of whether scientists can reduce the levels of causation to only one level since the mystics' concern is the oneness of being, not the possible oneness or plurality of structures. Mystics do not aim at a more comprehensive unification than scientists or pursue a Grand Unified Theory (contra Weber 1986: 10). When the physicist David Bohm says "The mystic sees in matter an immanent principle of unity" (ibid.: 144), he is certainly not referring to the Buddha or Shankara, and he admits that "some mystics" go beyond matter to the transcendent (ibid.). In some mystical metaphysics there is one source of all reality (hence, of both being and structures), and hence a deeper unity than in science, but this is still only a matter of metaphysical status of the entire world and is not about the number of structures. There is nothing in any classical mystical system suggesting any interest by mystics in attempting to work on unifying the structures at work in the realm of becoming. Any "Theory of Everything" in physics would be simply irrelevant to the mystics' concern since it would remain a matter of structures—it may capture a "unity," but it is still a unity of structure, not the unity of being that is the only unity of interest in both depth-mysticism and mindfulness. Nor is it a unity of both unity and being. So too, with any unity of structures on the quantum physical level: as long as the content in the quantum realm is in constant flux and connected, mystics have no further interest in it. Quantum physicists are simply not doing what mystics are doing. Similarly, any biological holism is a matter of the interactions of the different parts of an interconnected but differentiated biological whole, not a matter of the organisms' beingness independent of any structures. Nothing on this subject is disclosed in mystical experiences. Perhaps if more scholars used "*identity* of being" when discussing such mystical systems as Advaita (as, in its analogy, in the moon being totally reflected in each drop of water) and not "*unity*" (which suggests a unification of parts), fewer parallelists would be misled concerning "oneness."

It is not only that different states of consciousness are involved, or that mystics look inward while scientists look outward, or that mystics focus on the spiritual and scientists on the material. Mystics do not directly experience the same "truth" that scientists arrive at tentatively or approximately through the route of theory and experiment. Mystics do not reach "fundamental reality" while scientists fail to do so. Each endeavor, if each is in fact cognitive, reaches something fundamentally real but different: mystics experience unmediated beingness or its source; physicists discover the fundamental level of structure, or, under antireductionism, all scientists discover multiple, equally fundamental levels of structuring. Each pursues the depth of a dimension of reality, but not the same dimension. Neither is reducible to the other, and structures and beingness both appear to be equally real and fundamental. And whether there is a common source to both structure and being or whether one in fact is more fundamental than the other in some respect cannot be answered by either endeavor.

In short, scientists and mystics are doing basically different things. The *content* of science and mysticism will always remain distinct, and thus their theories and ideas can never *converge* into one new set of theories replacing theories in either science or mysticism. This also means that science and mysticism are not competing in the same arena: they are different endeavors, and based on science and mysticism alone, neither has any advantage over the other in knowing reality. Nor can one endeavor discredit, confirm, or replace the other. Mystics are not trying to conduct a scientific study of beingness: the contemplative approach of mysticism remains fundamentally non-scientific in nature—since beingness is common to everything, it is not subject to any way of testing. Conversely, scientific analysis is fundamentally nonmystical in nature, with its focus on how the differentiated parts of nature affect each other. Thus, one cannot incorporate the other. Nor can there be an integration of science and mysticism into one new, more comprehensive science—a new "integrated" science of nature (contra Schumacher and Anderson 1979; Weber 1986: 1-19)—since their content will always remain distinct.

Ken Wilber is one figure in this field who argues that science and mysticism are different endeavors and are not converging on one endeavor or one theory (1998).[4] In his view, in mystical consciousness mystics apprehend Reality directly and immediately; but when physicists look at quantum reality or space-time they are not looking at things-in-themselves (direct and unmediated Reality), but only at a set of highly abstract mathematical symbols of reality (1984: 7-8). Scientists, in effect, are looking at the shadows on Plato's cave wall while mystics are experiencing the source of the light and the real world. Thus, Wilber does not see the difference between mysticism and science in terms of "being" versus "structure" or any other distinctions of fundamentally different dimensions to reality—rather, there is only one aspect to reality, and mystics and scientists are apprehending that one aspect, either directly or indirectly.

The Fields of Mysticism

With its focus on the beingness of phenomena, mysticism's fields are the levels of phenomena, both internal and external, open to direct, contemplative experience. The insights into reality involved in mystical experiences are into the apparent impermanence, connectedness, and selflessness of the natural realm in mindfulness and the underlying oneness of beingness in the depth-mystical experience. The mindfulness mystics' insight involves the content of both their mind and macroscopic phenomena. Thus, mindfulness mystics have both an internal and external field of experience, while depth-mystics have the mind alone as their field.

But mystical experiences cover only what is *directly experienced*. Only by a non-experiential (metaphysical) extrapolation does the mystical insight cover all levels of phenomena in the realm of becoming. Mindfulness is a matter of the "such-ness" of the everyday level of the world, and the depth-mystical experience is a matter of the true self or the source of the everyday world's beingness—neither is a matter of any underlying levels of structures that scientists study to explain the changes in the everyday world. We will not learn anything about the structures operating in the subatomic or cosmological realms by meditating. The new scientific interest in emergence, chaos, and complexity of everyday phenomena would have relevance in highlighting the impermanence and interconnectedness of things, but mystical practices are not responsible for the development of theories in these areas. Nor do we need these sciences to see the impermanence and interconnectedness of the everyday realm. Seeing the thoroughness of impermanence in the everyday world may in fact be aided by complexity theory, but science here still remains a matter of trying to explain these observed features.

The most important point concerning external phenomena is that mindfulness remains exclusively on the everyday level—only that level can be *directly experienced*. There is absolutely nothing in the writings of the great Asian spiritual masters remotely suggesting that they were "quite adept" at seeing into matter and space-time, or that through meditation mystics realize that energy comes in discrete packets ("quanta") (contra Nisker 2002: viii, ix). Contrary to what Fritjof Capra says, mystics in higher states of consciousness do not have "a strong intuition for the 'space-time' character of reality" (2000: 171-72) or any other scientific explanatory structure.[5] Nothing in their writings suggest that mindfulness mystics become aware of the quantum realm or experience subatomic structures or experience anything other than the mind or the everyday level of phenomena in the external world. Connecting space and time certainly fits with Buddhist dependency, but the connection would be news to Buddhists—nothing in the Buddhist teachings would predict that time is connected to space. Theravada Buddhists in fact exempt space (*akasha*), but not time, from being "conditioned"—this makes space as *independent and absolute* as is possible within their metaphysics and precludes any encompassing holism. Space is merely the absence of anything; it does not affect anything, nor is it affected by anything. Nor did Nagarjuna or any other Buddhist connect space with time in their analyses. Nor do depth-mystics experience "the four-dimensional space-time continuum" of relativity theory or the "ground manifold state" out of which quantum phenomena emerge and are reabsorbed: the "space-time manifold" is no more "pure beingness" than is a grain of sand in the everyday world since according to physicists it too is structured. (That the scientific concepts are explanatory posits presents a problem itself—no one can experience a *concept*—but parallelists must assume some reality corresponds to such posits.)

Even if we accept that the brain is sensitive to events in the quantum realm, still that realm is differentiated and so this cannot explain the undifferentiated depth-mystical experience—calling the quantum realm "the One" or "Wholeness" does not change this (contra Schäfer 2008). Nor do we need anything other than the differentiations of the everyday realm to explain mindfulness. And even if there is a subatomic realm that is free of all structure, nothing suggests that meditation extends the range of human perception—as if mystical experiences involve some super microscopic power to experience that realm or confer magical powers revealing new scientific facts about reality. When the Tibetan Buddhist Tsongkhapa wanted to learn if a bell seller was selling solid bronze bells (see Mansfield 2008: 75), he could not use his advanced meditative states to determine the bells' molecular structure. Mystics do not "harmonize" their minds with subatomic structures or bring the "micro-level" and "macro-level" together (contra Weber 1986: 12). Mystics' claims, including those of interconnectedness and impermanence, remain thoroughly grounded in the experience of beingness on the everyday level of phenomena. Only commentators whose view of mysticism is distorted by their view of science (as discussed in the next chapter) could see things otherwise.

Or consider Advaita Vedanta's oneness of reality. This has nothing to do with any scientific findings about a "quantum field" or any "energy-filled vacuum" underlying the universe. Energy is not any more "mystical" or "spiritual" in nature than matter (contra Ravindra 1991: 41). We cannot equate "energy" with "spirit" simply because both are not solid (contra Schäfer 2008)—energy is just as much a part of the natural realm as matter and thus is not a gateway to the mystical in a way that material objects are not. Materially, it is like the "dead matter in motion" of the Newtonian worldview. Nor is it proof that the universe is an emanation of a transcendental source or anything else that would conflict with materialism. So too, the quantum field is simply part of the natural universe and thus does not give the entire natural universe its being—at a minimum, it cannot give itself existence. Even Capra realizes that the "underlying reality" of the "Eastern mystic" cannot be identified with the quantum field: the former transcends the natural realm and is beyond all conception, while the latter is a well-defined concept that accounts for only some physical phenomena (2000: 211). (However, he thinks the *intuitions* of the physicist and mystic closely parallel each other [ibid.].)

Whatever fundamental field scientists posit will be only one part of what to Advaitins is the "dream" realm (*maya*). Such a field will be structured by the forces necessary to explain why one specific physical state of affairs is the case, while Brahman, the reality behind the "dream" universe, is not. Brahman is free of structure—it is a featureless, partless, timeless, self-existent, and self-luminous consciousness. Brahman cannot explain why some things occur in the dream realm and others do not since it supplies being to all equally and has no structures to explain why something in the "dream" is the case; thus, it cannot be used as a posit in any scientific theory to explain the different phenomena and the order we see. Nor is it an extended "root consciousness *field*" within the world since this would still be one part of the objective natural universe—the "dream" realm. Rather, Brahman is not any type of objective reality. It is not an extended whole with no distinguishable parts (contra Raman 2008: 282-83), nor simply the totality of the natural realm. It is the still center underlying the surface-flux of things, not any type of dynamic and interrelated unity. (Again, it is better to refer to it as an "*identity* of being" rather than a "*unity* of being," which suggests a union of various parts.) Nor is there anything for Brahman to interact or interconnect with since it alone is real.

For depth-mystics in all traditions, what is experienced in the depth-experience is also changeless and not part of this world. Neither depth-mystics nor mindfulness mystics are experiencing *energy* in any scientific sense of the word when they see the impermanence of things or a depth-mystical source—electromagnetic energy or any other natural energy is as much a part of the "dream" realm as matter; it needs a source of its being as much as matter or anything else. Even if such energy is the source of everything else in the world, it still needs a source of being for its own existence. Treating a *metaphysical "power of being"* that keeps us from lapsing into nonexistence as a form of *natural energy* (as Adolph Grünbaum does [1996]) only leads to problems. Any transcendental source of the universe is not shooting natural energy into the world from another realm. Such metaphysical power is constant whether a law of conservation applies to natural matter/energy or not. Scientists' findings will always be about objective features within the natural realm and cannot in principle affect the issue of this realm's ontological status. In sum, whatever scientists find or do not find, the ontological status of the universe as a whole will be the same, and thus whatever scientists discover is irrelevant to the core claims of depth-mystics.

The "Emptiness" of Reality

Problems also arise with the different ideas of the emptiness in science and Buddhism. Physicists speak of the emptiness of phenomena on the subatomic and cosmological levels, and Buddhists speak of the emptiness (*shunyata*) of phenomena, and so parallelists conclude that physicists and Buddhists are actually discussing the same thing. The Buddhist ontological claim is, to use Ninian Smart's description, that the cosmos is composed of "a vast swarm of short-lived events." This claim is about *the lack of any permanent entities in what we experience in the everyday realm*—the emptiness of all phenomena of any "inherent self-existence" (*svabhava*) that would permanently separate one thing from another as distinct and self-existing realities. That is, nothing we experience in the everyday realm is self-created and self-contained. Rather, everything we experience in the natural world is impermanent and dependent upon conditions and other objects for its existence.

This lack of self-existence has nothing to do with scientific notions of emptiness: it is the *metaphysical* absence of any power of self-existence, not anything about the *material* absence of matter in some space Nevertheless, parallelists assert on two fronts that it does. First, some see Buddhist emptiness as connected to the near emptiness of the vastness of space on a cosmological scale (e.g., Kirtisinghe 1984b). The physicist Harry Lam wrote an entire book on the "amusing connections" between the notions of emptiness in Zen and modern cosmology without mentioning *self-existence* once (2008). He did mention "lacking reality, substance, meaning" once in connection with Buddhist emptiness—he takes the definition from an English dictionary and understands that Buddhist emptiness is more like this than physical emptiness (ibid.: 5)—but he still continued the discussion only in terms of physical emptiness. His basic point is that, since according to modern cosmology the universe was devoid of material particles at the beginning, modern cosmology is "more Zen than Zen Buddhism" because its notion of space is emptier (ibid.). He even wonders whether the Chinese Buddhist Hui Neng "knew about the universe being nearly empty at the beginning," but he does this by translating the line "nothing is really there" (which is about *the lack of self-existence*) into "nothing was *originally* there" (ibid.) to fit his way of thinking in terms of physical emptiness. He concludes that Zen and cosmology have no "direct connection" other than the term "emptiness," but that there are "subtle connections and links" (ibid.: 200). And at the end, he still thinks of Zen in terms of the near emptiness of space—he even has to say that "Zen acknowledges the presence of stars and galaxies but does not consider them ruinous to the emptiness" (ibid.). Nevertheless, the Buddhist idea of "emptiness" has nothing to do with how much matter occupies space or the physical absence of any objects.

More commonly, parallelists see Buddhist emptiness as connected to the near emptiness of matter on the other extreme of scale: the smallness of the quantum level. Here the scientific notion of "emptiness" comes from the idea that there are no solid particles in a sea of energy. Under the current theories, the "emptiness" of space-time is actually seething with "virtual" particles, and it only needs energy to get "real" particles out of it. Thus, "empty" space-time has field properties and hence is not actually *nothing*. Virtual particles are at most an example of the temporariness of things, but mindfulness mystics do not experience them—the mystics' claim stands or falls on the impermanence in the everyday world. As discussed in Chapter 9, Nagarjuna's "emptiness" is not the "quantum vacuum" out of which things arise (contra, e.g., Ramanna 1999: 163). Nor does this emptiness of "self-existence" have anything to do with space, time, and matter being *interactive* (contra Finkelstein 2003: 383). Nagarjuna says nothing about that issue, and so his ideas on impermanence of the experienced realm cannot even be seen "anticipations" of that issue. Nor did the Buddha twenty-five hundred years ago in any way set out the hypothesis that elementary particles are not solid or independent (contra Ricard 2003: 274). In fact, the early Abhidharma Buddhists posited *extremely minute uncuttable and undestroyable particles of matter unopen to sense-experience (paramanus)*, comparable to the atoms of the ancient Greek Democritus (Sadakata 1997: 20-22) and yet affirmed the impermanence of the experienced realm—such particles simply do not affect the impermanence that Buddhists are interested in. So too, the Madhyamaka conception of emptiness remains completely grounded in the everyday realm—i.e., with the complete impermanence and interconnectedness of what we actually experience.

Quantum physicists do find a realm of particles and virtual particles that is totally unlike the everyday realm, but this too has no bearing on the Buddhist ontological claims about the nature of our experienced realm. The wave/particle duality of electrons and other subatomic "particles" is often cited as proof that they have no "intrinsic properties" and hence are "empty" in the Buddhist sense. But that is simply wrong: electrons consistently manifest only wave features under one experimental set-up, and only particle features under another. That is, they do indeed appear to have "intrinsic structural properties"—some are manifested merely in one context, others in another. So too, atoms have some intrinsic properties, such as rest mass (Ames 2003: 301). But whether or not particles have stable "intrinsic properties," this does not affect what Buddhists are concerned with—the impermanence of what is experienced in the everyday world.

How Buddhist Abhidharmists analyze the "elements of reality (*dharmas*)" shows the difference between science and mysticism: physicists focus on the *objects* of the world and their constituents or causes, while mindfulness mystics focus on the elements of our *experience* of the world. As noted in Chapter 3, the *dharmas* are not "objective" bits of the world but more like qualities of our experience; thus, the dharmic analysis is nothing like a scientific analysis of matter. The world consists of such momentary, experiencable events, and to try to identify with such tropes as "me" or "belonging to me" with anything within the world is the fundamental error causing our suffering. To Abhidharmists, what is real is open to our immediate experience, unlike in physics, and the *dharmas* are momentary, unlike the unchanging atoms of classical physics (Ames 2003: 292-93). To think of the ephemeral *dharmas* as anything like small bits of matter—such as long-lasting atoms—is to start off in the wrong direction. And, as discussed in Chapter 9, even if physicists find permanent bits of matter on the quantum level, it would not refute a mindfulness tradition like Buddhism because it does not affect the impermanence of the "constructed things (*sankharas*)" of the everyday world that we actually experience. (See DeCharms 1997: 53-55.) Moreover, nature's laws and forces (e.g., gravity or magnetism) may exist eternally and unchangingly in some way, but, as previously noted, this permanence does not affect the Buddhist picture of reality any more than does the permanence of the law of karma since the Buddhist view is about the impermanence of *things we experience in the world*. Whatever scientists find about the permanence of laws, the world we actually experience—the natural world of interacting laws—still appears impermanent and constantly changing, and this is what mindfulness is about.[6] In short, everyday phenomena could have structural "intrinsic properties" and still be empty of self-existence and hence be "empty" in the Buddhist sense.

Much attention has been paid in recent works to the Madhyamaka tradition's concept of emptiness (*shunyata*). The Dalai Lama sees an "unmistakable resonance" between Nagarjuna's notion of emptiness and the new physics (2005: 50). (For introductions to Nagarjuna's thought, see Jones 2010, 1993: 79-97; Garfield 1995.[7]) But it should be noted that the Madhyamikas' emphasis on emptiness is only a shift in attention from the earlier Buddhists'—from the impermanence of *constructed things* to the emptiness of self-existence of their *parts*. What is important remains the emptiness of any sort of self-existence of what we directly experience. Early Buddhists emphasized that the *wholes* (*sankharas*) we experience are impermanent and their ultimate components (the *dharmas*) are without a self. They used the analogy of a chariot that keeps having parts replaced: there is no permanent, distinct reality called a "chariot" that exists apart from the temporary and changing collection of parts—it remains "the same chariot" only in a "conventional" sense, not in any "ultimate" sense. So too, there is no "self" to be found among the mental and physical parts we actually experience. The Mahayana Buddhists of the Prajñaparamita and Madhyamaka traditions reacted to the Abhidharmists' claim that the ultimate parts (the *dharmas*) exist by their own nature (*svabhava*) by shifting the emphasis to the emptiness of those fundamental parts. But again, the Abhidharmist analysis is not in terms of any physical analysis of matter but of the nature of the experienced world—it is a claim about the ontological status of everything we experience, and whatever physicists find about whether there are indestructible bits of matter or not on the subatomic level is simply irrelevant. Buddhists need not deny or affirm anything that physicists find in this regard. Again, Abhidharmists accepted indestructible atoms.

The interactions on the subatomic level may be responsible for the phenomena on the macroscopic, experiencable level. But even if so, the Buddhist notion of emptiness has nothing to do with them. Emptiness is part of the belief-system explaining why we suffer: for our happiness, we search among things we experience for permanence in what is intrinsically impermanent, and thus we have nothing but unfulfillable desires.[8] The nature of whatever occurs on the subatomic level causing everyday phenomena is simply irrelevant to this impermanence. It may be easier for some people to see the impermanence of reality by thinking about the subatomic realm, but the bottom line is that that realm is no more "mystical" than the impermanent everyday realm we actually experience. Nor do we need anything from that realm to confirm the impermanence in our world.

We may make a metaphysical generalization about the impermanence of all things that would encompass the subatomic level or we may speculate like the Abhidharmists did on atoms, but the focus of the classical Buddhist way of life is not about that issue—it remains firmly in what is experiencable. We do not merely need a correct view of the physical nature of reality to end suffering. Hence, there is no reason to be interested in physical structures. Like mysticism in general, Buddhism has no interest in the analysis of underlying layers of physical organization or in identifying the lowest level of physical realities. Buddhism has no *scientific* view of the nature of matter (contra Zajonc 2004: 5), and there is no such thing as a "Buddhist *physics*" (contra Wolf 1996: 169). Buddhism has never given a *physical* analysis of matter (contra Ricard and Thuan 2001: 107). At most, there was philosophical speculation comparable to Democritus's. Buddhists adopted the traditional Indic "physics" of earth, water, fire, and wind (e.g., *Samyutta Nikaya* II.94), adding space as a fifth element later (Sadakata 1997: 21-25). (As physical explanations, these four elements are not the earth, water, fire, and air we actually *experience* in the everyday world: they are *invisible elements* constituting all that we see. Akira Sadakata likens them to energy [ibid.: 21-22].) Identifying a new subatomic level will not lead to calming the mind of the discrimination of separate entities on the everyday level or to discerning what is ontologically real—if anything, it only increases the danger of discriminations for the unenlightened by introducing a new layer of possible objects and creating new distinctions. Physicists simply do not supply the type of knowledge needed to end the ignorance (*avidya*) at the root of our suffering—no scientific knowledge of the world does.

In sum, the Buddhists' metaphysical discussions of the nature of experienced phenomena should not be confused with the scientists' quest to identify the ultimate particles of matter or whatever natural reality may underlie them merely because the term "emptiness" comes up in both endeavors. The Buddhist *dharma*-analysis simply has nothing to do with what physicists find. In particular, Buddhist emptiness is not merely the opposite of *solidity*: an object could be solid and yet breakable and hence impermanent, or something could be in another state of matter where it is not solid and yet be eternal and hence permanent. Buddhist emptiness is not about the presence or absence of any *object* but about the impermanence, dependence, and constant change inherent in all experienced phenomena.

Consciousness and the Phenomenal Realm

Another common problem comes up with comparisons of consciousness and Brahman. For example, the physicist Amit Goswami gives consciousness a role in physics and also treats consciousness as the ground of being.[9] He claims that this resolves all quantum paradoxes (1997: 8). However, there is nothing in Advaita's *brahman/atman* doctrines about a subject's consciousness affecting, or interacting with, an object—there is only the underlying consciousness of Brahman and thus nothing to interact with. Brahman does not even cause the entire material realm since what is conscious cannot cause what is unconscious (*Brahma-sutra-bhashya* II.1.4-6)—root ignorance (*avidya*) is the cause of the realm of *maya*. In Advaita, Brahman is never portrayed as any type of causal agent in the phenomenal world but as the only reality constituting all phenomena; thus, to make it the cause of the wave-function collapse is to change its nature.[10] In Advaita's theory of sense-perception, consciousness does go out from the mind and "grasp" a sense-object (i.e., takes its form), but there is nothing in this act about perception creating the object or otherwise affecting it. In the end, Goswami has to distinguish "consciousness" from "awareness" (which he says implies an implicit subject/object split) to maintain both the unchanging background consciousness as a source and the act of awareness in his theory of how the quantum wave-function collapses (1997: 32-33). In mindfulness mysticism too, there is nothing about a subject's consciousness affecting objects: we "create" objects by imposing artificial *conceptual boundaries*, not by somehow *physically affecting* what is actually there. Nor do mindfulness mystics deny the reality of objects unless metaphysical considerations override. Buddhist mindfulness is not an emanationism in which the mind gives birth to matter. (Buddhists do see karma as creating the material world, although they are not always consistent on this point.) In general, Goswami tries to make his case by listing a catalog of isolated snippets of texts taken from their contexts in disparate mystical traditions from around the world and translating all the key terms from them as "*consciousness*" and then concluding that mysticism thus offers experiential proof of "monistic idealism" (1993: 49-54).[11]

Goswami's attempt to use consciousness to resolve the problems of quantum physics also ends up with the same fundamental circularity he sees with materialism only in reverse: he cannot explain how unconscious matter and multiple centers of consciousness (i.e., individual subjects) arise in the natural realm from consciousness (or, as he puts it, how the undivided consciousness divides itself into the subject/object reality), even if they are not self-existent entities; or how the underlying consciousness becomes physical energy in the phenomenal realm; or how matter and our individual mental phenomena could interact within the universe. He also admits that the Upanishads and Shankara have no explanation of how the fundamental illusion (*maya*) arose from consciousness or how it works (1997: 31). In sum, he is only substituting another mystery for the mystery within materialism of how consciousness arose. Nor is the problem of how the conscious part of the phenomenal universe can influence the unconscious part solved by postulating a transcendental consciousness as the source of both any more than by postulating matter as the common source.[12] Consciousness as the underlying reality may seem better than materialism, but individual minds, bodies, and matter in general are now the unexplained epiphenomena of consciousness. Even if physicists eventually end up accepting a form of idealism as the foundation of the material universe, this does not mean that they must accept any form of mysticism.[13] In particular, a universal observer to make the universe exist or to collapse wave-functions does not need any mysticism but only Berkelean idealism.

More generally, the idea that consciousness plays a role in the formation of the universe is no doubt appealing to many—it not only fits with a metaphysical holism, it also solidifies the place of conscious beings as central to the scheme of things. It places human beings at the center of things, as does making consciousness a cause in quantum events—the latter gives us a role in what may be the most fundamental level of physical interactions. The physicist John Archibald Wheeler suggests that consciousness and information are the dominant forces in producing the universe—we get "it from bit" (i.e., the material realm from information). Ours is a "participatory universe." The universe had to produce conscious beings to observe it so that it would exist, i.e., the existence of the universe depends on there being conscious beings who can observe it and collapse its wave-function. Thus, the universe began to expand with the Big Bang, but later acts of observer-participation gave "tangible reality" to the universe not only now but back to the beginning (1983: 194). In sum, the observer-participation of quantum theory is the mechanism by which the universe came into being. Obviously, there is a circularity problem here: how could we come along later in the history of the universe and yet produce it to begin with? Wheeler admits he has no explanation for this.[14] He also denies that quantum observation has anything to do with *human consciousness*. He accepts Niels Bohr's position that what actually does the observing is not the human mind, but the *experimental devices* used to do the measuring, just as Geiger counters detect radioactivity (ibid.: 207). Thus, in the end Wheeler too must resort, not to science, but to metaphysics—a form of idealism—to explain "existence itself."

The issue of consciousness also comes up with any faster-than-light signals posited to deal with Bell's nonlocality theorem: actions to one apparently independent particle that has been "entangled" in the past with another particle appear to influence the other particle at faster-than-light velocities even when they are vastly separated in space—e.g., one particle responds immediately to the change in the spin of the other. But such signals are not any more *conscious* than sublight signals. Conversely, making consciousness the locus to resolve this nonlocality problem in physics also has nothing to do with the Advaitins' idea of Brahman or any other mystical concept of a featureless underlying source. Any scientific posits to explain space-time may not be *in* space-time, but to be *explanations* of the differentiations within the space-time realm they too must be *differentiated*—the undifferentiated would have the same effect on all phenomena and hence could not account for any variations at all. Brahman is the same reality for all phenomena and thus cannot explain why one phenomenal state of affairs is the case rather than another. Thus, since Brahman is not differentiated, it cannot be a scientific explanation. Brahman is not an objective order of objects behind experience but an undifferentiated consciousness that we can directly experience. It is not one part of the natural universe, as any underlying field or other scientific posit is. If the universe was created so that consciousness can know itself, as Goswami asserts, he cannot escape the fact that all that the unenlightened, including scientists, see with our dualistic consciousness are the "illusions"—it is one part of the manifested realm seeing another, not the underlying transcendental consciousness seeing itself.

The New Physics and the Old

Some physicists have tried to develop a "hidden variable" theory to make quantum physics deterministic, but no physical theory has yet made consciousness the encompassing unseen reality. David Bohm's hidden-variable approach to quantum physics proposed in the 1950's is an example of a physical theory that is less popular with physicists than with those who see parallels between physics and mysticism (even though it treats particles as distinct entities). Although some physicists have recently expressed interest in his theory, most physicists do not like its dualism of "pilot waves" guiding old-fashioned Newtonian particles, that some of the variables describing the particles are hidden forever and thus can never be known, and that it requires signals traveling faster than light to maintain the hidden variables. The principal virtue of the theory is that physicists can rewrite quantum equations to look like Newtonian ones.

Bohm was friends with the Western-educated Indian mystic Jiddu Krishnamurti, and his understanding of Eastern mysticism may well have influenced his work in physics. (See Sharpe 1984: 48-49, 1993: 71-72; for Krishnamurti's disdain for science, see Weber 1986: 222-24.) But any such influence would have come only after he developed his hidden-variable theory and would relate only to his later idea of a hidden "implicate" order (a structure in which each part contains enfolded within it the totality of the universe) underlying the manifest "explicate" order we see. This order has no observable consequences or any predictions or calculations that differ from those in conventional quantum physics (Bohm and Hiley 1993: 350-90). His "new synthesis" also brought consciousness into the same implicate order as external events, but consciousness is not an all-encompassing underlying reality. Reality becomes "an undivided wholeness in flowing movement," and his later theorizing tried to explain this. He also saw meditation as a way to overcome the "fragmentary Western approach"—it leads "the whole process of mental operation non-verbally to the sort of quiet state of orderly and smooth flow needed to end fragmentation both in the actual process of thought and in its content" (1981: 19-20). Bohm saw this implicate order as paralleling Advaita's Brahman, even though the implicate order is one part of the material universe and even though such an underlying order would still be a matter of structure (to explain the differentiations we see) and not a source of beingness. Bohm's order does underlie quantum events, but it is of the same "physical" nature as the quantum realities with which it interacts. It is "nonmaterial" or "transcendental" in the sense that it is not part of the manifest world, but just because we ordinarily divide the everyday world into "material" and "nonmaterial" (i.e., conscious or spiritual) does not make Bohm's "nonmaterial" order a transcendental consciousness.

In mainstream cosmology, space is no longer seen as a huge, black, empty, featureless box through which things move. Rather, it is a reality that changes and affects other elements of the universe and in turn is affected by them. It is now seen as the foundation of the physical world, the substance out of which everything else is constructed (Wertheim 2002: 202). Cosmologists now debate whether space-time is continuous or whether there are atoms of space-time with literally nothing in between them. But it must be noted that space is still not any more *nonmaterial* or *spiritual* than any other physical realities. Matter has lost its primacy for defining what is "physically real" and is now seen as a manifestation of the space-time manifold or a quantum field. Thus, we now must get beyond an either/or choice between solid matter and spirit. The new theories remain fundamentally *physicalist*: matter may no longer be primary, but this does not mean that we are now talking about "spirit" or "souls" (ibid.: 204). We have to modify Democritus's old idea that reality is only atoms and the void, but the result is just as material as before. Atoms and their parts today are no more "mental" or "spiritual" than Newtonian particles, and they are still detected by scientists through physical interactions. The space-time manifold, whatever its ultimate nature, is, like any field in physics, still a physical reality that interacts with material objects. Fields in physics remain distinct entities. Changes in fields are regulated by laws and are a matter of natural causation and perhaps chance events. The situation is not even closer to a mystical view of emanation since the underlying manifold is also physical—only now physical objects are "emanating" out of another physical reality.

Overall, the universe of the "new antireductionist scientific worldview" is more creative, with the emergence of different levels of organization, and more complex, but it is no more *mystical* than the "old Newtonian reductive worldview" of the universe as nothing but matter in motion. Indeed, some who have studied the issues suggest that Newtonian physics is actually much closer in many ways to Asian mysticism than is quantum physics (Wilber 1984: 24). Physics and cosmology today are no more metaphysical than in Newton's time, despite the claims in the popular press that science today is "discovering God"—contrary to what the physicist George Smoot said, finding cosmic microwave background radiation, if you are religious, is not "like seeing God." Energy and the quantum field are as natural as the old material objects and space, and the new physics is not addressing religious "why" questions related to meaning and purpose but remains firmly a matter of "how" questions related to the workings of the natural realm. Metaphysical questions related to the universe as a whole (e.g., where everything ultimately came from or why there is any order at all) remain distinct from scientific "how" questions in cosmology. At best, the new interest in religion by some scientists only brings out *the difference* between metaphysical and scientific questions and shows the limit of scientific answers—the "reconciliation" makes room for religion, but it does not make science religious in nature or vice versa. In itself, the new science provides no grounds to believe in free will or life after death, and the natural realm can still easily be seen as a realm of blind chance and causation operating on natural realities. The uncertainty in complexity theory may only relate to our inability to calculate all the details—the physical processes may remain strictly deterministic. Emergence may involve laws of nature scientists have not yet found and may also be deterministic. Even if the mind is a causal force, it still may be merely the byproduct of natural processes in the brain—there are no grounds from science to believe that the mind could exist independently of a body. In fact, the new view overall may have the same *antispiritual* effect that the old physics allegedly had, only with a new twist: everything now becomes seen as just a byproduct of physical space and natural processes (Wertheim 2002: 205).

The Levels of Reality

The idea that the world is merely "an idea in the mind of God" is centuries old, but now the claim becomes quantum physics *proves* that "the universe is being created in a dream of a single spiritual entity" (Wolf 1994: 343-44).[15] Indeed, "quantum" has become the parallelists' favorite word. The reasoning is simple: if everything has a material base and quantum realities are the basis of physical organization, then everything is actually only a quantum reality. All things are just excited states of the underlying "quantum vacuum," and human beings thus are just ripples on the quantum vacuum's sea of potentiality (Zohar and Marshall 1993: 274). Thus, there is a quantum basis to the mind (e.g., ibid: 68-77, 82-85; see also Zohar and Marshall 1990 and Penrose 1994), and so there is a quantum basis to all things mystical and psychic. We now have "quantum meditation" at the interface of matter and energy. And there is Deepak Chopra's "quantum healing."[16] A remark by Chopra is typical: "The quantum field is just another label for the field of pure consciousness and potentiality" (quoted in Rothman and Sudarshan 1998: 184).

However, this type of reasoning misses something basic about reality: phenomena are organized into *different levels of structure*. Beginning with the various subatomic levels and leading up to the everyday world of our experiences and to cosmological levels, nature adds different levels of causal interactions. Thus, an atom may be constituted only by smaller parts, but it is "real" since it has causal powers as a unit—e.g., to explain Brownian motion. Structural reductionists and antireductionists disagree over the final number of ultimately real levels of structure. Under the structural reductionists' view, all phenomena are merely the result of extremely complex interactions of only one fundamental level of physical structure. All chemical facts about the elements are explainable by physical facts about their atomic structure—there is nothing non-physical about the chemical elements, and thus nothing but physics is needed in our final picture of the elements; so too with biological and psychological reductions. Under antireductionism, all levels of structures are equally real: higher-level events are not quantum events—everything may have a quantum base, but each level of interactions are causal realities in their own right. Thus, biological processes are not the consequence of physical or chemical laws and any initial physical conditions but are autonomous on their own level of operation. (See Jones 2000: chap. 4 and 5 and 2013: chap. 3 on reductionism and emergentism.)

But contrary to what most parallelists believe, a scientist need not be a reductionist to practice science, and reductionism is increasingly out of vogue in philosophy of science today (if not in philosophy of mind). Quantum physicists can still speak of "levels of being" (Malin 2001: 191-208). Scientists need not ultimately produce only one theory to compare to some composite, generalized mystical theory or to a mystical theory from one particular tradition. *Reductionism* must be distinguished from *analysis* of the parts of a whole. Scientists engage in such analysis to discern the structures operating in phenomena, and no one doubts the value of analyzing how the parts interact for figuring out how nature works. But reductionists make a further philosophical move: ontological reductionists reduce the reality to only one substance; structural reductionists reduce all causal structures to the minimal physical ones; epistemological reductionists argue that the properties of the parts exhaustively explain the properties of the whole, and thus we can learn everything about the whole by knowing all about the properties of the parts, and so all explanations are ultimately in terms of physics; methodological reductionists argue that analysis, not any form of holism, will ultimately be the only necessary scientific method. Parallelists, like most people, do not differentiate the various types of reductionism; the common conclusion is that, since naturalists are committed to an ontological reductionism (only one substance for everything that is real), naturalists are committed to all types of reductionism. But this is not the case: one can be an ontological reductionist and still be a structural antireductionist, holding that nature is not merely "matter in motion," but "matter in different levels of organization." Nor are all scientists committed to any reductionist metaphysics—many scientists, perhaps most, accept that different sciences reveal equally real features of the world, and in America at least, many reject even ontological reductionism and accept a theism or deism.

While reductionists see the parts as responsible for the properties of wholes, antireductionists see more to wholes than merely the interactions of parts. They do not think that the action of parts can explain how wholes emerge—i.e., forces governing the interactions of parts do not produce higher-level phenomena, and the question is how the parts actually relate to the wholes. To antireductionists, there is no one level responsible for everything. Instead, the world exists in a different way on each level of structural causes, with different laws of nature becoming operational at various levels of organizational complexity. Quantum phenomena do not explain DNA or other biological phenomena—each level has its own causal order and laws. Even a physical "Theory of Everything" would not explain the higher levels of the world—it would be only a "Theory of (one level of) Everything." Each phenomenon has multiple levels of organization, and thus a pluralism of sciences is needed to provide a complete scientific picture of reality's structures and hence of how reality works. No scientific account of one level will depict all the "real" causes at work in nature or provide the "real" explanation—there is no one scientific way the world "really is." Each science explains the same phenomena of nature in terms of a physical, chemical, biological, or psychological structure, but only one aspect of the phenomena is covered in a given field of scientific inquiry. Each science may give a complete picture of all of nature, but only for *one level of structure* ordering all of nature. This pluralism does not violate Occam's Razor: a complex world simply requires more than one account. The scientific accounts do not compete or contradict each other, but are supplements to each other, each revealing something different about reality and answering different questions. Physics encompasses the broadest levels—the same physics operates in brains as in rocks—but it does not encompass all levels of causation.

But antireductionists need not claim that the whole *produces* the parts—as parallelists interpret, for example, Chu Hsi's Neo-Confucianism to hold. Rather, for antireductionists a whole is a causal part of reality, but antireductionist scientists at present are looking at the role of the parts and other natural forces at work within the wholes. They do at least entertain the possibility that there may be more forces at work in nature than those currently recognized by physics. But, with a few prominent exceptions (such as the Nobel-winning chemist Ilya Prigogine), most scientists are still analytical "bottom-up" thinkers, not holistic "top-down" thinkers according to whom the forces at work in a whole affect or even create its parts. Thus, to learn more about how nature works, scientists can accept both the "analytical" approach and a "holistic" approach in which the whole is treated as a causal reality in its own right (and thus as different from simply the sum of the properties and interactions of its parts)—it is the structural reductionists who take the additional metaphysical step about the nature of reality in claiming only the whole's parts are actually real and doing all the causal work.

"Quantum Mysticism"

Ironically, parallelists too, even while disparaging reductionism, engage in a reductionism that treats the lowest physical levels as more real than the everyday world:

they bash "reductive science" and yet argue that everything must be remade in the quantum image. In a case of "physics envy" (Shermer 2005: 34), they make the lowest levels of physical interactions the only type of actions that are of value or are even real. For them, the types of events on those levels must become models for how we treat reality on the everyday level (e.g., Zajonc 2004: chap. 3). We must change our way of thinking about everything in light of what quantum physics demonstrates (ibid.: 50). Ken Wilber summarizes (and later criticizes) the parallelists' reductionism: "since all things are ultimately made of subatomic particles, and since subatomic particles are mutually interrelated and holistic, then all things are holistically one, just like mysticism says" (1984: 27). For parallelists, nonlocality on the subatomic level means that *all of reality, including the everyday level*, is interconnected in some way, and the Heisenberg's Uncertainty Principle (concerning our inability to measure the exact momentum and exact location of particles at the same time) means we cannot have certain knowledge *about anything*. The principle finally makes room for free human will (Ratanakul 2002: 118). So too, the wave/particle paradox in science means nothing has fixed properties and we must speak paradoxically about everything.

However, the only way to maintain this position is to deny the emergence of any new, genuinely real levels of causation and any genuine multiplicity of levels to nature's organization. In fact, parallelists want to emphasize *both* that new higher-level phenomena emerge in the everyday world *and* that the lowest level of physical organization dictates how we must see the world. They do not see the blatant contradiction. But the only way to make these two points consistent is to give a reductionist interpretation of emergence, chaos, and complexity—which parallelists do not do. Nevertheless, failing to distinguish levels of organization here means that biological and social phenomena are merely the complicated interactions of nonconscious, impersonal quarks governed by fixed physical laws and that ultimately human phenomena require no other explanations.

What initially drew the parallelists' attention to the possibility of parallels between science and mysticism was precisely the fact that our everyday notions do not apply to subatomic events. But oddly *the reverse* implication of this is somehow forgotten: obviously any theories developed specifically for the subatomic level will not apply to the everyday world for the same reason—in the macroscopic world, planets do not jump orbits like electrons, nor are their orbits a matter of probabilities until someone observes them and thereby makes them fixed, baseballs cannot be in two places at once, Schrödinger's cat is either alive or dead, Heisenberg's Uncertainty Principle does not affect determining the exact momentum and exact location of a speeding train at the same time, and so forth. Heisenberg did *not* point out that the *very act of measurement* interferes with what one was attempting to measure in all situations (contra Verhoeven 2001: 86)—there is no scientific basis to generalize his actual claim to all scales of reality and to all types of measurements.[17] Nor do we have grounds in physics to believe that Bell's nonlocality theorem and quantum entanglement apply to ourselves and the everyday objects we interact with daily. So too, we cannot generalize to conclude that quantum physics has brought out the intrinsic inseparability of subject and object, between the observed and the observer for all events (contra Raman 2002a: 191). Bell's Theorem and other quantum theories do not lead to the conclusion that the mind "is necessarily at the heart of *every assertion of reality*" (Wallace and Hodel 2008: 129, emphasis added). As Linda Wessels says, Bell's theorem has only minimal consequences for our conception of everyday objects and of most objects studied by science: it gives no reason to doubt that these objects can be treated as bodies or fields with objective properties; it only shows that our traditional model does not apply to all objects in nature (1989: 96).

Capra presents another common error in this regard: he speaks of the physicists' unification of "a non-ordinary level of reality" that parallels Eastern mysticism (2000: 149). But this fails to distinguish the fact that the higher levels in mystical experiences are levels of *consciousness* and have nothing to do with non-ordinary levels of *structure in external phenomena*. Internally, mystical experiences involve non-ordinary states of consciousness, but how can internal states parallel any external non-ordinary levels of physical organization? When it comes to external phenomena, nothing about depth-mystical oneness nor the mindfulness mystics' depiction of their experiences suggests that they are experiencing in "four dimensions" or "transcending the three-dimensional world" (ibid.: 150-51, 171, 179, 294) rather than simply experiencing the beingness of things free of conceptualizations. Only distorting mysticism by seeing it in terms of science would make anyone think otherwise. The experience of "now" has to do with the freedom from temporal categories in experience, not anything to do with the "block" interpretation of the universe in physics or experiencing the "full span of space-time" (ibid.: 186). It is not "in a way" like relativistic physics (ibid.: 187).

In sum, we cannot jump from the fact that everything has a material base to privileging the lowest level of organization as the sum of reality. Erwin Schrödinger in his *What is Life?* argued that the then-current physics could not account for life for the simple reason that the processes governing organisms are far too stable to fit with the realm of continuous fluctuations depicted by quantum physics. The everyday world may well have more interconnections than scientists are currently aware of and the role of consciousness may be much more significant, but events in the everyday world still do not behave like quantum events, whether because the effects of the mass of quantum entities simply cancel each other out or because some other factors are involved. Different levels of organization appear to have different levels of causal interactions—e.g., quarks do not interact with molecules—and the everyday world has its own level.[18]

Even if reductionists are correct, each level of organization and causal interaction has a reality that is not described by quantum physicists. Most obviously, whatever physicists find about the subatomic level, the fact remains that physical forces still produce solidity on the everyday level: the chair I am sitting in as I type still supports me and does not fall through the floor no matter what post-Newtonian physics says about the "emptiness" of the subatomic level of the world. Nor is the everyday world infinitely malleable and manipulatable because the quantum level is mostly empty space—we still do not create the world nor can we change it at will. The world simply is not under our control any more than it was under the Newtonian view. Solidity may be limited to only the everyday level of the world, but it is nevertheless a feature of reality that we have to deal with. Thus, whatever physicists find out about the cause of that solidity, it is not an illusion (contra Eddington 1958: 318) but just as real and nonnegotiable as properties on other levels. Arthur Eddington famously distinguished two levels of the phenomenal world with his analogy of two tables, the solid everyday one and the insubstantial scientific one (ibid.: xi-xiv), and, as the philosopher Gilbert Ryle noted, particle physicists do not describe tables and chairs at all. Schrödinger affirmed the reality of the everyday world more poetically: "Science cannot tell us a word about why music delights us, or how an old song can move us to tears."

If that is not enough, think of *human free will*. Do parallelists really want to claim that the quantum realm is mirrored in human action? This would mean that human actions are the result of a mixture of random events and a strict physical causation—no free will could enter the picture. Our acts would be random, not controlled. That is, if we deny the emergence of levels of organization that genuinely differ from what happens on the quantum level, we cannot affirm organized wholes that act as distinct units with some type of freedom, as we like to think human beings do. We would have no control at all—random events in the brain would dictate what happens.[19] Of course, it may be that our sense of free will is an illusion (as Einstein thought), but do parallelists think their own actions are determined by quantum randomness and a physical determinism?

To say "we must see reality differently in light of the physicists' new findings" can be ambiguous: we cannot treat the subatomic realm as being like the everyday realm, but this does not mean we therefore must see *all of reality* differently. Quantum physics is not "forcing" us to see all of the world differently (contra Capra 2000: 18, 138). Billiard balls still behave like billiard balls, despite what is going on on their subatomic levels. Nothing in science itself justifies making the colossal jump from a subatomic physics to an all-encompassing holism for all aspects of all phenomena of reality, regardless of the levels of organization involved. Even treating a subatomic holism merely as a model for how we should understand the rest of the levels of reality is not justified by what we know of the everyday world and certainly is not compelled by anything in science. In fact, trying to see everything as one big integrated whole even on microscopic levels can be misleading—it misses the different levels of causation. For example, atoms have their own level of causal interactions, and thus scientists still treat them as *entities*—they are not just empty connections and correlations (contra Capra 2000: 68-69) or abstractions or our reifications.

In short, the physics of the subatomic realm can no more be extended to the everyday world than vice versa—we could not see the everyday world as quantum events even if we wanted to. We cannot extrapolate ideas from one realm into the other in either direction. All the new physics shows is that our everyday understanding does not apply to *all* things in nature, not that everything in nature now must be treated like subatomic particles. Privileging the lowest level of organization as the only true level of reality is a metaphysical move that misses the fullness of reality. (Under antireductionism, it is very difficult to draw any metaphysical conclusions from one science for all of reality since there is a pluralism of different but equal sciences and theories.) That physicists at present have difficulty unifying *quantum theory* and *relativity theory*—the very small scale and the very large scale of things—should also be noted. There is a perceived indeterminism on the quantum level that cannot be easily reconciled with the perceived determinism reigning in relativity theory. In addition, quantum nonlocality apparently requires an absolute simultaneity that cannot be squared with relativity.

And of equal importance for the issue at hand, the parallelists' reductionism misses the fact that mindfulness mystics are dealing with the impermanence of the everyday world. If, as Capra admits, nonlocality can be ignored on the everyday level and so we can speak in fact of separate objects (2000: 310) and the same is also true of other subatomic theories, then mystics are *wrong* about the interconnectedness they claim—everyday separateness is precisely what mindfulness mystics deny. (See Wilber 1982: 166-67.) This alone should lead parallelists to concede that mystics are dealing with something other than a scientific subject and that the science of any level cannot be cited as support for any mystical claims.

Does the New Physics Have Implications for Society?

In sum, parallelists lose sight of the obvious and badly distort the situation when they require that we must revise how we see the everyday realm in light of new scientific findings. It is important to note that they think their position is *deducible* from quantum physics; they do not advance it as a metaphysics consistent with physics. Indeed, parallelists go even further: they extend this error to the realm of ethics and social organization.

To parallelists, the old Newtonian picture of separately existing entities is consistent only with individual selfishness and divisiveness in society—indeed, to them, the old worldview is a cause of selfishness. The old picture reinforces our innate tendency to project a sense of separate existence onto everything from photons to our own ego; in contrast, quantum physics and relativity tell us that all phenomena are interdependent and defined primarily by their relationship to other elements of the world and our observation (Mansfield 2008: 63-64, 161). And according to Capra, "the worldview implied by modern physics is inconsistent with our present society" (2000: 307). The new physics should be a model for society in general (ibid.: 7). According to Wei-ming Tu, the emergence of the new physics and cosmology has rendered many of the "social and cultural values" resulting from the Scientific Revolution "outmoded" or "at least problematic" (Zajonc 2004: 191). This claim is more than merely suggesting that we use the way phenomena are related on the quantum level as revealed by physics as a possible model for society.

Rather, these parallelists are claiming that our societies are *inconsistent with reality* and *must be made* to reflect reality as it truly is. Thus, science *compels* us to have a "quantum society" (Zohar and Marshall 1993; Goswami 1993). To parallelists, a thoroughly holistic society follows from the new physics, replacing the old atomistic individualistic one. In addition, an ethic of nonviolence, love, and compassion for others follows from the interconnectedness and impermanence of the quantum level (e.g., Weber 1986: 17).[20]

But why would we think that our society must be reconfigured along quantum lines when quantum concepts do not apply to the everyday physical level of the world? Nature on the everyday level clearly does not manifest nonviolence, love, and compassion. The asteroid that wiped out the dinosaurs reflects how much the universe cares. Earthquakes and tsunamis result from the interconnectedness of things on earth, but describing this situation as "harmony of the parts" does not really seem appropriate. Indeed, even on the quantum level, entities are constantly appearing and being destroyed in collisions—thus, not just bonding, but *violence* seems to be a value manifested, if the quantum level manifests values at all. In the animate realm, animals are well integrated into nature, but they still exhibit a nasty streak of selfishness and violence in their quest to survive. Evolution is a history of the suffering and death of individual animals and entire species. (This is not to deny that *cooperation* also figures prominently in evolution. But it should be noted that the "genetic altruism" of sociobiology fame is ultimately a form of selfishness: it is a case of helping another creature in order to help propagate one's own genes.) Charles Darwin expressed his dismay on seeing this suffering to his fellow biologist Asa Gray: "What a book a Devil's Chaplain might write on the clumsy, wasteful, blundering low & horridly cruel works of nature!" More recently the philosopher of biology David Hull agrees: evolution is cruel, haphazard, "rife with happenstance, contingency, incredible waste, death, pain, and horror"—all evidencing, not a loving god who cares about his creations, but the careless indifference of an almost diabolical god (1992: 486). That is nature "as it really is" independent of our attempts to combat it. In sum, it is hard to follow New Age thinkers to the conclusion that the universe is wise and compassionate or to follow theists in seeing the universe as an emanation of pure love.

In fact, before trying to develop social values from twentieth-century physics, it is worth remembering that the generation of physicists who devised the new physics was also the one that designed the atomic bomb. Also, Einstein's personal life was not the paradigm of concern for family members (see Ricard and Thuan 2001: 15). Granted, these physicists may well not have seen the philosophical implications of their physics for a new worldview, but it may be that the physics has far less of an impact on anything outside of science than parallelists think.

Moreover, even if the new physics does lead to seeing reality as impermanent and more interconnected, this does not mean that any particular basic *values* for society must follow. Universal compassion does not follow from a metaphysics of interconnection and wholeness (contra Mansfield 2008).[21] For example, killing human beings can still be easily justified by a metaphysics of wholeness: just as a cancerous limb must be removed because of its danger to the rest of the body, so too a dangerous person must be removed from any social whole—indeed, it is precisely because of the connection of the dangerous part to the whole that we must consider removing it permanently. It is also worth noting that holism flourished in the life sciences in fascist Nazi Germany (e.g., Gestalt psychology)—after World War II, German scientists quickly switched gears to emphasize that individual freedom was in fact compatible with holism (Harrington 1996: 207). More generally, we can exploit the interconnection of things to benefit our little node in the field without any inconsistency in belief about wholes and interconnectedness—i.e., we can still feel and act "selfishly" to improve the lot of our little node even though we know that we are connected and that there is no permanent, independent "self" to protect. So too, we can still suffer from natural events from diseases to tornadoes even though we are connected to them, and thus we cannot conclude that "all is good" merely because all is interconnected (or because all is the creation of God or is Brahman) without changing the meaning of "good" or admitting a mystery.

On the other side of the equation, no one can seriously claim that it was impossible to be moral or to be concerned with others' welfare *before* a "quantum worldview" was developed. Selfish action was certainly not a new byproduct of the Newtonian worldview. No doubt selfishness existed well before any science, and nothing in Newtonian physics leads necessarily to a lack of moral concern for other people. As the astronomer Victor Stenger puts it, reductionist classical physics has nothing to say about human beings except that we are made out of the same atoms as rocks and trees—just more cleverly organized by the impersonal forces of self-organization and evolution—and this is hardly a philosophical basis for selfishness and narcissism (1995: 291). And that same materialistic philosophy is still possible with quantum physics: the new physics does not change anything about the possibility of ontological and structural reductionism—naturalists can still treat everything as nothing but matter/energy and physical forces. Overall, values do not come any more from contemporary physics than from classical physics.[22]

And it must also be added that mystics throughout the world have not produced one universal, generic "mystical value-system" for societies to implement. Seeing the inherent impermanence and interconnectedness of the "such-ness" of things may lead to ending the frustration, dissatisfaction, and unfulfillment that Buddhists label "*duhkha*," but it need not lead to one particular set of values. Like mystical belief-claims, value-systems are a matter of the different encompassing religious ways of life and vary accordingly. A given mystical value-system will reflect cultural values, not merely mystical selflessness. Thus, it is hard to conclude that mystical experiences have fixed implications for social and personal values.

It should also be noted that not all mystics have even been moral or compassionate: mystical selflessness does empty mystics of all self-concern, but it does not necessarily fill the enlightened with any concern for others. Rather, realizing selflessness through mystical cultivation can also lead to a third option: *indifference to others*—if we come to realize that there is no reality in us to be selfish about, then we may also conclude that it is equally true that there is no corresponding reality in others to be concerned about. Even Buddhism has a "selfish" branch, even though there is no permanent "self" to defend. (See Jones 1993: 217-44, 2004: 149-79.) Or one may believe that one has attained a state where one is incapable of sin and thus unconstrained by religious precepts and secular laws; the result is an antinomianism or quietism where one simply lets the body do whatever it naturally desires. So too, some mystics may see no need for social reform: everything is "good" or even "perfect" as is. Asserting that a mystical experience is not "genuine" or enlightenment is not "authentic" unless the mystic is moral or hypernomian like some followers of the Kabbala traditions is simply question-begging. No ethical values come from mystical selflessness itself, and the overall relation between mystical experiences, mystical systems of thought, and ethical values is more complex than parallelists realize. (See Barnard and Kripal 2002; Jones 2004; Wainwright 2005.) The ethics one cultivates on the path plays a role in one's values of the enlightened state, and today, with our emphasis on individualism in our society, there is the danger that cultivation of mystical selflessness may actually result only in more "selfless" selfishness and narcissism.

Accepting the Reality of the Everyday Level

All in all, there are very good reasons to doubt the parallelists' enthusiasm for the idea that twentieth-century physics has major implications for a worldview, ethics, or a way of life. Physics, whether new or old, is certainly not grounds for denying the realities manifested on the everyday level of experience. Indeed, it was the *incongruity* of the everyday and quantum realms that was the starting point of the "new vision of reality" that parallelists envision. J. Robert Oppenheimer was correct in saying that discoveries about the structure of atoms do not logically necessitate any philosophical conclusions about the world at large. So too, Erwin Schrödinger was correct when he said that acausality, wave-mechanics, and complementarity on the subatomic level do not have as much connection with a philosophical view of the world as was supposed in his time (Jones 1986: 196), and now in ours. (The physicist Steven Weinberg [1996] sees only two legitimate implications of physics for philosophy: science sometimes reveals that topics like matter, space, and time that were once thought to be philosophical belong to the domain of physics; and nature is strictly governed by impersonal mathematical laws.) The physicists Albert Einstein, Arthur Eddington, Niels Bohr, and Werner Heisenberg, all expressed similar concerns about using their discoveries in philosophy and religion, and this concern should certainly be taken to heart here.

Notes

1. A generation earlier than the parallelists discussed here, Aldous Huxley made many of the same basic claims and the same mistakes. For a discussion of his ideas and the mistakes of the parallelists' "misty-science," see Deery 1996: 12-45, 147-49, and 158-61.

2. Parallelists throw around the term "unity" too easily in science too. For example, there is no "quantum unity" except in the naturalist sense that all things are made of the same substance and are governed by the same laws. There is a structured, interconnected, and impermanent realm, but no "organic whole" or "unity" as in the parts of a biological organism. It is not even as organized as a machine with interacting parts.

3. Naturalism also supplies an ontological unity to nature: everything that exists is made of only one type of substance; everything arose from the development of the Big Bang, and so everything is interconnected; everything in our solar system comes from the star dust of some earlier supernova; and all life on this planet is descended from the same earliest life-forms and so is related. In this regard, it may seem like mystical systems of oneness. But to Advaitins, all that the naturalists consider real is a product of the illusory "dream" realm.

4. More recently, Wilber speaks of "contemplative science" as being no different from natural science except in its subject matter (in Shear 2006: ix-xii). He has to treat meditative experiences as simply "experiments in consciousness," as if a disinterested knowledge of how the mind works is the objective of mysticism. He also must dismiss such problems as how one person can confirm the content of the mental state of another person.

5. Capra does acknowledge the idea of different levels to reality (2000: 204). The parallel he sees is that the way in which microscopic patterns are interrelated for physicists is *mirrored* in the way in which macroscopic patterns are interrelated for mystics (ibid.: 339). But in the end, he says that all that mystics and physicists have in common is that they explore levels of reality that lie beyond ordinary consciousness (ibid.: 338-39)—something no one would dispute, but which does not lead in itself to any great depth of convergence.

6. Buddhist apologists only began to refer to karma as a "natural law" in the late nineteenth century (Lopez 2008: 21), but it is an appropriate characterization.

7. To give a one paragraph summary: Nagarjuna was attempting to forge a path between the strong Advaitin sense of "exists" (what is unchanging and eternal) and "does not exist" (e.g., the horns of a rabbit or the son of a barren woman). He made no appeal to mystical experiences or indeed to anything other than reasoning and ordinary, everyday experiences. His method was a *reductio ad absurdum* (supplemented, it must be said, by some sophistry at some points): he showed that if we assume each thing exists independently by some inherent self-nature (*svabhava*), then any change is impossible, and this conflicts with what we actually experience in the everyday world. Thus, for any phenomenon (fire, motion, an agent, and so forth), if it has inherent existence, it could not change; so too, if it did not exist, it could not change; but we see change; and therefore any phenomenon is neither self-existent nor non-existent, but "empty" of inherent existence (*shunya*). Note that this result does not lead to the extreme of total nonexistence: things do exist in the usual sense of the word—they simply are void of any essence or substance that would make them self-existent. Thus, there are two levels of truth: in the conventional sense, things do exist, but in the ultimate ontological sense they do not (since they are not permanent and eternal). We can still use conventional language—even to state the ultimate truth of emptiness—but we should not be misled into thinking that the world is populated with discrete, permanent entities. Thus, "emptiness" does not mean "nonexistent," nor is it a new "essence" by which

things exist—it simply denotes the true nature of things. (See Jones 2010.)

8. Buddhists add other characterizations of the realm of becoming—e.g., we seek what is beautiful in what is inherently not—but it is *impermanence* that is prominent here.

9. Goswami studied the Upanishads from an early age and could not give up the idea that consciousness played a role in physics (1997: 28-29). Conversely, he also concludes, for reasons that are not made clear, that "quantum measurement is the key to understanding consciousness" (ibid.: 30). But it should be noted that not all Indians see parallels. C. T. K. Chari thinks that Advaita or any other Indian metaphysical system "does not require official endorsement by quantum mechanics," and that Advaita "cannot be validly or fruitfully used in solving the specific logico-mathematical problems of quantum mechanics" (1976: 55). "The glamour of the new physics must not lead to the metaphysical abuse of it" (ibid.).

10. Alan Wallace makes a similar claim for the physical "primal vacuum" of quantum physics and the underlying "primordial consciousness" uniting mind and matter in Mahayana Buddhism—indeed, he sees "possibly a meeting point at a very deep level between physics and Buddhism" here (Wallace and Hodel 2008: 191). But the Mahayana idea has nothing in it about a pool of energy from which particles emerge, nor does the physicists' idea have anything to do with consciousness.

11. Goswami is confusing idealism and mysticism here. He argues that because the moon is ultimately a quantum object (since it is composed entirely of quantum objects), it is not there when no one is looking at it (contrary to what Einstein said). But the claim that "there is no object in space-time without a conscious subject looking at it" (1993: 60) has nothing whatsoever to do with the metaphysical claims of any classical school of mindfulness, with Yogacara Buddhism perhaps being an exception. Nor is there is anything in the depth-mysticism Advaita about individuals controlling the appearance of an object in that way. The basic problem with any such idealism is the constancy of the world of objects: we do not seem to be able to change things or create things with our minds. Why do objects seen or unseen continue to obey the laws of physics? Why are the objects in a drawer always where we left them even though no one sees them when the drawer is closed? Bishop Berkeley at least postulated a constant transcendental observer (God) to make the everyday world reflect what we know. (For a realist interpretation of a panpsychic idealism as an explanation of extrovertive mindfulness experiences, see Marshall 2005: 261-68.)

12. Many New Age advocates see mystical experiences as a causal factor contributing to the evolution of mankind toward a higher plane of consciousness. Pierre Teilhard de Chardin is the patron saint of those who see evolution as involving both mind and matter and who also see the cosmos as evolving toward a higher goal. To these advocates, our consciousness participates in the process of an unfinished universe, and mystical experiences are crucial to the next step leading to more evolved beings or to a new level of evolution in which each person becomes a node in a social or even planetary consciousness. Such "consciousness evolution" is foreign to classical mysticism, but it does combine valuing the material universe and evolution with valuing mystical states of mind.

13. Some scientists interpret the same phenomena that lead parallelists to emphasize a fundamental role for consciousness in the universe in nonconscious, mechanical terms: it is *computation* and the *increase of information* fueled by natural selection that is programmed into the structure of the universe. There is nothing about the universe "becoming aware of itself" or any "cosmic intelligence" at work but only a nonconscious, material process at work—computation as mechanical as an adding machine's clicks—that leads to greater complexity and conscious beings.

14. Wheeler asks: "Does looking back 'now' give reality to what happened 'then'?" The astronomer Martin Rees suggests: "In the beginning there were only probabilities. The universe could only come into existence if someone observed it. It does not matter that the observers turned up several billion years later. The universe exists because we are aware of it" (quoted in Rosenblum and Kuttner 2006: 193).

15. Fred Alan Wolf imagines the soul to be "composed of spinning virtual, negative potential energy, electrons" that he calls "minisouls immersed in the Dirac sea-like vacuum of space" where the soul deals with virtual particles and real particles in the sentient body (1996: 152).

16. The movie *What the BLEEP Do We Know !?* centers on quantum mysticism. Amit Goswami and Deepak Chopra are two of the authorities featured in it. Goswami sums up its central theme: "I create my own reality"—we literally make the external reality through our thoughts and will. (For the book version, see Arntz, Chase, and Vicente 2005: 125-38.) The naturalist's response is blunt: "leap out of a 20-story building and consciously choose the experience of passing safely through the ground's tendencies" and see what happens (Sherman 2005: 34). For Goswami and Chopra, consciousness creates reality, and to create a better reality for ourselves we need to correct our consciousness, since our consciousness is infecting the quantum field (Arntz, Chase, and Vicente 2005: 113-51, 81). Even some people in the popular mysticism movement are embarrassed by this (see Huston 2004). So too, even assuming that mindfulness shows that we are integrated into the universe and that our mind is connected to a more pervasive consciousness, it does not follow that the universe is our "extended body" (quoted in Rothman and Sudarshan 1998: 169). We still cannot control the rest of the universe the way we control our body. Even if paranormal powers are real, this does not mean that we can look upon everything as an extended body: manipulating an object by our mind does not make it an appendage of our body even temporarily.

17. In itself, a photon or electron is neither a wave nor a particle, but a reality that manifests such properties in different settings that physicists create by their experiments. The subatomic realities "in themselves" are never revealed in experiments. That is, an electron is *not* both a wave and a particle but something that exhibits wave-like or particle-like behavior in different settings (Barbour 2000: 77). Whatever is there behaves like a particle under some conditions and behaves likes a wave under other conditions that physicists create. The act of observation becomes part of the quantum event. When subjected to one experimental set-up, what is real consistently reveals wave-like properties, and when subjected to another set-up, it consistently reveals particle-like properties, and we cannot observe both properties simultaneously. In addition, the mathematics of quantum physics produces one consistent account. In short, if we do one thing to the reality that is there, wave-properties appear; if we do another, particle-properties. What we see is always a combination of the reality that is there and our intruding experimental procedures. Thus, what appears depends on different combinations of things, including what we do; if we did not interfere, the reality is unaffected and these properties may not exist. That x (what is there) plus y (one set of conditions) does not equal x plus z (another set of conditions) is not paradoxical or even surprising.

18. "Lower" levels do support the "higher" level activities by providing, for example, the chemical base in which DNA information is carried. There is also some interlevel causation, as when radiation causes a cell to mutate or a Geiger counter to click.

19. For free will to work, there also would need to be a *causal order* on the everyday level of things—otherwise, we could never predict what consequences our choices would have in actions since things would happen randomly. But there could be no *determinism* of

physical events in the brain or we would have no choices at all.

20. Mansfield tries to justify universal compassion with particularly bizarre reasoning. Since all electrons are absolutely indistinguishable from each other, and since human beings are absolutely alike in wanting happiness and avoiding suffering, therefore all human beings are interchangeable, and quantum physics grounds a universal compassion (2008: chap. 2). He is not claiming quantum physics proves Buddhist truths (ibid.: 31). Yet we are totally indistinguishable with regard to the truth of suffering, and so the universal principle of quantum indistinguishability is relevant to Mahayana ethics and the universalization of compassion. But since we human beings are in fact different in all other regards, as Mansfield admits (ibid.: 32), it is hard to see quantum indistinguishability as relevant even by analogy, even if we do all want happiness and to avoid suffering. This also ignores the issue that different people have different ideas of what happiness is.

21. Mansfield's logic seems to be this: since (1) quantum physics and relativity are in "thoroughgoing agreement" with Madhyamaka Buddhism on emptiness, "not just in broad outline but in terms of the most fundamental principles," and (2) Mahayana Buddhism integrates wisdom (*prajna*) with compassion (*karuna*), then modern physics naturally leads to universal compassion (2008: 162, 90-92, 166). But there are problems with the first premise (as discussed), and the second premise involves a value-judgment that does not follow from the factual premise (see Jones 2004: 189-93). Mansfield could modify his conclusion from claiming that quantum interdependence "must express itself in universal compassion" (2008: 164) to claiming simply that interdependence is *one way* to ground "more compassion in our cruel world" (ibid.), but the value-choice would still remain independent of the factual claim.

22. It should also be added that the philosophy of *naturalism* is not necessarily a basis for *selfishness*. Indeed, exclusive self-interest is *inconsistent* with naturalism's metaphysics: realizing that we are part of one integrated universe is no basis for self-centered desire. One cannot see oneself as a separate entity to be valued over everything else if we are interconnected with everything else (i.e., physically we are products of star dust and biologically all life on earth has evolved from the same original life-forms). In addition, we are not born alone (we could not be closer to another) and cannot survive alone. In such circumstances, choosing a concern for others is more reasonable than "looking out only for number 1."

— 7 —

Distorting Science and Mysticism

Much of the reasoning in the parallelists' comparisons of science and mysticism is embarrassingly bad.[1] For example, they argue that time is "unreal" in both mysticism and science, and so the two endeavors are converging, even though the underlying ideas are very different: in mystical experiences, the sense of time vanishes and so the experience feels timeless; in relativity theory, time-frames are relative to motion and so no time-frame is absolute, but the temporal succession of causally-related events is still part of the scientific picture. This reasoning is on the order of concluding that if A cannot be visualized and B cannot be visualized, then A and B must have something significant in common, or they in fact must be the same thing, without any analysis of the underlying content of the different claims or any discussions of the philosophical problems in comparing two different endeavors. (See Jones 1986: chap. 8 and 9.) Usually the comparisons are of isolated statements without much background on the contexts that make their meaning clear. Thomas McFarlane's *Einstein and Buddha: The Parallel Sayings* (2002) is the extreme in this regard: he quotes merely the isolated statements with nothing at all to give them any context. Because the wording in bits of translations looks like something a parallelist is familiar with from science, he or she concludes without further research that the passage must be referring to the same scientific subject—however, if we look at the context, inevitably we see that the wording clearly does not refer to anything we would consider "scientific." In short, parallelists make mystical teachings into something they were never meant to be.

But another aspect of their methodology deserves special comment: the way parallelists *distort* both science and mysticism from the beginning of their comparisons.[2] Whenever we attempt to understand anything new we all have previous beliefs, and there is a very real danger in comparing science and mysticism of misreading one endeavor in light of our prior commitment to the other. The danger is that we will end up seeing mystical ideas in the scientific ideas or vice versa and not in terms of their own endeavor. That is, our understanding of one endeavor may become "contaminated" (Restivo 1983: 24) by our understanding of the other endeavor, and thus the comparisons may not be of the genuine article. This contamination of the subject under study can occur in either direction, and we can end up distorting one and thus end up with an artificial commonality that does not reflect the genuine article of either subject. Indeed, we can contaminate both: first we contaminate mysticism with our view of science, and then revise our view science in light of the new view of mysticism, or vice versa.

Distorting Science

Distorting their understanding of science in light of their beliefs about mysticism is a persistent error among parallelists. Consider quantum physics. Although its mathematics is well-established, there are conflicting interpretations among physicists on how the quantum realm should be understood. (There are at least nine different ontological interpretations of quantum physics [Rosenblum and Kuttner 2006: 156-66]. For an accessible explanation of how quantum physics works without *any* such interpretation, see Feynman 1967: 127-148.) The danger is that parallelists will pick a particular theory that fits their theories about mysticism or a "new vision of the world" and present that theory as the one interpretation generally accepted by the scientific community. It may not even be a mainstream theory but quite unorthodox. In particular, they pick the theory making consciousness a cause in quantum events that Eugene Wigner developed following John von Neumann's lead, even though mainstream physicists have not pursued this approach for generations. (But see Malin 2001: 119-24.) Or they will mash together parts of conflicting theories and present the resulting amalgam as the one accepted interpretation (e.g., Griffiths 1989: 16-21) in order to show how modern science allegedly is coming around to see the world as ancient Vedic rishis or some other seers saw the world. (See Spector 1990 for a discussion of the parallelists' general mistakes in their understanding of quantum physics. Also see Clifton and Regehr 1990; Crease and Mann 1987, 1990.)

Also note that comparisons are made to specific scientific theories, and this leads to another problem: science is not so much *a body of theories* held at any given moment as *a way of questioning nature to learn more about how things work*—an approach to reality that will remain different from the approach that mystics use to accomplish their ends, regardless of the belief-claims used for comparisons at any given moment. In short, the distinction is between science as a knowledge-giving enterprise—a way of knowing—and science as a body of specific claims at a given time. Science as a way of studying nature cannot be reduced to the results of that approach at a particular point in history. But since the nineteenth century, parallelists, while acknowledging the different natures of mystical experiences and the "scientific method," focus on the content of the then-current scientific theories in order to find mystical metaphysics "scientific." But that some of the content of, say, traditional Hindu cosmology might converge in broad outline with contemporary scientific cosmological beliefs does not make the Hindu beliefs *scientific*. (In Chapter 9, comparisons of scientific theories with some traditional Asian cultural beliefs will be covered. If we reduce science to the current body of theories, a problem also arises when those theories change; this will be discussed in the next chapter.) The question is how those beliefs were arrived at and the reasons for holding them—just because they cover the same terrain or have some similar belief-content is irrelevant. If the "scientific method" as a way of knowing reality was not applied, consciously or unconsciously, any general similarity of content does not make a cultural belief *scientific* in nature. Even to call such cultural beliefs "*anticipations*" of modern science is misleading: it changes the cultural context of the beliefs if they were not originally at least proto-scientific in aim (i.e., exhibiting some interest in understanding the causes at work in nature). That is, the mind-set then becomes that of looking at other cultural beliefs through the lens of modern science rather than seeing them in their own terms. Any abstract "similarity" or "convergence" of claims (e.g., that there are other realms in the universe with conscious inhabitants) does not make the traditional Asian mystical ideas "anticipations" of science in method, aim, or actual content—mystics were not trying but failing to make a scientific theory about how nature works or having a vague sense of what scientists will find.

Another danger is that parallelists often ascribe everything they like to the "new physics" and see Newtonian physics as the source of everything wrong with the world when in fact many of the things they see as innovations of twentieth-century physics have always been a part of modern science. Three points in particular stand out. First, Newton did not see the world as "static" (contra, e.g., Matthieu Ricard in Ricard and Thuan 2001: 278), and we did not have to wait until Einstein to see the world as "dynamic." Science has always been about change. For example, in mathematics Newton devised the calculus—the "method of fluxions," as he called it—to work with changes in speed. Modern scientists have always seen the world as fundamentally dynamic, and their basic task has been to identify patterns in the changes and to explain them in terms of underlying and apparently unchanging structures. In fact, it was not until *relativity* came along that a *static view of the universe* was introduced into science: the universe as a four-dimensional "block" in which the causal sequence of before-and-after is not denied, but in which time is not a component—the universe does not *happen*; it just *is*.[3]

Parallelists are confusing the concept of *fixed laws* with the concept of a *static universe*, but a scientific world having fixed laws is no more static than a mystical one having fixed laws of karma and Buddhist "dependent arising." Scientists attempt to detect structures underlying the flux of the world by measuring changes in the interaction of objects—even "mass" and "inertia" are determined by measuring an object's resistance to changes in motion. Nor are post-Newtonian laws any less fixed than Newtonian ones (although some are in the terms of probabilities), and thus the new physics is the same as the old in this regard. Second, Newton and other early modern scientists had a profound sense of *the unity* of God's creation. Newtonians in general saw the world as integrated by laws into one ordered whole, not as fragmented or disjointed. Such a "clockwork" world is fully interlocked, with every piece determining the movement of other pieces—indeed, clockworks only works if *all the parts fully mesh*. Nor did Einstein invent the idea of gravity as one encompassing force integrating everything. That idea too was part of early modern science. In fact, some early modern Christians rejected the idea of gravity precisely because such a universal force seemed like a rival to God. The "field" may be, as Einstein said, the most important concept introduced into science since Newton's time, but it did not introduce the idea of a framework of an ordered, interconnected, and dynamic whole. Third, twentieth-century physicists did not make the discovery that the fundamental workings of nature are different from those of the everyday world. Indeed, the idea that "nature loves to hide" goes back to the pre-Socratic Greek Heraclitus.

Parallelists also claim that contemporary physics frees us from the Newtonian world that was *deterministic* and thus did not permit a genuinely open future or human free will. But many of the physicists today in fact still believe in a physical determinism of the universe. Nothing in relativity is incompatible with determinism, and many physicists are turning to deterministic interpretations of quantum physics (Hugh Everett's multiworld theory, David Bohm's hidden variable approach). Einstein accepted determinism and, following Spinoza, also denied free will. So too, chaos and complexity theories are open to a deterministic interpretation—the unpredictability involved in these theories is a matter of limitations only on our *epistemic abilities*, not necessarily a matter of ontological indeterminism.

All in all, while the revelations in the twentieth century on the subatomic scale and the cosmological scale were most certainly very significant, and new theories in science are eclipsing the old, this does not change the fact that many basic parts of the new framework were not elements of only the new innovations. Although Newtonians did see interactions of parts as mechanical, and a reductionism of levels did seem a natural metaphysical position for such a view, not everything that parallelists see as scientific sins can be attributed to Newton.[4] The contrast of the old and new physics is not as great as many parallelists like to believe. Indeed, Einstein and some historians of science see the changes not as "revolutions" at all but only as the "evolution" of earlier ideas (Jammer 1999: 34-37).

The Kantian distinction between a thing-in-itself (*noumenon*) and a thing-as-we-observe-it (*phenomenon*) is embedded in most current theories of the quantum realm. The Kantian framework is part of the standard position labeled the "Copenhagen Interpretation," in which quantum physicists cannot know the nature of the objects they study "in themselves" but only as they are exposed to our experiments.[5] This makes quantum physics a matter of the correlation of observations, but this does *not* mean that the quantum realm is structureless or that science is only a matter of our experiences in the macroworld—reality still plays its determinative role in the results even though we cannot separate out our everyday level of involvement in the experiments. There are correlations in the classical macroworld and we cannot ascertain their quantum-level correlata (Plotnitsky 2003), but this does not mean that there are no quantum-level realities at work. And nothing suggests that the quantum realm is structureless: the successful replication of experiments suggests that something real is fixed and is being hit by physicists. In addition, an event such as the collapse of the Schrödinger wave-function into a definite position is still a physical event even if there are permanent barriers to our finding out everything about it. (And this does not make the wave-function into some ethereal physical reality—it remains only a summary of the mathematical probabilities of all the possible states a system can be in.) In sum, even if quantum physics is a set of mathematical rules for predicting observations, it is not merely about correlating our subjective experiences: something on the quantum level is responsible for the correlations, even if we cannot know the causes in themselves.

Mystics, on the other hand, claim to have had *direct experience* of what they assert knowledge of. It is possible to see Brahman as a Kantian noumenon, although it would be a featureless and structureless noumenon. But mystics believe they have gotten to reality-in-itself, unimpeded by any mediation. (Philosophers following Kant deny this is possible, as will be discussed in Chapter 14.) If so, they are doing something quantum physicists say is impossible for what they study. But again, mystical experiences involve being and not the structures that appear through experiments and indirect observation. In short, it is not the case that mystics have an experience of what quantum physicists are studying. In fact, mystics could agree that we never have direct experiences of the scientific structures since such structures would be part of the differentiated realm and not a matter of beingness.

Most importantly, the world of the new physics remains as "objective" as under the old physics, despite what the parallelists might think. Consistently getting the same experimental results means that physicists are studying structures that exist independently of our minds: they are irrevocably real aspects of the world—i.e., something that we simply cannot get around, whatever we think, and hence are "objective" in that sense. That we have to interact with the structures to learn about then does not change this. Nor would any role that consciousness might play in quantum physics or any pluralism of frameworks in relativity theory change this. There may be limits to our knowledge of these structures, but even empiricists acknowledge that something in the objective world is responsible for the reproducible changes we observe, although they insist that we cannot know what it is without experience of it. And the actions of the unseen realities are as rigorous as with Newtonian particles. Physicists have replaced the precise Newtonian language of particle trajectories with the precise quantum language of wave functions (Weinberg 1996). The objects in the everyday world may be impermanent and thus "illusions" in the Indian mystical sense of the word, but it still remains true that the structures operating in the "illusions" are objective. If, as science critics argue, the old physics produced an estrangement between human beings and nature, the new physics will not repair it. As science critic Theodore Roszak said, the tunes have been altered but the mode of the music is the same.

Distorting Mysticism

Turning to mysticism, problems of distortion also frequently occur. First, parallelists treat the altered states of consciousness of *mystical experiences* as the end-all and be-all of mysticism rather than the transformed *state of an enlightened person*. This would not distort mysticism too badly if these altered states of mind were the point of the comparisons to science, but it is the mystical *doctrines regarding the nature of the world and a person* in various Asian schools that are used in the parallelists' comparisons, and for this, mysticism cannot be reduced to its esoteric experiences or states of consciousness alone. The conflict of doctrines discussed in Chapter 15 concerning the nature of what is experienced cannot be dismissed.

Approaching any pre-modern culture today presents a basic problem: we always bring our own modern beliefs to the table. We may well read pre-modern texts out of their original context and through the light of modern Western Enlightenment beliefs and values. This is especially true when parallelists have only a superficial understanding of Asian traditions based on Western popularized accounts or are enchanted by a romanticized idea of "the mystical Orient." To point out the obvious, not all Hindus and Buddhists are mystics. In Hinduism, three of the four "aims of life" are for a householder's life—the mystic's path is relegated to the end of life, and needless to say, not all Hindus adopt it. Nor do all Hindus follow Advaita Vedanta—indeed, Advaita was never prominent until the encounter with the West producing Neo-Vedanta. Most Hindus are theists of one stripe or another. So too, comparatively few Buddhists adopt the full-time life of a monk or nun, and not all who do are serious about a quest for enlightenment—showing proficiency in learning doctrines and performing rituals is more the norm in Buddhist monasteries today than meditating to achieve selflessness (see Pyysiäinen 2006).

The very real danger of an anachronistic reading is enhanced when parts of a religious way of life's belief-framework are ripped from their full cultural and religious contexts for the purpose of a comparison to modern scientific theories. Taking mysticism out of its context reflects our modern compartmentalization of areas of knowledge, but we may end up with only a deformed understanding of a full way of life. In science-and-mysticism studies, there is also the more specific problem of understanding mystical concepts and traditions through the prism of modern science. Using *modern* mystics such as Vivekananda or Shri Aurobindo for comparisons presents a related problem: the mystics themselves bring their understanding—contaminated by modern science through their study of science and modern philosophy—to how they understand the significance of their own mystical experiences and their own traditions. But more typically, classical mystical systems have been the subject of comparisons.

Another problem is that there may well be religious motives for advocating a parallel between a science and a South or East Asian mystical tradition—i.e., wanting to put the imprimatur of physics on religious ideas of one's own tradition. Or, because of the prestige of science within our culture, parallelists may consciously or unconsciously want to see science as proof of mysticism, or at least want to claim that mysticism leads to the same knowledge. Conversely, conservative Christians and Jews who distrust mysticism in general may reject any such parallels—mischaracterizing Buddhism and other Asian religious traditions in the process—and instead advocate a philosophy of quantum physics that maintains a proper theistic distance between creator and creation (e.g. Barr 2007). (Of course, one may see parallels between *Western* mystical traditions and quantum physics too. Victor Mansfield's physics colleague at Colgate University, Shimon Malin [2001], gives an interpretation based on Plotinus's Neoplatonic emanationism.)

Simply seeking the imprimatur of science need not lead to distortion, but the enthusiasm for science may lead to misunderstanding mysticism in its aims, methodology, and doctrinal content. Science may well filter what is seen and how classical mystical traditions are understood. As mentioned in Chapter 3, this may effect a rethinking of mystical metaphysics. But there is also a great danger of circular reasoning: cleansing a mystical tradition of anything that might conflict with current scientific claims as simply "nonessential" cultural accretions (e.g., Buddhism's "flat earth" cosmology with various heavenly realms above and hells below), and then miraculously finding a remarkable convergence of mysticism and science.[6] The tradition can then be seen as having been "essentially scientific" all along. This does not require remaking a mystical tradition entirely in science's image—i.e., expunging all things non-scientific (e.g., mythological cosmologies or unseen supernatural beings)—but obviously in letting science set what is deemed "essential" to the mystical tradition in the first place, the result is blatantly circular. At a minimum, the comparisons are selective. For example, at a meeting between the Dalai Lama and scientists at MIT, the Western Buddhists deliberately edited their presentation: they focused on the empirical and rational aspects of Buddhism and minimized its more esoteric and explicitly spiritual dimensions (Zajonc 2006: 232). Scientists sometimes were unable to make relevant connections with Tibetan Buddhists who spoke out of their full religious context (ibid.). Looking at only selective aspects of a tradition is certainly legitimate, but parallelists tend to reduce the spiritual tradition to only those aspects and to view even the selective aspects through the lens of science, thereby making them into scientific concepts when they are not scientific in content or purpose.

This problem is exemplified by the work of the Buddhist scholar K. N. Jayatilleke who knocked out everything in Buddhism that was inconsistent with any currently accepted cosmological theories as not really "essential" to Buddhism in the first place and then concluded that the early Buddhist conception of the cosmos is, in essence, similar to the modern conception of the universe and that Buddhism is scientific to its core (1984). So too, Akira Sadakata sees "a surprising number of similarities between Buddhist cosmology and modern science," but then he says that we have to "remove the graphic, the dogmatic, and the mythological from the expressions of Buddhist cosmologies" to be "left with a series of concepts that resemble in no small way the conclusions of modern science" on such matters as galaxies, the birth and extinction of nebulae, and the birth of heavenly bodies from cosmic dust (1997: 181)—but only if we read the Buddhist texts in light of modern cosmology would we think that they had anything to do with those matters. The danger here is similar to a common practice among liberal Christians: first expunging all portions of the Bible that conflict with science by giving them a nonliteral reading, and then concluding there is no conflict between Christianity and science. Here parallelists distort mystical doctrines to fit science and then those doctrines become "anticipations" of specific physical and biological theories—i.e., interpreting a mystical doctrine so that it looks scientific and then seeing it as a premonition of modern science. For example, parallelists reinterpret the Chinese notion of the Way along the lines of modern field theory in physics and then see science as confirmation of the Chinese anticipation.

Equally important, parallelists lump all Asian mystical traditions together as if they were in fact only one system of thought or one tradition sharing the same set of beliefs. However, there is no abstract "Asian mysticism." Parallelists play down or ignore entirely the fact that Advaita's depth-mystical doctrines are very different from Samkhya's, which in turn are very different from the mindfulness doctrines of the different Buddhist traditions, and so on. Indeed, Buddhism can be seen as having arisen as a reaction *against* Hindu metaphysics of eternal entities. Parallelists also have ignored the various theistic Indian *bhakti* mystical traditions. Some Asian traditions share enough commonality to categorize them under the heading of "mystical traditions" even though most followers of these religious traditions are not mystics, but this does not change the fact that there is no one abstract "mystical tradition" but only many traditions and subtraditions, many of whose doctrines conflict with those of other traditions. Most significantly, the parallelists' approach distorts Advaita by making its claims related to the realm of change (*maya, lila*) its central ontological claim in order to connect it to the mindfulness idea that change is central to reality (e.g., Capra 2000: 194)—even though Advaitins take what is changing to be *unreal* (an illusion, the "sport" of Brahman) and emphasize the *unchanging reality* of *brahman/atman* as central. At least those parallelists emphasizing Brahman as an unchanging consciousness get that much right. We have to be cautious even concerning generalizations about Buddhism: there are some common core ideas, but there also are conflicting ideas between the different substraditions. No tradition is completely monolithic, and there interactions with science may differ. (Nor is science monolithic. There may be features that all modern natural sciences share that permit generalizations about "science," but when it comes to specific theories, the sciences can conflict.)

All in all, parallelists today are like the nineteenth century Christian missionaries who went to India with the mind-set that a trinity was central to religion—not surprisingly they found their trinity (Brahma the creator, Vishnu the preserver, and Shiva the destroyer), even though for the vast majority of Hindus do not see things that way. Today, parallelists are finding quantum physics and modern cosmology—everything from the virtual particles of the quantum field to the Big Bang to relativity to multiple worlds. They are reading Hindu and Buddhist teachings through a prism of scientific knowledge that distorts or screens out the original intent and meaning of these teachings and substitutes alien ideas in their place.

Was the Buddha a Scientist?

The filtering problem can occur in another way: the emphasis on any type of *experience* as the source of knowledge becomes seen through the lens of modernity as *scientific in nature or method*. For example, Buddhist claims now become seen as a matter of tentatively-advanced, empirically-tested hypotheses. All meditative exercises become scientific experiments on the mind. To modern eyes, the basic point that the Buddha exhorted his followers to rely on their own experiences and to examine phenomena dispassionately meant the Buddha must have been a scientist—that he was actually trying to get them to follow the path to ending his followers' suffering (*duhkha*) themselves and was not interested in learning about phenomena just for the sake of knowledge is missed entirely.

More importantly, there is nothing "scientific" in the Buddhist aim or purpose. In the *Kalama Sutta*, some villagers expressed to the Buddha their confusion about the conflicting religious doctrines they had heard. He exhorted them not to rely upon reports, hearsay, the authority of religious texts, mere logic or influence, appearances, seeming possibilities, speculative opinions, or teachers' ideas, but to know for themselves what is efficacious and what is not (*Anguttara Nikaya* I.189). But he was not exhorting them to conduct mental experiments over a range of inner states and see what happens: the villagers were told what would work—the Buddhist prescribed path to enlightenment (involving ethics, meditation, and the cultivation of wisdom)—and the Buddha already knew what the villagers would find. What they will find is set before any mental exercises are undertaken, unlike in science where scientists do not know beforehand what in their experiments will disclose, even when testing predictions. Buddhists have a goal established in advance and are not exploring the unknown.

Thus, Buddhism is prescriptive in a way science is not. Pinit Ratanakul may say "Buddhism has a free and open spirit of enquiry and encourages the search for truth in an objective way" (2002: 116), but this is deceptive: it is not fresh research since the Buddha already knew what the villagers would find. The Buddha had already discovered the path to the end of suffering, and there was nothing new to be discovered on this front. In the *Kalama Sutta*, the Buddha is merely saying that the villagers will then know for themselves because they will have *experienced it themselves*. We have to distort Buddhism to see this as "anticipating the skeptical empiricism of the modern scientific method" (Verhoeven 2001: 90). Finding something out for yourself through experience that you did not know before does not necessarily make you a *scientist*—sometimes it is only a matter of following a path that others laid out for you. In short, we cannot equate everything based on experience with a "scientific method." (As discussed in Chapter 9, Neo-Buddhists want to restrict what scientists may find. This also damages the claim to "free and open inquiry." It should also be noted that the Buddha's exhortation did not prevent Buddhist schools over time from accepting *the Buddha's testimony* [*shabda*] as a means of valid knowledge [*pramana*], along with perception and inference—in the end, Asian Buddhists considered the words of the Buddha's discourses as all but supremely authoritative [McMahan 2004: 927 n. 3]. Faith in the authority of the Buddha is a theme of the widely accepted *Lotus Sutra*.)

In sum, Buddhist meditation is less an open-ended inquiry than a method of discovering for oneself the truths authorized by the tradition (McMahan 2008: 210). Nevertheless, in the Buddhist apologetic literature, the Buddha is revered as the greatest scientist of all time. In the parallelists' eyes, the Buddha also regularly becomes seen as a biologist (e.g., Nisker 1998). But even in a proto-scientific sense, let alone a modern sense of "biology," this claim is simply wrong: the Buddha did not have a scientist's interest in understanding how nature works but another interest: ending the suffering entailed by perpetual rebirth. The Buddha cannot even be seen as "a scientist of the inner world" of consciousness since he was not interested in establishing a scientific understanding of consciousness. He simply was not studying the subjective or objective world to learn how things worked. The Buddhist parable of the poisonous arrow (*Majjhima Nikaya* I.63) again applies: the need for a cure, not any scientific knowledge about the arrow, is all that matters. He did not use the "scientific method" to test various hypotheses to create a scientific picture of the inner world. His method does involve empirical investigation and objective (disinterested) observation of inner mental states, but the objective is not learn more about the world: just as the one flavor of saltiness permeates the entire ocean, so too the Buddha's teaching has only one "flavor"—how to end suffering permanently (*Majjhima Nikaya* I.22). There is no need for a thorough, systematic understanding of all aspects of the human psyche to end suffering, nor was the Buddha out to describe whatever he found in this quest in order to contribute to a scientific study of the psyche. At most, he can be likened to a *technician* who was using trial and error to find what worked for a practical goal he already had in mind, not to a scientist who is out to find how nature works. Later practitioners followed the steps the Buddha devised, but at most they could confirm only that the techniques worked to end a sense of self, not that the theory of the mental life advanced by Buddhists and disputed by other mystics is correct. That is, they may be able to replicate the requisite state of mind, but that is all.

Granted, science throughout its history has usually been under the control of religious, political, and economic masters—to use the medieval Christian term, science has usually been the "handmaiden" of some other enterprise. But that is not what is happening here—it is not as if the Buddha wanted to practice science under the guise of a religion. Buddhism need not conflict with science and certainly could incorporate scientific facts as part of its view of the world, but this does not make it *scientific* in nature. Instead, a *personal transformation* is the objective: the Buddhists' interest remains squarely focused on its one "flavor"—ending suffering by ending the process of rebirth—and not on a disinterested scientific quest to learn how things work. Buddhists may encounter mental phenomena in their quest that interest scientists and may let scientists monitor their meditation, but this does not mean that Buddhists are leaving the path leading to the end of suffering to take time to study those phenomena for their own sake. Presenting mediation as a freestanding mode of inquiry and analysis also neglects its ritual, social, and even magical functions within Buddhism (McMahan 2008: 209-11).

As noted earlier, mindfulness does involve disinterested observation as does scientific observation, but this is not grounds to conclude that even to just this extent Buddhism is "a science of the mind" (contra Dalai Lama 2003: 101-102). Buddhists did not develop a systematic first-person methodology for exploring all or even some inner states in order to explain them. Seeing inner states as if from a third-person point of view, free of one's beliefs and preferences, and cultivating a general attitude of impartiality and objectivity does not make mindfulness a scientific study of the mind. That may lead to a useful phenomenology of experience, but another interest is needed for science: understanding the processes at work for their own sake. The Buddhist quest is not scientific "research" guided by empirical findings (contra ibid.: 102). Again, mindfulness involves cultivating selected mental states only for a particular purpose and with a particular goal. In science, experiments and observations are directed by theories to particular phenomena, and thus scientific observation too has a particular purpose and goal, but there is a difference: in science, results are not laid out in advance—something genuinely new and novel may be obtained by observation and experimentation. There is trial and error exploring, but here it is to find out how nature works. In fact, the impartiality of mindfulness would actually *interfere* with science here by disconnecting observation from making any phenomenon a priority.

Granted too, learning something about the working of our mind and our environment may well become part of any quest, and the Buddhist theorists did devise theories of perception and analyses of phenomena. Nevertheless, we can make the Buddha into a scientist only by ignoring the central point of his teachings entirely: scientists end up focusing on what, from a Buddhist point of view, is at best a subsidiary point and missing the central point completely. Buddhism does not become a "science of the mind" merely because practitioners are searching for a state of consciousness that lessens desires. Buddhists do have spiritual exercises where they use reason and analyze states of mind. This is part of a mystical way of life, although not meditation in the more common mystical sense since it involves utilizing the analytical mind, even though these exercises are often called "analytical meditation." Nor is it science: Buddhists are examining harmful states of mind (e.g., greed or hatred) to overcome them, not to establish a scientific understanding of how they operate.

Nor are Buddhists "experimenting" in the scientific sense at all or testing scientific hypotheses. Trinh Xuan Thuan points out that the only instrument Buddhists use is the mind; that they attempt to examine the mechanisms of happiness and suffering in order to discover the mental processes that increase inner peace and compassion and to eliminate those processes having destructive effects; and that science can only provide us with information and not the personal transformation in how we see the world and act on it as is required in Buddhism (2006: 119). But he is completely wrong in seeing the experiential nature of Buddhism as "thought experiments" (ibid.: 103). The Buddhists' inner experiences are nothing like physicists turning over in their minds hypothetical scientific experiments that they have not physically conducted or may not be capable of being conducted (e.g., Galileo dropping balls of different weight from a tower, or Schrödinger's famous cat). Thought experiments in science and philosophy (e.g., John Searle's Chinese room) are not real experiments at all; they are merely proposed experiments—some of which are impossible, as with Einstein's thought of riding a beam of light—to test an idea or to show its consequences. The Buddhists' actual meditative work on their minds is nothing like that. The Buddha did not "experiment with ideas, not things" (Spencer 1984: 18). His claims are not *hypotheses* in the sense that scientists test new ideas: simply because unenlightened Buddhists have not yet experientially realized their goal of enlightenment themselves does not mean they are "testing hypotheses scientifically" by their meditative practices and behavior in any scientific sense. And that others have achieved this goal does not mean that the Buddha was offering a "scientific hypothesis" that he and others had "verified" (contra Jayatilleke 1984: 15; Wallace 2003: 8-9). Having to follow a path oneself does not make the path a scientific hypothesis. Moreover, to think that the Buddha was setting out a "hypothesis" about *unexperiencable subatomic particles* (e.g., Ricard 2003: 274) only compounds the error. Any "direct experience of spiritual truths" makes mysticism *experiential*, but it does not make it scientific in the sense of being experimental or involving a scientific method. In short, not everything experiential is *scientific*. Just because mysticism involves experiences other than revelations does not automatically make it "scientific." Nor, as discussed in Chapter 15, can we speak of Buddhist metaphysics as "a verifiable system of knowledge" (contra ibid.) when alternative systems in other traditions that conflict with Buddhist claims are "verified" by the same experiences.

Naturalizing Brahman

Nor does Buddhism become "scientific in character" simply because the traditional Indic cosmology it adopted has some very general similarities with contemporary scientific cosmological views. (See Jones 1986: 180-84.) One does not become a scientist simply because the cultural ideas that one grows up with happen to have vaguely similar counterparts devised later in science (e.g., that the universe is ancient or goes through cycles of birth and death). Parallelists also distort the role of cosmology in mystical traditions to make them sound scientific. The pre-scientific and proto-scientific traditional cosmologies that mystical traditions incorporate as the cosmological part of the factual framework of a way of life become treated as essential to the mystics' teachings themselves—at least after pruning out the parts that obviously conflict with current cosmology. The remaining parts are then seen through the prism of modern scientific cosmologies and thereby become transformed into concepts from modern cosmology or physics.

For example, the Sanskrit term translated "space"—*akasha*—in classical Indic culture can refer to an ethereal fluid pervading the universe, but it has nothing to do with scientific theories of quantum fields. It is an element of nature in addition to earth, water, fire, and wind (Sadakata 1997: 24-25). It is a substance pervading the world and not "empty space," but it is not *the source* of the other four elements or anything else—it is not any type of "field" connecting everything with everything else, but another element separate from the rest. Nor can *akasha* be equated with Advaita's Brahman (contra Laszlo 2004: 140-41): Brahman is nonspatial—indeed, it has no physical dimensions—but transcends the phenomenal real, and no terms from phenomenal reality apply to it.[7] Nor does anything in Advaita or the Upanishads suggest that Brahman is a medium for "encoding" or otherwise conveying or conserving "information." Recording any information would involve differentiations, and thus the medium storing it would have differentiations too—precisely what Brahman does not. Nevertheless, Ervin Laszlo makes *akasha* the basis for his "informational Theory of Everything" by reading the modern ideas that he needs into the pre-scientific concept. Laszlo is not "*rediscovering an ancient tradition*" (2004: 112) at all. Nor is he doing a scientific analysis of an ancient concept—all *akasha* and his idea of an underlying informational field have in common is that they pervade all of space. Instead, he is imposing totally alien ideas onto the Indic concept. It is a clear case of letting modern understanding dictate what is meant by an ancient term.

Central to the parallelists' approach is that the depth-mystical experience, if they even acknowledge that it is distinct from mindfulness, becomes *naturalized*, i.e., what is allegedly experienced is no longer transcendental but part of the natural world.[8] In no mystical tradition is consciousness seen as merely the product of a naturalistic world, and no depth-mystical tradition eliminates a reality transcending the natural universe. But to create parallels, all mystical experiences, not merely mindfulness, become experiences of the natural universe, not an experience of a possible base of the true self or of the being of everything that transcends the creation and expiration of the natural realm. More generally, the "timeless," "uncreated" transcendental reality in different mystical traditions ends up being identified with simply some part or the whole of the natural order rather than the source giving being to all parts. Thereby, the naturalized depth-mystical experience can be connected up to science.

Laszlo's equating Brahman with *akasha* and with a physical quantum-level field is an instance of such a naturalization. But the two most important characteristics of Brahman for the issues at hand are first that it is featureless—in Advaita terms, it is without qualities (*nir-gunas*)—and thus devoid of structure (and hence cannot be a scientific explanation for why one state of affairs is the case and not another), and second that it is open to direct inner experience but not to being probed by objective experimentation the way features of the natural realm are. Any quantum-level reality does not share these features: it is structured enough that concepts apply to the differentiations, and it is not the subject of the depth-mystical experience any more than any other structured reality beyond the everyday world. The quantum realm remains a temporal realm of change, unlike the timeless Brahman. A quantum-level field is a sea of potentiality out of which pairs of particles and antiparticles arise from energy fluctuations. But this ground state or any other source of particles is as much a part of the natural realm as those particles. Thus, it needs a source of being—a "power of being" supplying its existence in the natural realm—as much as the entities arising out of that field. Even under an emanationist metaphysics this is true: a quantum field is at best the first material reality to emanate from the transcendental source—it still has the features of an objective reality needing a source and is not the featureless source itself.

Another basic distortion of mysticism in most comparative studies is oversimplifying it. Again, parallelists do not differentiate the two types of mystical experiences or the difference between the "vertical" metaphysics of depth-mystics and the "horizontal" metaphysics of mindfulness traditions. Thus, they do not notice a common ambiguity in the use of such terms as "nonduality" and "illusion" as noted in Chapter 1: the same terms may be used in different mystical traditions, but there are differences corresponding to the type of mysticism involved. There is the Advaita type of nonduality (the nonduality of the source of the self and of the experienced "dream" realm) and the Buddhist type (the absence of a plurality of independently existing, "real" entities within our experienced world). These produce different senses of "illusions": in Advaita, the whole natural universe is an unreal dream when compared to the transcendental source; in Buddhism, the illusion involves our conceptualizing distinct entities from the real flow of things. These different senses cannot be conflated. A depth-mysticism such as Advaita might use the same terminology as a mindfulness tradition such as Buddhism does, but this does not mean that the terms refer to the same thing in both traditions or that their ideas can be used interchangeably. Indeed, Advaita has no meaningful comparisons with scientific theories devoted to a realm of multiplicity and change; this leads parallelists either to ignore it completely or to naturalize Brahman and distort the doctrines of Brahman and *maya* to make them "in full accord" with whatever are the latest theories in physics or biological evolution.

Causation and Buddhist Dependence

A concept that figures prominently in recent discussions—causation—also illustrates these problems. Parallelists contrast the external, linear, mechanical causation of the old Newtonian physics (the paradigm being one billiard ball striking another) with the "mutual causation" of the new physics in which each entity affects the others (e.g., two atoms bonding into a molecule, thereby creating a new entity and affecting the properties of the atoms themselves in the process). This affects how they interpret the Buddhist doctrine of dependence.

Buddhists do affirm a causal relationship between phenomena, and their metaphysics affirms that the course of nature has an objective order (*dharmata*). (See, e.g., *Samyutta Nikaya* II.25.) Indeed, a fundamental belief in Buddhism is that existence is orderly (Ratanakul 2002: 115). While Buddhists accept natural orderliness (ibid.: 116), they are not interested in the causal laws of nature on any level of organization except as they may pertain to enlightenment—they have never expended "considerable energies" examining "the laws of nature" (contra Ricard and Thuan 2001: 209). That is, Buddhists are interested in the law governing actions and their consequences upon the actor (karma) and inner mental phenomena related to ending suffering but not in the laws of external material phenomena. Just because the Buddha was interested in the cause of suffering does not make Buddhism "scientific in character" (contra Chan 1957: 310-11)—it remained totally different in aims, interests, central experiences, and justifications. Buddhists simply showed no general interest in a causal understanding of nature or the mind that would characterize science.

Buddhism also has a central concept of *dependence*: every component of the experienced world (*dharma*) except space and nirvana is impermanent and arises dependent upon other conditions. The fullest statement of this dependent arising (*pratityasamutpada*) is a twelve-step process showing how suffering, death, and rebirth are all ultimately dependent upon our root ignorance (*avidya*) of seeing permanence in an inherently impermanent world; conversely, by removing the condition at the base that is necessary for the process to proceed (our root ignorance), the cycle is broken and rebirth is thereby ended. This process is the type of "law of nature" that Buddhists are interested in. However, it is very misleading to translate "*pratityasamutpada*" as "*causation*." Pratityasamutpada is about the necessary *conditions* for a process and how to remove a condition so that the cycle does not continue. The difference is not merely semantic: causes are all the necessary conditions coming together, but *pratityasamutpada* only delineates one necessary condition in each step. Nagarjuna places this distinction between cause (*hetu*) and conditions (*pratyaya*) at the very beginning of his most important philosophical work, the *Mulamadhyamakakarika* (Garfield 1995: 103-104). If *avidya* were *the cause* of desires, then once it arose desires would have to arise; there would be a deterministic chain with no way to break it; thus, once we are unenlightened, we would remain unenlightened forever. But under *pratityasamutpada*, once *avidya* arises, desires are not automatically caused. That is, our root ignorance does not *cause* desires, but it is a *condition* for desires. Thus, by removing this ignorance, desires cannot arise, and the chain of conditions leading from one rebirth to another is broken. This is not an instance of efficient causes as in science (or of any other type of Aristotelian causation), and to approach the interconnectedness and conditionality of all phenomena with a prior mind-set in terms of scientific causation is to set off on the wrong track. The focus should remain on our inner life and how to end suffering through removing our active misapprehension of reality (*avidya*), not on anything like the efficient causal course of inanimate objects in science.

Moreover, parallelists have now taken to misrepresenting *pratityasamutpada* to be an instance of *mutual* causation—i.e., A is dependent upon B which in turn is dependent upon A. The Madhyamaka tradition in particular is portrayed this way. (See Ricard and Thuan 2001; Macy 1991.) Later Tibetans did move from unidirectional dependence to a mutually dependent network of events (Jinpa 2012: 874-75), but there is no suggestion in the basic Buddhist conception of dependent arising of any sort of mutual causation, and Nagarjuna is in full accord with this. There are chains of dependence, but later links do not somehow affect prior ones. We cannot simply jump from the concept of "dependence" to the concept of "interdependence" and then to the concept of "mutual causation" and then claim Buddhism is like quantum physics. In Buddhist dependent arising, the root ignorance is a necessary condition for desire, which in turn is a necessary condition for the next step in the process that eventually leads to a new rebirth. Thus, ignorance in one life is ultimately a necessary condition for ignorance in the next life, but this is not any kind of loop in which the ignorance in a later life causes ignorance in the former—there is a temporal succession of the links of the chain in this dependence. Nor does *pratityasamutpada* mean that "everything affects everything" in one big interconnected whole: the Buddhist concept of "arising through dependence on conditions" does not interconnect different chains of dependence—in particular, one person's chain of dependence is not dependent on what happens in another's. (There are later modifications of this part of the doctrine in some Buddhist traditions concerning help from others.)

Nor does *pratityasamutpada* have anything to do with Bell's theorem concerning the nonlocal connections of distant quantum particles that had earlier been "entangled" (contra Thuan 2006: 107). Buddhist interdependence has to do with the *impermanence* of all things and the fact that things arise and fall *dependent upon* other things—not any connection of previously independent particles that have become entangled. In no way is such entanglement part of the conditions from which things arise according to Buddhist metaphysics. The two ideas have nothing in common. In fact, if the nonlocal connections of particles are *permanent* (or at least continuing), this would present a problem for Buddhism. Yet to Victor Mansfield, the Madhyamikas' "denial of independent or inherent existence precisely parallels the arguments in physics that establish quantum nonlocality" (2008: 88).

All in all, *pratityasamutpada* is more like "linear" Newtonian physics than the new physics in its connections. But trying to see any of this in terms of any type of scientific causation, let alone the relation of events on the quantum level of organization, can only mislead. It would be a clear instance of circularity—i.e., remaking a mystical concept in scientific terms and then claiming to have discovered a parallel between science and a classical mystical tradition.

An Illustration: Fritjof Capra

Fritjof Capra's work illustrates another problem: the risk of *theory-change* when one attaches one's position to a particular theory. In the 1970's, Capra championed Geoffrey Chew's S-matrix theory in quantum physics in which there are no fundamental entities or laws of nature: properties of entities are dependent upon the properties of all the other entities on their level of organization, thereby creating a self-consistent web of relationships. Thus, each particle helps to generate other particles which in turn generate the first particle—in short, each particle "bootstraps" itself. This theory had the advantage of having no unobservable entities such as a quantum field. However, the S-matrix's competitor—the *particle approach* of quarks, leptons, and bosons—won out. Nonetheless, Capra still adheres to the S-matrix theory while other physicists have made advances in the particle approach. Indeed, under the recently proposed "loop quantum gravity" theory in cosmology, even *space* is seen as consisting of discrete, particulate "atoms." But incredibly, Capra sees nothing that has developed in physics in the intervening twenty-five years as invalidating anything he wrote (2000: 9)—to physicists, he is simply in denial (Woit 2006: 152). And not only has he not refined his approach to science and mysticism in any way in his latest edition of *The Tao of Physics*, he has now expanded the parallels he sees to mysticism to include biology and psychology (2000: 9).

Capra considers "the bootstrap philosophy as the culmination of current scientific thinking," even though it is "too foreign" to "the traditional ways of thinking" of most members of the physics community to be "seriously appreciated" (2000: 316-17). Granted, there are problems with the quark theory—it keeps getting more and more complicated—but a deeper particle approach, "superstring" theory, is looking more and more appealing to many physicists. Thus, quantum physics is still "particle physics" even if the "particles" do not have the properties of classical hard and solid everyday objects. Of course, the bootstrap approach may come back into vogue—old ideas do sometimes return in science—but Capra's comparisons to mysticism at present seem dated and awkward. His own drug-aided mystical experiences (ibid.: 12) and his beliefs concerning "the worldview of Eastern mysticism" apparently have dictated what scientific theories he accepts (Sharpe 1993: 69-71)—or it could be that his views on science and his views on mysticism are bootstrapping themselves, leading to an encompassing vision of the impermanence and interconnectedness of nature.

Capra also illustrates the other problems discussed above. He views all of the Asian traditions as variations on one system of thought: Hwa Yen Buddhism. This he selects because of its doctrine of mutual causation. He sees this tradition as the "culmination of Buddhist thought" and "the core of Mahayana Buddhism" (2000: 105). This claim will come as a surprise to Buddhist scholars. All Buddhist traditions accept impermanence and dependent arising, but not the doctrine of mutual causation. Indeed, the current batch of parallelists barely mention Hwa Yen, if at all, and instead focus on Madhyamaka Buddhism, the philosophical foundation both of Zen and (along with the Yogacara) of the Tibetan traditions. (Tibetan Buddhism, it should be noted, has become the current flavor of the month, although most parallelists actually rely on doctrines common to most Mahayana traditions, not doctrines unique to Tibetan Tantric schools.) It is as if Capra searched through various Asian texts, found one that fit the beliefs he developed on other grounds, and crowned that text the "epitome" of all Asian mysticism. (Capra sees no reason to differentiate the beliefs of different mystical traditions because he believes there is a common "perennial philosophy" to all spiritual traditions, whether we are talking about Christian mystics, Buddhists, or Native Americans [1996: 7].) In fact, Capra distorts even Hwa Yen by not presenting all of its doctrines—including its principle of separate things or events—that would show the complete context of the one doctrine he selects as central (Wilber 1982: 258). He simply selected a popular image from the *Avatamsaka Sutra* that illustrates well any view of a holographic interpenetration of things: Indra's net of jewels, each with countless facets, which is arranged so that when we look at any one jewel we see all the other jewels reflected in it.[9] This selectivity ends up making his comparisons very narrow and not at all representative of Buddhism as a whole, let alone of all Asian thought or all mysticism. In addition, his knowledge of Buddhism was apparently drawn, not from the basic practices and texts, but from apologists such as D. T. Suzuki who wanted Buddhism to appear "scientific." Thus, his parallels are contaminated from the start.

Caution and Criticism

Ironically, Capra has become a little disenchanted with "Eastern mysticism" and has shifted his focus to Christian mysticism (Capra and Steindl-Rast 1991) because he found that "many Eastern spiritual teachers . . . [are] unable to understand some crucial aspects of the new paradigm that is now emerging in the West" (2000: 341). Why this should be so would be hard for him to explain since he believes the "new paradigm" is simply the expression of the "essence" of all Asian mystical traditions—how can these teachers not understand themselves? He does not consider the possibility that he might be *distorting* Asian teachings by seeing them through the lens of modern science. But mysticism cannot be made into a type of natural science. Nor, as discussed in Chapters 3 and 6, can science be made into a spiritual path to mystical enlightenment. Nor, even if we ignore the fact that parallelists tear mystical doctrines from their spiritual context, can mystical ideas be made into pale copies or anticipations of theories in modern physics, cosmology, and biology.

It should also be noted that in the Buddhist community today it is Westernized Buddhists who see a natural fit between mysticism and science. Prior to World War II, Asian Buddhists had presented Buddhism as compatible with science or vindicated by it (McMahan 2004). But as a result of the war, some Asian Buddhists began to express caution and concern about connecting Buddhism to science. For example, D. T. Suzuki began to stress the differences and that religion supplied something science cannot. Today some Buddhists express the same caution: they do not think that Buddhism should be reduced to a "mere school of thought" or a set of doctrines about nature or that religious truths need scientific validation; there is also the danger that Buddhism could be absorbed into a Western materialistic view of the world, thereby changing its character (see Verhoeven 2001: 91-93, 2003: 44-46, 50-51). They also are concerned that letting science determine what is "essential" to Buddhism means that the Buddha's enlightenment is being submitted to a higher epistemic authority—science (McMahan 2004: 928). Indeed, the parallelists' "physics envy" (Shermer 2005: 34) can lead to *scientism*: mystical experiences may end up being taken seriously only if mystics' knowledge-claims are validated by science. In the end, only science leads to truth, and so mysticism needs scientific support. But to do this, parallelists would have to distort the nature of mysticism as its own way of knowing reality.

Notes

1. Gary Zukav gives a paradigm of such reasoning. He claims that light has no properties independent of our observation, and then continues: "To say that something has no properties is the same as saying that it does not exist. The next step in this logic is inescapable. Without us, light does not exist" (2001: 105). It is one thing to realize that light has no particle-like or wave-like properties independent of our act of observation; it is another thing altogether to conclude that therefore it has *no properties at all and does not exist*. Our experimental observation may affect what is there, but it absurd to say that nothing was there to begin with or that we created some physical reality. Nor are the properties of light arbitrary: physicists always get the same properties by the same procedures, and so some things in light are indeed fixed even if we cannot observe them directly. Nor is there anything the slightest bit mystical or spiritual about this effect of the experimental process.

2. The Buddhist apologists (e.g., any essay in Kirtisinghe, ed., 1984) will not be discussed in detail. Buddhist apologists claim, for example, that "[t]hat can be no question that Buddhism is the one system, excepting perhaps science itself, which achieves an objective and detached view about the nature and destiny of man" (Spencer 1984: 17), but apologists in other traditions say the same about theirs. For example, to Vivekananda, only Advaita could stand the test of modern scientific reasoning.

3. Under this interpretation , the universe is a four-dimensional block in which our sense of the "flow of time" is merely an illusion our consciousness foists on us. There is the before-and-after causal sequence of events on a line through space-time, but there is no additional element to reality of "past," "present," and "future"—no "time." Events are like the still frames of a motion picture: there is nothing in reality corresponding to the motion. The sense of motion—"time"—is only an illusion in our minds. The past, present, and future all currently exist "timelessly." (This view does not explain why there is a "now" at all, or how our consciousness is roaming over the block universe.) But this view of a differentiated universe still distinguishes it from the contentless timelessness of depth-mysticism. And even with mindfulness, the experience of "now" involves an experience free from all temporal

categories, including the before-and-after sequence. Nor does the sense of change in mindfulness fit well with this static view in which events simply *are* and do not *happen*.

4. Incidentally, Newton himself would have rejected a "Newtonian worldview"—he believed that human actions were initiated and directed by a nonmaterial soul and that God had to intervene in his creation to maintain order in the universe. In addition, his idea of "action at a distance" does not easily fit the "mechanical" picture that parallelists paint. Indeed, he rejected the mechanical point of view most of his life.

5. What exactly the "Copenhagen interpretation" is is open to dispute—it was a title its opponents created, and neither Niels Bohr, the originator of this view, nor anyone else ever set forth a formal statement of it. But the idea that we cannot know what quantum-reality-in-itself is was central to what Bohr was saying. That is, physicists should stick to the mathematical formalism of quantum physics, embrace antirealism about the "wave-function" and other physical terms, and remain agnostic about what is "really happening" in quantum events apart from their experimental results. The theory's mathematics, in Bohr's words, "merely offers rules of calculation for the deduction of expectations pertaining to observations obtained under well-defined conditions specified by classical physical concepts." It is pointless to ask what reality is "in itself"—we cannot talk about what reality does when we are not observing it. So too, the quantum realm appears random to us, but it in fact may be *deterministic*—we simply cannot tell. Many physicists were happy to ignore the ontological elements of all theories in quantum physics—they were content to "shut up and calculate"—and adopted Bohr's interpretation. But beginning in the 1980's, many physicists did become more willing to say more about possible properties of quantum particles.

6. After the rise of modern science, Buddhist apologists started to see the heavenly and hellish realms as other places within the natural universe (i.e., galaxies or planets). That would be a naturalistic revision of this cosmology since such realms under traditional Buddhism are not part of the natural universe. Rather, the various "realms of form (*rupa-lokas*)" and "formless realms (*arupa-lokas*)" are created by our mental activity and are not out there in space to be traveled to. The natural realm (*kama-loka*) is also created by us—by our desires—but it is not the locus for the other realms. To revise these doctrines in light of modern science and then turn around and say that this cosmology "anticipated" modern science is obviously circular and a distortion.

7. Laszlo apparently relies upon the thought of the Neo-Vedantin Vivekananda, whose thought was shaped by his early education in modern science and Western philosophy and who was expressly looking to make classical Indian thought look scientific.

8. The Buddha too becomes naturalized: he is seen as merely a human being. However, in Mahayana Buddhism, the Buddha has three bodies: his physical body, a "body of enjoyment" that appears in Pure Land realms, and a source-like transcendental "body of *dharma*"—the Buddha cannot be reduced, in the Dalai Lama's words, to only "a nice person" (Lopez 2008: 195).

9. The idea that "each thing is in each other thing" can also be employed in theistic traditions to ground the commonality of being in a transcendental source. (See Nicholas of Cusa's *On Learned Ignorance*, Book 2, chap. 5.)

— 8 —

What is the Alleged Relation of Scientific and Mystical Claims?

One persistent problem in science-and-mysticism studies is the lack of clarity over what precisely parallelists are claiming. Parallelists see "profound similarities" between scientific and mystical claims, to quote Fritjof Capra, but they are vague on what exactly is the alleged relationship of these claims. Parallelists throw together an amalgam of different ideas: science and mysticism "share the same insight" or have "common ground;" or scientific claims "mirror" mystical claims; or scientific claims are "implicit" in mystical insights; or each endeavor has "implications" for the other; or the two have a "synergy;" or one "anticipates" or "resonates" with the other; or one "validates" or "verifies" the other; or they are "harmonious" or "consistent;" or science and religion can be "reconciled" through mysticism; or the two endeavors exhibit a "correspondence;" or a "fusion" or "integration" between the two should occur; or a "confluence" of science and mysticism will produce something new—all without specifying how exactly, for example, science can verify a mystical metaphysical claim.

The most commonly used terms are "parallels," "converging," "complements," and "confirms."[1] But parallelists use these terms without precisely defining them, and without realizing that these concepts are very different: if mystical claims *parallel* scientific claims, then the claims are fulfilling analogous roles in different conceptual systems but their substantive content is different, and so they cannot *converge*; if the claims are *converging*, they are not separate *complements*; if the claims are *complements*, they are not *confirming* each other; indeed, if science and mysticism are *complements*, they cannot directly *influence* or *affect* each other because each then is a *separate* endeavor that in some way adds something that the other omits; one system cannot both *complement* and *reveal* the other's truths at the same time. (See Jones 1986: 173-74.) Nevertheless, parallelists throw these terms haphazardly into the same paragraphs, sometimes the same sentence (e.g., Ricard and Thuan 2001: 276), in a "dialogue" between scientists and mystics.[2]

Different Endeavors

Parallelists observe that science and mysticism both entail problems with language as their participants move away from everyday knowledge, that both involve experiences, and that scientists find impermanence in the interactions among the content of the quantum realm while mindfulness mystics see impermanence in the content of the everyday realm. Indeed, they find great significance in these points—they find scientific and mystical claims paralleling each other and confirming each other and converging on a new worldview based on the impermanence and dependency of things upon other things. The most popular way to reconcile mysticism and science is to claim that mystics are dealing with the "depth" of reality and scientists with the "surface" of the same aspect of reality. That is, mystics and scientists are using different approaches to reality, but they apprehend the same thing rather than apprehend fundamentally different aspects of reality: mystics simply turn objective observation inward and arrive at a deeper level of the same truth that scientists reach observing external phenomena (See Wilbur 1998; Capra 2000.) Since science and mysticism both lead to the same basic knowledge, we only have to choose the route that is more agreeable to our disposition.

However, parallelists do not see the consequence of this position: either mystics are giving a more thorough account of what scientists are studying—i.e., they get to the root of the same subject and therefore are doing a more thorough job than are scientists—or scientists are examining the same subject as are mystics but with more precision. Either way, this means that one endeavor is superseded: either mysticism's thoroughness renders science unnecessary, or science's precision replaces mysticism's looser approach. Why would *both* be needed if they are studying the same thing and one is doing a better job?

On the other hand, if scientists and mystics are studying different things both endeavors in the end would be needed for our fullest knowledge of reality. If, as is being argued here, scientists and mystics do not focus on the same aspect of reality but on fundamentally different ones, then neither can render the other superfluous. It is not as if all we have to do is push further in science and we will end up mystically enlightened, or push further in mysticism and we will end up with a unified theory for physics—scientists and mystics are doing different things. Scientists are not even investigating areas that "border on the mystical" but another aspect of reality altogether. Science and mysticism, of course, can be said to have a "common pursuit of truth" and to be "united in the one endeavor of discovering knowledge and truth about reality," or, as noted in Chapter 6, both "seek the reality behind appearances." But this only places both endeavors into a common, more abstract philosophical category of being knowledge-seeking since they are not pursing the *same truths*—they are focusing on different aspects of reality, and neither discipline learns new truths of any value to the other. Mystics do come "to recognize an aspect of the universe that is ordinarily hidden from our view," and in this sense a mystic is "not unlike the physicist becoming aware of aspects of the universe ... through the instrument of mathematical analysis" (Raman 2008: 275-76): both mystics and scientists encounter aspects of reality we do not normally experience. But this in itself is not grounds for any further, more substantive commonality—the differences here in what is experienced and in how it is experienced foreclose any greater convergence.

So too, mysticism and science may share a general ideal methodology—i.e., careful observation, rational analysis, open-mindedness, and having background beliefs (e.g., Wallace 2003: 1-29). But this is so only on an abstract level: in actual practice, the differences in objectives between cultivating mystical experiences versus scientific observation and explanation cause very different implementation of any common abstract general principles. Mystics and scientists are engaging different aspects of reality differently for different purposes. Together they are indeed studying reality, but they are not becoming united in any substantive way into one way of knowing or converging on the same claims about reality. That science and mysticism are both concerned with discerning truth does not make mysticism a form of science or vice versa. At best, the parallels between aspects of each endeavor are "parallels of analogy," not "parallels of identity" (see Balasubramaniam 1992), since the endeavors remain focused on different aspects of reality and have different goals. In the end, the only commonality may be features that any enterprise intending knowledge of reality would have—knowledge based on experience, and so forth—and the fact that these endeavors encounter things we would not expect from our ordinary experience in the everyday world. They value types of experiences (conception-free experiences versus concept-driven observations) and value conceptualizations very differently (becoming free of conceptualizations versus coming up with better conceptualizations of how nature works), and this alone precludes any deeper convergence in "method."

Obviously, scientific and mystical claims will always be "harmonious," "compatible," and "consistent" on basic claims since they are dealing with different aspects of reality and hence they cannot intersect at all—scientists and mystics talk past each other. However, being *compatible* with science does not make mysticism *scientific* in nature. (See Geoffrey Redmond and Victor Mansfield in Redmond 1995-96.) Claims in one endeavor are simply irrelevant to claims in the other—logically, they cannot confirm or conflict even in principle. This makes reconciling mystical metaphysics and science very simple as long as the mystical side is confined to claims about a transcendental self or ground of reality. (See, e.g., Haisch 2006.) The metaphysics of naturalism would be ruled out, but nothing from science itself could in principle present a problem. However, as discussed in the next chapter, mystical traditions also have *more metaphysics* that always reflect concerns and ideas other than mystical experiences alone. Problems arise when a religious tradition's metaphysics specifies something of the nature of the natural realm—in particular, when a transcendental reality is seen as an *active power* in nature. Such metaphysics may well not relate specifically to the mystical experience of beingness, but may still be adopted by mystics into their total way of life.

Parallelists make much of the problems with language that practitioners in the two different endeavors have when encountering phenomena outside of the everyday realm of experience, but they cannot make any substantive convergence out of these problems. Just because both scientists and mystics have problems expressing what they encounter does not mean they must be encountering the same thing. For example, both mystics and scientists must use metaphors when they encounter the unexpected outside the everyday realm or the realm of ordinary experience. But this is not a very profound commonality since philosophers and linguists now point out that *all* of our thought is permeated with metaphors. All the use of metaphors means is that mystical and scientific thought is human thought when encountering something new—it tells us nothing about whether scientists and mystics are talking about the *same thing*. Of course, parallelists can take mystical claims out of their context and reinterpret the language used by mystics to describe a reality to fit scientific descriptions of nature. But to do so, parallelists must distort what the mystics really mean—e.g., reinterpreting "Brahman" to refer to the quantum realm and then seeing mysticism and science as converging. Mysticism and science may even share some abstract vocabulary, but the terms in the actual contexts of their systems of thought show that their referents diverge.

So too, paradoxes appear in both mysticism and science when the practitioners are confronted with contradictions between their expectations shaped by their everyday experiences and what they now experience or observe. But paradoxes do not function in the same way in mystical and scientific discourse: in mysticism, the aim is to abandon conceptualization altogether to experience beingness or its source free of the analytical mind, while in science the objective is to push through a paradox and to replace an inconsistent conceptualization with another one that consistently reflects what has been observed. Paradox may provoke more research or new theories in science; in mysticism it may evoke an experience, but no new conceptual systems. This points to a central difference: the centrality of formulations in science versus the need to transcend formulations for mystical experiences—the former reflects science's concern with differentiations and conceptualizations, and the latter reflects mysticism's goal of getting beyond them to experience beingness unmediated by any conceptual or emotional framework.

An example of an alleged parallel between Buddhism and contemporary physics—indeed, one that Alan Wallace finds "profound"—is that both "propose that all phenomena are illusory appearances arising from space and consisting of manifestations of space" (Wallace 2009: 159-160). But using the word "space" as the point in parallel is ambiguous at best: in the case of physics, it is physical space; in the case of Buddhism, it is a subjective, substrate consciousness. Seeing a parallel here also can easily lead to misconstruing the basic ideas: it makes the underlying consciousness of Buddhist metaphysics appear spatial in nature, and it makes physicists committed to the reductive claim that "all phenomena are illusory appearances." Misusing a word obviously generates only an artificial parallel or convergence, not an agreement of any substance. It is like diplomats intentionally drafting a treaty ambiguously so that each side to a dispute thinks it says what they want it to say—in the end, there is no agreement and nothing is resolved.

The Insubstantiality of Alleged Convergences

It is telling that Capra introduces the topic of parallels with a visual: pictures of mathematical equations and Sanskrit (2000: 128-29, 283). They do indeed look similar—if we squint, never look at them in focus, and ignore all the "details." Their rough similarity in appearance is certainly no basis for any substantive convergence of content. And in light of the basic divergence of science and mysticism, the "convergences" that parallelists see are not of any greater significance.[3] First, at most the alleged epistemic convergences merely reveal that people have problems when dealing with anything outside our normal view of things. Mysticism and science "converge" in both being "experiential," but this does not change their divergence in the types of experiences that are central to their endeavors: conception-free experiences versus concept-driven observations. Second, any convergences on the metaphysical level at best show that reality is more impermanent and connected than we normally suppose, but for mindfulness it is a matter of the everyday world of change that is open to our experience, while in physics it is a matter of subatomic realms. Third, as discussed in Chapter 10, we do not need any mystical experiences to see the impermanence and interconnectedness of things in the everyday realm—naturalists can easily accept these claims.

Nevertheless, while mystics focus only on the *beingness* of reality (both internal and external) as it is independent of our conceptual systems, parallelists read all of contemporary physics and cosmology on *structures* into the view of reality of a mindfulness mystic. Even a mainstream Buddhist scholar says that "[i]t is an event of tremendous historical importance when seventy-five years of research on the front lines of particle physics confirms the Buddhist conception that the world is never the same twice, that there are no mutually independent contemporaries, and no separately and independently existing parts" (Jacobson 1986: 28). It is a principal claim of parallelists too. For example, the Buddha is seen as having made claims about subatomic levels of structures that are only now finally being confirmed by scientists. Buddhists have "uncovered at least the basic principles of subatomic physics through their meditation practices" (Nisker 1998: 18). Modern physics "echoes" the investigations of Buddhism (Ricard and Thuan 2001: 10). That is absurdly wrong. Nothing remotely about the scientific principles actually involved in the features of quantum structuring is revealed in any sense in mysticism. As discussed, mindfulness mystics do not experience anything other than the everyday level, nor do depth-experience mystics experience anything about scientific structure. Nothing about the quantum realm's structures is a subject of mystical interest even though those structures are responsible for producing the physical conditions of the everyday world. Our experiences on the everyday level—including mindfulness—would predict nothing about the nature of the parts or the nature of their interactions. That some Buddhists postulated unbreakable atoms once again shows that mindfulness does not require a metaphysics of impermanent parts. Conversely, quantum physics cannot either confirm or disconfirm any of the mystics' claims about the everyday level of the world.

In sum, claims in one endeavor cannot in principle support or challenge claims in the other—science cannot confirm or refute, or indeed say anything about, the mystics' "essential teachings," or vice versa. Nor can these two endeavors converge on the same claims in any substantive way: to "converge" means to arrive at the same point, but science and mysticism are dealing with different aspects of reality and thus cannot converge on the particular claims of either endeavor. Mysticism and science are not aiming at the same thing, with mysticism transcending but incorporating scientific insights, or vice versa. Einstein equating mass and energy may remind some people of the *atman/brahman* equation in Advaita (Finkelstein 2003: 381)—they are both instances of equating two things that appear disparate on the surface. But this parallel is not grounds to equate *atman/brahman with mass/energy*. Such a substantive move is of an entirely different order. At best, mystical and scientific claims can "converge" only on an abstract level when one constructs an overarching metaphysics that "harmonizes" the two as revealing reality's impermanence or dependence. But no "synthesis" or "fusion" or "conceptual unification" or "synergy" of the two endeavors is possible because of their disparate subjects. There can be no "collaborative effort" (contra Zajonc 2004: 7) because scientists and mystics are doing different things. Mindfulness claims about the impermanence and interconnectedness of the experienced everyday realm in no way "validate" or "verify" scientific theories of anything beyond this realm, let alone the quantum realm, or vice versa (contra Nisker 2002: vii-viii).

Nor did the Buddhist doctrine of dependent arising "anticipate by twenty-five centuries the analysis of modern high-energy physics" (Jacobson 1986: 27). We can say that Buddhist metaphysics by extrapolation from the experienced realm anticipated finding *impermanence among the parts* of the quantum realm (again, with the qualification that some Buddhists accepted immutable atoms) but nothing about the *scientific structures* involved on that level. Nor more generally did Asian mystics "anticipate in an intuitive way" the findings of modern science. It is one thing to note that, say, the notion of "fields" is highly intuitive to the Chinese today because of their attention to context and environment; it is another thing entirely to assert that classical Chinese *anticipated* the scientific analysis, let along specific theories, in any way. The Chinese attitude simply did not relate to how a natural world separate from human culture works: their approach would make "fields" seem obvious once the scientific idea was introduced to them, but their attitude on its own would never lead to modern Western science. (See Nisbett 2003: 24.) And to say that they in any way "intuited" something on the subatomic level is absurd. At most, they are only extrapolating their experiences in the everyday realm—it would only be an act of speculation, not of any experiential intuitions.

We might say that the ancient Greek Parmenides anticipated the contemporary cosmological view of a "block universe" in which time is unreal or that Democritus anticipated modern scientific atomic theory (or set Westerners on the path leading to it)—or even that H. G. Wells in *The Time Machine* anticipated parts of special relativity—in that they did have the general idea that was later developed by scientists.[4] But there is nothing comparable in Asian mystical thought: they did not anticipate anything about what scientists would find concerning any scientific structures or the general nature of the quantum realm. Asian mystics were dealing with something else entirely—what is experienced in the everyday realm—and in no way did they anticipate any scientific findings about *structures*.(It is also worth noting that parallelists never see the mystical texts as *predicting* some new theory in physics or biology—it is only *after the fact* that parallelists see something as anticipating something of the science of the day.) Mindfulness remains about only actually experienced interactions of parts on the everyday level. That even the more mystically-minded physicists saw their mysticism and science as separate (see Wilber 1984) makes perfect sense. When physicists and astronomers finally finish scaling the peaks they are climbing, they will *not*, contrary to what parallelists are fond of saying, find mystics and seekers sitting there waiting for them.[5]

Moreover, if we examine the alleged convergences more generally we see that they are only of a very general nature. In fact, many alleged parallels are as superficial as the physicist Murray Gell-Mann adopting the Buddhist term "The Eightfold Path" but none of its content to describe a property in quantum physics—Gell-Mann also took the term "quarks" from James Joyce's *Finnegan's Wake*, but this does not mean that quantum physics and literature have anything significant in common. Because they differ in their subject matter (structures and beingness), the *specifics* of particular scientific theories and mystical beliefs cannot reveal any alleged convergences at all—no one can actually read contemporary physics from say, the Buddhist doctrine of dependent arising, or vice versa. Nothing in the claims can support the stronger claim of a "convergence" on the specifics of *how* the world is constructed according to different scientific theories and different mystical claims. In sum, we cannot infer a scientific theory from any mystical doctrine or vice versa.

At most, all that the theories of the two disparate endeavors have in common is the general metaphysics of impermanence and interconnectedness (as discussed in Chapter 10), not the *specifics* of any theories in mysticism or science. Their "common ground" is the impermanence and interconnectedness of the components of reality (e.g., Kohl 2007), but the mindfulness mystics' claim remains fully within the realm of what we experience in the everyday world, while quantum physics is a matter of theories and postulates about underlying causes. Thus, all that mindfulness mystics "mirror" of quantum physics in their doctrines is the more abstract principle of impermanence and interconnectedness—they do not provide any new insights into the subatomic structures that would be of any actual help to physicists. Similarly with depth-mysticism: science and the metaphysics of some depth-mystical traditions may converge on the idea of dependence, but the depth-mystics' claim involves experiencing something transcending the natural universe, while the scientists' involves only the dependence of appearances on another part of the natural universe.

Indeed, the idea that science and mysticism are "converging" can severely *harm* both mysticism and science. By naturalizing depth-mystical experiences or tying any mystical theory to a scientific one, we may go from seeing science as supporting or confirming mystical claims to arguing that science has *supplanted* mysticism. Thus, it may become the basis for *rejecting* mysticism altogether. Or we may believe that because science and mysticism are achieving the same knowledge through different routes there is in fact no reason to bother with the strenuous way of life that serious mysticism requires—all we have to do is read a few popular accounts of contemporary physics, cosmology, and biology on "the unity of things" or complexity and we will know what enlightened mystics know and hence be enlightened. All that matters is learning a post-Newtonian way of looking at the world, i.e., "shifting the paradigm" to the "new worldview," not experiencing reality free of all points of view. Conversely, by the same reasoning, scientists need not go through the expense and trouble of conducting elaborate experiments to learn about structures—mystics have already "intuited" what physicists would find and in fact have achieved the same knowledge with even more thoroughness through their experiences. They already know what scientists will find on the quantum level of organization in the future, so there is no need to conduct any more experiments. Hence, all that scientists need to do is meditate. That mysticism and science may involve different dimensions of reality that result in completely different types of knowledge-claims—and also require different ways of knowing and different states of consciousness—is missed entirely.

Complementarity

Parallelists who see a similarity in content but a difference in method or vice versa speak of a "complementarity."[6] For many, mysticism is a function of the left hemisphere of the brain and science the right, so only by utilizing what comes through each hemisphere do we have "the full-brain approach" (e.g., Nisker 2002: vii.) (Actually, the left and right hemispheres work *together* in most brain functions, not work *separately* to complement each other.) However, difficulties also arise here too. The idea is adopted from the quantum physicists' idea of the complementarity of wave and particle features of light and matter in different experimental set-ups. In physics, complements thus are two mutually exclusive ways of looking at the same object that result in different phenomena; only by accepting both ways do we have the most we can know of subatomic "particles."

But it is difficult to fit the relation of science and mysticism into this model. First, science and mysticism have different functions: science is only about gaining knowledge of reality, while mysticism is a total way of life geared toward a religious goal. Because of these different functions, religion in general and science are not of the same "logical type" and thus do not fit the scientific model (Barbour 2000: 77). Even restricting mysticism to only a way of gaining knowledge of an aspect of reality, it is still hard to see how to fit that model: science and mysticism have nothing corresponding to the unifying mathematics of the complements in physics; at best, a theory uniting them would be metaphysical, as discussed in the next chapter. (See Jones 1986: 176-78.) The two endeavors involve different dimensions of reality rather than different approaches to the same phenomena on one level of reality. Accounts of one aspect of reality do not relate to accounts of the other aspect.

Mysticism and science do not separate into different compartments neatly. It is not as if mysticism is about the "inner world" of consciousness and science is about the "outer world" of material objects, a standard trope in Buddhism/science discussions (Lopez 2008: 29): mystics work on consciousness, but they are interested in the beingness of all of reality, including the beingness of the "outer world." José Cabezón elaborates the complementarity position: science deals with the exterior world, matter, and the hardware of the brain, while Buddhism deals with the interior world and the mind; science is rationalist, quantitative, and conventional, while Buddhism is experiential, qualitative, and contemplative (2003: 50). But he realizes there are limitations: Buddhism too is concerned with the external world, and science too can study aspects of the mind (ibid.: 58). It is also hard to see natural science as "rationalist" rather than "experiential." But as discussed in the next chapter, mystical analyses of external phenomena—such as that by Buddhist Abhidharmists—do reveal an interest in external phenomena, but they do not reflect scientific interests. Limitations on any compartmentalization of all elements of mystical ways of life from science due to mystical ways of life embracing more than mystical experiences will also be discussed there.

The physicist Victor Mansfield sees the wave/particle complementarity as the same as the *yin/yang* complementarity in traditional Chinese thought (2008: 18). But in the latter, as one complement increases the other decreases, and neither complement is totally devoid of the other (as represented by the small dots of each in the other). In the former, it is case of all of one or the other, depending on the experimental set-up: there is no mixture of the waves and particles, nor does one complement affect the other in any way. At a minimum, the two senses cannot be thrown together as if they obviously are saying the same thing, just in "different languages" (e.g., ibid.: 88, 141, 162). So too, Capra is wrong in claiming that scientists and mystics "are really expressing the same insight—one in the technical language of science, the other in the poetic, metaphorical language of spirituality" (2000: 8) when they are dealing with different aspects of reality and doing different things.

In short, science and mysticism are not tied together in the way scientific complements are. But at least the idea of complementarity does affirm that science and mysticism involve irreducible *differences* (e.g., Cabezón 2003: 49-56). There are also other senses of "complementary." But the sense of complements in geometry does not apply: the expansion of knowledge in either mysticism or science does not shrink knowledge in the other. Nor, since each endeavor is irrelevant to the other, does knowledge in one endeavor expand the other's knowledge or affect it in any way at all.

Of course, since science and mysticism do different things, they "complement" each other in a looser, nonscientific sense—like, say, science and art. Science and mysticism deal with different dimensions of reality, and, if we accept both as ways of insight into reality, together they form a more complete picture of reality by supplying noncompeting explanations of those different aspects of reality (as discussed in Chapter 16). Each supplies a type of knowledge the other is missing, and thus they supplement each other. Each endeavor has theories that give an account of reality that is complete in the sense that it covers all of reality, but the accounts are of different dimensions of reality (structures versus beingness). Mystical doctrines are not competing accounts of structure that lead to inconsistencies when we try to affirm both scientific and mystical doctrines. Nor, since mysticism is not another scientific approach, do mystical doctrines fill in deficiencies in scientific accounts of structures and thus do not complete scientific accounts, or vice versa. There is no mutual influence or synthesis between them. Since they involve different dimensions, they are logically independent; thus, changes in the claims from one do not necessitate any changes in the beliefs of the other. Neither mystics nor scientists need to dismiss the other endeavor. If, however, mystics do reject science or scientists do reject mysticism, practitioners of either endeavor do not see their own endeavor as missing something that the other one supplies. Nothing in either endeavor calls for the other type of knowledge. Most importantly, mystics reject knowledge of the "differentiations" as reflecting reality at all and thus attempts at a nonmystical reconciliation of science and mysticism are at odds with all classical mystical ways of life.

In the end, there can be no "deeply-rooted connection" or convergence of the substantive claims of these two endeavors. At most there is an agreement on the abstract claim that an aspect of reality is impermanent and interactive, even though they differ on the aspect of reality they are referring to.

The Dangers of Claiming Convergence

At the end of the epilogue to *The Tao of Physics*, Fritjof Capra does state the correct relation between science and mysticism in one respect: mysticism and science are entirely different approaches involving complementary manifestations of the mind. "Neither is comprehended in the other, nor can either be reduced to the other, but both of them are necessary, supplementing one another for a fuller understanding of the world. . . . Science does not need mysticism and mysticism does not need science; but man needs both" (2000: 306-307). More generally, he thinks that we need both the "dualistic" point of view of science and everyday life for survival and the mystical point of view to be at home in the universe and to attain peace and joy. (He sees the relation of mysticism and science in terms of the "depth" and "surface" of one aspect of reality—i.e., mystics and scientists are using different methods, but they apprehend the same thing rather than fundamentally different aspects of reality.) However, in the actual body of his work, he still insists that we need "a dynamic interplay" between science and mysticism. He goes to unsupportable views, speaking of "convergence" and "confirmation" (e.g., ibid.: 114, 161, 223)—and he even does so in the epilogue just quoted (ibid.: 305). Elsewhere he speaks of modern physics "making contact" with mysticism, and that this shows "the unity and complementary nature of the rational and intuitive modes of consciousness" (1983: 47-48). And unfortunately the same tendency toward vagueness and inconsistency on what exactly is the supposed relation between science and mysticism is still the norm among parallelists today.

In fact, advocates of the convergence of science and mysticism should be very wary of any convergence of specific theories, as Capra's case with the S-matrix illustrates. There is a danger in tying a claim to any current theory: the convergence may be very temporary. That science is an ongoing enterprise and cannot be reduced to the theories of a given moment must again be remembered. When the French mathematician Henri Poincaré surveyed the history of science around the turn of the twentieth century, he saw only "ruins piled upon ruins" and thus the "bankruptcy of science." That may be an overstatement, but it is true that theories in science are constantly being modified and even replaced—twentieth-century physics taught us that the only certainty in science is that no theory is absolutely certain. Scientists speak with more tentativeness about their theories—seeing their theories as partial and open to revision—than do the parallelists. (Mysticism also contrasts with science here: classical mystics are much less tentative about their own mystical interpretation being the best or least inadequate among competitors. This is true of depth-mystics even when they contend that there is more to a transcendent reality than can be conceptualized.) Today much attention has shifted to complexity, emergence, and theories of self-organization. For example, some theorists speak today of a "self-organizing quantum universe" (Ambjørn, Jurkiewicz, and Loll 2008)—without an S-matrix and without giving up the idea of linear causality of a specific temporal sequence of cause and effect in favor of mutual causation. But there's the rub: if the theories that parallelists had favored are rejected, as so many scientific theories in the past have been, doesn't that mean we have to reject all *mysticism* since it supposedly is making the same claims? But if advocates contend that a mystical theory would still remain viable, then it must not have been the same claim as the scientific theory to begin with.

That science is an on-going inquiry into reality must also be remembered. Its theories remain tentative, provisional, and ultimately temporary. Dean William Inge long ago warned of the danger of wedding a theology to a particular physical theory: "the Church who is married to the spirit of this age will be a widow in the next." Arthur Eddington purposely did not offer "a God revealed by the quantum theory, and therefore liable to be swept away in the next scientific revolution" (1958: 353). Jeremy Bernstein echoes this admonition with regard to mysticism: "to hitch a religious philosophy to a contemporary science is a sure route to its obsolescence" since "the science of the present will look as antiquated to our successors as much of nineteenth-century science looks to us now" (1979: 8). More recently, Victor Mansfield said the same: since physical theories are intrinsically impermanent, it is a guarantee of obsolescence to bind Buddhism or any philosophical view too tightly to a physical theory (2008: 6-7). More generally, the Buddhist Walpola Rahula has noted that it "is incongruous and preposterous to depend on changing scientific concepts to prove and support perennial religious truths" (quoted in Verhoeven 2001: 92). Today, the inconsistency of quantum theory and relativity leads many physicists to believe that our current theories are not the final ones but are only approximations—hardly the basis for a comparison of any substance. So too in quantum theory: the element of randomness and the general statistical nature in our understanding of the quantum realm suggests to many quantum physicists that their science simply has not yet captured the true causes at work on that level. On the other hand, if claims from assorted mystical traditions can be attached to whatever the currently-accepted theory in quantum physics happens to be, then there must be very little substance to the alleged convergence. Or parallelists will pick one tradition whose doctrines they see as paralleling the new scientific views as representing the "essence" or "epitome" of Buddhism or all mysticism only because of they see a parallel to science in it.

It is also well to remember that books were written in the late nineteenth and earlier twentieth centuries in America and Europe that portrayed the Buddha as a good Newtonian. In the 1970's when interest in Buddhism and science revived, the Buddha had become an Einsteinian. Indeed, in the century and a half that people have claimed that Buddhism and science are compatible, the claim has remained remarkably similar in both content and form despite majors shifts in both science and in what we mean by "Buddhism" (Lopez 2008: xii). In biblical studies, there is the danger of creating a different Jesus for each generation or each political point of view, and the same danger occurs with mystical traditions with regard to scientific theories. Trying to see a mystical tradition in light of current science inevitably distorts that tradition and downplays its real substance. Indeed, the comparisons may eviscerate any substance to the mystical traditions by making them pale copies of current scientific beliefs.

Notes

1. Postmodernists would rule out the possibility of any comparisons or commonality or collaboration between science and mysticism because they are different endeavors. But others would disagree: to the extent that mystics make claims about the nature of the natural universe in their metaphysics (as discussed in the next chapter), conflict and commonality cannot be ruled out prior to an actual investigation. (For criticism of "the dogma of postmodernism" on this point, see Wallace 2003: 20-25.)

2. The term "dialogue" is common in recent discussions (e.g., Payne 2002, Wallace 2003). Usually it is meant to suggest that practitioners of both mysticism and science can learn from the other enterprise, and so practitioners in each endeavor should listen to practitioners in the other. But while a dialogue between scientists and mystics may help members of both groups see the *nature* of their own endeavor more clearly, whether mystical ideas can *influence the content* of scientific theorizing or research is a very different question. That is, discussions with mystics may well help *scientists* see the nature of science as a human enterprise more clearly—its philosophical presuppositions, that it is only one way to approach reality, its limitations, and so forth—but whether mysticism can affect the actual *content of science* is the more important question for science itself. And the same holds for science's possible effect on mysticism.

3. The idea of convergence is not always based on mystical experiences but on other religious ideas. For example, Raja Ram Mohan Roy (1999) sees modern physics and cosmology encoded in the Vedas and his job is to decode them. For example, the primal void of certain Vedic creation myths (like Genesis 1:2) becomes the quantum void, and domestic animals become bosons. How could Vedic thinkers now modern scientific theories? Roy claims that they arrived at their conclusions through reasoning about everyday phenomena and self-knowledge. This claim, however, does shade off into the idea that Vedic seers learned their physics through meditation. (See Nanda 2003: 115.)

4. Even with the Greeks, we can go too far with the idea of "anticipation." It is hard to say that Parmenides on the denial of *motion*, which is of one piece with his denial of time, anticipated modern science. So too with the Renaissance Italian natural philosopher Giordano Bruno's speculation about multiple worlds within this universe: the general idea of multiple worlds is not itself scientific, and it is hard to see how Bruno's speculation was an "anticipation" in a historical or any other sense. Some speculation is just speculation.

5. Varadaraja Raman gives an example of this claim when he wonders if the Vedic seers of ancient India had "tumbled upon some profound truths about the unperceived world that, because of their very nature, cannot be expressed adequately even in sacred Sanskrit" (2002: 90). "Could it be that now, at long last, after countless tortuous turns of experimentation, mathematics, and microscopes, we are slowly beginning to get a glimpse of what the sages were speaking about?" (ibid.).

6. Sometimes "complement" and "converge" are combined—i.e., complementary routes converge on the same claims (e.g., Raman 2002: 90-91).

… 9 …

How Science and Mysticism May Intersect

Since mystical experiences are about an aspect of reality that scientists *qua* scientists cannot examine, mysticism would always be in harmony with science if mystics could stick only to making claims about the source of beingness and the general impermanence and interconnectedness of the realm of everyday experience—their claims would then only be about being and could not in principle conflict or concur or even intersect with scientists' claims about causal structures. That is, both types of claims would then be about reality but about different dimensions of reality, and so their paths could never cross. Neither endeavor would be a possible help or danger to the other. Any "dialog" between them would become simply a matter of "show and tell," as José Cabezón says (2003: 59).

However, it must be remembered that *mysticism* is more than just *mystical experiences*. Mysticism cannot be reduced to mystical experiences for two reasons: to incorporate their own mystical experiences into their lives, mystics must understand these experiences once they return to the realm of differentiations, and hence they need conceptualizations and knowledge-claims; and mysticism as a way of life for cultivating selflessness involves a factual component that includes an understanding of the nature of both a person and the world that makes the way of life's path and goal seem reasonable to its practitioners. In sum, mystics themselves need to understand both the cognitive significance of their own experiences and also their place in the world. Thus, mystics are interested in the nature of reality and not only their experiences, and therefore mysticism cannot be limited to matters of experience or "higher levels of consciousness" alone.

But this means that science and the totality of a mystical tradition's metaphysics are not isolated and independent of each other—mysticism, in making claims about the nature of the world beyond a general impermanence and interconnectedness, intrudes into the domain of science. What Alan Wallace says of Buddhism can be expanded to mysticism generally: mystics are not scientists, but they address questions of what the universe, including both objective and subjective phenomena, is composed of and how it works (2003: 9-10). The "how it works" part, however, is limited: with the inward turn of mysticism, mystics are interested in matters related to mystical experiences and to cultivating a mystical way of life (e.g., karma); for other parts of a worldview, it appears that they typically simply adopt the general beliefs of their culture into their ways of life. Historically, all of the known mystics have belonged to religious or philosophical traditions. Thus, the distinctly mystical element of mysticism—the mystical way of knowing the beingness of reality—for these mystics is subsumed within a broader religious way of life and its factual beliefs, some of which impinge on the scientific domain. In this way, science and classical mystical traditions may intersect.

The Metaphysics of Mystical Systems

Thus, mystics do not limit themselves to making claims only about the experiential nature of the experiences themselves; they more often make claims about the nature of what is experienced and also the nature of the world and a human being. This is the metaphysics of each mystical tradition. Parallelists do not advance a new interpretative framework for mystical experiences. Rather, they utilize doctrines from various Buddhist, Hindu, and Daoist traditions, sometimes claiming that there is a "perennial philosophy." On the other front, it must also be remembered that metaphysics is always more encompassing than any scientific theory. This is so even if the scientific theory encompasses more than one level of causal interactions or is a comprehensive Theory of Everything.

Metaphysical claims about the nature of the world adopted by mystics from their culture are not strictly "mystical" since they are about more than matters related to mystical experiences, although it is not always simple to isolate claims about the nature of the world from claims about what is experienced in a mystical experience.[1] Nevertheless, these factual claims, or claims logically entailed by these claims—i.e., both explicit and implicit claims—can agree or conflict with scientific claims. In particular, how mindfulness mystics in different traditions envision various structures in the realm of becoming related to consciousness or how consciousness may play a role in external reality may in principle intersect with a scientific picture of reality. These claims venture outside the context of being and advance other metaphysical principles. This also applies to how a given tradition specifies the interconnection of things. Depth-mystical metaphysics are more insulated since they involve the source of the world or self and the ontological status of the entire natural realm, not what happens within the realm common to scientific explanations and mindfulness. With their views of reality adopted from traditional societies, mystics of both stripes may also affirm paranormal powers that scientists are either unaware of or at present reject.

In sum, even though the core mystics' claims are not about the structures that scientists study, the total metaphysical picture of reality presented in any mystical tradition may still concur or conflict with the picture of reality advanced in a science today. A claim in a mystical tradition's metaphysics adopted from the general culture may "resonate" in the mind of someone familiar with a particular theory in science or vice versa, and this resonance may help that person understand the theory from the other endeavor. Nevertheless, this still does not mean that there is any substantive identity or convergence of the specifically mystical ideas and scientific theories—i.e., the true substance of the claims. And the danger of misunderstanding a doctrine in light one's other beliefs still remains.

Because of these difference in interests, much of the metaphysics in mystical traditions may be immune to empirical findings and thus neutral to any possible scientific theories. But not all metaphysics is necessarily in that category. Consider four areas of science: quantum physics, consciousness, cosmology, and biology.

Quantum Physics

It is quantum physics's alleged "confirmation" of Buddhist claims of impermanence and interconnectedness that prompted the recent surge in science and mysticism comparisons. But it must be reiterated that neither depth-mystics nor mindfulness mystics are making predictions about the subatomic realm. The depth-mystics are not making any claims about natural structures but about the source of the self's or nature's beingness, and mindfulness mystics such as the Buddha are concerned with the level of the world that is actually experienced. The impermanent and interconnected "such-ness" of things has nothing to do with structures orchestrating changes within the realm of becoming but only with what is open to experience. Finding subatomic impermanence does not at long last finally confirm the Buddhist view of the world. The Buddha and Nagarjuna did not have to wait thousands of years to have their ways of life vindicated by science.

Conversely, even if some *permanence or independence* were established on a subatomic level—permanent, eternal, immutable nuggets of matter on some lower level of organization as yet undiscovered—it is hard to conclude that the Buddhist way of life to end suffering is invalidated. And, physicists do speak of a permanent (albeit dynamic) ground: an energy field out of which subatomic particles arise and return. But parallelists misidentify this "quantum vacuum" with the Buddhist emptiness (e.g., Zohar and Marshall 1993: 238).[2] Some Mahayana traditions do step into the metaphysics of depth-mysticism and envision a source of the experienced realm (the *dharmakaya*), although this source is *experiencable* and is devoid of the *structuring* that scientists theorize for a quantum vacuum.

Nagarjuna, however, had no concept of a "Void." He did not reify emptiness (*shunyata*) into any kind of entity or reality—in fact, avoiding the reification of any concepts is a major theme of his strategy. Emptiness itself is not a self-existent reality, but is also empty of any inherent self-existence. That is, Buddhist emptiness is not an *"essence"* by which things exist or a reality that is the *source* of anything—the term simply denotes the true *state of things,* i.e., the absence of anything that would make a phenomenon permanent and independent (*svabhava*). Parallelists who equate Brahman in Advaita with a theistic god now routinely reify emptiness into a cosmic "Void" or "Absolute Reality" analogous to Brahman as an underlying source of phenomena. People raised in a theistic culture no doubt think in those terms, but "emptiness" is not a reality out of which things arise: it is not an inherently existing continuum out of which we carve conventional entities—each phenomenon is empty, and the totality is empty too (Garfield 1995: 199 n. 67). And to reify the mere *absence* of anything that could give "self-existence" into any *reality* of any kind would make emptiness into what Madhyamikas see as a type of entity—and according to Nagarjuna, anyone who does this is *"incurable* (*asadhyan*)" (*Mulamadhyamakakarika* 13.8; see Jones 1993: 80-81).

In addition, the permanence of relativistic four-dimensional space-time does not present any more of a problem for Buddhists than an eternally existing universe (which they accept), as long as *the content* of space-time that we experience remains *impermanent*. Even if there is some permanent physical ground that produces the impermanent everyday world, the unsatisfactoriness of what we actually experience (i.e., *duhkha*) would still be an irremovable part of our lives. Thus, finding permanent, eternal bits of matter on a subatomic level would not *falsify* the doctrines (contra Cabezón 2003: 60): emptiness would still apply to the content of the realm of experience—i.e., the doctrine would not be falsified in the context for which it was designed and would still be useful in lessening a sense of self. And, as noted in Chapter 6, Hinayana Abhidharmists in fact did accept the existence of extremely small and undestroyable particles of matter (*paramanus*). They could do this because such particles did not present any problems for their Buddhist way of life, let alone falsify it, since the aggregates we experience are still impermanent. For example, the assertion that hatred and greed cannot ultimately be grounded in reality—because there would still be nothing permanent for us to grasp and thus nothing to crave or hate—would remain intact as long as the everyday realm is impermanent, regardless of underlying causes.

Thus, whether physicists find permanent entities or not, Buddhists would have some metaphysics to handle it. Buddhism simply does not stand or fall on whether physicists find permanent entities on a subatomic level; Buddhism could not be refuted since its claims remain applicable to the world of direct experience. And, as discussed, impermanence on the quantum level does not confirm mindfulness mystics' claims of impermanence on the everyday level either. Indeed, if such *permanence* cannot in principle *refute* Buddhist claims, then as a matter of simple logic, the converse is also true: finding the opposite of permanence (*impermanence*) on the quantum does not *confirm* Buddhist claims about the everyday world but is equally irrelevant.

Also consider efficient causation within the quantum realm. That quantum physics currently involves *acausality* and thus conflicts with the Buddhist emphasis on *causality* greatly troubles the parallelist Victor Mansfield (2008: 98-129). But since this does not challenge the causality on our *everyday level of phenomena*, this does not affect the Buddhist way of life. As long as billiard balls behave like billiard balls, there is no problem. In the end, Mansfield concedes that the divergent views on causality between Buddhism and quantum physics does not contradict Buddhist arguments on emptiness (ibid.: 124). At most, such quantum acausality would limit the scope of Buddhist metaphysics to only the everyday realm and would preclude its expansion into matters of unexperienced levels.

Nor do the Buddhist doctrines entail that the subatomic or any other realm has no intrinsic physical properties or does not obey fixed laws of nature; the situation would be no different than with the law of karma. In sum, the Buddhist way of life has nothing to do with the physics of other levels of organization. Buddhists have no interest in the structures of the world independent of their soteriological concern with suffering, and to transform the metaphysics of their ways of life into a system making predictions about what will be found outside of the everyday realm through experiments distorts their interests badly. The Buddha would no doubt leave all such questions unanswered since they are irrelevant to the problem of suffering, just as he did with questions of the age and size of the universe (*Digha Nikaya* I.13, III.137; *Majjhima Nikaya* I.427; *Anguttara Nikaya* II.80).[3]

The Abhidharmist lists of elements would not lead anyone to conclude that Buddhists had any interest in physical structures, let alone subatomic ones. As discussed in Chapter 6, the lack of a self (*atman*) or self-existence (*svabhava*) is not about the absence of matter or objects, but about the lack of any substance that would give an entity permanence or independence: no phenomenon has any inherent self-existence, but is impermanent and dependent upon conditions. The "emptiness" that Buddhists emphasize thus is connected to the impermanence of objects, not "empty space" without solid particles on other levels of phenomena. As also discussed in Chapter 6, parallelists now make much the Madhyamaka notion of the emptiness of the components of the experienced world (*dharmas*).[4] As just discussed, this means that the components of what we experience are void of anything that would give them permanence, self-existence, or independence from other phenomena.[5] But again, it is the emptiness of the components of *experience* delineated in the Mahayana metaphysics that is actually the subject of this claim, not the *physical emptiness* within either atoms or outer space. Even if parallelists expand Buddhist claims of selflessness and emptiness into an all-encompassing metaphysical system to embrace the physical objects on the levels of nature that we do not directly experience, it would still not be about physical emptiness. And since Buddhist selflessness is about the components of the experienced world, this metaphysical move would depart from Buddhism—it would go from a worldview about the beingness of things to claims about unexperienced realms.

The shared insight in this situation would be about impermanence, interconnectedness, and dependency. The claims may be parallel, but the fact remains that Buddhists are not making a claim about scientific structures on unexperienced levels of nature—parallelists are seeing the Buddha do something he never did. It is simply not a subject of interest to the classical forms of this mystical way of life. And to pull the Buddhist doctrines out of their soteriological context in order to see the Buddha as making a prediction about subatomic physical structures is a distortion.[6] In addition, if physicists did find any subatomic permanent objects, it would only show that the Buddhist doctrine of emptiness is not parallel to an aspect of nature that is was never designed to cover in the first place. So too, such a metaphysical extrapolation would go against the *experiential nature* of the Buddhist tradition and mysticism in general. Even if one wants to argue that technology is extending our perception, such instrumental readings of quantum-level events are only indirect experiences—the only actual human experience is reading the instruments in the everyday world. Still, in the hands of the parallelists, it seems that only today can we finally take Buddhism seriously because of what quantum physicists are finally discovering about the subatomic level of the world.

Consciousness

Parallelists also note a theory in quantum physics that gives a role to the observer's consciousness in causing quantum events and jump to a convergence of science and mysticism on consciousness (e.g., Goswami 1993). Seeing a role for consciousness in quantum physics is much more popular among parallelists than among physicists themselves—the vast majority of physicists think of "observation" in terms of the physical action caused by the experimental set-up and not the *consciousness* of the observers making the readings. (See Stenger 1995 for criticisms of the alleged role of consciousness in quantum physics.) Even Bruce Rosenblum and Fred Kuttner, two physicists who defend the admittedly minority position that consciousness is related to quantum measurements, do not think that quantum physics supports mysticism (2006: 152)—quantum physics does support the idea that mysteries still exist, but that is all.[7] The "observation" of quantum events involves a physical interaction between the light that physicists shoot into the quantum realm and what is there—human consciousness does not bring any physical events into existence.[8] Observers do choose the experimental set-up, but their mental state in making observations does not enter into the quantum events. Indeed, the human act of looking at what occurred may not occur until long after the experiment has taken place. In sum, there is a confusion over what exact an "*observation*" is in quantum physics: the *physical interaction* with the quantum realm versus the *human reading* of the results. Heisenberg rightly pointed out that quantum theory has led physicists "far away from the simple materialistic views that prevailed in the natural sciences in the nineteenth century" (1958: 128). But he meant that quantum particles are no longer seen as tiny, solid billiard balls. Parallelists cannot jump from this claim to claiming a role for *consciousness* in quantum theory—they cannot go from a refutation of one materialistic view of particles to a repudiation of all *materialism*.

Parallelists correctly note that consciousness figures prominently in both depth and mindfulness mysticism. The depth-mystical experiences lead depth-mystics to believe that they are aware of a fundamental reality having the nature of consciousness, but the interpretation of this event differs—e.g., Advaitins see consciousness as the only reality; Samkhya-Yogins see it as plural (each person having an independent source of pure consciousness) and as separate from matter. To the extent parallelists accept the distinctiveness of depth-mystical experiences at all, they focus on the former interpretation, often naturalizing Brahman, and combine it with a consciousness-centered interpretation of quantum physics to conclude that science has proven consciousness is the fundamental field of all reality.

But what mystics say about the nature of consciousness has nothing in common with its alleged role in physics (as discussed in Chapter 6). Nothing mystics say suggests that consciousness is one causal force among other forces operating within the universe on the quantum level or any other level. For mindfulness mystics, we create illusory "entities" in the everyday world by erroneously separating off parts of the flux of reality with our analytical mind—it is a matter of conceptualizing our everyday perceptions and beliefs and has nothing to do with the idea that consciousness is a possible *causal factor* in events. Depth-mysticism also has no parallel. For Advaitins, consciousness is not one element of the universe but is the only reality: it is not a causal energy in the material realm interacting with material objects.[9] It is not that mystics go further than physicists on observation (contra Capra 2000: 331)—what depth-mystics are claiming is fundamentally different from any alleged interaction of the observer and observed in quantum physics. And even arguing "all is consciousness" may be misleading: objectifying Brahman into a *field of conscious energy* in which we all participate goes against the Advaita tenet that Brahman cannot be any type of object among objects or anything experienceable as an objectified reality.

The various emanationist positions also conflict with materialism: consciousness is more fundamental, with matter emanating later. Indeed, all classical mystical positions conflict with the materialists' belief that consciousness is only a product of matter appearing recently in the evolution of the universe—i.e., the brain simply generates consciousness like a magnet generates a magnetic field. Materialists and Buddhists do "*converge*" on a "no self" doctrine, but this does not negate the profound *conflict* between the transcendental and naturalistic metaphysics on consciousness. As noted in Chapter 5, there is an issue of whether consciousness studies can be separated from the current materialist metaphysical framework. Can scientists study consciousness as a causal reality, or must it be treated as a product of matter? But even if neuroscience itself can be neutral to competing metaphysical frameworks, the conflict of transcendental and materialist metaphysical accounts of the fundamental nature of consciousness remains. To traditional Buddhists and Hindus, consciousness is still not merely an evolved product of nature: mind only comes from mind, not from matter. To them, consciousness is coeternal with the universe: it is causeless and uncreated, not tied to the body, not a product of matter, and is present in any cycles the universe may go through—in fact, to Advaitins, it constitutes all of reality. This causes Buddhists and Hindus to reject both the current scientific version of evolution (which has no role for rebirth or karma as a cause) and any claim that neuroscience as currently practiced can explain the origin or nature of consciousness.

There is no "intelligent designer" organizing the universe who is responsible for consciousness: since consciousness has always been around, things did not have to be organized for its existence. But Buddhists and Hindus need not endorse any form of panpsychism—the opposite of Samkhya's dualism—in which matter, no matter how simple its organization, always has some form of consciousness and in which consciousness evolves in degrees from elementary sensing to more complex forms as the organization of matter becomes more complex. (See Clarke 2004 and Skrbina 2005.) Buddhists distinguish "gross" consciousness that is dependent on matter for its appearance from "subtle" consciousness that is not (Ricard and Thuan 2001: 161-82). But their metaphysics does not explain how the "gross" forms arise. Nor does this resolve the basic conflict with materialists over whether any form of consciousness is coextensive with the material universe.

The idea of rebirth also complicates any view of evolution and neuroscience. Reconciling karmic guidance with any form of *genetic* evolution may be difficult—e.g., one is born blind because of one's own karmic actions in a previous lifetime, not because of purely material events in this life beginning with conception. The idea of the "collective karma" of a group or nation further complicates the picture. Complicating the total picture even further is the idea that karma can affect the course of natural events—e.g., the bad acts of kings can cause droughts. All in all, these views on consciousness differ radically from those of modern science, no matter what parallelists might say about "convergence."

Cosmology

The picture in cosmology is also complicated by the fact that in Indic cosmology there is a beginningless cycles of rebirths, with consciousness always existing and with karma shaping the course of a sentient being's path through the history of the universe. Moreover, karma plays a role in producing the material universe as a whole, and this also dramatically separates Indic cosmologies from modern Western cosmology. On the other end of time, there is the Advaita doctrine that since the natural universe is the product of ignorance (*avidya*), it will slowly disappear as more and more individual selves are enlightened by ending our root ignorance and thereby are removed from the cycling of rebirths.

Both the depth-mystical experience and mindfulness involve a sense of *timelessness*, i.e., beingness outside of the category of time. This can lead to a total lack of interest in the cosmological questions about this realm, as with the Buddha dismissing unanswered the questions of whether the universe is eternal or not, has an origin or not, or is spatially infinite or not, since such questions are not based on direct and immediate experience and are not germane to the quest to ending suffering (*Majjhima Nikaya* I.427).[10] Or the idea of timelessness can easily become translated in the metaphysics of religious traditions into a historical claim—the *eternity* of the universe, i.e., the universe existing throughout all time. For example, the universe may be taken to be the eternal emanation of a timeless source. This would in principle be neutral to any scientific account of the physical or biological evolution of the universe—it is a matter of a "vertical" cause of being, not of any "horizontal" causes operating within the realm of becoming.[11]

Nor does the emanation of the universe become part of a scientific theory simply by calling it a "singularity," such as the Big Bang is currently considered under mainstream theories. Of course, seeing emanation from nothing as a single event like the Big Bang is natural (see, e.g., Matt 2005: 134-39)—how else can we think of emanation from nothing except as a historical event? We think either the universe would be fully laid out spatially as in the book of Genesis or expanding from a single point as with the Big Bang. Thinking of emanation as eternal and thus not an event in time is not easy. But approaching the metaphysics of emanation through science can only be misleading since emanation does not have anything to do with any physical event. Emanation is neutral to any scientific theory—it is about the source of the being of everything constituting the universe, including the matter and energy in the expansion that began with the Big Bang or in any other way. Emanation is related to the issue of where the stuff came from that "blew up" in the Big Bang expansion, and looking at emanation through the science of cosmology does not add to understanding this metaphysical problem. Nor is the Big Bang in any way proof of emanation from an underlying source—it may be part of a series of "crunches" and "bangs." Nor are mystical metaphysical explanations of emanation any sort of evidence of a Big Bang. More generally, correlating mystical concepts with any scientific ones (e.g., "beingness" with "energy") misses the difference in dimensions involved in the two endeavors and can lead to a focus on science that misses the transcendental dimension entirely and leads to a naturalization of mysticism.

Also consider the fact that a mystical tradition may simply adopt the cosmology of their culture. The religious cosmologies in mystical traditions present more problems than parallelists realize. Since physical cosmology was irrelevant to their religious problem, Buddhists got along perfectly well for millennia with a "flat earth" type cosmology consisting of concentric circles of realms with Mount Meru in the center and various heavens and hells above and below. (See Dalai Lama 2005: 75-80; Sadakata 1997: 26-30; see Lopez 2008: 39-72 on the fate of Mount Meru in modernized Buddhism.) But a physical cosmogony and cosmology for this world simply do not figure centrally in Buddhism as they do in Western beliefs about God: Buddhists are more interested in processes of the mind than in creation and questions of origin (Payne 2002: 162). But even though physical aspects of a cosmology may not be integral to a given tradition's mystical way of life, Buddhists accept the notion of an *eternal universe* because of their belief that consciousness is eternal. Thus, Buddhists today are willing to accept the Big Bang. However, it should be noted that prior to the discovery of empirical evidence supporting the Big Bang over its rival—the "steady-state" theory—Buddhists had no trouble endorsing the latter (Kirthisinghe 1984a: 85-86). The scientific dispute is simply irrelevant as long as the universe can be eternal. But this does mean that Buddhists do reject the idea that a Big Bang could be the actual *origin* of the universe. They prefer either an "oscillating universe" or a "multiple worlds" hypothesis since these are more likely to assure the eternity of the phenomenal universe and consciousness. (See Zajonc 2004: 88, 95-96, 182-83.)

The current scientific cosmological hypotheses also fit better, at least on the level of abstract generalities, with the traditional cosmology of India in which the god Brahma "rolls out" and "rolls in" the universe. These cycles occur throughout eternity. (Currently, science does not support the idea that our particular universe is oscillating; rather, the amount of matter/energy in it suggests that it will expand forever.) But again, even if there is a convergence in broad outlines between modern cosmology and parts of a traditional cosmology, the convergence is not substantial. First, any elements in conflict with science (e.g, human beings living an incredibly long time in earlier ages) must be jettisoned, even though these elements are just as central to the cosmologies as the elements allegedly converging with science. Second, the fact that the universe ends in both the Hindu myth (being reabsorbed into Brahma) and in modern cosmology does not make Shiva a "mythic symbol" of a thermodynamic heat-death (contra Raman 2002a: 188)—all they have in common is that the universe ends. Adopting Shiva today as such a symbol does not mean that a heat-death is what the early Indians intended or that there is any other convergence of science and mythology here. Only by looking at mythology through the prism of modern science could we connect Shiva with thermodynamics. Of course, if we take modern cosmology as the controlling model and jettison everything in a culture's myth that does not comport with it, obviously we will end up a convergence, but the blatant circularity of this exercise is obvious.

Third, and more importantly for science-and-mysticism studies, Buddhists and Hindus give consciousness (which is eternal and not a product of matter) a central role in literally making this universe—e.g., basic to Buddhist cosmology is that this universe (*loka-dhatu*) came into existence, is sustained, and disintegrated by the karmic acts of sentient beings (Sadakata 1997: 25, 182). When one world-cycle comes to an end, the universe dissolves, but the karma of its sentient beings starts another world-cycle. That this world, the heavens, and the hells (collectively the *kama-dhatu*) and various realms of form and formless realms (the *rupa-dhatu* and *arupa-dhatu*) are made by our ordinary and meditative actions further complicates the picture. This role of consciousness keeps any apparent convergence of Indic cosmology with current Western science from being very deep. Still, the Indic idea that the entire natural realm is a product of the collective desires and actions of all sentient beings is a part of metaphysics that science has not and probably cannot deal with, but it is a part of the Buddhist way of life that would be hard to remove—it is the natural cosmology of a consciousness-centered metaphysics.

Victor Mansfield believes that Madhyamaka Buddhism and relativity theory "could not be more compatible" on relativity (2008: 141). The Madhyamikas make the same point in their language as physicists make in theirs (ibid.). However, Buddhism is not about relativity of frameworks or a "universal relativity principle" (contra Finkelstein 2003): objects could have *self-existence* (*svabhava*) and still be subject to the relativity of physical frameworks; conversely, objects could be free of self-existence, but for all that Buddhists say, there still may be no *relativity of frameworks*—Buddhist metaphysics simply has nothing to do with this scientific issue but is about the basic impermanence of phenomena. The relativity of time in different frameworks may eliminate the idea of an independent "now" (Mansfield 2003: 309, 2008: 141), but even this is different from the Buddhist analysis for the same reason: the Buddhist analysis of time does not rely on the ideas of different frames of reference but, as with objects, on the lack of self-existence: even if there were an "objective now," Buddhists would still argue that their analysis applies—i.e., there is no self-existent reality called "time." It is simply the standard Buddhist analysis of any alleged objective, substantive, self-existent entity. Thus, Buddhists and physicists reject the idea of "now" in different ways and in different senses. Indeed, the relativity of frameworks may actually *conflict* with the Madhyamaka analysis: under the Buddhist analysis, for the future to be contingent on the present and the past, it would already have to exist in the present and the past, which clearly it does not (*Mulamadhyamakakarika* 19)—but the idea of different temporal frameworks at least introduces the problem of whether the future (in one framework) is in fact currently present in the past (in another framework). At a minimum, the scientific and Buddhist analyses are completely unrelated, and the latter does not "anticipate" or "converge with" the former.

Biology

Evolutionary biology is a historical science that does not receive as much attention from parallelists as physics and cosmology, but since its structures do not go as deep as quantum ones, it may seem more relevant to the impermanence and dependence of the everyday level that is emphasized in mindfulness mysticism.[12] Capra, for one, has moved toward incorporating biology and ecology into his vision of a mystical "deep ecology" (1996).

But biology is open to the same sort of distortions as the physical sciences. In Hindu circles, the avatars of Vishnu—first as a fish, followed by a turtle, a boar, and semi-human forms (a man-lion and a dwarf) before taking on various human forms—are seen as an "uncanny parallel with our current views on biological evolution," if not the exact stages of an evolutionary process (Raman 2002a: 189), even though the Hindu story has nothing whatsoever to do with the development of new life-forms from other life-forms and makes no suggestion of it. Such "Avataric evolution" is another instance of looking at mythology through the lens of modern science and distorting what is seen.

So too with Buddhism. Evolution is seen as "a complete spiritual path," and the Buddha becomes a "biologist" or "spiritual biologist" (Nisker 1998: 15, 17, 21), even though he showed no interest in scientific questions about the development of life-forms. The becoming (*bhava*) involved in rebirth becomes a "law of continuity" to make it sound scientific (Jayatilleke 1984: 11). The Buddha is seen as discovering evolution before Darwin because of the cycling of rebirths involves not just human beings but also animals (Thurman 2004: 5-6), even though our *spiritual evolution as a person* (or, better, as an impermanent karmic stream) through different life-forms has absolutely nothing to do with the possibility of the *biological evolution of one species into another*. Rebirth does connect animals and human beings; it would be the natural subject for Indians to mention something to do with evolution if they had any inkling of it. But that a human being today may be reborn as a dog or a cow or another animal has nothing to do with the evolution of life-forms. The two notions do share the abstract principle of "life-forms changing over time," but to claim that the Buddha discovered anything even tangentially related to the scientific theory of how life-forms are connected and change over time is simply wrong. Also, as noted above, the Buddhist doctrines that consciousness and rebirth have existed eternally are not easily reconciled with cosmological or biological evolution (but see Cooper 1996).

Some scholars see Advaita's nondualism as a basis for "reverence for nature" and an environmental concern. Lance Nelson dismantles that position: classical Advaita only encourages attitudes of devaluation and neglect of the natural universe and has "the potential to seriously undermine environmental concern" (1998: 62). Neo-Vedanta, with its modern Western influence, is another matter, but in classical Advaita the world is to be feared and despised; liberation from the world is only goal (ibid.: 67). Advaitins yearn for the unchanging and radically unitary; this leads to a radical antipathy to the realm of change and multiplicity (ibid.: 68). Reverence for nature is hardly warranted—a "positive disgust" common in ascetic traditions is the attitude of enlightened Advaitins (ibid.: 75). Only the transcendental God or Brahman is fully real to orthodox Hindus; the divine is untouched by the pollution of the world, and the natural universe is ultimately unimportant (ibid.: 81). Thus, every day Indians can dump millions of gallons of raw sewage, hundreds of incompletely cremated corpses, and huge amounts of chemical waste into the sacred Ganges River, and yet say, in the words of a Benares taxi driver, "The Ganges is God and [God] can't be polluted" (ibid.: 80).

Buddhist dependent arising (*pratityasamutpada*) also has become recruited as a basis for contemporary environmental concern, even though classical Buddhists showed no such concern, since it was unrelated to a fundamental cure of suffering. The Buddhist concept and a concern with ecology do share on an abstract level the principle of dependency of some phenomena upon other phenomena. But trying to apply Buddhism to biological and ecological issues would be yet another case of removing the distinctly nonnaturalistic metaphysics of a mystical way of life and re-envisioning it to fit a nonmystical interest. (See Jones 2004: 363-65 on reinventing the Wheel of Dharma.)

Mystical Metaphysics and Science

Thus, the metaphysics of India's mystical traditions do not fit as seamlessly with scientific theories as parallelists suppose, particularly because of the place of consciousness in the scheme of things. Mystical ideas may remain a potential source of ideas for scientists to work into scientific hypotheses, but the difference in substance of mystical metaphysics from science's subject matter will curtail any further role in devising theories in science. In fact, the *conflict* with contemporary science of some Indic metaphysics concerning consciousness forces a *rejection* of parts of science in evolution, neuroscience, and cosmology. There are some factual claims about the world and the nature of a person that classical Buddhists, as well as mystics of other traditions, simply cannot give up and still retain their religious way of life. In particular, that consciousness is not a product of matter is the Buddhist and Hindu counterpart to the Christian and Jewish fundamentalists' stand on a literal reading of the Genesis myth in the face of modern science. Thus, there are limits beyond which mystics cannot reformulate their fundamental doctrines and still maintain their mystical ways of life. At some points, they have to choose between their belief-claims and science's. To capitulate to science as the higher epistemic authority would lead to a new naturalized mystical religiosity. (Of course, parallelists could attempt to devise a new naturalized mysticism, but they could not then say that they have *reconciled* science and say, Buddhism, or that they have found *parallels* in the two endeavors.)

But some Buddhists apparently are prepared to let their beliefs trump science. Buddhists offer no empirical data on scientific issues in physics, but according to Neo-Buddhists, to use the term the Dalai Lama's followers use for those interested in science (Zajonc 2004: 88), the Buddha *already knew* what physicists would find on lower levels of physical organization. Neo-Buddhists advance philosophical arguments for impermanence that allegedly refute "the idea of distinct particles that are supposed to constitute matter" (Ricard and Thuan 2001: 63-64). For example, Alan Wallace advances a simple argument with roots in disputes over Abhidharma doctrines to refute the very idea that there can be irreducibly small particles: any particle has a left and a right *side*; therefore, it must have *parts*, and thus it is not independently real because of those smaller parts (Wallace and Hodel 2008: 121-22). Thus, in principle nothing physicists find could not have smaller parts but must be a complex, dependent whole.[13] No empirical studies are needed to establish this fact, and physicists would be wrong if they thought they found independence at any level. So too, the strong belief in a causal order in the Buddhist tradition leads the Dalai Lama to be convinced that there are "hidden variables" in quantum physics (Zajonc 2004: 47-48; Dalai Lama 2005) producing a determinism, even though the

Buddhist interest in causal order relates only to our *actions and subjective states* rather than the interaction of inanimate objects. In this way, he accepts the parallelists' claim that Buddhist metaphysics extends to realms beyond our immediate experience into the quantum levels, even though the scientific issues about the quantum realm are irrelevant to the Buddhist quest to end suffering.

In short, Buddhist philosophy dictates in advance the general nature of what physicists will find. The Buddhist metaphysical doctrines, of course, do not supply any specific on the actual structures to be found, and no one has suggested that physicists do not have to bother conducting experiments. Nevertheless, Donald Lopez rightly notes that the claim that the Buddha, "an itinerant teacher of Iron Age India," understood the theory of relativity, quantum physics, or the Big Bang theory seems "preposterous" (2008: 3). While Buddhist apologists have made that claim, parallelists claim only that there is a convergence of the *metaphysics* or *general worldview* between modern science and Buddhism, not that even an enlightened Buddha knew the specifics of the theories in modern physics and cosmology. Nevertheless, Neo-Buddhists expect impermanence and causation and will not be satisfied unless both are established. The Dalai Lama did not need to know much about quantum physics to conclude this: he could "sense, at a very deep level, a certain number of convergences between the quantum view of reality and the Buddhist understanding of interdependence, but I do not yet have a very clear understanding of this quantum view" (1996: 199).

Can Mysticism Constrain Science?

As noted in Chapter 4, philosophy can guide research and theory-making at the frontiers of science, and Neo-Buddhists want Buddhist philosophy to do that (e.g., Bitbol 2003). In fact, they want mysticism to *constrain* scientific theories.[14] (See Ricard and Thuan 2001 and Zajonc 2004.) Buddhist ideas cannot force experimental results to conform to a particular belief any more than any other ideas can, but those ideas can become a criterion for the interpretation of experimental results and thus for which competing scientific theory scientists finally accept. Buddhist metaphysics was developed in conjunction with meditation. Thus, through this metaphysics, *meditation* under the Neo-Buddhist view in effect supplies *evidence* for a particular scientific theory (e.g., Ricard and Thuan 2001: 268-69).

The Dalai Lama does not want scientists to abandon their critical investigation of nature or otherwise replace science with meditation. He does not want "to unite science and spirituality," but instead considers them "two complementary investigative approaches," and he wants "to explore two important human disciplines for the purpose of developing a more holistic and integrated way of understanding the world around us" (2005: 4, 208-209). He starts his book *The Universe in a Single Atom: The Convergence of Science and Spirituality* apparently approaching science with openness and humility, giving science a free hand and asserting that Buddhism must conform to its findings: "if scientific analysis were conclusively to demonstrate certain claims in Buddhism to be false, then we must accept the findings of science and abandon those claims" (ibid.: 3).

However, the Dalai Lama, for all his enthusiasm for science, seems as ready as some conservative Christians in America today to have religious beliefs function as "control beliefs" guiding the course of science—i.e., beliefs constraining scientific research and theorizing based exclusively on nonscientific considerations (here, religion and philosophy) that dictate the outcome in advance of research. (See Jones 2011: 108-10.) He can readily abandon the Indic folk cosmology (2005: 80) since it does not affect any central Buddhist doctrines, but he is not ready to give up anything that would cause a radical reformulation of Buddhism—e.g., treating consciousness as a product of matter that expires with the death of the body. Instead, he is ready to assert that, firstly, the Buddhist philosophical analysis of the experienced phenomena of the everyday world rules out physicists finding any bits of permanence in the subatomic realm or any other type of permanent objects, although the Dalai Lama does admit that early Buddhist Abhidharmists in fact did have a theory of indivisible, partless atoms of matter (ibid.: 52-55).

Secondly, in cosmology the Dalai Lama denies that the Big Bang is the origin of the universe rather than merely the beginning of a new cycle within an infinite universe (2005: 82-84).[15] He favors any scientific account with a recurring universe on religious and philosophical grounds, not from scientific data or any study of the scientific issues. In his view, the entire process of the unfolding of the universe is a matter of the natural law of strict causality (ibid.: 90). The idea of an infinite regress of natural causes fits well with the Buddhist metaphysical belief of dependent arising according to which everything that happens depends on other things happening (Flanagan 2007: 69). The Dalai Lama also accepts that past beings' karmic residues survive the Big Crunches and Big Bangs into each new cycle (or into other worlds within a multiverse if this world expires) and thus that karma is one of the strictly causal factors shaping the material universe, although Buddhist Abhidharmists have not said much on how karma connects to the evolution of the physical cosmos (2005: 90-92)—issues scientists obviously have not yet even considered. In his own Tantric tradition, no creator god or Brahman-like source is involved here: the world simply appears out of the accumulated individual karmic impressions present at the origin of each cycle (ibid.: 153-54). Neo-Buddhists also reject the idea of any "Anthropic Principle" that guided the evolution of the universe so that consciousness would appear (Ricard and Thuan 2001: 42)—since consciousness has always been present in the universe, things do not have to be organized for it to arise (at least in its "subtle" form).

Thirdly, in biology the Dalai Lama's belief that consciousness has existed since the beginning of time requires him to deny that Neo-Darwinian theory is even a potentially complete explanation of the history of life on earth. The human body may be the result of evolution (2005: 97), but natural selection acting on the random mutation of genes to increase the genes' chances of survival or any other material explanation is not the way consciousness came to appear in the natural universe.[16]

The Dalai Lama realizes that any materialist explanation of evolution leaves no room for karma since all effects would be entirely accounted for by their physical constituents (Hayward and Varela 1992: 241). He accepts that Neo-Darwinian theory gives a "fairly coherent account of the evolution of human life on earth," but he insists that karma must have a central role in understanding the origin of human sentience (2005: 111, 115). Moreover, there must be a "hidden causality" behind the apparent randomness of mutations that biologists currently accept that assures the appearance of conscious beings—that mutations are purely random is "unsatisfying" (ibid.: 104, 112).[17] (But it should be noted that in evolutionary theory "*random*" does not mean *uncaused*. Genetic mutations do have physical causes. Rather, "randomness" means that these mutations are *undirected* and have no *goal*—they occur without regard to their usefulness to an organism, and thus there is no intentionality behind the process of evolution. That is, they are random from the point of view of the history of life, but they are not uncaused; indeed, there may be a physical determinism here. Thus, this randomness is not inconsistent with the Buddhist emphasis on *causation*. Perhaps Neo-Buddhists want some form of teleological causation to be at work.) He also thinks that karma would explain why a particular sentient being would enter the womb of a particular mother (Hayward and Varela 1992: 243)—an idea that goes against any material explanations of evolution. In addition, under traditional Buddhism, human beings devolved from celestial beings through a karmic process (2005: 107-108)—it was truly "the descent of man"—and not evolved from less complex life forms.

For similar reasons, the Dalai Lama's beliefs affect the theoretical part of neuroscience. His religious and philosophical beliefs require him to deny that materialism can adequately account for the origin or existence of life and consciousness. Metaphysical beliefs may affect the course of neuroscientific research—e.g., for materialists, seeing the mind as an epiphenomenon of matter eliminates the mind as a cause or the possibility of the mind influencing the body. But the Dalai Lama rejects any theory that would reduce human beings *in toto* to nothing more than "biological machines" or the product of pure chance in natural events. Buddhists "cannot accept" the idea that consciousness arises from a material cause (Hayward and Varela 1992: 153). In fact, *consciousness causes matter*: the world of sentient beings arises from the mind, and the diverse habitats of different types of beings also arise from mind (Dalai Lama 2005: 109). Treating the mind as a cause may radically affect the basic research program in neuroscience. As things stand today, the doctrine of karma and other ways that mind may affect matter conflicts with the way neuroscience is practiced.

This issue extends to a central issue of traditional Buddhism: rebirth. The Dalai Lama claims that if science one day definitely proves that there is no rebirth, then Buddhists "must accept it and we will accept it" (Flanagan 2007: 233 n. 1). Such a finding would render traditional Buddhism pointless: the problem Buddhists see as central—the dissatisfaction (*duhkha*) permeating life—would be over with our death no matter what: there would be no cycle of future rebirths to avoid. This problem deals a major blow to the common claim that Buddhism fits better with modern science than Christianity (e.g., Abe 1985)—Christians can give up the dualistic idea of a soul distinct from the body and return to the biblical view of God miraculously resurrecting the body, but without rebirth the central problem of Buddhism dissolves. Of course, we could engage in meditation to make our life better or follow Buddhist ethics, but the traditional Buddhist motive would be rendered groundless. Stephen Batchelor argues that today one can be a Buddhist and even take a Bodhisattva vow to help all creatures while being agnostic on the issues of rebirth and karma—to him, such beliefs are part of the old traditional Indic folk cosmology that can be jettisoned because they do not affect behavior (1997). It may be true that these beliefs have no direct effect on behavior—Buddhists could still follow their ethics and practice meditation—but jettisoning these beliefs does remove the purpose and framework of the traditional Buddhist way of life. It certainly is hard to argue that this is the traditional Buddhist stance. (See Thurman and Batchelor 1997.) If Buddhist doctrines are reduced to merely methods of stress reduction or for other physiological and psychological effects, it would be a case of the decline of the Buddhist teaching forecasted by many Buddhist schools (Lopez 2008: 211-12), as would reducing Buddhism to a form of naturalism.

Thus, permitting the possibility of science knocking out a fundamental belief-claim for the traditional Buddhist way of life would indeed be a major concession to science. However, there is a major caveat: the Dalai Lama distinguishes between what is *negated* through science and what simply *has not been observed* through a scientific method (Jinpa 2003: 77). In fact, he gives rebirth as an example of the fact that science not finding evidence for something is not finding evidence that it does not exist (Flanagan 2007: 81, 234 n. 2). Thus, the Dalai Lama's seeming openness to the possibility of scientific falsification may only be because he does not see science as a genuine threat here: he adopts a mind/matter dualism—indeed, he thinks that "pure luminous consciousness" has *no neural correlates at all* (ibid.: 87-88)—and thus he would reject any findings from a materialist-based neuroscience as really disproving rebirth.[18] As Owen Flanagan says, this caveat permits a Buddhist to believe pretty much whatever he or she wants, especially if the demand is that there is disproof where "disproof" means something actually demonstrated (ibid.: 88, 234 n. 2). At a minimum, this Buddhist control belief restricts what Neo-Buddhists would accept about what neuroscience can in principle reveal.

In sum, the Dalai Lama has concerns about independence and causation on the quantum level, any theory of an origin of the universe, current evolution as a complete explanation of the history of life, and materialism as the origin of consciousness. True, the Dalai Lama is "not subject to the professional or ideological constraints of a radically materialistic worldview" (2005: 93), but he fails to see that Buddhist religious beliefs can also act as control beliefs. His religious control beliefs certainly differ from those of contemporary conservative Christians and Muslims who favor "intelligent design," but his position is just as much an instance of wanting beliefs that are held solely on grounds unrelated to scientific findings to constrain the outcome of science. The problem is not simply the philosophical framework underlying current science, or that empirical data do not constitute legitimate grounds for developing a comprehensive worldview (ibid.: 13). Rather, Neo-Buddhists must reject parts of science itself as it is currently practiced: they must deny the possibility of a natural explanation of the origin of consciousness and any major role for unrestricted randomness in the evolution of consciousness; in addition, they must at least limit the scope of neuroscience's domain. This limits the Dalai Lama's stated aim of incorporating "key insights" from evolution, relativity, and quantum physics within a Buddhist worldview (ibid.: 3-4)—the insights must be modified and restricted by religious considerations. This also limits the popular claim that Buddhism is uniquely compatible with modern science—a claim made since the nineteenth century (McMahan 2004: 898).

But those who lament any influence of Eastern thought on Western societies and who are hysterical about the "easternization" of science, as Colin Campbell (2007) calls it, can rest assured that science remains to date a matter of empirical analysis and rational thought. Science has not been "coopted" by the New Age (contra ibid.: 365-66). Even if mystical thought contributed to the shift from a Newtonian "mechanical" approach to reality to a more "organic" one in physics in the early twentieth century, nevertheless the theories of the new physics were rigorous tested and are still being tested today. New Age scientists such as Capra are not controlling science and are ignoring the advances of traditional approaches (as discussed in the case of Capra in Chapter 7). (Even Campbell admits there is little "New Age science" but rather a particular interpretation of science by New Age advocates to support a "philosophy of nature" [ibid.: 139].) Any new suggestions for topics of research, theories, or general approaches to reality are still being greeted with skepticism and tested in the same way as such ideas have always been tested in modern science. And if anything of value is found, so much the better for science.

Science, Mystical Experiences, and Mystical Metaphysics

But even if we reject any control beliefs from mysticism, mysticism and science may nevertheless interact through the metaphysics that mystics must supply to understand their experiences, the world, and their place in it. Again, this is not an interaction of *mystical experiences or insights* with modern science but a matter of the encompassing *metaphysical beliefs* of particular mystical traditions. Mysticism and science as ways of knowing may be totally independent, but the claims from total mystical ways of life and science about the world are not.

One point that comes through this discussion is that it is not "science and mysticism" in the sense of "scientific approach to nature and mystical experiences" that is the real subject of the parallelists' studies. Rather, it is "*scientific theories* and *Asian metaphysics*." Mystical experiences informed mystical systems of thought, but they are not tied to any particular metaphysical system. Parallelists end up not looking at mindfulness or the depth-mystical experience *per se* or Western mystical ideas but looking at various schools of Asian metaphysics or forging an alleged "perennial philosophy." For example, the experience of mindfulness involves seeing the world as it really is, free of our conceptual and emotional constraints—even if we follow Buddhist meditative techniques, we do not have to follow the Buddhists' metaphysical analyses involving how dependent arising leads to new rebirths, but it is the Buddhist metaphysics that parallelists look at. Parallelists should realize that it is the Asian metaphysical ideas or a constructed "perennial philosophy" that they find congenial. (As noted earlier, it is also possible to give a *Western* mystical interpretation of quantum physics [see Malin 2001], and parallelists may become interested in that.) But, as noted in Chapter 2 and the next chapter, many, if not all, of mystics' metaphysical ideas are common to nonmystics—even naturalists can give naturalistic versions of many of the points that parallelists think are vouched for only by mystical experiences.

Indeed, if Richard Nisbett is correct the difference that parallelists see between scientific and mystical thinking is actually between Western and East Asian ways of understanding and perceiving the natural world (2003). He argues that Westerners typically engage in "analytical thinking" that involves detaching an object from its context and categorizing objects by their attributes, while East Asians typically engage in "holistic thinking" that involves an orientation to context and environments as a whole. Analytical thinkers explain and predict in terms of rules governing an object's attributes; holistic thinkers explain and predict in terms of the relation of an object to its context and to other objects. The former utilize chronological and historical relationships; the latter, causal patterns. The former are drawn to objects; the latter, to a perceptual field as a whole. The former decontextualize an object and manipulate its environment; the latter adjust themselves to their environment. The former try to understand the whole by how the parts work; the latter understand the parts by starting with the whole. The former see a logical contradiction between true and false; the latter see some merit on both sides and look for a middle way between them. The former naturally see distinct objects; the latter see a common substance. The former look for causes and agents; the latter, for relationships. The former come up with models simplifying how things work by removing things from their environment; the latter accept the complexity of the world. Western thinking fed Greek curiosity about how the world works and led naturally to the type of science that developed in the West.

But note that nothing that Nisbett says makes the holistic approach tied to having mystical experiences or to altered states of consciousness. He is not saying that everyone in a given culture thinks the same way, but what parallelists focus on may be a matter of general *cultural patterns of thinking* rather than anything tied to *mysticism*. Even if mysticism influenced Asian religious traditions more than Western ones, it may only be because the way that Asians already thought permitted greater influence from mystical experiences. While Nisbett says that Daoism and later Buddhism, along with the more nonmystical Confucianism, shaped the Chinese orientation to life (ibid.: 12-17), he did not need to refer to mystical experiences (and he did not) to explain the East Asian approach to the world. Thus, the "convergences" and "parallels" that parallelists see may be more a matter of general ways of thinking than the result of anything particularly mystical at all.

Notes

1. Metaphysics in mysticism starts out as a way to remove mental clutter, but there is the danger that the metaphysics may ossify and become a block to mystical experiences by becoming a new form of mental clutter. Such a hindrance is especially possible when the metaphysics that is adopted from a culture deals with broader, nonmystical matters.

2. Danah Zohar and Ian Marshall equate the quantum vacuum from physics not only with the Buddhist Void but with all other religious concepts of a source: God, Meister Eckhart's Godhead, and Being—the quantum vacuum and these are all names of the same thing since they are all names of the source of our being (1993: 240, 275). Even leaving aside the issue of whether the different religious terms are interchangeable, this is an instance of translating transcendental concepts into a natural one.

3. Buddhist give three possible reasons for why these questions were left unanswered: any answer would be misconstrued and would have adverse consequences for the student; asking these questions is not conducive to the successful practice of the Buddhist path and one should focus one's mind on more soteriologically efficacious issues; and they are metaphysically misguided because they involve incoherent "essentialist" presuppositions (Garfield 1995: 197 n. 65). Thus, even if science could show that the universe does not have an eternal past, it would still be pointless to ponder the origins of rebirth.

4. The Abhidharmists arrived at the idea of indivisible *dharmas* for the experienced world the same way as they arrived at indivisible atoms of matter: the need for a foundation—otherwise, there would be an infinite regress of divisible entities, and nothing would ever arise. Thus, they share the scientific search for basic building blocks, but this does not change the difference between the elements of the experienced world (*dharmas*) from the material atoms (*paramanus*). The Madhyamikas did not deny the foundational approach of the *dharmas*; they only denied that even these fundamental elements were self-existent.

5. It is interesting to note that the Buddhist doctrine arose in a culture that developed the concept of a *zero*—in fact, the Buddhist word for "emptiness" (*shunya*) was later adopted as the name for "zero." The concept of "zero" precedes the Buddhist concept of "emptiness," but it is not obvious that this is a case of mathematics influencing a mystical concept—the Buddhists probably developed their idea of "emptiness" on other grounds. (The Chinese independently developed the concept of "zero." The Greeks considered the concept but rejected it on philosophical grounds: "zero" meant "non-existence," and if we employed the concept, this would mean it exists; but that would lead to a blatant contradiction—how could the non-existent exist? Greeks also had trouble with irrational numbers and negative numbers while the Indians did not.)

6. Alan Wallace argues for an antirealist, instrumental approach to science and also argues that Buddhism rejects any realism about the physical reality of any entities postulated in a scientific theory; he then turns to a Madhyamaka view of reality (1989). But, as discussed, whether the Buddhist way of life and goal would collapse if permanent or otherwise real entities were postulated on the quantum level is questionable. Thus, whether Buddhists must be committed to antirealism about theoretical posits here is also questionable. In addition, most quantum physicists espouse a common sense metaphysical realism

(i.e., that there is a world existing apart from our ideas) that makes antirealism about theoretical entities, while appealing to philosophers, hard to maintain in the long run—experiments seem to hit something that can be duplicated by others and thus is *real*, even if there are no permanent discrete entities. Moreover, equating realism with materialism or the belief in solid objects (Ricard and Thuan 2001: 113) misconstrues the philosophical issue of realism: there still may be a world existing apart from our thoughts and having definite, definable features, even if it is not populated with permanent solid objects.

7. Rosenblum and Kuttner are "disturbed, and sometimes embarrassed, by cavalier, perhaps intentional, misuse of quantum ideas" (2006: 152). They say that a "touchstone test for such misuse is the presentation of these ideas with the implication that the notions promulgated are derived from quantum physics rather than merely suggested by it" (ibid.).

8. To preserve a holism in which consciousness is essential, New Agers have to overcome a major problem: the universe existed for billions of years apparently without any conscious beings in it. This leads to the idea of a cosmic consciousness transcending all conscious beings or a panpsychism.

9. Asian mystical traditions typically also have practices connected to paranormal powers, but parallelists are not claiming that such alleged powers play a role in scientists' consciousness in quantum events.

10. The Buddhists' belief in the thoroughly causal nature of the natural realm led them to accept that the universe was eternal—otherwise, there would have been *an uncaused first moment*. Their refutation of the idea of a creator god is simple: such a god must be either immutable or not—if it is immutable, it cannot change and thus is unable to decide to create or to act on the idea; if it is not immutable, it is within the realm of time and thus did not create the realm of time, and so the ultimate origin of the universe is not addressed.

11. Indic cosmology attaches numbers to the age and size of the universe, but these numbers only indicate that Indians thought the universe was *truly vast*. To treat them as even speculation on the *exact age and size* of the universe or to try to reconcile them to the numbers in contemporary cosmology would be a mistake.

12. There are a few books comparing DNA and the *I Ching* (e.g., Walter 1996). They have the character of books by Christians trying to correlate the days of creation in Genesis with the eras of the evolution of the universe as depicted in astronomy. Traditional Asian medicine also gets some attention. American medical schools are becoming more open to "holistic medicine." But one problem with testing the claims of, say, acupuncture or Ayur Veda medicine is that these traditional sciences operate according to different physiologies involving *the spirit* in addition to the body and mind. (For Tantric physiology, see Lopez 2008: 202-203.) This makes no sense in light of modern Western scientific beliefs. But these claims may prove testable. Still, even if these practices produce positive results for our health, Western scientists will look for other explanations (e.g., a placebo effect). That is, Western scientists may end up incorporating methods having any positive results but maintain the same materialistic science without modification.

13. This is on the same order as the philosophical argument in early modern science establishing that there are no indivisible particles. René Descartes argued that perhaps there are particles that we human beings could not divide, but God could not in principle create a particle that he himself could not divide, and therefore there are no indivisible particles.

14. In India today, conservatives in the nationalism movement have the political clout to try to change the face of science. The Vedas are seen as scientific texts, and encoded in them are all the ideas of modern science, e.g., some Vedic verses that ostensibly refer to domestic animals are really referring to bosons (see Nanda 2003: 111). In this way, the Rig

Veda is really a book of particle physics (see ibid.: 114). Metaphysics become translated into physics. For example, the three qualities (*gunas*) from Samkhya's metaphysics—brightness/purity, inactivity/ignorance, and activity/passion—become simply "other words for" the three components of an atom. Alternatively, modern science is seen as part of Western colonial imperialism, and so nationalists insist that holistic sciences based on India's traditions must be developed. The idea of "Vedic mathematics," "Vedic physics" (see Nanda 2003: 111-19; Roy 1999), and "Vedic creationism" (see Nanda 2003: 119-21; Cremo and Thompson 1998) has been adopted by the Bharatiya Janata Party, and such things as Vedic astrology is now being taught in government schools and India's Department of Defense is sponsoring research into magical weapons mentioned in the classic epics (Nanda 2003-2004).

15. It is important to remember that, while there are broad features that are the same for all Indic cosmologies, the actual cosmologies of different groups differ. The Abhidharma Buddhists' cosmology reflects a different metaphysics and different religious practices than does the Mahayana Buddhists' cosmology. (See Sadakata 1997.) Most significantly, Mahayana Buddhists gave the Buddha a cosmic function—a Buddhist analog to a creator god (ibid.: 143-57). Also, the view of the hells changed as material life became easier, and the Buddhist view of suffering (*duhkha*) also changed in the modern period (ibid.: 173-77). Parallelists can choose among the various Buddhist cosmologies to find one to their liking. But it should be noted that among Buddhists themselves many treat their cosmologies (including the idea of *rebirth*) in the words of Akira Sadakata, as "old ceremonial garments" that are no longer worn but that still retain an attraction (ibid.: 177).

16. In Christianity, the Catholic church has a similar official position: although it rejects unplanned and unguided evolution, it will accept the evolution of the body, if science establishes it, but not the evolution of the transcendental soul—God implants the soul in the body at conception.

17. Many people see karma and rebirth as providing a satisfying answer to what we see as the uneven and often unfair distribution of fate and fortune (e.g., Raman 2002a: 190), i.e., the problem of evil. Rather than genetic chance, the Hindu doctrines teach that our identity and destiny are determined by the law of karmic action and effect (ibid.).

18. This raises the issue of whether the doctrines of the supposedly enlightened Buddha are actually being subjected to a higher epistemic authority (i.e., science). But according to David McMahan, there has not been any large-scale jettisoning of Buddhist doctrines in the Buddhist community (2004: 927-28).

— 10 —

Are Science and Mysticism Converging on One Worldview?

The basic conclusion to the chapters of Part II so far is this: since mysticism is a matter of freeing the mind of conceptions to approach beingness while science is a matter of changing distinctions concerning structures responsible for changes in the natural realm, any substantive convergence in scientific and mystical theories is precluded. It is not the case that mystics reach enlightenment from the "inside" (i.e, through inner experiences) while scientists reach the same enlightenment from the "outside" (i.e., through observations and reasoning). Since different dimensions of reality are involved, it is simply a mistake to believe that approaching reality through the "unknowing" of mindfulness and through the concept-driven observation and experimentation of science could even in principle converge on a set of concrete claims about reality. Even sciences of the everyday level (e.g., evolution or ecology) cannot converge with a mindfulness claim about the beingness of the everyday level since these theories too are about the causes of how things work.

But although the sciences and mystical traditions are not converging on a particular scientific or mystical theory of things or merging into one new endeavor or being integrated into either of the two existing endeavors, can they at least be subsumed under one new common worldview? That is, do they converge, not on a, but at least on a more general metaphysical theory of reality? Are mystics and scientists at least growing closer together in their understanding of reality on the level of metaphysics, if not in the "details" of their theories? If so, parallelists could shift their usual claims and admit that science and mysticism do not converge or confirm the specifics of either's theories, and argue instead that it is only in more abstract features of a way of viewing the world that science and mysticism are consonant. Perhaps these diverse claims "converge" on more abstract claims about the general nature of the world that are logically entailed by specific scientific theories and mystical doctrines. In sum, do science and mysticism at least share one broader worldview? For example, the metaphysics in which Buddhists set forth a specific system of the relation of things in the realm of becoming does not converge with the particulars of quantum physics or any specific scientific theory, but are the abstract entailed claims of impermanence, connectedness, and dependency also entailed by scientific accounts of different levels of phenomena?[1] Can they both be included within a picture of a dynamic and impermanent reality? Or could some particular mystical system of thought at least provide a metaphysical foundation for physical and other scientific theories?

The New Worldview

So, perhaps parallelists can be seen as attempting to construct, not a new science or a new mystical system or a new composite system, but a more general philosophy of nature encompassing insights from different sources—quantum physics, cosmology, biology, complexity theory, and mindfulness mysticism all thereby become instances of the one shared worldview. This is not to say that all people who claim parallels and convergences between science and mysticism share one set of beliefs—just as mystics do not have common set of beliefs, neither do parallelists today. But this approach gives the most positive interpretation of their claims. And since parallelists are all over the map on what they say about the relation of science and mysticism, some of their remarks do suggest this approach. For example, Fritjof Capra argues that "Eastern mysticism" and the new physics share the same worldview and that the former provides a consistent and harmonious framework for the new physics and other sciences (1983: 78; 2000: 25, 327).

To parallelists, the mechanistic worldview of earlier modern science may have served a valuable purpose in liberating mankind from outdated religious dogma, but that approach to reality has outlived its usefulness, and today a new worldview is emerging. It is a worldview that goes beyond the Newtonian way of looking at things—i.e., beyond a "world as a machine" universe of an independently-existing space in which independent entities operate externally on each other to a "world as an organism" model. The new worldview instead emphasizes change, impermanence, interconnectedness, inseparability, contingency, and dependency. "Systems theory" has also influenced this new vision. (See Capra 1983; Macy 1991; Laszlo 2004.) The idea of systems emphasizes the relational nature of reality and that reality cannot be fully understood in terms of its parts alone.[2]

However, the alleged commonality of the insight encompassed in this new vision is only on an abstract level. The insight is the general claim that all of reality is one undivided, thoroughly integrated whole that is in constant flux with no permanent components. In other words: a fluid web of interconnected events, devoid of self-existent parts (including a "self"), with the parts being understandable only within the web of relationships. Nature is not seen as a machine with merely external, mechanical connections but as a system with interdependent, organism-like connections. Scientists can still discern patterns in the dynamic flow of events and can postulate structures to explain them, but there are no independent, self-existing elements in the mix. The laws that scientists discern may be eternal and permanent and as fundamental as the material that is ordered, but there are no permanent material parts in the process of constant change. Specific theories *per se* in science and mysticism may not warrant any particular idea. Indeed, that quantum physics and relativity theory currently *contradict* each other over determinism and absolute time is irrelevant—all that matters is that everything in the universe is seen as impermanent and interconnected. Such an organic worldview fits everything scientists have found so far on submicroscopic levels (even though advocates of the new vision favor interpretations of physics involving consciousness) and also to mindfulness mysticism in general. It is clearly an exercise in metaphysics building rather than being part of any science or mysticism.

Ludwig Wittgenstein once remarked that what Copernicus really achieved was not the discovery of a true theory but a fertile new point of view, a new way of looking at things—Copernicus got most of the specifics about a heliocentric universe wrong (the sun is not the center of a small universe, planetary orbits are not circular, and the solar system as a whole is moving), but he did provide a new orientation in cosmology by moving the earth out of the center of the universe. And, if parallelists are at all correct, something like that is the case here with this new metaphysical vision. The common insight may be too abstract to give concrete help to science, but parallelists insist that adopting this metaphysics has direct, practical consequences: it will change our "dualistic" point of view of ourselves and our relation to others and to nature; thus the new worldview will have major personal and social consequences. (Whether such philosophical changes are in fact a necessary consequence of science was questioned in Chapter 6.)

Creating a Worldview

Since the new metaphysical vision moves to an all-encompassing holism, it does not have the authority of either science or mystical experiences behind it. The worldview is more general than any specific theories or doctrines in science or mysticism. Indeed, it is not deducible from any scientific theory since the new worldview changes the focus from the underlying causal structures to the impermanence of events. Instead, it has all the problems associated with metaphysics. Some parallelists may also incorporate depth-mysticism here by advocating an underlying core of unchanging consciousness as the source of everything, perhaps under an emanationist interpretation. But the new vision does not explain why or how the interconnected realm arose in the first place. Nor does it offer any explanation of why nature has the specific scientific structures it has. No findings concerning laws and structures would support or conflict with this worldview as long as the theories maintain the impermanence and interconnectedness of objects.

Thus, finding the quantum realm to be impermanent and interconnected is the key, not any particular scientific structures posited to explain quantum events.

That is, this metaphysics covers the general impermanence and interconnectedness of *phenomena*, not the scientific *structures*. Thus, it is not a "scientific worldview" generated by science, nor do any specific scientific theories flow from this worldview—at best, this worldview is consistent with scientific theories, but it is not any more helpful to what scientists do.[3] The metaphysics does not provide any new scientific insights or predictions, but it does provide an encompassing framework for theories. Capra uses some scientific terms, but he admits that he is using them in a *nonscientific* sense. For example, he is now using the term "ecological," but he admits that his use is in a "broader and deeper" sense than its common use—it is now a *philosophical* term (2000: 326). Any scientific theory that suggests permanent entities is rejected, but other than this the actual content of specific theories from different sciences is not necessary. Indeed, if all mindfulness mystical traditions, the physical sciences, and biology are all converging on one viewpoint, then obviously the specifics of any one particular theory in any of the sciences or mystical traditions are not the core beliefs or substance of the vision. Instead, the new vision must be extrascientific, i.e., metaphysical. It cannot say anything specific about the nature of the interconnectedness of reality—that is for scientists to find—but only that reality is interconnected and dynamic and not a set of static, permanent, isolated objects connected only exteriorly and mechanically. This does move beyond the Newtonian worldview (in which the world is dynamic and interactive and objects still may be impermanent) to a view of things as interconnected, including even space. But mainstream science at present does not compel believing that objects are interconnected internally or that consciousness plays a role in determining physical events.

Science may have been responsible for us moving beyond the Newtonian worldview, but we do not need to study much current physics or biology to see the commonality highlighted by this new worldview. None of the "details"—i.e., the *real substance* of any theories in science or doctrines in mysticism—matter. We certainly to not need to know the mathematics of quantum physics. No particular current scientific theory needs to be advocated. Capra tied the vision to a specific theory in quantum physics (the S-matrix), but, while he still feels compelled to advocate it, that theory has been discarded by other physicists—nevertheless, the vision continues. Advocates of the new vision see any permanence or isolated parts as now permanently removed from science: specific theories may come and go, but scientists will not be going back to some idea of permanent, distinct entities at any level, not even at the lowest physical level of interactions, any more than science will return to a cosmology with an unmoving earth at the center of a small universe. Thus, parallelists are predicting that no theory of permanent components in string theory or any other scientific theory will be accepted.

However, some advocates will argue for a more thorough holism that would affect science. In order to make everything interconnected, theories that require a role for *consciousness* become the only theories in physics that advocates would accept even though these are far from mainstream. They may also add the metaphysical idea that all phenomena arise from a "cosmic mind." In neuroscience, they also insist that the mind is a cause, not merely an epiphenomenon of matter. But at least as long as these theories in physics and neuroscience are not ruled out on scientific grounds, this position is not inconsistent with science. In a case of metaphysics affecting the course of science, this metaphysical vision might also play a role in determining which theories end up being accepted. And since mysticism influenced the metaphysics of an underlying consciousness in this vision, mysticism would be influencing science. Otherwise, the new vision will remain at best only a matter of a metaphysical interpretation of the existing science.

Problems with the New Vision

However, this metaphysics still has to twist both science and mysticism to fit the encompassing vision. As just noted, advocates of a thorough holism want particular theories—in particular, a role for consciousness in physical events—and thus they stand apart from the current mainstream in physics and neuroscience. So too, advocates would have to edit mystical systems. Mysticism in the hands of parallelists becomes one unified system. The diversity of mystical beliefs and practices throughout history is ignored—one tradition is deemed the "essence" or "epitome" of all mysticism, or a "perennial philosophy" becomes a control belief for how mystical traditions are construed. Mysticism becomes about a generic "unity of reality" and all mystical experiences become cases of a *unio mystica*. Depth-mysticism all becomes one system of thought: all phenomena are manifestations or emanations of a basic conscious source. This fits the Upanishads' emanationism but not Advaita's "identity" metaphysics or Samkhya's dualism. In sum, the "new vision" certainly does not express the "true essence" of all "Eastern mysticism," let alone of all mystical traditions of the world. Thus, the new vision is a normative position with regard to mysticism.

Under this vision, all mindfulness traditions also become one: the "mutual causation" of Hwa Yen becomes the worldview of all mystical traditions (see Capra 2000: 329, 1983: 142), despite the fact that no other mindfulness tradition has such interpenetration as a central doctrinal tenet. But, as noted in Chapter 6, it must be remembered that Hinayana Abhidarmists exempted space (and nirvana) from being "conditioned" by other elements of the experienced world; they also accepted uncuttable and undestroyable bits of matter. This means that mysticism does not necessarily require the holism of the new worldview at all. Making this part of Hwa Yen central to all mysticism shows the selectiveness and distortion that results from making an alleged common vision dictate what is selected as "essential." But, as with scientific theories, even if this Hwa Yen doctrine is rejected as essential for all mysticism, the more basic metaphysical vision of impermanence, interconnectedness, and interdependency remains intact.

Equally important, to include consciousness in its holism, this vision must naturalize depth-mysticism: to keep everything mutually interconnected, the depth-mystical experience must now be taken to be only an experience of some material or nonmaterial portion of the natural universe that is also open to scientific study, not an experience of a possible transcendental source. There can be no *unchanging* transcendental source—otherwise, there would be only a one-way dependence and not reciprocal interaction. So too, giving the underlying consciousness a role in determining specific physical events forces a revision to traditional forms of depth-mysticism. The changeless consciousness, under such interpretations as Advaita's or Samkhya's, is simply not open to holistic interpretations.

Advocates of the new vision may now also want to include in it a *purpose* or a *goal* to the evolution of the universe through some type of design or an evolution of consciousness, as with Aurobindo and Teilhard. (The Neo-Buddhist rejection of the Anthropic Principle was noted in the last chapter.) But mystical experiences themselves cannot support this: mysticism is about the beingness presented to us in experiences with no conceptualizations or expectations. There is no sense of time, development, or a goal to the realm of becoming—the natural realm just is. Everything is what it is, and we can experience all of its being at any one moment in history. Any theory of anything outside of the "now" of experience must come from other sources. A concern for the purpose must come from sources other than mystical experiences. Thus, mystics who see a purpose to the universe or to human life must take this from their religious traditions.

Mystical experiences of being also do not by themselves justify the idea that all things in the universe *mutually influence* all other things or bring about each other's existence or are mutually interconnected the way the jewels of Indra's net are. And the idea of mutual influence is easy to doubt. It is one thing to say that all empirical phenomena are impermanent, depend on others things, and are parts in one interconnected whole; it is another thing to say that, for example, all human actions on earth somehow even indirectly or infinitesimally affect what goes on in the interior of a star a thousand light-years from here. We may be thoroughly integrated into the universe rather than be isolated realities, but this does not mean that we are each interacting with each item in nature. This vision goes beyond the everyday interconnectedness we see, and neither science nor mystical experiences justify the idea that everything interacts with everything else. It is a matter of metaphysics, not either science or mystical experiences.

In fact, it should also be noted that there is nothing particularly *mystical* about this new vision. The metaphysics that some mystics have adopted may fit the new vision, but there is nothing on what is unique to mysticism—the unmediated experience of the dimension of beingness and the transcendental quests of various mystical ways of life. In addition, virtually every claim that mystics have advanced nonmystics have also advanced for philosophical reasons totally unrelated to mystical experiences. For example, a chain of rebirths driven by ignorance and desire is accepted in nonmystical Indian traditions. The impermanence and interconnectedness of the external world is obvious to anyone upon some reflection.

We do not need the mindful state of conscious to see this, nor any science. Nonmystics have argued that things are impermanent ever since Heraclitus first noted that we cannot step in the same river twice—part of what constitutes the river will have changed by the time we try stepping into it a second time. So too, we need not have a mystical experience to realize that there is no permanent substratum to a "person"—the mind and body are constantly changing, giving rise to the perennial issue in philosophy of personal identity over time. Many in science and philosophy also reject the idea of a unified center to consciousness—the sense of a "self" separate from the rest of the world is merely something concocted by the brain to help us deal with the world and does not correspond to anything real. Moreover, even if mystical experiences lie at the historical root of our ancestors' initial sense of a "cosmic wholeness," nevertheless that all things share the same being and that the universe is interconnected with no independent parts are points that nonmystics can readily accept today. Naturalists can certainly agree that everything is connected, impermanent, and dependent upon other things, even if they do not see any point in emphasizing this by constructing a metaphysics since this general claim does not help scientists devise new theories. In fact, naturalists argue that we, along with everything else in our solar system, are natural products made only of star dust with no permanent, independent selves—the sense that we are each a distinct, self-contained entity is, in Albert Einstein's words, an "optical illusion of consciousness."[4] Even consciousness is made of the same stuff as everything else—we divide the world conventionally into observer and observed only for practical purposes.

Certainly no altered states of consciousness or special experience is needed to understand any of these points. Thus, there is no need to credit mysticism as the source of this vision. Mindfulness may highlight impermanence and interconnectedness, but experiences of beingness are not necessary to validate the new vision. Nor, as discussed, does a mystical experience offer a new insight into the organization of scientific structures. Nor is adopting this framework by itself going to induce any mystical experience—in fact, we can remain as unmystical as before. The philosopher Derek Parfit finds the neuroscientific denial of any "self" within our mental makeup quite liberating without any resulting hint of mysticism. The difference with the mystical states of consciousness is that the beingness of things is brought into awareness, and then the impermanent and interconnected beingness of all of the everyday realm of becoming (including the alleged "self") is seen more clearly and becomes prominent. In short, mystics realize something experientially and make the framework of their lives, not merely see some logical points about nature that nonmystics also may acknowledge as true and accept as a belief.

Because of these issues, few may be interested in trying to reconcile science and mysticism by approaching them through the construction of an abstract metaphysical vision covering both science and mysticism that one can accept without mysticism and without any particular scientific theory—the unique experiential nature of mysticism becomes downplayed or entirely lost, as are the specifics of science's understanding of the structures of the realm of becoming. In sum, a metaphysics of becoming is certainly possible, but it washes away what is most distinctive about both mysticism and science.

Notes

1. One common generalization is that the "modern mind" informed by science and modern philosophy forms worldviews in a different way than does the "traditional mind" informed by mysticism and mythology. The former starts with the natural world as given and looks for what knowledge we can attain through experience and reason. The latter starts with the primacy of transcendent realities as given; it sees the natural world as a product of supreme transcendent realities and sees human beings as participating directly in transcendent realities. Through the latter approach, societies come up with competing comprehensive metaphysical views. Through the modern approach, we need not end up with a metaphysical system that denies all transcendental realities—i.e., a form of naturalism—but our starting point remains different.

2. "General Systems Theory" was a philosophical school in the mid-twentieth century that never gained wide support. But today even mainstream biologists are taking the idea of "systems biology" seriously. Along with help from computer specialists and physicists, they are using the idea of systems to try to determine how whole organisms work—e.g., how an embryo gets from a few cells to a full human being with cells organized into specialized functions, or how the genetic code assembles proteins into an embryo in the first place.

3. There is an ambiguity about the phrase "scientific worldview." As discussed in Chapter 12, we do need to make certain metaphysical commitments to practice science, but there is no such thing as a "scientific worldview" in the sense of *a total picture of all that is real that is required by science*. We can adopt a worldview that is consistent with current scientific theories or otherwise is informed by science without adopting the philosophy of naturalism that treats the scientific picture as potentially exhaustive. To do otherwise does not mean that we are not taking science seriously. It only means not extrapolating the approach appropriate for studying the efficient causation within nature into one, all-inclusive approach to reality—a move that is not required to value science. This also leaves aside the question of whether in fact all scientific theories are consistent with each other in how they explain different aspects of phenomena and thus could even be integrated into one view of things—in particular, there is the problem of finding a way to make quantum physics and relativity consistent, since they are equally fundamental but currently conflict. A comprehensive "scientific worldview" in this stronger sense is not a matter of science alone but is a *philosophical* move: no scientific theory or the practice of science in general dictates that our complete view of the world must be reduced only to what science reveals. All worldviews, including ones incorporating science, remain metaphysical in nature.

4. Neuroscience suggests that there may not be a self—i.e., no one unified center of awareness, and no one locus in the brain to our sense of "self." Rather, there may be multiple "selves"—i.e., each conscious type of mental functioning can produce a self-awareness of that activity, but there is no one command center overseeing all such acts of self-awareness.

— 11 —

Where Do We Stand?

Since the 1970s, some scholars discussing mysticism and science have become more knowledgeable concerning at least the doctrines of some Buddhist traditions and also have followed the current developments in the sciences. Some are also less prone to broad generalizations about all of mysticism and tend to stick to individual mystical traditions and specific scientific theories. In this regard, these studies are more nuanced and sophisticated (Cabezón 2003: 56-58). Unfortunately, the recent works have not progressed *philosophically* from earlier comparative studies on the issues discussed here in Part II. And the enthusiasm of most parallelists for science still causes them to see mystical traditions through the lens of science, thereby distorting spiritual traditions by seeing them as making modern scientific claims. Overall, they reflect the same approach as the popular books in the 1970's that introduced a generation to the field of "science and mysticism."

The only substantive advances in science-and-mysticism studies have been in exploring the neurology and physiology of religious experiences through the scientific study of meditators, as discussed in Chapter 5, and in Neo-Buddhists engaging scientists in discussion. While most in the cognitive sciences still view mysticism with suspicion, more scientists today are willing to accept mystical experiences as something other than merely the product of a brain malfunction or wishful thinking, even if they dismiss mystical claims to insight or show no interest in them. That many of the scientists involved in such discussions are themselves practicing Buddhists or meditators makes them more sympathetic to mysticism, but it does not help with understanding the philosophical issues in comparative studies. And there still seems little interest in philosophy or religious studies in studying the issues arising from comparing science and the mystical strand of religiosity.

The search to find commonality and convergences still drives thinkers in this field, even if parallelists acknowledge in the introductions or conclusions to their works that scientists and mystics do different things. (See Clarke 2005.) But that scientists and mystics are concerned with different aspects of reality and have a different set of interests is still more fundamental than any abstract "parallels" and distortive "convergences" that parallelists may construct. And it is these irreducible *differences* that must be the starting point for addressing the relation between the two actual endeavors rather than contaminated or truncated distortions of them. Science and mysticism address different mysteries underlying our everyday world—the what-ness and how-ness versus the that-ness of things. (See Jones 2009.) This basic divergence cannot be overcome by attempts to find a "synthesis" of science and mysticism or a new metaphysical "vision of reality" common to both endeavors. To revise Rudyard Kipling's saying, science is science and mysticism is mysticism, and never the twain shall meet—at least, as ways of knowing reality and in their basic knowledge-claims.

There is also value in highlighting the differences between the endeavors: it reveals what is unique about science and about mysticism and how each may contribute to our fuller view of reality. The search for a common worldview, on the other hand, ends up missing each endeavor's distinctive way of knowing by reducing them simply to two ways of voicing the same alleged abstract metaphysical vision. If science and mysticism each can in fact contribute to a fuller view of reality, another approach is needed than attempting to reconcile science and mysticism either through seeing specific scientific theories and some mystical metaphysics as converging or through developing a purported common metaphysical worldview that eviscerates what is unique about both science and mysticism. An alternative will be suggested in Part III.

Part III

Reconciling Science and Mysticism

— 12 —

Can We Take Mystical Experiences Seriously Today?

In the modern world, we start with science as the authoritative way of knowing the world. How then can we take mystical knowledge-claims seriously? Is there an accommodation that accepts both science and mysticism as different ways of knowing reality? Embracing a view of knowledge that rejects either science or mysticism is certainly much easier: if only one way is accepted as providing knowledge of reality, it is easy to dismiss the other out of hand as fundamentally misguided and not really knowledge at all, or at best as not necessary in the end—what is the Age of Enlightenment for science is the dark age of the Kali Yuga for mysticism, and vice versa. Trying to find a place for both science and mysticism in a scheme of knowledge is more challenging, but it is possible. What was discussed in the first two parts of this book suggests a way: science and mysticism both provide us with genuine knowledge but fundamentally different types of knowledge, and together they give us a more complete view of reality—i.e., knowledge of reality's causal organization and of its beingness.

However, before presenting an outline of this approach in Chapter 16, the decks must be cleared by dealing with certain preliminary points: (1) *whether people with a modern Western outlook can even take mysticism seriously today as a possible source of knowledge*; (2) *whether natural explanations of mystical experiences undercut mystics' cognitive claims*; (3) *whether constructivism can be applied to mystical experiences*; and (4) *whether there are good philosophical grounds to rule out mystical experiences as having any cognitive significance*. The first of these topics will be the subject of this chapter.

Naturalism

It is not obvious at first glance that scientific and mystical ways of knowing can be reconciled with each other. From what has been discussed, we can see why classical mystics would dismiss science as at best a waste of our valuable time and at worst as wrongheaded. So too, we can see why anyone accepting the importance of science may not warm up to mysticism as a way of knowing; from this point of view, nothing cognitive is added by mystical experiences, and the experiences may end up misleading the experiencers into believing in transcendental realities. It is not that science logically refutes the possibility of mystical knowledge or otherwise proves all depth-mystical knowledge-claims wrong or impossible; rather, science seems to render such claims implausible or unneeded and hence obsolete. We have turned to objective, this-worldly knowledge only. We no longer need to think in terms of transcendental agents or causes for any natural phenomena—science is slowly but surely answering all the legitimate questions we can ask of the world, including everything about mystical experiences. Science cannot supply an answer for the ultimate mystery—why does anything exist?—but then again there is no use in postulating a transcendental cause here either since naturalists can just turn around and ask why God, Brahman, or any other transcendental reality exists. (See Jones 2009: chap. 5.) Either way, we end up with a mystery, and so we should accept the natural realm as final since we at least know that this exists.

Certainly anyone trained in the analytical and controlling stance of science may well have trouble accepting an undirected, contemplative stance as revealing anything about the world. In particular, taking depth-mystical experiences seriously as cognitive of anything transcendental goes against the spirit of the modern age—we are not "thinking like a scientist" if we take the idea of transcendental realities seriously. People who have passed through the Western Age of Enlightenment have trouble taking any other type of claim to enlightenment seriously. For many, mystical cognitive claims are simply unreasonable in the modern world, and any attempt to make them somehow reasonable will have to transform them into something they are not. Of course, if meditation can be rigorously tested and shown to have demonstrable health benefits or to help us focus our awareness, we in the modern world may embrace it for these effects. But whether we can accept the claim that mystical experiences give insights into the nature of reality—i.e., have cognitive significance—is another matter. How can anyone commit to a reality transcending the natural order as the best explanation of any experience today? Even mindfulness adds nothing to science and so is cognitively valueless.

Any claim of a mystical insight into any transcendental reality goes against the most prominent metaphysics of our time in scientific circles: *naturalism*.[1] The success of scientists in understanding nature has led many to conclude that only what scientists can study is real—indeed, science can become so ingrained in our view of things that we may do not even see naturalism as a form of metaphysics at all but simply as the view of the world given by science itself. Edward O. Wilson is one naturalist scientist who acknowledges that his preferred type of naturalism, "scientific materialism," is "a metaphysical worldview, and a minority one at that, shared by only a few scientists and philosophers. It cannot be proved with logic from first principles or grounded in any definitive set of empirical tests"—rather, it is "no more than an extrapolation of the consistent past success of the natural sciences" (1998: 9). But only such a metaphysical extrapolation would negate the alleged cognitive content of mystical experiences since the knowledge mystics allegedly give is of something that cannot be empirically checked. Nevertheless, many scientifically-minded moderns see the world through some form of naturalistic glasses, even if they do not realize they have them on.

Under naturalism, what is real is only the world of space-time—both the phenomenal world and the underlying scientific structures ordering what we observe. It can be defined by what it denies: there is no transcendental realities or transcendental dimension to the world or to a human being.[2] Scientists may not be able to disclose all of the natural realm—i.e., some mysteries about how nature works may always remain—but no realities exist that in principle are not open to scientific investigation. Ethical and aesthetic values are usually deemed noncognitive since there is no possible scientific study of them except social studies of what values people actually hold. But whether alleged mathematical realities should be included in the naturalist's inventory of what is real is controversial. Consciousness also presents a problem since naturalists want to consider it a natural product, but as noted in Chapter 5 how to study it empirically is difficult to envision. Scientists can identify the neurological bases, but they still cannot figure out how or why consciousness arises or how to study the subjectivity of consciousness itself. Not all naturalists are materialists, but this problem has led many within the naturalists' ranks to reduce the mind to the body or to deny the reality of consciousness altogether. But for all naturalists, consciousness is considered merely a product of the natural order even if scientists will never be able to study it.

By definition, naturalists accept that the space-time universe alone is real, and thus it is constituted, formed, and controlled only by spatio-temporal processes. Our brain has evolved in a purely natural environment only to aid with our survival and nothing more. Thus, naturalists are committed to denying any experiential knowledge of any alleged transcendental reality—first, because they deny any such realities exist; second, because they accept only science as a way to knowledge, and so even if any transcendental realities did exist, they would not be open to any sort of empirical checking and thus could not be known. In short, if we accept naturalism, we must reject all alleged depth-mystical cognitive claims. Depth-mystical experiences are then seen as the result of either a pathological brain condition or at best the bare monitoring activity of the mind that continues to function even after the mind is emptied of all sensory and conceptual content.

It is possible to give a *positive* naturalistic interpretation of both types of mystical experiences—i.e., accepting that such experiences give an insight either into the nature of our mind (perhaps revealing our purely natural consciousness free of all intentional content) or into the being of the natural world, rather than any transcendental reality. Mystics experience something previously unknown about the nature of our reality. In sum, under this interpretation mystical experiences may provide insights into natural phenomena and cannot be explained away any more than any other cognitive experience. In fact, much of mysticism can actually be reconciled with naturalism and even with a reductive materialism. (See Angel

2002.³) But while this approach treats a mystical experience as a positive occurrence rather than a brain malfunction and can also preserve much of mystical ways of life, it still must reject the transcendental elements of traditional mystical metaphysics, thereby negating the depth-mystics' claims.

In any case, the fact remains that mysticism does not characterize the spirit of our age. Even if we ignore depth-mysticism's transcendental element, to modern inquirers mysticism still reflects only passivity, quietism, the obscure, the irrational, and powerlessness in an era when the assertion of self-will has come to dominate our culture. Few people want to give up their sense of individual existence or do anything that would render the ego meaningless—inducing any type of selflessness is precisely what most people do not want today. Buddhist teachings on selflessness become transformed in psychotherapy into a way to enhance the proper sense of the self through "self-realization." Overall, the typical response of most who take science seriously today is to lump mysticism proper in with everything occult or weird, and then to dismiss it out of hand without bothering to examine it.

It is not merely the unfathomable "occult" entities and forces of a particular pre-modern mystical tradition's worldview that is the problem. It is the conflict of any naturalistic worldview with any transcendental worldview that would incorporate depth-mysticism: people who ascribe to the occult have simply not assimilated the scientific way of bringing order to experience—they are not living in any meaningful way within the paradigm of science—and in fact it would be suicidal for our society to embrace mysticism (Hutcheon 1996/97). Any worldview based on traditional mystical doctrines would render pointless any social reform to remedy poverty, disease, and hunger since under traditional religious doctrines the world and society are accepted as is or are not considered ultimately real or valuable. (It is also worth noting that "perennial philosophers" often have nothing but contempt for modern society.) Indeed, any premodern worldview or ethos will not reflect the concern with the rights and dignity of *individuals* that arose in the Age of Enlightenment in the West. Rather, any traditional view will manifest an indifference to the fate of individuals in light of an other-worldly goal.⁴

Under naturalism's denial of transcendental realities, this world takes on a reality it would not have as the product of a transcendental source—it is not, for example, merely the stage upon which the drama of our eternal salvation is worked out. Rather, it is an end in itself. Even if naturalists could affirm the possibility of a transcendental deistic source, the focus of our attention would still be on this universe and our own efforts since such a source would still be uninvolved with our problems. Either way, only this universe is of value to us. Philosophers as diverse as Friedrich Nietzsche and John Dewey criticize any transcendental desire as a hindrance to our growth and to living fully in this world. Mysticism becomes seen as an other-worldly opiate that keeps us from the this-worldly salvation that is attainable through science and reason.

Indeed, to naturalists what could possibly motivate any scientifically-minded thinker to be anything other than a naturalist (Shear 2004: 85)? Even if we reject the naturalists' metaphysics, they still insist that taking only an agnostic stance toward anything not supportable or refutable by empirical evidence is the only position consistent with science. Only what can be based on scientifically checkable experiences, either directly or through the winnowing process of collective testing and clear logical reasoning, can count as knowledge. Thus, all claims to knowledge must ultimately be based on empirical evidence and scientific explanations, and mystical "intuitions" fail this standard. In such circumstances, we may remain open to the possibility of mystical knowledge and agnostic about particular transcendental claims, but this is no basis to adopt a mystical way of life or even to devote time to cultivating mystical experiences.

"Modern Epistemic Standards"

So does the popularity of naturalism present good grounds to reject mystical cognitive claims? Matthew Bagger makes an argument based on our social situation in the modern world against the possibility that the "quintessentially modern inquirer" could countenance any explanation of mystical experiences based on the impingement of a transcendental reality (1999). Today supernatural realities are no longer accepted as part of good explanations of anything, including mystical experiences. In fact, it is no longer even *rational* for people in the modern world to hold any supernatural explanations since natural explanations of the occurrence of religious experiences either now exist or can at least be envisioned—indeed, even if no good natural explanations were a prospect at present, it would still be irrational to look for a supernatural explanation because of the epistemic values we in the modern world hold today. Supernatural explanations no longer represent good explanations of lightning and earthquakes or any other natural event, and a mystical experience is merely another natural event—it just happens to be one occurring in the brain. Thus, even modern members of theistic religions should abjure supernatural explanations of these experiences. Theistic modern believers cannot segregate the explanations of mystical experiences from all other explanations—i.e., giving them a special status to which our general epistemic values do not apply—simply in order to protect them from assault. In short, only a natural explanation of a mystical experience is acceptable to the modern mind. We in the modern world reject supernatural explanations of alleged miracles, and mystical experiences are simply small, internal, alleged miracles. Invoking the actions of a god or other transcendental reality to explain the occurrence of any event, internal or external, is a "god of the gaps" type explanation—i.e., invoking the supernatural to explain something in the natural order that science cannot at present explain—and such a strategy is no longer acceptable to the modern mind.

Bagger presents no philosophical arguments against the validity of any mystical claims. Indeed, he does not even attempt to prove that scientific explanations are superior to all other types of explanations for everyone. In fact, he advances no arguments other than his basic sociological claim that what type of explanation is "culturally prevalent" in a given society determines what type of explanations must be accepted as "rational"—and since naturalistic arguments happen to be prevalent in our society today, *ipso facto* transcendental explanations of mystical experiences must be rejected out of hand. The modern inquirer simply assumes everything must be ultimately explainable in naturalistic terms alone.

Bagger's position ends up being a standard postmodern cultural relativism. He is not arguing that modern Western culture is epistemically superior to other cultures, but only that epistemic standards are relative to a particular culture and era. He presents no arguments against the idea that transcendental explanations of mystical claims might be rationally held by members of another culture or era having its own internally coherent logic and set of values. We are left with no way to argue for or against a mystical cognitive claim on any philosophical or even scientific grounds. Indeed, the question of whether mystical cognitive claims are true for all people in every culture and era is rendered meaningless. There is no way to adjudicate between "culturally prevalent" standards, and so a society's own standards are conclusive for that society. Each culture simply devises epistemic standards that are supreme for it. Naturalists routinely accuse advocates of mystical experiences as cognitive of employing a "protective strategy" by arguing that claims based on depth-mystical experiences require a different type of justification than claims based on sense-experiences, but Bagger's relativism insulates "modern epistemic standards" and all other cultural standards from any criticism from other cultures and from any criticism in terms of a purported cross-cultural rationality.

Bagger's sociological claim about our society, however, is open to doubt. Forget about all the devotees of astrology in American society. Instead, think only about scientists. Polls of American scientists throughout the twentieth century have consistently shown that a significant percentage of working scientists, especially in physics and mathematics, are either theists or deists. (See Larson and Witham 1999.) They range from fundamentalist Christians to deists such as Paul Davies. Those scientists who are theists accept that a transcendental reality in fact is active in the natural realm; deists affirm some transcendental source to this world and its order, but one totally uninvolved with the world's activities. Both theists and deists accept a transcendental explanation for why the universe exists, even though naturalists reject the question since it cannot be answered scientifically. In fact, some scientists are interested in mysticism and accept different mystical traditions' transcendental claims.[5] In sum, a significant percentage of scientists do in fact accept supernatural explanations of some aspects of the universe, although the vast majority do maintain that scientific explanations must be in terms of natural, efficient causes. This means that there is in fact no one settled position on the alleged rationality of supernatural explanations for *all aspects* of the universe even in the modern scientific community.

It is also doubtful that any epistemological questions can be settled simply by a show of hands. Certainly Bagger cannot merely appeal to one segment of modern Western society—those scientists and philosophers who are secularists—and claim on sociological grounds alone that all modern thinkers therefore must conform to that segment's normative standard in order to have a rational belief today. There simply is no one society-wide norm. And even if there were, tying rationality to any social standard misses something very important: social standards have changed and may well change in the future. We are not prisoners of old points of view. We can at least partially abstract ourselves from our cultural situation—otherwise, there would be no changes at all. We can see beyond the accepted position of one segment of a society (or, indeed, all of a society) and see other points of view. As the social anthropologist Ernest Gellner claimed, "[t]ranscendence of custom is the most important fact in the intellectual history of mankind." This is so, even if the new point of view seems "irrational" by the old standards.[6]

And if the vast majority of academics end up rejecting naturalism and incorporating non-naturalistic elements into their worldview, all Bagger can say is that mystical cognitive claims would then be considered rational. Thus, in the end, all Bagger has done is point out the obvious: mystical cognitive claims conflict with naturalism, and many academics today are naturalists. He has presented no reasons why naturalism is epistemically superior—indeed, under his sociological approach, this question is rendered moot since there can be no standards transcending a particular cultural point of view.

Science and Naturalism

In addition to the problems with a purely sociological argument, there are philosophical grounds to reject the position that science demands that we all become naturalists and dismiss depth-mystics' transcendental claims out of hand. But, again, naturalism is a philosophy, not science *per se*. That naturalism goes beyond science itself into the realm of metaphysics can be seen by asking one simple question: what experiment in physics or observation in any science can establish that only what scientists can study is real? None. No scientific account of the universe can establish even in principle that it is a complete account of all that occurs in nature or that it has captured all that there is to reality. Rather, the naturalists' worldview that the natural universe is the only one and that consciousness is realized by the brain is only an inference to what naturalists themselves consider the best explanation (Flanagan 2007: 93).[7]

But anyone, including scientists themselves, can fully accept science and yet reject metaphysical naturalism. The modern common sense of *science* does not tell us that the world as studied by science is all there is—only the *philosophy* of naturalism claims that. And whether we should impose standards from science on everything in a culture is questionable. It requires an argument more than just that science is successful in its own domain. Nor is it a protective strategy to see mystical experiences as requiring a different treatment when they differ in nature from the experiences accepted as evidential in science and may also require a different function of the mind. This leads to an alleged conflict between science and mysticism that does not actually exist. The idea behind the alleged incompatibility is that to practice science one must be committed to a "scientific worldview." In one sense this is true: to practice science, one must accept certain metaphysical claims—that an objective world exists, that scientists are detecting an objective order to nature rather than imposing our subjective order, that the past is like the present and that other regions of the universe are like our own (at least until we discover otherwise), and that the world outside our observations and experiments is like what is revealed in our observations and experiments. Quantum physics presents problems for the last point because of the nature of observing on the scale of the subatomic realm. Empiricists reject the idea that scientists are finding unobservable structures, but they do not reject the objectivity of the observed order.

However, there is no "scientific worldview" in the stronger sense—that only what scientists in principle can study can be real. This is the metaphysical position of naturalism. The epistemological correlate of this is scientism: science is the only means of knowledge about what is real, and only experiences that are relevant to scientific knowledge are cognitive. (See Sorrell 1994.) Polls show that many of the elite scientists in America are atheists, agnostics, or simply not interested in religion. Many of today's public voices of science are committed to naturalism or scientism or both, and many such as Richard Dawkins, Stephen Hawking, and Edward O. Wilson are vocal about their atheistic or agnostic beliefs. If one spends all of one's time looking only for natural causes, it is not surprising that one may end up looking at all of reality that way. Thus, consciously or unconsciously, many scientists end up embracing naturalism or scientism or both and do not even see that these are philosophical rather than scientific positions. But again, polls also show that many rank and file working natural scientists in America are in fact religious—the majority in some fields—being either theists or deists. (See Larson and Witham 1999 for polls of elite and rank and file scientists). While the percentage of elite research university scientists who are religious is significantly lower than the population as a whole, still a great many have a religious affiliation and are religiously active (Ecklund, Park, and Veliz 2008). That significant numbers of natural scientists are theists or deists makes it difficult for naturalists to claim the "scientific mind" requires naturalism. (It also makes it difficult for parallelists to rail against mainstream science as necessarily reductionist, materialistic, deterministic, or anything else that is incompatible with transcendental realities.)

The natural sciences are by definition "naturalistic" in the methodological sense: scientists are interested only in "natural" phenomena, i.e., events occurring within the experienced order of causes and effects and posits within space and time to explain these events, since only these can be replicated, and thus only theories involving natural phenomena can be tested. This makes all scientists naturalists in the methodological sense. But this does not make science is a form of naturalism in the stronger metaphysical sense that "metaphysical naturalists" intend. Methodological naturalists treat the universe as closed for the limited purpose of finding scientific laws and explanations, but they can remain neutral on whether in fact there is more to reality than what scientists can disclose—i.e., this method does not require that they must be *metaphysical naturalists* who reduce reality to only what science reveals. One can practice science without thinking that if something cannot be studied scientifically then it must not be real. Again, that so many scientists in America do accept transcendental realities is evidence of this. In short, we must accept that not all actual scientists adopt the alleged metaphysical "scientific worldview." Thus, the successes of science are not in any way evidence that there is not any more to reality than what scientists can in principle find.

Under a realistic interpretation of scientific theories, scientists do detect, however darkly, real structures causing the regularities in nature we observe—but this does not mean that scientists are committed to the view that those underlying mechanisms are *all* the causes at work in reality. Under antirealism, we know even less about what causes are at work in nature. (On the issue of realism, see Jones 2009: chap. 3.) Either way, there may be levels of realities in our natural world (including consciousness) that are not open to scientific study but are nonetheless real, or there may be realities at work in nature that are outside the scope of lawful conditionals of causes and effects and thus beyond scientific testing. Science *per se* cannot make any pronouncement one way or the other on whether such natural forces are real. Nor does science compel us to believe that the natural realm must not be dependent for its existence or its order on a further, transcendental reality.

In short, one can be a practicing scientist without claiming that science produces the final picture of all of reality or that the natural realm is closed off from transcendental realities. Science is metaphysically leaner than naturalists suppose—it is only about discerning the causal workings of nature. Scientists can readily admit that there is more to reality than what is studied or found by science and still be scientists. Indeed, they can even admit that there are in fact transcendental causes at work in nature—i.e., *miracles*—and not just the repeatable natural causes that they study. Miracles simply cannot be studied scientifically because the causes cannot be controlled and repeated.[8] (Thus, "naturalism" is technically is a misnomer: if a transcendental reality's actions were repeatable and thus testable, it would be a candidate for being a scientific explanation. But a personal being such as theists believe God to be cannot be forced into testable predictions and so cannot be a scientific explanatory posit.) And if the depth-mystical experience is simply a small miracle, it cannot be ruled out as cognitive simply because the "subjective" side cannot be studied scientifically.

The distinction between science *per se* and the philosophy of naturalism must be kept in mind when relating mysticism to science. Many thinkers see mysticism conflicting with science because of the faulty assumption that science is based on the metaphysics of naturalism. They give science a metaphysical dimension it does not have. But, again, the successes of science in explaining events do not compel us to accept naturalism. Rather, the metaphysics of naturalism and the epistemology of scientism are both based on science, not vice versa. Naturalism and scientism both present philosophical problems for mystical experiences and mystical belief-systems that science itself does not. But naturalism is merely one philosophical way of interpreting science's significance, one that adds the extra metaphysical claim that only what scientists can potentially study is real. Science can also be fitted into metaphysical frameworks that include transcendental realities. And since science can be practiced without a commitment to either naturalism or scientism, these philosophical positions do not present barriers to a positive relationship between science itself and mysticism.

If we reject naturalism and scientism, science is then seen as only one particular way of approaching the universe and in itself entailing no further metaphysical commitments. The distinction of science and philosophy also becomes clearer. Any decision to deny reality to what does not come through what in the final analysis is only a filter must be a philosophical decision. The scientists' way of approaching reality has proven extremely valuable to our knowledge of nature, but this does not mean that reality must be, or even can be, reduced to only what scientists find.

The Issue Survives

In sum, we can understand part of reality by means of science without concluding that this is all there is to reality. On this issue, science is neutral. This neutrality, in turn, leaves open the possibility that mystical cognitive claims are veridical but involve aspects of reality that scientists simply do not study. Thus, scientists can reject naturalism and scientism, embrace all of science, and still be open at least to the possibility that mystical experiences are cognitive. Obviously, to accept that mystical claims are in fact cognitive would require an additional, positive argument. So too, there may be excellent grounds to affirm metaphysical naturalism. But for that, an argument beyond merely accepting science would be required, and such an argument would a philosophical one. All that is being argued here is that accepting science itself does not require rejecting the very possibility that depth-mystical experiences are cognitive and involve a transcendental reality.

Thus, neither sociological observations about our society nor science *per se* rules out the possibility that mystical experiences may involve contact with a transcendental reality. And perhaps the transcendent is not as dead in intellectual circles as some naturalists in academia believe. Of course, that some physicists and other scientists are interested in mysticism is not grounds to accept any mystical claims to knowledge—their interest is not a scientific argument for the validity of these claims. But this is at least sufficient grounds, especially when combined with the fact that science is compatible with the denial of naturalism, to forge ahead with attempting to see how both scientific claims and also mystical claims to transcendental knowledge may be accommodated in our scheme of knowledge.

Notes

1. "Naturalism" in this sense is more completely called "philosophical" or "metaphysical" or "ontological" naturalism, not "*methodological naturalism*" as discussed below.

2. Some Christians and Jews today, trying to become more in keeping with the spirit of the age, have become "religious naturalists." (Their counterpart among contemporary Buddhists are those who are agnostic about a belief in rebirth and karma. See Batchelor 1997.) They argue that there are no transcendental realities that enter the natural world or the human psyche and that there is no life after death. Thus, there are no miracles. Some religious naturalists may be deists, who affirm a reality that created, ordered, and sustains the natural realm, but none are *theists* since there is no transcendental god who is actively involved with his creation out of concern for his creatures. Thus, there is no god who could answer prayers or otherwise be active in our lives. They must also disallow the possibility of an experience of any transcendental reality since such an experience would mean that the reality would appear in the natural realm. That is, there may be an absentee creator god who designed and created this realm, but there is no "living God" open to experience, mystical or otherwise. Rather, religious naturalists attempt to make a natural god that could fulfill the psychological and social needs of *Homo religiosus*. They take religious language that describes a transcendental reality and reinterpret it as being only about an attitude or orientation toward the natural world, or they translate terms traditionally referring to a transcendental reality into terms referring to natural phenomena (e.g., the fundamental forces of nature), or the deists among them accept a transcendental realm but treat it as a total mystery.

3. Leonard Angel argues that the phenomenology of the "universal self consciousness mysticism" (i.e., the depth-mystical experience) can be explained even assuming that the only causal factors involved are physical (2004: 20-26). Angel argues that strong evidence supports the principle of the physical completeness for all human psychological functioning, but whether this is only a metaphysical assumption based on experiences where possible nonnatural causes are not an issue (e.g., sense-perception) is still a question.

4. See Kripal 2002 for the interesting case of the Neo-Vedantin Vivekananda who was influenced by modernity, secularism, and individualism, and who attempted to forge a modern, socially-minded mysticism. Kripal contrasts Vivekananda here with his teacher, Ramakrishna, who adhered to a more traditional world-denying form of mystical Hinduism and attached little importance to reforming this world. And, as Kripal points out, Vivekananda returned to the more traditional mystical stance late in life.

5. Some theistic scientists advocate a "intelligent design" and want to change the nature of science to permit teleological causes and intermittent interventions by a designer. Whether this is "science" will not be discussed here. (See Jones forthcoming: chap. 8.)

6. Of course, postmodernists see any changes in standards as completely arbitrary, no matter what standards are adopted or how they are adopted. Realists think changes may be guided by reality. But whichever group is right, the point is that the standards may well change, and Bagger's position does not help determine if mystical claims are rational in any sense other than conforming to current standards.

7. A similar problem arises for scientism: how can the claim that all knowledge of reality is scientific be proved scientifically?

8. Contrary to popular opinion, science cannot in fact rule out miracles, i.e., a transcendental reality's intervention in the otherwise autonomous workings of the natural order. First, we can never know all the factors operating in any event—transcendental causes may

be part of events for all we know. No empirical examination of any past event can ever be 100% complete and rule out the possibility of transcendental action. Of course, a plausible scientific explanation does render believing in a miracle less warranted. Overall, we do not know if the universe is deterministic or if only natural forces are at work. Naturalists simply rule out miracles *a priori* because miracles allegedly conflict with a scientific view of reality. Second, science is about discerning recurring causal relations—whenever all the necessary conditions x come together, then event y will occur. Miracles do not contradict this since the natural conditions that scientists study for their conditionals would not be the total set of conditions present in an event involving a miracle—God's action would be part or all of the causal conditions. That is, miracles would fall outside possible scientific study. A miraculous event is not uncaused, but its cause is not controllable and thus is not repeatable by human beings, and therefore is simply not open to scientific study. The problem here is not that God is a transcendental reality, but that his acts are those of an *agent with free will*. His actions would fall outside of the purview of science because there is no way to establish a causal conditional to test—we do not know when, where, or how God would act, nor can we force him to act in way to test the consequences. And since a transcendental cause could not in principle be part of a repeatable causal conditional, it could not be part of a scientific law. However, science only gives the causal skeleton of nature, not a complete picture of everything that might be happening in nature. Science does presume a "law-bound universe" in the sense that effects follow lawfully from causes, but not in the sense that the universe is a closed and gapless chain of natural causes. Of course, since a transcendental cause would be involved, miracles would conflict with the metaphysics of naturalism; if scientists did detect any anomalous events, naturalists would simply chalk them up to chance. But scientists can reject this metaphysical position without giving up science since the miraculous acts do not conflict with causal lawfulness depicted in science. In addition, if a transcendental reality injects energy into nature to effect actions, a miracle would conflict with the law of the conservation of energy that scientists postulate. However, if this law is taken to preclude any such input from the transcendent (rather than as simply covering the interactions of purely natural objects, as the law was designed to deal with in the first place), then the law is merely a restatement in more scientific terms of part of the naturalism's idea of the closure of natural forces—no scientist has attempted to track whether the total energy of the universe is constant, and it is only an assumption that it must be. In sum, while the mystery of *how* miracles could occur may be unanswerable, miracles themselves are in fact compatible with science. The proper scientific attitude in such circumstances is to remain open to at least the theoretical possibility of miracles since science does not rule them out. (This only shows the compatibility of miracles and science—whether it is reasonable to conclude miracles *actually occur* is another matter.)

— 13 —
Scientific Explanations of Mystical Experiences

Even if we accept that a transcendental explanation of a depth-mystical experience is acceptable today, we still have to ask whether scientific explanations of mystical experiences in fact defeat mystical claims to knowledge. The issue is whether a mystic has a cognitive experience of a transcendental reality, or whether the claims connected to a depth-mystical experience can be explained away by natural explanations of the experience. The same can be asked of mindfulness: does a natural explanation of this state of consciousness undercut its cognitive claims? Arthur Deikman's explanation of mindfulness in terms of the "deautomatization" of the mental structures that organize, select, and interpret perceptual stimuli may well explain how a mindful state occurs (1980), but does this by itself explain away any possible cognitive claims to the unreality of a self and our connection to everything else in the universe? Deikman thinks the available scientific evidence tends to support the view that all mystical experiences are only an "internal perception" (ibid.: 259). So too, does James Austin's theory—that during meditation the circuits of the brain associated with self-awareness and those associated with monitoring the environment are simply deactivated (1998), leading to a sense of selfless connection to the world—render any mindfulness claims groundless? With such an explanation, can we conclude that such unawareness does not mean a self does not exist, any more than the fact that a mystical experience seems timeless means it does not last a certain amount of time, and thus that the state of mindfulness is not grounds to reject belief in a self?

But consider only the depth-mystical experience and mystics' claim to knowledge of a transcendental reality. Naturalists argue that these experiences can be exhaustively explained in terms of purely natural phenomena.[1] That is, no supernatural causes need to be included in the chain of causes in the explanation of any depth-mystical or other religious experience for the explanation to be complete. Any allegedly transcendental reality is not a causal factor in a depth-mystical experience, and mystics are simply confused by the emotional power of the experiences into thinking that a transcendental reality must be involved. Instead, naturalists attempt to identify the actual set of necessary natural processes at work in the experience that collectively are sufficient to product it. They then argue that, not only will the physiological bases permitting mystical experiences to occur have been identified, thereby *explaining* how the depth-mystical experiences can occur, but the experiences themselves will be *explained away*—i.e., any supernatural explanations will be rendered groundless, and thus any claim to have had a cognitive experience of a transcendental reality should be rejected.

If successful, naturalists would be able to duplicate "the experience of the transcendent" without any transcendental realities actually being involved. The natural explanation of sense-experience (e.g., seeing a tree) does not undercut the possible validity of the experience (i.e., that the tree exists), but naturalists distinguish this from natural explanations of mystical experiences. In the case of sense-experience there is no alternative explanation to a sense-object existing externally to our mind as part of the causal chain leading to the perception (unless one wants to endorse idealism or solipsism), while in the case of mystical experiences natural explanations (if successful) provide an alternative to transcendental realism, and a transcendental reality would thus not be necessary for these experiences to occur. Being able to produce mystical experiences from purely natural events also makes the occurrence of such experiences much more tightly predictable, further solidifying the claim that the experiences are nothing but natural events. Indeed, naturalists argue that the transcendent is not a possible cause at all: the experiences' complete explanation in terms of necessary and sufficient natural causes means that there is no place for a transcendental cause to act, and so it renders any causal role for the transcendent impossible even if a transcendental reality exists. Depth-mystical experiences would thus be successfully reduced to natural phenomena only, and their alleged cognitive claims explained away.

For naturalists, other experiences and nonexperiential factors prevail over mystical ones on the cognitive issue. Thus, even if naturalists had depth-mystical experiences themselves, they would then understandably dismiss their own mystical experiences (and, *mutatis mutandis*, out-of-body-experiences and near-death experiences) as merely hallucinations of a transcendental reality—no matter how vivid, strong, or "real" the experiences feel. Or the experience may cause them to rethink their position but not change their minds, as A. J. Ayer's near-death experience toward the end of his life caused him, not to change his belief in the lack of a life after death, but to weaken his "inflexible attitude" toward that belief.

Proponents of mysticism may argue that nothing even in principle could sway a convinced naturalist since for naturalists other experiences always outweigh the alleged cognitive significance of mystical experiences, and thus naturalists are being dogmatic in letting their metaphysics overrule experiences. That is, counter-evidence to their metaphysics is impossible, and so no argument against naturalism is in principle possible; this makes naturalism "metaphysical" in the worst sense. But naturalists can reply that in constructing their metaphysics they are in fact weighing all experiences, including mystical ones, and simply reaching other conclusions than do classical mystics. There is nothing dogmatic about this process, and everyone—including the mystics themselves—must weigh all types of experiences in constructing any metaphysics. That naturalists reach different conclusions about which experiences are cognitive than do mystics does not make them any more dogmatic than those mystics who dismiss everyday perceptions as illusory in the most fundamental sense.

Natural Explanations and Naturalistic Reductions

Natural explanations come in three varieties: scientific, sociocultural, and philosophical. (See Jones 2000: 271-97.) A scientific reduction would result in religious experiences being nothing but electrochemical activity in the brain or some other biological phenomenon.[2] Sociocultural reductionists find social or psychological mechanisms responsible for these experiences.[3] In a philosophical reduction, mystical experiences are shown not to add any cognitive content to the mystic's prior cultural beliefs; this will be discussed in the next chapter. Naturalists argue that natural explanations of religious experiences will always be substantively reductive: the only realities involved in the experiences are the experiencer and elements of the natural world, not anything supernatural. This means that, even if a transcendental reality does happen to exist, a depth-mystical experience reality is still not an experience of anything but natural phenomena. Thus, the alleged cognitive content of the depth-mystical experience—i.e., any transcendental beliefs based on it—will be radically discredited. In sum, naturalists deny the very possibility of depth-mystical experiences being a potential source of knowledge of transcendental realities. Thereby, the rationality of participants in a religious way of life centered around such experiences is called into question. In addition, even if no reduction is successful, a plausible natural explanation of mystical experiences nevertheless would neutralize these experiences as *evidence* of a transcendental reality or as *justification* of the truth or rationality of religious beliefs.

But before this conclusion can be reached, certain problems with naturalistic reductions must be countered. (See Jones 2000: 279-88.) As an example of the problems, consider only part of one point: whether neurological explanations and religious explanations of depth-mystical experiences are in fact compatible, i.e., that one can accept *both* a natural explanation *and* the validity of some mystics' claims about transcendental realities. Naturalists argue against such compatibility: if scientists can identify a set of natural conditions in the brain the activation of which causes a mystical experience, then obviously the transcendent cannot be a causal factor in the chain of events producing the experience, and so the experience is totally natural. Naturalists claim that by demonstrating that all features of the experience can be replicated by natural causes (e.g., by electrical stimulation of the brain), mystics cannot claim to have experienced a transcendental reality.

Advocates of mysticism, on the other hand, will contend that a transcendental reality is in fact a causal factor in these mystical experiences—e.g., theists will argue that God simply works through the natural apparatus of our brains to bring about a mystical experience. Thus, if there is a transcendental reality, an explanation of the depth-mystical experience in natural terms is still possible, and the explanation is not counter-evidence. Proponents of mystical claims to knowledge might argue that experiencing the transcendent is not a mini-miracle initiated by a transcendental reality, but rather that the mystic alone is active and is participating in a reality that is always already there (as the ground of the self or of the universe). The mind alone is active as in sense-experience and self-awareness; the transcendental source is not any more active in these experiences than in any other experience we have. No new energy or information is being injected into nature by a transcendental reality and only natural processes of the brain are involved. This would affirm the existence of a transcendental reality and that it is open to experience, but it would not violate the causal closure of nature any more than does self-knowledge. Thus, there would be a purely natural basis for the mind knowing the transcendent, but the experience would still be cognitive.

Thus, defenders of mysticism will argue that, even if scientists can duplicate every feature of a mystical experience by some natural triggers so that the natural experience is phenomenologically indistinguishable from an allegedly "genuine" mystical experience, the naturalistic reduction does not follow. (In Chapter 5, it was noted that believers challenge whether laboratory-produced experiences do in fact duplicate all the "subjective" features of a genuine mystical experience.) If experiences of the transcendent do occur, then obviously some mechanism in us permits them to occur, and all that scientists will have done is identify the neurological bases involved. All that scientists can do is identify the locus where a transcendental reality acts in the brain and then stimulate it artificially. Thus, no matter how complete the neurological explanation, all that scientists have done is to demonstrate how to stimulate the neurological mechanisms at work in the brain by means other than the impingement of the transcendent. This demonstration cannot in itself rule out the possibility that other causes—transcendental ones—may also produce the same physiological effects. Thus, a complete natural account cannot invalidate the claim of a genuine mystical experience of a transcendental reality or that depth-mystics might gain an insight into reality.

The pro-mysticism argument is that if during a depth-mystical experience our brain produces a certain chemical, then scientists may well be able to identify this chemical and to administer a drug that will substitute for its natural production in the brain during a genuine depth-mystical experience; this drug can then produce the same physiological effects when it is artificially introduced into the brain. But naturalists cannot conclude from this that during a mystical experience occurring outside of the lab a transcendental reality does not cause the brain to produce this chemical naturally—i.e., that a transcendental reality somehow uses the normal neurochemical channels of our physiology in producing the mystical experience. The transcendent would then be a cause working "behind" the chain of natural causes that scientists can detect—a "primary" cause, not a "secondary" one, as it were. Empirical findings would only mean that the chemical conditions that are necessary to set up the experience of the transcendent have been identified, not that nothing more is involved. There may also be a difference in the "subjective" side of the experience since the transcendent would be present in a "genuine" depth-mystical experience but may or may not be present in one stimulated artificially.

And the pro-mysticism argument is the stronger one here. Naturalists cannot, without more, conclude from the fact that some chemical is involved that the resulting experience must be a purely natural phenomenon and that no nonnatural factors can possibly be part of the set of causes. In fact, the drug, whether administered artificially or generated by the brain, may permit *genuine* experiences of a transcendental reality. Or the experience with or without artificial stimulation may in fact only be a source of a *delusion*—the chemical base alone will not determine this. Scientists will at most be able to demonstrate that a particular chemical is involved in the brain during a certain experience, but they cannot demonstrate that this is all there is to the experience or determine its cognitive import.

In sum, neurological demonstrations will at best only reveal a set of sufficient causes for the mystical experience to occur—they cannot eliminate the possibility of other sets of sufficient causes. No amount of artificial stimulation of mystical experiences can prove that the experience cannot be caused by another means and thus that it is a purely natural phenomenon. In sum, even if the natural causes duplicate every feature of a mystical experience exactly, scientists can never demonstrate scientifically that they have located its *necessary* causes, thereby eliminating the possibility of a transcendental reality as another *sufficient* cause. There is simply no way of demonstrating scientifically that another type of cause is not possible. It is the naturalists' metaphysics that requires that natural conditions are the only possible causes and thus that natural conditions in fact encompass all the necessary ones. But nothing in the actual scientific demonstrations requires this philosophical judgment. Thus, the science itself will always remain neutral on the philosophical issue of whether there are transcendental causes or not.

Can Scientific Studies Confirm or Refute Mysticism?

The last point leads naturally to the central philosophical issue: can scientific studies of meditation either confirm or refute the claims of a specific mystical tradition or at least the more general claim of the possibility of a mystical insight? Whether these experiences produce an *insight* into the nature of reality is an issue that scientists can simply ignore in their work. It is the *physiological states* of the body during mystical experiences that are of interest to scientists trying to understand how the brain works or trying to study the "secular" effects of meditation related to lessening stress and pain, increasing good health (e.g., enhancing the immune system) or general well-being, or to aiding concentration, not alleged insights into a transcendental reality or the beingness of this realm. Scientists *qua* scientists can ignore this issue since the purely physiological effects apparently occur regardless of the meditators' religious or philosophical beliefs or their religious affiliation. According to Herbert Benson, nothing about the beliefs of any tradition are relevant to the health effects of meditating—one can belong to any tradition or have no religious beliefs and the benefits remain the same (1975).

Nevertheless, do the scientific studies still have philosophical implications? Can the study of physiological states at least in principle bear on the truth of mystics' alleged insights? This issue has not received as much scholarly attention as the studies themselves. Typically, believers and scientists simply conclude without discussion that the studies obviously validate or invalidate religious beliefs, depending on their prior convictions. Materialists do not even see an issue here: if material bases to mystical experiences are identified, then those experiences are only brain events. On the other hand, those seeing parallels between science and mysticism enthusiastically conclude that scientists studying the physiology of meditators have validated age-old mystical claims—e.g., science has proven that mystical experiences come from the right hemisphere of the brain or has otherwise shown that these are genuine experiences and not fabrications.

However, it follows from what was just discussed that we cannot conclude either way. The science at best establishes the physiological base for the experience, and this is ultimately irrelevant to whether or not any claim is true. Science can only locate the site of neural activity; it cannot establish whether any genuine insights into the nature of reality accompany this activity. Perhaps, for example, mystical experiences are grounded in the right hemisphere of the brain functioning without contact with the left, but this does not determine if the alleged mystical insights are genuine or whether in fact the experiences are no more than the brain malfunctioning by the disconnection in this situation and thus are incapable of any true insight into reality.

More generally, how science could test the claim of an insight into transcendental realities is not at all clear since transcendent realities cannot be tested scientifically—such realities, if they exist, are not an object in the universe and thus cannot be presented for examination by others or even by oneself subjectively. It is certainly difficult to see how any possible scientific studies of consciousness could establish a metaphysical claim like Advaita's that consciousness constitutes all of reality and is in fact the only reality. Producing measurable physiological effects in Advaitin meditators does not confirm this claim—it is simply irrelevant to it. Nor is it clear how such studies could more generally determine one of the competing alternative interpretations of the cognitive significance of the depth-mystical experience as superior to others. Even proving that mystical experiences are "genuine neurological events" and not speculation or wishful thinking does not settle which interpretation of its significance is correct. Nor can research on the circuits of the brain that enable mystical experiences to occur tell us anything even in principle about transcendent realities, if that is indeed the cause, no matter how often research on the neural bases of religious experiences and spirituality is called "neurotheology." There is simply no way of bringing a transcendent reality (if it exists) into a lab to test alternative interpretations. Nor is such research "bridging the gap between mysticism and science" or "uniting religion and science"—the two endeavors still remain distinct, as noted in Chapter 5. Of course, scientists may step out of their role as scientists and, *qua* philosophers, devise a metaphysics based on Advaitic oneness or some other belief-system. But the point is that nothing in the science itself would require that interpretation. Establishing objective physiological changes is simply not the basis for affirming any meditator's religious claims.

But even though science is neutral to the competing religious interpretations of mystical experiences, can science at least rule out naturalism here? Or is it also neutral to the more basic epistemic claim that mystical experiences are potentially insights into reality at all? Can science determine that a transcendental cause must be at work, or that all the causes are strictly natural? Is there any way a complete neurological account could help establish that the experience is either a genuine experience of the transcendent or is a delusion? Or is science also neutral between all transcendental options and naturalism? Advocates of mysticism believe the depth-mystical experience "feels so real"—indeed, even more in touch with what is fundamentally real than experiences in ordinary consciousness—that it must be rooted in a transcendental reality and thus is not merely the subjective product of our brains. This is especially so since the experience still seems cognitive to mystics when they return to our baseline state of consciousness (Newberg and Lee 2005: 485). It does not have the feel of a hallucination, which is seen to be delusory after the experiencer returns to a normal state of consciousness; rather, the memory of mystical experiences has the same sense of reality as memories of ordinary "real" events (Newberg, d'Aquili, and Rause 2002: 112). To advocates of mysticism, that scientists can in principle identify the neurological correlates no more explains away the insights than a neurological explanation of perception explains away claims based on sense-experiences. In fact, neurophysiology arguably actually helps the mystics' case by showing that the experiences are grounded in the normal mechanisms of a healthy brain and are not the product of speculation or a faulty brain—why else would our brain have the capacity to achieve these experiences unless they were cognitive? Meditative techniques simply rewire the brain to permit certain insights that are unrelated to the survival functions of the brain to occur more easily.[4]

Critics of claims of mystical insights, however, are not impressed: mystical experiences only establish that mystical experiences occur—they do not determine what is the best explanation of them. Critics see no reason to believe that there are any insights into reality involved, no matter how powerful the experiences may feel or what there emotional impact is. They have what they take to be a plausible alternative: the depth-mystical experience is the result of a brain disorder, i.e., the malfunctioning of a brain system that has some legitimate function (e.g., Saver and Rubin 1997). Even if no disorder is involved, the depth-mystical experience at most is simply the brain spinning its wheels in a type of feedback effect when it has no mental content to work on. That is, our brain has evolved under the pressure of the natural environment only to produce an intentional consciousness to deal with problems of survival; thus, when the mind is "on" but has no content to work with, it malfunctions badly, producing the delusory sense of mystical oneness, timelessness, infinite space, and so forth. The area of the brain connected to the sense of a distinction between oneself and the rest of the world (the junction of the temporal and parietal lobes) receives less input and thus is less active during mystical experiences; this also affects our temporal and spatial orientation. In addition, the area connected to tagging events as significant (the limbic system in the temporal lobes) is more active. Thus, it is only natural that there is no sense of a boundary between the self and the world and also a sense of great importance to the experience. The sense of ineffability results simply from the temporary dominance of the brain's non-linguistic right hemisphere over the left when the two hemispheres are not operating properly in tandem. Thus, at best, what is experienced is our own consciousness. But consciousness is only the product of the brain, and hence the depth-mystical experience is not an experience of a transcendental reality. The "pure consciousness" event of the depth-mystical experience is not even an insight into the nature of consciousness since the brain is malfunctioning during this experience. Of course, the experience may well have a powerful impact on experiencers, even causing a transformation of their personalities, but this is no reason to believe that any transcendental realities are involved. Mystical selflessness could end a sense of self-centeredness and self-importance and lead to a sense of a selfless connection to the rest of the universe, but there is no need to invoke any transcendental reality to explain this. Mundane brain activity explains it all.[5]

Thus, according to critics, mystical experiences present no reason to accept any reality to consciousness apart from the material base that produces it. If scientists one day do exactly replicate everything about the experience that supposedly requires the transcendent, then the obvious conclusion for them is that the experience is only a product of natural factors—if we can replicate something by natural means that is presented as being caused by God, why would we now think it has a divine origin? Mystical experiences may reveal an innate human mental capacity and may be the same across cultures and eras, but this is only because our brains are basically all the same, at least with regard to these experiences. And the fact that the experience is open to such diverse interpretations by the mystics themselves shows that no alleged transcendental reality is involved that could actually shape the content of the experience—mystics simply are unaware that they are making up the cognitive claims out of a mixture of cultural beliefs and unusual but purely natural brain events. Thus, these experiences and the claims based on them are not merely explained but explained away.

So, does the scientific study of meditators itself then provide a stronger empirical case for either side on this philosophical dispute? No. Granted, if it turns out that people who have mystical experiences *all* have brain lesions or otherwise have *defective or damaged brains* or suffer from other *pathologies*, then the naturalistic approach becomes a plausible argument that no transcendental reality is involved, even if no one particular natural explanation has yet gained a consensus.

It is hard to argue that a physically damaged brain can gain a new insight into reality that a healthy brain misses—that God, as it were, only discloses himself to people with defective brains. Rather, if only something malfunctioning in the brain produces these experiences, we should conclude that they are most likely delusional. (No less an authority than William James argued that, for all we know, an abnormal brain state is in fact needed for some insights—a fevered state "might be a more favorable temperature for truths to germinate and sprout in" [1958: 30]—but he may well have accepted limits in this regard.) If, however, these experiences are common among people who are free of pathological conditions and have perfectly healthy brains, this argument fails. And there is no evidence that mystical experiences only occur in people with physiological damage. Indeed, there is empirical evidence that these experiences are not uncommon and not restricted to pathological persons (Hood 1997). And even if it turns out that mystical experiences are associated with parts of the brain that normally produce only hallucinations, advocates of mysticism can turn this situation around and argue that the *hallucinations* are the product of the *malfunctioning* of brain mechanisms that enable *veridical mystical experiences* to occur when functioning properly. For example, some psychologists argue that dissociative states of schizophrenia and some psychoses result from the same implosions of the transcendent that occur in mystical experiences but that the patients are not equipped to handle them; mystics, on the other hand, have a belief-framework and the training or psychological preparation needed to handle them—e.g., mystical selflessness apparently is a more coherent mental state, and mystics do not conclude that the experiencer alone is God. (See the discussion in Brett 2002. But that the depth-mystical experience is *devoid of dualistic content* distinguishes it from these states.[6])

Critics of mysticism may also argue that physiological explanations of mystical experiences counter the claim to insight in a way that physiological explanations of sense-experiences do not: in the latter case, we can corroborate claims about an external source (sense-objects), and so the physiology of perception is irrelevant; but in the former case, there is no object to present to others and so how the experiences arise becomes important. But the critics' argument here is not very strong. The situations are not parallel in one critical regard: transcendent realities cannot be presented for inspection, and in such circumstances we cannot expect the possibility of a third-person corroboration; thus, we cannot impose standards where there can be observations by others on this situation; thus, third-person corroboration is not required, and so its absence is not counter-evidence. Advocates of mysticism can also add that since the transcendent grounds all of reality, there may not be any physical receptors to carry a sensory signal into the brain or anything else special to find. No special "God receptors" are necessary since the transcendent is also the ground of the self and so is already present in the brain—it is not a matter of any sort of signal being sent from a transcendental realm into the natural realm or any sort of interaction with an outside source as with sense-experience; instead, the reality can act directly upon the relevant parts of the brain in another manner. That is, a transcendental reality may simply use the normal cognitive apparatus of the brain: even if the brain is only a natural product that evolved to help in our survival, there still may be a configuration of the brain's parts that is also able to function as a receptor of a transcendental reality, or indeed for all we currently know of the brain there may be a dedicated circuit in the brain that has evolved for the purpose of enabling religious experiences.

Thus, transcendental realities may in fact be among the causal roots of these experiences. At present, not only can this possibility not be ruled out, it is not unreasonable to accept it (at least as far as the scientific considerations go). And naturalists must admit that scientists are currently split over the locus of relevant brain activity and the mechanisms involved in different mystical experiences. Given our present state of knowledge of the brain, all that naturalists have is a commitment based on metaphysics that a naturalistic explanation of these experiences in terms of the brain will someday be forthcoming and will suffice, thereby explaining away mystics' cognitive claims. On the other side, advocates of mysticism have no way of testing their claim. They will need to provide a defense of the cognitivity of the depth-mystical experience that will require an appeal to factors other than the science or the experience itself—a philosophical "best available explanation" argument. Thus, their position will remain as metaphysical as the naturalists' commitment. In addition, members of each particular religious tradition will then also have to advance a defense of their particular interpretation of what is experienced in mystical experiences.

Science Versus the Philosophical Assessments of Mystical Claims

Also note that even if a complete physiological account of the experiences is eventually given, naturalists once again are confronted with the problem that advocates of mysticism can readily agree that there must be some neurophysiological base for these experiences to occur—again, they are human experiences. And, as discussed above, this leads to a problem for naturalists: being able to duplicate the experiences in the lab does not foreclose the possibility that the experiences could be caused alternatively by a transcendental reality. If, for example, certain drugs stimulating an area of the brain can cause the depth-mystical experience, how do we know that awareness of a transcendental reality does not also stimulate the same area during a traditional mystical experience? How do we know that the chemical reaction of the drugs in the brain does not simply reproduce the same chemical reactions mystics have when they are aware of a transcendental reality? That is, does a genuine awareness of a transcendental reality merely produce the same necessary chemical reactions in the brain? Ingesting the drugs may be a sufficient cause, but how could the science itself show that another sufficient cause is not possible? Moreover, stimulating certain parts of the brain may be necessary, but this does not mean that natural events are all that is involved—perhaps by their actions on the brain, the drugs merely permit the transcendent to enter the subject's consciousness. Or perhaps a stimulation prepares the brain, but something more is still needed from the experiencer for a genuine mystical experience to occur.

In this way, being able to produce a mystical experience by stimulating an area of the brain artificially does not foreclose the possibility that a transcendental reality is an alternative cause—at most, this merely identifies the location where the transcendent may also work in veridical experiences of the transcendent. Thus, the possibility of an awareness of the transcendent cannot be ruled out even if a neurophysiological account identified all the circuits involved.[7] Only if the natural explanations by themselves could in principle rule out the very possibility of a transcendental reality being a factor in a mystical experience could natural explanations definitely be grounds for a naturalistic reduction of the experience, and there does not appear to be any way that any natural explanation could accomplish this. In short, the science alone cannot, even in principle, refute the mystical claim to cognitivity. Such a reduction will have to be a philosophical move related to the metaphysics of naturalism and the best available explanation.

Thus, our ability to duplicate a mystical experience by external means (assuming scientists are in fact duplicating all aspects of the training-induced and spontaneous experiences) simply does not touch the broader philosophical question of whether the experience is still an insight. (Also see Jones 2000: 273-88.) Even if neuroscience can be taken as verifying that mystical experiences occur, it does not either validate or invalidate any mystical knowledge-claims related to selflessness.[8] Merely establishing the nexus of the event and the mechanisms involved is irrelevant to the issue of whether the stimulated area of the brain *permits* a depth-mystical experience of a transcendental reality to occur or whether the experience is no more than an internal *function of* that mundane brain activity. We are left with a metaphysical question: does our brain naturally cause us to create these experiences (e.g., somehow to aid in our survival or because of malfunctioning), or did a transcendental reality create our brain to permit genuine experiences of the transcendent? To oversimplify: if the brain is not malfunctioning, we may be hard-wired for religious experiences, but did God wire us to experience the transcendent, or did evolution wire us just to think so because it somehow aids in our survival?[9]

Some scientists who study meditators agree that their research cannot answer such questions and thus cannot prove or disprove the existence of a transcendental reality (e.g., Ramachandran and Blakeslee 1998: 185; Newberg, d'Aquili, and Rause 2002: 143, 149-51, 178-79; Newberg and Waldman 2009: 4-5). It is not that they consider the broad issue of whether a transcendental reality exists to be a philosophical one that cannot be settled by science.[10] Rather, it is something more specific: the neuroscientific study of religious experiences cannot settle whether these experiences are veridical or not, let alone the validity of any specific religious interpretation. Scientists studying the same data or even colleagues working together may draw diametrically opposed conclusions on the epistemic and metaphysical implications of the data (as has also happened with near-death experiences). Such conclusions are simply not part of the science of the mechanisms, nor are they determined by the science. In sum, the reality of the transcendent cannot be *proved or disproved* one way or the other by studying what happens to people's brains when they have mystical experiences, as many scientists see (e.g., Beauregard and O'Leary 2007: ix, 38, 276). Advocates of mysticism may lower the standard and argue that demonstrating that specific brain states are associated with mystical experiences would show that at least it is *reasonable to believe* that mystics are aware of a transcendental power. But the demonstration does not show either that such experiences are nothing but the result of brain states or that such a power exists. At a minimum, naturalists are just as reasonable in their denial.

One basic problem is a conflict of metaphysics. Mario Beauregard rightly points out that for a convinced materialist who sees the mind as simply the workings of the brain and who is determined to deny the existence of God, it is unlikely that anything can constitute a proof of the existence of a spiritual world (2007: 289). However, those who start out already assuming the existence of God have the same issue: what would convince them that there is no transcendental reality? So too, mystical experiences may be quite common (ibid.: 290-91), but this does not mean that a transcendental reality is involved—a demonstrated commonality would bear on the question of whether mystical consciousness is a more normal mental state than materialists typically accept, but not on the question of their proper explanation. In turn, this means that the frequency of such experiences is irrelevant to the philosophical question of whether there is some naturalistic explanation that explains away mystical claims to insight.[11] In addition, there are still the conflicting interpretations of mystical experiences in the different religious traditions to contend with. Thus, to those so inclined, these physiological studies may reenforce the reality of the mystical experience and support a broad "mystical spirituality," but they must bypass the doctrines of any particular religious tradition and theism in general. And they will not convince the nonreligious: naturalists offer a plausible scenario, as discussed above.[12]

In the end, the situation here appears to be a case of conflicting metaphysical systems offering different interpretations of the significance of the empirical data. Mystical experiences *per se* and their scientific study *per se* cannot resolve those conflicts. Thus, unless there is a finding of pervasive pathology in mystics, science, regardless of any findings, does not remove the basic philosophical mystery surrounding mystical experiences, even in principle. Accounts of the brain wiring itself, no matter how complete, will remain neutral on this matter.

Applying Occam's Razor

The compatibility of neurological explanations and the possibility of depth-mystical insights means that there is no forced either/or choice between neurological events and authentic encounters with transcendental realities—experiences may in fact be both. Naturalists might concede this point and admit that science is neutral in this strong sense. But they would then turn to philosophical grounds and counter that under Occam's Razor it is improper to invoke a transcendental reality when an ontologically simpler explanation in terms of natural factors alone does the same job.[13] If we can duplicate all aspects of a mystical experience by drugs or other natural means, why should we think that a transcendental reality is ever involved? In addition, the naturalists' position also brings coherence to our picture of the mind: no special mental function for these experiences is needed—mystical experiences are explainable in terms of the same ordinary mental capacities that explain all our other experiences, even if naturalists have to argue that the brain is malfunctioning during these experiences. To cite a previous example: when neural input is cut off to the part of the brain responsible for the sense of a self and our separation from the rest of what we experience, then of course we will feel more connected to the rest of the world; but not being aware of our separation does not change the fact that we are distinct entities. This, they argue, at least puts the burden of proof on the religious to show that transcendental explanations are needed when plausible natural explanations either already exist or at least the inklings of them are being established and it is only a question of when, not if, a complete natural explanation will be forthcoming. Thus, they argue that even if the scientific accounts do not absolutely rule out a transcendent cause as *impossible*, they do at least render such causes *more unlikely* since ordinary natural factors can accomplish precisely the same thing, and thus there is no reason to invoke a transcendental reality. Natural explanations will still remain the best available explanation.

And naturalism does seem to have the initial advantage on this point. Surely a laboratory duplication of *all* of a mystical experience through natural means (if in fact this is possible) would at least count *prima facie* against the idea that some experiences have a non-natural, transcendental cause. In addition, the naturalists' monism is ontologically simpler than religious dualisms of this world and transcendental realities, and, everything else being equal, we do believe that the universe is more likely set up with a simpler ontology. (It is interesting to note that William of Occam originally justified parsimony on *religious* grounds: it would be vain for God to use a complex way of constructing things when a simpler one would suffice.) In naturalism, no new entities or processes are involved. The religious, on the other hand, introduce an entirely new order of reality, and with it a new mystery that the religious probably never will be able to solve: how the transcendent could act in nature. Naturalists have no corresponding mystery.

But the religious will counter that Occam's Razor applies only when everything else is *equal*, and everything else is *not equal* here—reality in fact is more than merely the natural realm, and mystical experiences do involve the transcendent as a cause, and so reference to the transcendent is still needed for a complete understanding of mystical experiences. We make exceptions to Occam's Razor when we think we have reasons to believe that it does not apply. Most obviously, we think sense-experience requires reference to sense-objects to be complete, even though idealism and solipsism are ontologically simpler. The religious will argue that a similar exception is needed here: explanations of the neurological mechanisms of experiencers undergoing mystical experiences do not cover all that is actually involved in the experience, and the naturalists' economy is no more warranted here than solipsism is to be favored simply because of Occam's Razor. To naturalists, this is precisely the type of situation where Occam's Razor should be invoked, but to the religious any argument in favor of a naturalistic reduction on these grounds merely reintroduces the basic metaphysical dispute. The naturalists' metaphysics does not account for why the natural universe is here; to theists, the universe is a creation, and the explanation for why it is here is pertinent to explaining everything, especially exotic things like mystical experiences. In other words, without an explanation for why there is a universe at all, naturalists are not in a position to rule on whether a transcendental reality is involved or not.

In addition, everyone agrees that it is not a violation of Occam's Razor where a more complex phenomenon requires a more complicated explanation. And the religious will argue that the depth-mystical experience is indeed a unique mental event, and so it obviously requires its own explanation—to treat it as any other experience would distort it. Thus, they argue, asking for a unique explanation of this experience is not a strategy designed simply to protect certain religious beliefs, but something that reflects what needs explaining. The religious argue that naturalists consider their explanations satisfactory only because these explanations account for all the aspects that naturalists think on metaphysical grounds are actually involved. Naturalists want to domesticate the depth-mystical experience and make it like every other experience when in fact it is a unique mental function and thus requires its own explanation. Naturalists consider the fact that they can predict on physiological or sociocultural grounds when a mystical experience is likely to occur to be the end of the matter—it shows that only natural factors are at work—but the religious consider that fact to be simply irrelevant to the issue. The religious may also argue that the lack of predictive power in religious explanations need not count against their possible validity. After all, not even all scientific explanations are predictive. The key to any explanation is that it makes us believe that we understand why what occurred did occur. That is, a successful explanation "makes sense" of the occurrence to us. The transcendent is an explanation in that way, even though the fact that the transcendent cannot be empirically tested forecloses it as a possible scientific explanatory posit.

Since naturalists think in terms of scientific explanations only, there will be a permanent dispute between the religious and naturalists here. Scientists triggering a mystical reaction by artificially stimulating parts of the brain may explain all that naturalists want to explain about a mystical experience, but it does not mean that it was actually explained everything about a genuine mystical experience. Thus, the religious accuse naturalists of engaging in a circularity in invoking Occam's Razor here. At a minimum, the principle of parsimony should be taken as favoring naturalism only if we have other grounds to favor naturalism. Standing alone, the principle is merely located at the center of contention.

The Principle of Credulity

Some Christian philosophers and theologians today also invoke "the principle of credulity" under which we should accept the *prima facie* claims of experiencers until it can be shown that the experiences are based on some unreliable mechanism. The idea goes back to Thomas Reid's common sense retort to David Hume's skepticism: our beliefs about the existence of the external world, the past, and other minds are not the product of rational arguments or any inferences; rather, we simply have innate capacities that generate such beliefs; when these capacities are operating properly and under the appropriate circumstances, it is rational for us to accept the beliefs they produce. The skeptics' unanswerable demands for certainty can simply be ignored. Thus, these thinkers reverse Cartesian doubt and argue that we should believe experiential claims unless we have good reason not to. They argue that this principle shifts the burden of proof to the naturalists to show that all mystical experiences are somehow pathological and not reliable cognitive experiences (Franks Davis 1989: 101), not merely to show that natural mechanisms are at work enabling the experiences to occur. And apparently the depth-mystical experience does occur in physically and psychologically healthy persons without damaging their well-being (Hood 1997; Byrd, Lear, and Schwenka 2000). But naturalists think that these purely natural experiences mislead experiencers into thinking they have experienced something transcendental shows ipso facto that the experiences' mechanisms are obviously unreliable in these circumstances. Thus, they see this principle as a "principle of gullibility" unless mystical claims can be justified as veridical on other grounds. Thus, they contend that the burden is not shifted to naturalists at all.

However, as discussed, we cannot determine on neurological grounds alone whether a depth-mystical experience is an authentic experience of a transcendental reality or whether experiencers merely mistakenly take it to be so. What will constitute an adequate explanation is decided for both sides prior to constructing an explanation. In short, each argument will be construed within one's metaphysical position, and the issue of which position is correct will become one of adjudicating between competing metaphysics. Naturalists, of course, will argue that there are in fact other grounds to reject all transcendental explanations offered by the religious—in particular, the problem of natural suffering, the atrocities committed in the name of God by the religious, and the conflicting belief-claims of different religious traditions. The religious will make counter-arguments. But the point of importance here is that the scientific study of people undergoing mystical experiences will not contribute one way or the other to the argument.

Natural Explanations and the Question of Evidence

Discussions of whether mystical experiences are an insight into the nature of reality degenerate quickly into a war of metaphysics—first religious versus naturalistic metaphysics, and then among the doctrines of the different religious traditions. Against the naturalists, classical mystics will insist that the depth-mystical experience is a direct experience of a reality in a way that no experience of anything in the natural realm is, but they then disagree among themselves about the nature of what is experienced.

But, naturalists will ask, why should we accept a transcendental cause to the depth-mystical experience when today we reject other forms of divine intervention into the natural order, i.e., miracles? Perhaps the sense of "the presence of God" in a numinous experience is only the left hemisphere of the brain becoming aware of the right hemisphere's activity but mistakenly thinking it is a distinct, conscious being separate from oneself.[14] Certainly, the naturalists' contention that the depth-mystical experience is nothing but mental gears spinning without engaging mental content is plausible: the brain evolved to help us survive in the natural world, and when we succeed in removing all sensory and other content from the mind while remaining awake, the brain will simply malfunction badly; at best, it is simply consciousness aware of consciousness and not anything more profound. Alternatively, naturalists may see the experiences as self-induced delusions that seem so powerful to the experiencers that they cannot help but consider them to be insights: if we concentrate hard enough and long enough on nothing but the mental image of a dancing purple gorilla in the corner of the room where there is none, our mind will eventually become stressed out enough and *see* a purple gorilla dancing in the corner—and, according to naturalists, the same may be happening when mystics meditate for years with some mystical goal in mind.

Perhaps naturalists can advance plausible natural explanations for each element of both types of mystical experiences. However, from what has been discussed so far, we can see that scientific accounts cannot be used by themselves as evidence against mystical claims. EEG examinations of scientists doing research are irrelevant to their observations, let alone to the truth or falsity of their theories, and the same holds for meditators. The truth or falsity of a claim is simply independent of accounts of the mechanics involved in forming the claim (at least if the brain cannot be shown to be malfunctioning). Truth and falsity turn on other considerations. We must reject any broader naturalist version of the genetic fallacy: a scientific or sociocultural account of an experience or the formation of a belief is, without more, no reason to reject the beliefs involved. As discussed, the naturalists' proposed reduction is not a scientific argument but an extra-scientific move. Their conclusion that depth-mystical experiences are purely natural and thus that the transcendent, even if it exists, is not a cause in them is a metaphysical position and must be defended as such. The reduction follows only if the argument contains naturalistic metaphysics as a premise. Naturalists cannot merely cite the scientific studies of meditators for this belief without arguing in a very tight circle. The defense of their position, and their underlying commitment to science, will have to rest on considerations that are philosophical in nature.

But natural explanations do render mystical explanations *less probable* in the sense that at present an apparently equally plausible alternative explanation of the occurrence of mystical experiences is now in principle available—i.e., traditional transcendental explanations of these experiences are no longer the only candidates, but now must contend with a plausible competitor. This in itself is not evidence *against* religious explanations of mystical experiences. However, this does neutralize mystical experiences as uncontested evidence of contact with the transcendent. Some mystical experiences may be veridical experiences of a transcendental reality, but if scientists can duplicate all the phenomenological features of the experience by means of drugs or other artificial stimulation, how can we know? We are left, not with proof that the religious explanations are wrong or proof that a reductive explanation is right but in a more uncertain situation.

Thus, the most direct damage that scientific explanations cause is to the mystical experience's potential value as *evidence* in a philosophical argument in favor of the transcendent. The religious can reply that just because mystical experiences are not unambiguous evidence, it does not follow that they may not be genuine encounters with a transcendental reality, and thus they still can be used in a broader argument about the best available explanation. And the religious would point out objections to the plausibility of natural explanations, thus raising the issue of whether today there is an "equally plausible" reductive alternative to religious explanations. They will argue that at most natural explanations mean that mystical experiences cannot be used to ground a simple deductive proof, not that mystical experiences cannot be treated as an experience of a transcendental reality as part of an argument about the best explanation of mystical phenomena.

The dispute can be taken one step further. Mystical experiences and scientific explanations are not evidence except in the context of a total explanation, and therefore we should look at other elements of the arguments. We have to see how the depth-mystical experience figures in the arguments in conjunction with the other elements. The plausibility of the entire argument becomes important. Only if one side can show the other's overall argument to be implausible, or at least less plausible, will it win. However, neither side appears markedly more plausible by any criterion that is not biased in favor of that side already. In such circumstances, both sides appear at least plausible, and neither has an upper hand in commanding our assent. Thus, in today's religious epistemology, holding either position would be deemed rational.

This appears to be the end of the argument. There is no obvious way to resolve the dispute. For example, if our ordinary consciousness has evolved for our survival, how can a state of consciousness empty of all differentiable content possibly permit a cognitive insight into reality? How can it be anything other than the result of the brain malfunctioning, or at best a useless spandrel, an evolutionary by-product of some useful adaptation of the natural brain? But on the other hand, how could it not be cognitive when we have also evolved a capacity for it? Even if it is not a product of some feature useful for survival, this in itself does not mean it cannot be cognitive—it must still be shown to be the result of some malfunction. Ordinary consciousness evolved for our survival and thriving, yet we are able to learn at least something about the scientific workings of nature underlying what we actually see even though this is not necessary for our survival. Advocates of mysticism could also cite *mathematics* here: it is something that is not related to evolution or our survival, and yet we still have the mental capacity to come up with ideas that seem to reflect the structures of the universe.[15] So too, the capacity to have mystical experiences also arose. So how, without the support of a philosophical argument, can we give ordinary consciousness priority in determining all matters of what is ultimately real? Evolutionary psychologists might give a plausible explanation for how religion functioned in the past to help with our survival, but the religious will still argue that such explanations do not explain why we have the physiological capacity for mystical experiences to begin with. Or consider aspects of the mystical experience other than the alleged insights. For example, the bliss or joy of mystical experiences: does this mean that mystics are connected to a fundamental reality, or are mystics simply "blissed out" when the brain is not functioning properly because of the lack of differentiated content? Any scientific account of the brain events occurring during this sense of bliss will not help answer this question. So too, for the depth-mystical experience in general: the question of the alleged cognitive claims remains distinct and intact.

In the end, advocates of mysticism will appeal to the principle of credulity until depth-mystical experiences have actually been demonstrated to be the result of the brain malfunctioning or a pathological state, while naturalists will argue that, all things considered, naturalism is the best explanation. In addition, if we could get beyond the basic hurdle of naturalism versus transcendental metaphysics, there is still the second level—that mystical experiences cannot offer a justification for any particular mystical doctrine since competing alternatives to each claim advanced by one mystic are offered by other, apparently equally qualified, mystics. Mystics will naturally see their experiences as supporting their own tradition's doctrines, but the verdict must be that the competing claims that mystics have advanced about the nature of what is experienced cannot be resolved by the experience itself and that no neutral criteria to resolve the disputes are apparent. So too, attempts to argue what is the "best overall religious explanation" will not be resolvable since the various parties will dispute what the proper metaphysical considerations are. Of course, naturalists see the confusion of voices over incompatible truth-claims as evidence that mystical experiences do not convey any true knowledge at all. How could the depth-mystical experience be a source of any knowledge if conflicts of claims have persisted unresolved for millennia? To naturalists, this indicates that obviously doctrinal mystical claims must come from other sources.

Naturalists have a point here. Even if we accept that what mystics experience does give them the insight that there is more to reality than meets the naturalistic eye, their conflicting truth-claims does indicate that they do not know the *basic nature* of what is experienced any more than do nonmystics. Depth-mystics may be in a privileged position on the issue of whether there are any "pure conscious events," but whether the depth-mystical experience is noetic is another matter, and, as argued in Chapter 15, mystics are not privileged as to whether their experiences offer genuine insights into the nature of reality. They are aware of something nonmystics are not—thus, they *know* something we do not in that sense. But the claims about its specific nature are in the same class as all claims about reality: any truth-claims about the nature of what is real, even those resulting from these experiences, are not given by an experience itself. Issues of true-claims here encompass more than any one type of experience, and the resulting disputes remain a philosophical matter for discussion outside the depth-mystical experience.

The Neutrality of Science

So, is the mystical experience a purely natural phenomenon, or have scientists merely identified the conditions that make a person receptive to the infusion of the transcendent? The bottom line is that science cannot answer this. The brain during a depth-mystical experience may be malfunctioning, abusing some legitimate functions, or using a natural capacity to experience a transcendental reality. There is a gap that science cannot close between the experience and the epistemic judgment of its significance. Identifying the mechanics of how an experience occurs is one thing, and the judgment of whether an alleged insight is veridical is another. The former question is scientific, and the latter is a philosophical one concerning which science will remain neutral except in circumstances where the brain is damaged.

Most scientists and academics reviewing neuroscientific studies of religious experiences dismiss visions, arguing that they have been successfully reduced as subjective delusions or merely as interpretations of ordinary experiences. At most, there is a vague sense of presence that is structured by experiencers according to their beliefs. However, many scientists remain open on the issue of mystical insight, and there does not appear to be a way to resolve the dispute on scientific grounds. We live in what John Hick calls a "religiously ambiguous" universe (1989: 226), and this situation is likely to last. We are left with two alternative groups of metaphysical systems—religious and naturalistic—neither of which is more compelling at present and probably for the future as well. Which option one chooses concerning what natural explanations actually accomplish will depend on one's prior commitment to naturalistic or religious metaphysics, and thus will depend on other arguments and ultimately on one's intuitions of what in the final analysis is in fact real. But the conclusion for the issue at hand is only this: our choice regarding what natural explanations can, at least in principle, accomplish will turn on metaphysical considerations—the scientific explanations themselves will not determine this choice.

Notes

1. Naturalists also claim that religious experiences other than mystical ones can be explained away as self-induced delusions. To give a example: they can point to the "laughing rapture" occurring in some Christian Pentecostal circles in North America as an example of how social and psychological mechanisms can easily explain away a religious experience. That is, if we put people in a setting where it is conducive to do what others are doing and one person starts to laugh, others will join in and eventually most will be laughing. The actual religious beliefs of the participants are irrelevant to this purely psychological response. Thus, the experiences are psychologically real and the experiencers feel they are not acting voluntarily but are being acted upon, but there is no reason to think the "Holy Spirit" is descending upon the Pentecostals or that any other transcendental factor is involved in this "rapture," even though the participants believe otherwise. Similarly, "speaking in tongues" and any other phenomenon in such ceremonies are, to naturalists, equally the product of purely natural factors. But how far one can extend this approach from what is arguably a worse case scenario to all other religious phenomena is more debatable.

2. The phrase "naturalistic explanation" can have two quite different meanings: the scientific account (a "*natural explanation*") or one possible philosophical conclusion (a "*naturalistic reduction*" discrediting the mystics' claims to insight). The point here is that the former does not logically entail the latter.

3. Sociocultural explanations note that people with certain psychological dispositions are more inclined than most people to have mystical experiences, or that members of certain social groups are more likely to have these experiences, or that some types of experiences (e.g., a child feeling he or she was previously an adult and is now reborn) come mostly from cultures that traditionally accept certain ideas. (See Fales 1996a, 1996b, and 2001 for an example.) These explanations are not as exact in their predictions as physiological explanations. Nor are they as strong. Whether religious beliefs have a positive or negative value for a group's survival does not bear on the question of whether a transcendental reality exists or not—we would have the same beliefs whether the alleged reality is real or not. Nor does the social origins of religious beliefs and practices in general explain why we have a *physiology* enabling *mystical experiences* to occur in the first place. That mystics typically adopt or adapt a religious explanatory scheme from their culture to understand what they experienced does not change this. Any evolutionary or otherwise natural explanations of *religious faith* are not explanations of why we have the capacity to have mystical experiences at all; however, they may be relevant for the matter of why the religious give transcendental explanations of mystical experiences. Nor does noting that, for example, certain groups are more likely to have members who have mystical experiences impress many people as the final explanation of the experiences any more than the fact that some social groups may be more likely to produce scientists undercuts the validity of science. Sociocultural reductionists believe that their explanations render supernatural explanations redundant and thus dismissible as superfluous. But while these social and psychological conditions may have a bearing on whether someone is inclined *to have a mystical experience*, we can still ask what bearing such conditions have on whether a mystical experience is *a genuine insight or not*. The same with other types of experiences. For example, does the fact that a society that already has a belief in rebirth is more likely to produce children who tell of being reborn prove that the stories are untrue? We could just as easily turn the claim around: parents in societies that do not have a belief in rebirth would tend to dismiss their children's stories of their former lives as daydreams, and if the children persisted in telling them the parents

would tend to tell the children to grow up. In other words, societies with the belief would encourage the stories, and societies without it would tend to suppress them—how then do the prevailing social beliefs bear one way or the other on whether the stories are true or not?

4. The brain apparently has more plasticity than was once believed—it can structurally rearrange itself in response to events—and meditation is one way that we can rewire the brain. (See Newberg and Waldman 2009.) The brain can be retrained to manage destructive emotions and to activate neurological centers associated with happiness, well-being, and compassion (McMahan 2008: 205).

5. It may be that having a mystical experience does not depend solely on neurological changes in the brain but also on the *personality* of the subject (e.g., being open to new experiences)—i.e., the experience is not produced by physiological changes alone, but occurs only in people predisposed to have them. If it is established that only people with certain personality traits have mystical experiences, this may not be good news for advocates of mysticism. Theists may object that God would not allow only some people to experience him and not everyone. In addition, naturalists can then claim that this is evidence that no god is involved in these experiences.

6. Naturalists may look at works on the connection of mystical states and psychosis (see Brett 2002) and conclude that mystical experiences are only a perfectly natural, if abnormal, state of mind resulting from a problem with the brain: psychotic breakdowns and mystical states result from the same material processes and cannot be differentiated in content (e.g., the loss of subject/object boundaries) but only in form—mystics simply have the mental training and framework of beliefs to handle the disintegration of the mundane worldview and so can successfully reintegrate into the normal world (ibid.: 335-36). However, it should be noted that these studies involve states of mind with *visions and auditions*, not the *contentless* depth-mystical state. In addition, the *mindful* perception of the world can be explained without appealing to psychoses (e.g., Deikman 1980; Austin 1998).

7. A second possibility arises if the transcendent's action in a mystical experience is not analogous to a physical object affecting another object but is instead analogous to software guiding the course of physical events in a computer. (For the analogy to hold, the software represents a different level of causation than the causation within the hardware—information rather than another electrical cause.) A physical account of the electrical events in the computer's hardware can be complete and yet it tells us nothing about the program operating in the computer. By analogy, something similar may be occurring with the transcendent in a depth-mystical experiences: complete physiological accounts of these experiences would be only accounts of the "hardware" of the brain areas involved and not touch the role of the "software" (the transcendent).

8. Charles Tart, after fifty years of studying paranormal phenomena (telepathy, clairvoyance, precognition, psychokinesis, and psychic healing) concludes that there is evidence of a non-materialistic element to human beings and of life after death. But beyond that, he does not think the evidence warrants drawing any other conclusions about the fundamental nature of reality or of a human being (2009: 338-39).

9. Herbert Benson believes that we are "wired for God," but he realizes that his study of the concentrative meditative techniques he labels the "relaxation response" is neutral to the issue of whether a god exists. He believes faith in God is good for our health whether a god or evolution caused this wiring, i.e., religious faith may be valuable to our evolution even if no transcendental reality exists. The same philosophical dilemma appears in the socio-scientific research into religion. For example, if church attendance proves to have health benefits, is it because of a divine influence on the body or because a social support-

group combined with a positive outlook on life produces beneficial effects? Is it simply because church goers usually have a healthier life style (e.g., smoking and drinking less)? Does thinking that one is in touch with God have a placebo effect? There is also the danger in looking for simple answers. For example, church attendance is obviously an easy variable to measure, but it is not a simple measure of faith—some unbelievers may attend church simply for social reasons such as trying to enhance their standing in the community. So too, the fact that those who attend church are by definition well enough to leave their homes gives church attendees an initial advantage over the population as a whole on issues of health for the trivial reason that the latter group also includes those who are bedridden at home or in hospitals. But this does not mean that church attendance makes people healthy. Rather, the causal arrow is reversed: health makes church attendance possible in the first place. Those who engage in recreational activities such as going to the movies have an even bigger initial advantage in assessing health since some people no doubt attend church out of a sense of need or duty, even when they are not feeling totally well—something that would not apply to the more frivolous activities. But no one concludes that going to the movies makes us healthy or that going to movies should be encouraged for its health benefits.

10. Neuroscientists may engage in poor philosophical reasoning here. For example, Eugene d'Aquili and Andrew Newberg cannot automatically equate "Absolute Unitary Being" with God without engaging in more argument. Simply because the "Absolute Unitary Being" transcends the natural realm and in the West this means God is not enough. It should be noted that "Absolute Unitary Being" is only their posit—none of their subjects report achieving a state of being one with it while being observed. Based on their empirical findings, their posit is not a personal being with thoughts and concerns, nor does it have the traditional attributes of a theistic god (omnipotent, omniscient, and omnibenevolent) or all the attributes a believer today may read in. Nor is a "vivid" subjective sense that what is experienced is real (1999: 191-93) the only criterion for what is objectively real, especially when there are types of experiences with possible third-person testing. D'Aquili and Newberg attempt to distinguish mystical experiences from hallucinations by arguing that the former retain their vivid sense of reality after the experience, while the latter do not. But the experiences of people suffering from schizophrenia seem real to them—we reject the claims because they do not conform to the consensus sense of ordinary reality. The depth-mystical experience has no such checking procedure since the alleged realities experienced transcend the natural realm and neither conform with or conflict with what we observe in the world.

11. Alister Hardy found that roughly a third of adults in England have had mystical experiences (1983). One problem inherent in any such survey is that the participants may not mean the same thing that the questioners mean by such terms as "religious," "transcendent," "mystical," "feeling," "oneness," and so forth. For example, an experiencer may label a premonition as being momentarily "one with God." Such surveys are also typically framed with a theistic bias; for example, classical depth-mystics would not speak of a "presence" of a transcendental reality as if it set off apart from us.

12. It should also be noted that the field of the neurological study of religious experiences is populated with many advocates either for or against religious experiences rather than scientists conducting experiments just to find out the results. These proponents tend to give at most only a brief account of their opponents' position or to ignore any data or theories that would conflict with their position. For example, Beauregard and O'Leary 2007 contains no discussion of the significance of drug-induced mystical experiences for the issue of whether mystical experiences can be duplicated; they find out-of-body experiences and near-death experiences more important to discuss, but here too they ignore studies that

conflict with their position.

13. Occam's Razor becomes involved only when there are *competing* explanations. If theists offer a "theology of science" in which they argue that God set up the order of nature to endow it with some purpose and then let nature proceed by natural forces alone, then this explanation is not competing with any scientific theories: God is not considered a cause within nature and so is not offered as a science-like explanation. Science is given a free hand in finding what order God designed. The religious explanation is of a different order than scientific explanations, and so we do not have to choose the religious explanation over science or vice versa. But for the issue at hand, there are competing and conflicting explanations of *the true source of a mystical experience*.

14. Julian Jaynes offers a sweeping (and admittedly highly speculative) explanation of the entire history of the gods, the soul, and other supernatural phenomena—indeed, the entire origin and subsequent development of religion—as the products of auditory hallucinations in the evolution of the two hemispheres of the brain in these terms (1990).

15. As Eugene Wigner asked, isn't it a miracle that the musings of mathematicians, not rooted in any facts, turn out to be so much in harmony with the structure of the universe? Mathematics is an artificial language we have invented by the free use of our minds and yet it leads to new insights about reality in realms we cannot directly experience, such as the unpicturable quantum realm. Indeed, it may be the key for understanding basic structures of reality—to Galileo, God's "book of nature" is written in mathematics. Does this show that our mind is more than an evolved survival machine? Or is there an evolutionary explanation? And it should be noted that there is opposition to the whole of idea that mathematics reflects what is real. For example, the mathematician Brian Davies believes that mathematics is a human cultural creation and that our mathematized theories in science are unlikely to survive long. And while mathematics plays a major role in new scientific discoveries, it should be noted that there are still many aspects of nature that have proven resistant to all attempts at mathematization—failures, indeed, so far outnumber successes—and conversely that there are many mathematical ideas that apparently do not have any application to nature.

— 14 —

Constructivism and the Claim to Mystical Knowledge

As discussed in Chapter 2, mystical experiences in the classical religious traditions are cultivated, not for health benefits, but to gain insights into the fundamental nature of reality. Mystical experiences allegedly give us the ability to know reality free of our culturally-created images, thus enabling us to align our lives in accord with the way things truly are. But, as also discussed, the depth-mystical experience itself does not determine how mystics interpret its significance—i.e., the actual *knowledge* that is allegedly gained in the depth-mystical experience will involve elements of the mystic's beliefs *outside* the experience itself. Indeed, that the depth-mystical experience is taken to be an insight at all—rather than just an interesting and potent exotic mental state—depends on factors outside the experience. Even if mystical experiences affect the mystic's worldview, nevertheless judgments of the status of the depth-mystical experience can only occur outside of the depth-mystical experience in a "dualistic" state of consciousness when the experience itself becomes an object of intentional consciousness.

Some interpretation must always be given the depth-mystical experience for a mystic to integrate it into his or her life, whether the experience occurs spontaneously or occurs to those who have been cultivating it in a particular tradition. Of course, the interpretation may be ready-made by the mystic's own tradition prior to the experiences (even if the tradition's doctrines have to be adapted), but those outside any tradition will also need to work with their prior religious and philosophical beliefs to understand the significance of the experience.

Constructivism

Naturalists point to the great diversity in the interpretations of mystical experiences occurring in mystical traditions from around the world and throughout history as an indication that no reality is actually experienced. Mystical interpretations are not converging on one set of doctrines, as with theories of a phenomenon in science. This suggests that only a mystic's cultural beliefs are involved in the cognitive claims. Just as visions of the Virgin Mary occur only to Roman Catholics and visions of Krishna only to Vaishnavites, so too mystical experiences in different religious traditions are always taken as confirming the basic doctrines of the tradition that the experiencer was trained in. Buddhist monks and Franciscan nuns in a certain study exhibited similar physiological changes, but the Buddhist monks described their experiences in terms of selflessness while the Christian nuns described theirs as "a tangible sense of the closeness of God and a mingling with Him" (Newberg, d'Aquili, and Rause 2002: 7), just as their traditions would dictate.[1] The interpretations may only be applied after the experience or the interpretative elements may actually penetrate the meditators' altered states of consciousness, but either way the experiencer's cultural beliefs control their claims.

This position leads to the contemporary philosophical reductionism of constructivism. (See Katz 1978, 1983; Proudfoot 1985. For criticism, see Forman 1990; Sullivan 1995: 56-57; Studstill 2005.) The key idea here is that the alleged cognitive content of all mystical experiences is reducible to the experiencer's *prior religious beliefs*. The experiences can have a huge emotional impact on the experiencer and can be taken to be cognitively significant, but they are void of any independent cognitive content, and so the experiencer can read in many different philosophical doctrines—indeed, doctrines from the experiencer's religious background must be read in precisely because the experience is void of any of its own doctrinal content. That is, even if there is some amorphous, experiential "given," it does not determine or even figure in the alleged cognitive content of the experience—only learned cultural beliefs do. Thus, the experience itself makes no cognitive contribution to the belief-framework. Nothing cognitively significant would remain if the doctrinal and cultural contents were removed from these experiences (Marshall 2005: 271).

The basis of this reduction is the view virtually universally held in philosophy today that all our experiences are conceptually structured. Constructivists contend that all conscious experiences, even mystical ones, must have an intentional object. There can be no "pure consciousness" events: there are no experiences when there is no phenomenal content in the mind—the "light" of awareness is "on" only when there are objects to be illuminated. In short, "contentless consciousness" is an oxymoron: we can only be conscious if there is something there to be conscious of. There can be no content-free experience of beingness—a structureless "now" experience. Rather, even our experience of the present is always a combination of our recollections, our prior reactions, and also our anticipations for the future. Our mind does not reflect reality "as it really is"—it only approaches reality through its own conceptual filter. That is, the concepts we create become part of a mental filter by which the mind processes information in every experience. There is no "objective" experience in the sense of an experience free of any structuring framework originating from a particular experiencer. Sensory input is structured into perceptions of sense-objects by the concepts developed within the perceiver's culture of what types of objects make up the world. And the same process of structuring applies to mindfulness and the depth-mystical experience. In sum, in the words of Wilfrid Sellars, "all awareness is a linguistic affair."[2]

Extreme Constructivism, Moderate Constructivism, and Nonconstructivism

That sense-perception has such a conceptual element is certainly well-entrenched in philosophy today. The roots of the claim lie in the Kantian view of perception as an active process of selecting and relating what is experienced to our concepts and beliefs rather than the passive registering of an external reality. But moderate constructivists still insist that the external world plays a role in constraining our creations—concepts are structuring the experiences, but reality surprises us and resists our expectations, and thus how we conceptualize an experience is not infinitely malleable. Culture might explain why religious visions are of Mary or Krishna, but it does not explain all of the experience—in particular, why there is some "sense of presence" to experience in the visions in the first place. A content independent of the form is still part of the content of the experience. For moderate constructivists, this content can affect the experiencer's beliefs—beliefs shape the form of the experiences, and the experiences in turn shape the beliefs.

Extreme constructivists, however, go further and add a second premise: *all* the belief-content of depth-mystical experiences is supplied solely by the mystic's existing tradition—the transcendent, even if it exists and is in fact experienced, contributes nothing. In the case of sense-experience, moderate constructivists give the world a role in knowledge-claims. Extreme constructivists, following postmodernism, deny that the world ultimately plays any role at all: the world-in-itself, if there is such a reality, is amorphous and we can cut it up with our concepts any way we want.[3] Thus, in the end an external "real" world, if there is one, does not figure in determining our knowledge-claims; instead, our concepts exclusively shape our knowledge-claims. (On postmodernism and realism, see Jones 2009: chap. 3.) And when constructivism is combined with naturalism, the issue of a role for a transcendental reality does not even come up.

Thus, for extreme constructivists depth-mystical experiences cannot add anything at any point to the beliefs or values of a mystical tradition. The religious beliefs that mystics bring to their experiences are not merely one of the components contributing to their experiences but are the *only* cognitive component. Extreme constructivists thus assimilate knowledge-claims totally to the nonexperiential and the cultural. Some may apply extreme constructivism to depth-mystical experiences even when they would not apply it to sense-experiences. (There are, however, constructivists in sociology and science studies who apply extreme constructivism to scientific theories, facts, and observations.) Mystical experiences are merely an intense feeling of our previous beliefs. They become, in the words of Robert Gimello, "simply the psychosomatic enhancement of religious beliefs and values" (in Katz 1978: 85). If mystical experiences are grounded only in the part of the brain connected to *emotion* rather than *thinking* (see Ramachandran and Blakeslee 1998: 179), it would help the argument that mystical experiences simply reenforce the experiencer's prior religious beliefs. The conceptual framework of a religious tradition brought to the experience controls the experience entirely and thus constitutes the experience's complete cognitive content. The cognitive substance of any mystical experience is thereby reduced to the purely cultural.

In effect, extreme constructivists go from the fact that we create concepts to the conclusion that this is all there is to the cognitive content of experiences. Moderate constructivists in this field, such as John Hick (1989), argue that the mind contributes to every genuine religious experience but that the transcendental realities do too. Thereby, the total cognitive content of religious experiences is not reducible to an experiencer's prior doctrines, and the depth-mystical experience can offer cognitive input constraining our knowledge-claims. Moderates argue that reality and the structuring we supply are inextricably mixed in our experiences and our knowledge, but extremists conclude that concepts are simply our creations and have no connection to anything but the other concepts we create. Extreme constructivists thus reduce the content of any depth-mystical experience, while moderate constructivists do not. Extreme constructivists need not deny that some reality exists independently of individual consciousness, but like other postmodernists they contend that any configuration of concepts will do for coping with the world—we can make any "web of beliefs" fit if we make enough adjustments to its parts—and so in the final analysis reality does not constrain our creations. Thus, even if there is a transcendental reality that mystics actually experience, our conceptions of that reality are infinitely malleable; hence, the mystics' knowledge-claims are controlled totally by their concepts, and so in the end the reality itself drops completely out of the epistemic picture.

Philosophers devised constructivism without first seriously considering mystical or other religious experiences, but the idea arguably can be extended to at least some religious experiences. Most scholars would agree that people who undergo mystical and other religious experiences bring their prior religious and nonreligious beliefs to their experiences and that these shape their understanding of the experiences they undergo. It certainly seems plausible that these beliefs inform the actual experience of religious visions, shaping their content: experiencers may sense only a vague, amorphous presence, but they *see* Jesus or some other figure from their own religious tradition. Such numinous religious experiences are enough like perceptions that they may be open to an analysis similar to ordinary sense-perceptions. The only alternative is that there are multiple gods and spirits, a scenario that conflicts with modern views on religion.

Mindfulness too seems amenable to constructivism: mystics can admit that the mind in mindful states (including enlightened ones) contain conceptualizable differentiations in all but a pure state and thus may be structured by prior beliefs.

The mindfulness state's content and structuring would depend in part on concepts and beliefs from each mystic's tradition. Thus, there would be multiple mindfulness states, and understanding the states themselves would depend in part on understanding each mystic's religious framework.

But whether constructivism can be extended to the *depth-mystical experiences* is open to dispute. Nonconstructivists in mystical studies deny even moderate constructivism with regard to this experience and contend that it is different from all other cognitive states—a contentless state of consciousness free of all conceptualizations. As noted in Chapter 1, the experience is not truly "contentless," but it is allegedly free of any differentiatable content. Obviously, mystics retain *something* of the sense of the experience after it is over, even if the sense can be expressed only in abstract terms—a sense of the direct awareness of beingness, oneness, fundamentality, power, immutability, and permanence. This is so even though experiencers cannot step back during the experience itself and make a mental object out of what they are aware of. If mystics retained nothing whatsoever from their depth-mystical experiences, they could make no claim about the nature of what they experienced and could not reject any other claims as objectionable. To constructivists, the conflicting claims that mystics make are merely a matter of doctrines formulated outside the experience, with the depth-mystical experience only intensifying a mystic's prior belief. But nonconstructivists tend to agree with mystics that the depth-mystical experience is still cognitive. They may also argue that the experience is an unmediated, direct experience of the noumenon of what is experienced (contra Kant): any post-experiential intentional object is the product of the memory and a conceptual scheme, but the experience itself is a direct experience of a noumenon.

Moreover, if a truly "pure consciousness" event devoid of all phenomenal content does occur then logically all such experiences must be phenomenally equivalent (Shear and Jevning 1999: 199-200). That is, if there is an experience that is indeed truly empty of all differentiable content that could shape it, it would have to be, as a matter of simple logic, phenomenologically *identical* for all experiencers regardless of culture and era (assuming we all have basically the same mind in this regard). It would be a truly culture-free and history-free experience. Constructivists respond by denying that in fact such a thing as a "structureless experience" is possible. There are no pure, unmediated experiences period (Katz 1978: 26).[4] They believe that all experiences are intentional and must have some conceptual content. Thus, the depth-mystical experiences, contrary to the mystics' own claims, must have at least some conceptual content or mystics would not be conscious. Beliefs and concepts penetrate the experiences themselves and are not simply applied after the fact in a separate act of interpretation. No mystical experiences are the same across cultures: each mystic's experiences are conditioned by different elements, and so they are phenomenologically different from others'. Meditation does not involve emptying the mind of a culture's framework, thereby permitting new cognitive experiences, but simply helps the meditator to internalize fully the culture's beliefs and values. Thus, yoga properly understood is not an *unconditioning* or *deconditioning* of consciousness, but rather a *reconditioning* of consciousness, i.e., a substituting of one form of conditioned consciousness for another (ibid.: 57). Enlightenment is merely the final internalization of a religion's framework of beliefs—the culmination of long periods of intense study, practice, and commitment to those specific beliefs and values.

The second part of extreme constructivism, in sum, rules out the possibility that mystics have any knowledge of a transcendental reality, even if mystics do experience such a reality: nonexperiential cultural belief-systems control everything about the experience's cognitive content. Thus, there is no such thing as "*mystical knowledge*" in any real sense. There is no possibility of any independent experiential input from a transcendental source: any such experiential input is totally shaped by our concepts and cannot provide any cognitive content about reality—it simply has no independent cognitive component. Mystical experiences thus are not sources of any potentially fresh cognitive input in anyone's system of belief. Prior mystical experiences cannot even shape the conceptual framework one's brings to later mystical experiences since the prior ones also are totally controlled by the tradition's beliefs. In sum, alleged experiences of a transcendental reality cannot enter the cognitive picture at any point. All mystical experiential claims thus can be dismissed as groundless: even if they are experiences of a transcendental reality, how could they be used to justify beliefs about that reality when the total cognitive content comes only from cultural beliefs?

Is Constructivism Applicable to the Depth-Mystical Experience?

Thus, under extreme constructivism all mystical experiences are no more cognitive than, to cite an especially egregious example of the instances naturalists love to relate, when Roman Catholics see the face of Mary in a rusted refrigerator on a back porch. And many who think that extreme constructivism is absurd in cases of sense-experience—obviously there is some sensory input, and reality provides constraints on our constructions—find extreme constructivism attractive when it comes to mystical experiences. Extreme constructivists neatly combine a popular philosophical position (constructivism) with two popular academic views on religion (natural explanations of religious experiences and the reduction of religion to belief-claims). Extreme constructivism also reflects academics' general love of all things linguistic and their unease over any claims of ineffability.[5] Naturalists, who already reject the alleged cognitive content of religious experiences, thus see no problem in reducing mystical experiences in this way.

Extreme constructivists offer no reason for their position on the depth-mystical experience other than the claim that ordinary experiences are structured. Their position is based on Kant and not on any empirical investigation of mystical experiences.[6] That there may be a cognitive state of consciousness without an object is simply logically impossible to philosophers who address the situation with the preconceived idea that all mental states are intentional. And, of course, such philosophers do not have any qualms about telling mystics they are wrong, despite their experiences. Constructivism is simply applied to mystical experiences without seriously examining the possibility that the depth-mystical experience may in fact be unique. This means that when extreme constructivists claim that the depth-mystical experience must be structured, they are in effect making only an assumption concerning this experience based on ordinary experience, not reaching a conclusion based on any empirical research on mystics.[7]

But nonconstructivists have a very strong case against both moderate and extreme constructivism here. First, there is empirical evidence against the constructivist interpretation of the depth-mystical experiences: a "pure consciousness" event may in fact be possible (Hood 1997: 227-28). Even a materialist who thinks the brain and mind are identical and that no transcendental reality is involved in a depth-mystical experience can argue against constructivism and for a genuine pure consciousness event: the monitoring activity of the mind continues in the absence of any representational processing; thus, after the mind is emptied of sensory, conceptual, and ideational content, a lucid conscious states results (Peters 2000).

Second, there is an argument that makes sense of what mystics actually say. In ordinary perception, we do not experience a patch of colors and *interpret* it as a rug. There is only *one act*: seeing a rug. This may apply to mindful states of consciousness and visions, but in the case of the depth-mystical experience, the mind is allegedly *empty* of all differentiations, and it is only *after* the event that mystics interpret its significance. Thus, depth-mystics clearly "perceive" the transcendent, but they cannot "grasp" it like an object until the experience is over—the gleaming transcendent shows itself, but what it is is only grasped after the experience. As Teresa of Ávila put it, only after her mystical experience did she know that it was an "orison of union" with God—during the experience itself she said the soul sees and understands nothing, but afterward the soul sees the truth clearly, not from a vision, but from the certitude God placed there (*Interior Castle* IV.1.9). After the fact, one can believe that an experience was an experience of *x* without the *concept of x* being present in the experience itself—this is true of sense-experiences, and it can also be true of the depth-mystical experience. (So too, any *certainty* that the experience itself apparently gives is at best a memory or aftereffect.) Interpreting sense-experience occurs in the same state of consciousness as the experience itself; thus, it is harder to see if there is conceptual structuring in the experience itself. But in the case of depth-mystical experiences, one must change one's state of consciousness to see its significance. It is therefore clearer to mystics that there is a difference between the experience and its conceptualization, which leads to claims of ineffability. This also leads to the issue noted in Chapter 2 of what role religious doctrines play in claims of mystical knowledge.

Thus, if mystics are correct, *two* acts occur here, unlike in sense-perception: the depth-mystical event and the later act of interpretation. The later can be separated from the depth-mystical experience itself. Thus, the experience of the alleged reality must be distinguished from conceptualizations of it and beliefs about its ontological status, and we cannot infer that the latter must be informing the former. Indeed, we cannot imply anything about the phenomenology of the experience from the mystic's later understanding of what was experienced. Mystical claims are "based on experiences," but there is both a direct, nonpropositional awareness and something inferred (the interpretation of the nature of what is experienced), each with its own epistemic status. This is not to suggest that there is such a thing as an "ineffable insight"—we must know what the alleged insight is, and thus the insight must be statable. Indeed, even if the experience is free of a mystic's cultural beliefs, something must be retained from it that is prior to the mystic's later conceptualization and understanding of it. Thus, even if the experience is free of any conceptualizations, it can still be a fresh awareness with cognitive import. This also means that mystical "emptying," "unknowing," and "forgetting" is a process of deconditioning consciousness, not reconditioning it.[8] If so, the mystics' accounts of their own experiences are at least prima facie evidence against constructivism and in favor of the idea that the depth-mystical experience is a "pure consciousness" free of all differentiable content. Thus, nonconstructivists defer to the mystics here: only mystics are aware of both differentiated experiences and the depth-mystical experience, and they claim the latter is radically different in type.

Nonconstructivists can agree that the images and interpretations of the experience that mystics form in their dualistic consciousness after their depth-mystical experience are shaped by the beliefs of a particular mystic's tradition. But, they ask, if this experience is in fact free of all differentiations—as many mystics (including some theists) claim—then what is present to structure it? They also point out that the content of mystical experiences often comes as a surprise and even a shock to mystics—their expectations do not control the experience. This strongly indicates that their doctrines are not controlling their experiences. So too, some mystical experiences occur spontaneously to people with no mystical training or no religious background; this unexpected event can radically alter the experiencers' worldview, expanding their sense of what is real; it can also alter their values and can lead the nonreligious to adopt a religious way of life. In addition, mystics within the same tradition interpret the same basic texts differently, sometimes heretically. Visionaries, on the other hand, are less frequently heretical. Moreover, the heavy-handed interpretations that such mystics as Shankara and Eckhart give their scriptures suggest that it is more likely that mystics interpret their tradition's revealed texts to fit what they have experienced than vice versa.

Extreme constructivists claim they are being empirical, although they must dismiss any reports by mystics themselves of the depth-mystical experience being empty of differentiable content. But obviously it would not be empirical for constructivists to argue that these reports must be false on the ground that no experience in principle can be free of content. Indeed, with the constructivists' strategy, nothing mystics say could even in principle provide counter-evidence to constructivism: whatever mystics say after their experiences will reflect their religious and philosophical tradition and will then automatically be interpreted by extreme constructivists to fit their preconceived theory. Even if constructivists had depth-mystical experiences themselves, the transitional state back to ordinary consciousness will be filled with content from their beliefs and expectations, and constructionists may well see their post-experiential interpretation as permeating the depth-mystical experience itself. Hence, constructivism applied to the depth-mystical experience ends up being unfalsifiable by that experience in practice.

Can the Dispute be Resolved?

Are there grounds to resolve the constructivism dispute? The problem is that mystics cannot present a depiction of the depth-mystical experience free of the mystics' conceptual commitments, and all depictions can occur only outside the depth-mystical experience in a different state of consciousness. That is, in order to communicate, mystics will have to be in a state with the differentiations of language, and in that state they will use whatever conceptual scheme they have adopted. And this is all we will ever have. To use an analogy: in mystics' report, we are presented with a colored light without being able to examine the light's source. The light may be a clear light with a colored shell (the object-free depth-mystical experience, with an interpretation applied after the experience is over), or the light itself may be colored (the constructivist position with the concepts embedded in the experience)—but all we can see is the colored light from the outside, and by itself it cannot resolve the issue at hand. Nonconstructivists operate with the premise that mystics are in a privileged position for the issue of whether the depth-mystical experience is free of intentional content, and so nonmystics should accept their word on there being an experience free of all conceptual and other elements. Constructivists argue that people may well misconstrue their own experiences and that constructivism fits better with the generally accepted philosophical view of the nature of experience and also with naturalism; thus, they think constructivism is the best available explanation.

Constructivists correctly point out that there is no one abstract "mystical worldview" but instead a variety of more specific mystical systems—usually more than one even within the same religious tradition. The diversity of mystical accounts, however, does not support constructivism over nonconstructivism: nonconstructivists have no problem agreeing that there are conflicting doctrines, but they argue that this diversity only reflects the diversity of the interpretations that mystics apply after the depth-mystical experience is over. That is, mystics do bring their cultural beliefs and values to their experiences, and these do influence their later understanding of their own experiences, but this does not mean that the concepts must be active during the experiences themselves. The diversity only reflects the diversity of mystical and religious metaphysics of the different religious traditions of the world, not a difference within the depth-experience itself.

The dispute thus comes down to whether we give more weight to what the mystics say or to what philosophers say about the nature of other experiences. In the end, whether one subscribes to a philosophical reduction based on extending constructivism to depth-mystical experiences may depend as much upon whether one has a prior commitment to reducing mysticism than anything inherent in the depth-mystical experience itself. But it must be said that constructivists do not present a strong case. Their case is built only on imposing ideas onto mysticism that were developed from the study of other types of experiences, not studying mystics first and then devising constructivism. Nor is their position the result of any first-hand experiences. Thus, they have no reason other than an argument based on the psychology of other experiences to rule out the possibility of an event of a "pure," object-free consciousness. This is a very risky way to rule out the very possibility that mystics might not have a genuine insight into the nature of reality.

Notes

1. John Hick thinks this difference in the conscious states reported by the Tibetan monks and Christian nuns is hard to reconcile with a direct brain-to-consciousness causation (2006: 75). But if the differences in the reports reflect a post-experiential interpretation and not differences within the experiences themselves, then the monks and nuns had the same experience and only interpreted it differently (the nonconstructivist view), and the fact that the physiological effects are the same is only to be expected. On the other hand, if the subjective structuring affects the experience itself (the constructivist view), then the physiological effects again might be exactly the same regardless of whatever structuring is present: the physiological effects only reflect the fact that some structuring was present in the experience—what the specific structuring is is irrelevant to those effects.

2. Whether our linguistic concepts penetrate our *sense-experiences* is in fact open to question. And even if there is structuring to our sense-experiences, is it linguistic in nature? Once we taste a banana we do have something in our minds for that taste to which we affix a linguistic label, but are our subsequent experiences of bananas then affected by the label? So too, Ptolemy and Copernicus differed radically about what occurs in a sunset, but whether they actually *experienced a sunset* differently is another question.

3. This is not to say that constructivists necessarily follow postmodernists in their suspicion of all "grand metanarratives" or that no interpretation of reality is any more true than any other. Here the claim is only that we have no direct, unmediated access to reality—all experiences are permeated with some conceptualization.

4. Katz cannot accept that any part of a mystical experience is unconstructed and still maintain what he wrote. Mediation must permeate the entire experience or there would be a cultureless core to the experience that would give nonconstructivists an opening.

5. All experiences are ineffable in one sense: how do we describe, say, the taste of licorice to someone who has not experienced it? The idea that mystical experiences are *ineffable* in a stronger sense is that they can be given a linguistic label but they cannot be expressed by any concepts or doctrines the way ordinary dualistic experiences can be at least crudely "captured" by language. Both what is experienced and the experience itself seem beyond all our concepts, not merely that we do not currently have the right concepts—no

concept can apply to what is undifferentiated. (See Jones 2009: chap. 7.) Not surprisingly, many mystics assert the ultimate inapplicability of any "dualistic" terms to the "nondual" transcendent—i.e., since all terms must make distinctions, none can apply to what is free of distinctions—and that any terms make what is experienced into an object of consciousness, which it is not. They also use "ineffability" to indicate the profound otherness of the reality—since it has no phenomenal content, it is unlike anything else we experience. Yet most often mystics continue to talk about the nature of what is experienced, even if the concepts used are of an abstract nature (e.g., oneness) or terms from their religious tradition. Those theists who think God has revealed something of his nature to us through other experiences (revelations and prayers) have a more positive theology: we know some definite things about God—he is a personal, loving, moral creator. God is indescribable only in that he is *greater* than we can know, not because we know nothing of him. Theistic mystics, thinking that they have experienced God, know that his mode of existence is different than that of creatures and so believe that all terms mislead: we make God into *a being* like worldly beings, which he is not. Even just denoting the transcendent as "the transcendent" or "the Real" makes it an object like other objects, which "it" is not. Thus, mystics deny the adequacy of all terms. Indeed, the medieval Christian Marguerite Porete said that God is so much greater than anything that can be said that everything that is said about him is much more like *lying* than speaking the truth. But the fact that mystics, both theistic and nontheistic, still distinguish what is an appropriate description from what is not does indicate that what is experienced has some distinctive character even when seen through a grid of traditional doctrines after the experience. That is, something is retained from the depth-mystical experience, and therefore this experience is not ineffable in a strong sense. Thus, any claim to strong ineffability should be rejected. (See Jones 1993: 101-23.)

6. For Kant, certain categories (such as space, time, and causation) structure the noumena that affect our sense-organs into perceived phenomena for all people—i.e., sensations become conscious perceptions through the structuring of these categories; no unmediated experience of the noumena is possible. But constructivists focus on another layer of structuring: our *cultural* beliefs and concepts. Nonconstructivists contend that depth-mystical experiences do not involve either layer of structuring but are "intuitions" of whatever it is that is experienced in such experiences unmediated by any learned cultural concepts or any unlearned Kantian categories.

7. Epistemologists in classical Indian traditions also accepted that concepts play a role in everyday experiences, but they held different views on mystical experiences.

8. The traditional goal of meditation is the discovery of reality through personal experience, but that mystics rely upon a tradition's teachings to understand their experiences does complicate the picture. The process of emptying is still to overcome cultural conditioning and decondition the mind, but the resulting knowledge-claims are determined by the tradition's teachings or the authority of a master. (See McMahan 2008: 212-13.)

— 15 —

Does the Depth-Mystical Experience Have Cognitive Value?

If what has been argued so far is correct, then neither alleged cultural epistemic standards nor natural explanations nor constructivism makes a strong case for rejecting out of hand the possibility that mystics have insights into reality. The next step then is to accept the possibility and determine if a credible case can be made that mystics in fact do gain knowledge of a transcendental reality through the depth-mystical experience. In short, should we accept a mystic's claim to knowledge? The religious want to argue that the alleged transcendental realities are not merely unexperiencable posits postulated to explain things about the natural world but are realities that impinge upon our minds. According to the religious, not only are the transcendental realities experiencable, the experiences offer evidence justifying the rationality of practicing a particular religious way of life and holding its doctrines. Many (but not all) religious people accept mysticism as one of the prime experiential bases, along with revelations and such personal experiences as prayer and worship, for holding their beliefs and practices.

All of this raises some of the most central questions in religious epistemology. Do depth-mystical experiences qualify as "objective evidence," i.e., grounds that even opponents concede are a reason in favor of accepting a certain belief (even though the opponents will not accept them as compelling)? Do these mystical experiences *prove* the existence of a transcendental reality? Or, if not, do they at least make belief in such a reality *rational* to all of the faithful or at least to the experiencers themselves?[1] Two basic questions must be distinguished here: (1) do depth-mystical experiences offer evidence of the existence of *some transcendental reality*, and if so, (2) do they offer evidence for the *particular doctrines of some specific religious tradition* regarding its conceptions of transcendent realities? That is, is the depth-mystical experience a veridical experience of a nonnatural reality, and if so, what exactly is it an experience of?

Is the Depth-Mystical Experience Evidence?

Consider the first issue. First, there is the problem of natural explanations: if scientists can duplicate all of an actual depth-mystical experience by natural means, then this experience can occur whether the transcendent exists or not, and therefore these experiences lose any epistemic presumption that they might otherwise have had. Even the mere possibility of a natural explanation is enough in the eyes of many when naturalists can make a viable case for accepting naturalism. As things stand today, the experience is not unambiguous evidence of the existence of a transcendental reality because naturalistic reductions cannot be ruled out as a legitimate possibility. Thus, the experience is not an objective warrant of belief in the existence of a transcendental reality when a naturalistic explanation seems viable.

Second, there is no objective way (i.e., from outside a particular mystic's own experience) to test whether a mystic is in fact in contact with a transcendental reality. Nor does a psychological test work. The depth-mystical experience does not have a uniformly positive psychological effect on all people—not all who have had mystical experiences turn out healthier or live more effectively in the natural world. Meditation can end up aggravating negative mental conditions and personality traits. And to naturalists, any positive effects are irrelevant to the question of insight: any positive character changes merely indicates that the mystics *think* that they are in contact with a transcendental reality, not necessarily that they actually are. Any positive transformative effects of the experience are no guarantee that the insight is veridical when a purely natural cause for the change cannot be ruled out. So too, with any moral test: while all enlightened mystics shift toward selflessness, not all enlightened mystics fill their newly found selflessness with a moral concern for others—they cannot be ego-centered, but they can exhibit a "holy indifference" to the welfare of others. (See Jones 2004.) So too, they can be judged by their "fruits" only by the standards of different religious traditions, and this ends up being circular since the same values shape how the mystics see their experiences in the first place.

All in all, while there may be other grounds for preferring a particular transcendental interpretation over any naturalistic interpretation of the depth-mystical experience or vice versa, the depth-mystical experience itself will remain neutral on whether it in fact involves a transcendental reality

The Problem of Religious Diversity

The last point leads to the second question: even if we grant for the sake of argument that depth-mystics are in fact in touch with a transcendental reality, which religious tradition has the proper understanding of it? Consider the fact that religious doctrines in the world religions conflict with each other in at least some central claims. It is difficult to argue that the depth-mystical experience is unambiguous evidence supporting any particular religion's beliefs or even, say, theism in general when all the traditions have doctrines that seem equally well-supported in experience and reasoning. The various theistic and nontheistic religious traditions have no trouble interpreting the significance of the depth-mystical experience to fit their doctrines—articulating mystical doctrines and establishing their coherence with the other doctrines within the religious tradition are the subject of theologians and their counterparts in the nontheistic traditions.

It is impossible to speak of mystical experiences *verifying* one tradition's doctrines when nothing internal to the experience itself clearly favors one interpretation over alternative explanation from other traditions. Unlike with revelations, with mysticism other experiencers may be able to verify empirically the existence of *states of consciousness devoid of content*, but whether they can verify mystics' *various claims about the nature of reality* is another matter. Of course, mystics in the various traditions see their experiences as confirming their own tradition's doctrines and not the doctrines of other traditions. So too, different traditions have developed verification procedures to recognize the genuineness of a depth-mystical experience. However, the meditation masters who determine if a student is enlightened or not will utilize their own tradition's doctrines. This way of testing might be able to confirm if a student is enlightened (i.e., truly selfless), but it in no way helps to determine which tradition's interpretation of the depth-mystical experience's significance of this selflessness is correct (or "best" or "least inadequate"). Trained Buddhist meditation masters will still see any experiences as confirmation of Buddhist doctrines within their school, not as possible confirmation of Islamic theistic claims. The "peer review" is limited to confirming at best only that a student has achieved the intended proper state of mind, not that a discovery about reality has been replicated (contra Wallace 2003: 9). How do we distinguish a Buddhist meditator's "discoveries based on their first-hand experiences" from those of Christian or Hindu contemplatives who through "repeated experiments" have confirmed (and had verified by their superiors) that there is in fact an eternal soul beneath the fleeting apparitions of the personality (McMahan 2008: 210)? There is no scientific way to adjudicate between the Buddhist doctrine and these conclusions (ibid.). There is no convergence or commonality as with trained observers in science, and therefore mystical claims about the nature of what is experienced cannot be checked or disconfirmed as with scientific claims.

Thus, the lack of third-party checking of mystical claims is an issue here.[2] When it comes to conflicting claims involving sense-experience, others can test the credibility of the evidence for our claims—no such procedure is possible for mystics' claims. Naturalists will rule out the depth-mystical experience as possibly cognitive precisely because any transcendental reality cannot be presented for checking by others. Such cross-checking is essential in science, and thus according to naturalists and advocates of scientism it is essential for all cognitive claims. Of course, none of anyone's inner experiences can be presented for others to see, but in the case of, say, astronomical observations, others can look into the telescope and confirm (if trained) an observation or disconfirm it. Masters in meditative traditions may have tests to determine if a practitioner is enlightened, but from the scientific point of view those tests are still subjective and indirect. In sum, a mystical experience is not the kind of experience that can be checked the way sense-experiences can, and the judgment of whether this rules out the possibility of mystical experiences being cognitive will depend upon whether one believes the standards of science apply to all cognitive claims. Obviously, this is simply a return of the basic conflict of naturalist and religious points of view.

This might be less of a problem if there were one agreed-upon interpretation from the different religious traditions of the world of what is allegedly experienced, but there is no convergence of doctrines and none is in sight. There are theistic and nontheistic monisms and dualisms, all supported by mystics. Abrahamic theists themselves are split. Mainstream Christians see the depth-mystical experience as supporting a christocentric or trinitarian view of God, while Muslims and Jews see it as supporting a divine unity. In theisms, there is also the problem that the depth-mystical experience has been interpreted as either an experience of God or the experience of only the root of the self. Of course, theologians within any tradition will be able to advance reasons to prefer one interpretation over others, but equally obviously members of other traditions will not be convinced. This diversity would not be a problem if there were neutral criteria to adjudicate the disputes here, but there are none, as discussed below.

It is because the depth-mystical experience does not give its own interpretation that it is open to being seen as supporting these diverse claims. However, this has one major consequence: even the *experiencers themselves* are not justified in accepting their mystical experiences as conclusive confirmation of their tradition's doctrines. Arguably, mystics are being *rational* in accepting that they have had an experience of a transcendental reality and in accepting the doctrines of their own tradition as confirmed, but other mystics can just as reasonably conclude that their interpretation is confirmed and so they are being equally rational in accepting their doctrines. In such circumstances, none can claim any more objective confirmation from the experience itself.

The problem of conflicting interpretations has a similar consequence for the "argument from religious experience" for God's existence and attributes for those who have not had mystical experiences. Theists take mystical experiences as positive evidence, or even conclusive proof, that a transcendental source exists and has certain features. Christians see the transcendent in terms of the Christian conception of a god and so see an argument for any transcendental source of the world as an argument for the existence of a Christian version of the transcendent. (See Franks Davis 1989; Alston 1991; Swinburne 1991; Yandell 1993; also see Gellman 1997, 2001.) Opposition to the very idea that mystical experiences are insights at all is, of course, also alive and well. (See Martin 1990; Gale 1991.)

But seeing mystical experience as supporting the specific doctrines of any particular tradition requires *discounting the accounts from mystics in other traditions* and arguing that those mystics really are experiencing something other than what they think. Religious theorists are just as willing as extreme constructivists to tell mystics that they are mistaken about the content of their experiences. The Christian Caroline Franks Davis, for example, has to twist the Advaitins' and Buddhists' experiences to claim that mystical experiences really support a "broad theism"—i.e., Shankara was really experiencing God although he explicitly argued that the impersonal Brahman alone is real. She ultimately has to claim that all mystics, despite what they say, really experience "a loving presence ... with whom individuals can have a personal relationship" (1989: 191)—just as one would expect someone raised a Christian to see the true "common core" of the experience to be. But we cannot simply translate one tradition's "highly-ramified concepts," to use Ninian Smart's phrase, depicting the transcendent into another tradition's equally highly-ramified but different concepts, nor can we say that all low-ramified concepts about the mystical experience supports our chosen highly-ramified theological concepts over other interpretations and then conclude that all mystical traditions really support our own tradition's doctrines although the outsiders do not know it. Theological arguments on other grounds would be needed.

And it must be admitted that nontheists could just as easily apply the same contorted maneuvers to the claims of Christian mystics to affirm that the transcendent is nonpersonal in nature, the experience of the mystic's own transcendental self, or whatever. In fact, it would be quite easy to give an Advaitin interpretation to Meister Eckhart's thought. Christians may reject the evidential support of mystical experience for nontheistic doctrines because the latter are "intertwined with bizarre and fantastic elements" (Gellman 2001: 37), but non-Christians could do the same with Christianity, starting with the core idea of a transcendent creator who was incarnated through an immaculate conception as a human being who yet remained fully God while being fully human, who died as a ransom for all human beings or otherwise to reconcile us to himself for the sins committed by the original two human beings whom he specially created, and who then rose from the dead and ascended into heaven. Overall, the vast majority of religious believers will end up seeing the depth-mystical experience as objective support for the tradition they just happen to have been raised in. But in such circumstances, the depth-mystical experience remains neutral on the matter of which interpretation, if any, is valid.

Thus, religious theorists looking at mystical experiences may easily end up arguing in circles—starting with one tradition's ideas, then interpreting the mystical writings of the world to fit those ideas, and finally claiming that all mystical experiences are objective confirmations of those ideas. But theology cannot bootstrap itself in this way. If the depth-mystical experience is open to what mystics in different traditions depict it as, no one theological framework of highly-ramified concepts and theories can be imposed on the experience's actual content. First, there are the contentious issues of whether the transcendent is personal or nonpersonal in nature or whether it is the source of all elements of the universe or only the self. Second, that the depth-mystical experience suggests the complete simplicity of the transcendent causes problems for Abrahamic theologians. Certainly the traditional "omni's" of a theistic god—omnipotence, omniscience, omnibenevolence—are attributes that cannot be justified by any experience. What mystics encounter may seem to be the most powerful reality that a human being could possibly experience, and this may make it reasonable to *infer* that it has the maximum amount of whatever a particular tradition values, but it hard to see how those qualities could be *experienced*. How we could know from *any* experience that the reality is *all*-powerful, *all*-knowing, and *all*-good? Or that it has *infinite* power, knowledge, and goodness? Nor is it at all clear how a mystic could know from the experience that the reality experienced is a designer or that the designer must be the same as the ontological source of the world. So too, what we experience may seem to be the source of our reality and make us feel secure in the world, but how can we tell it is the source of all of reality or does not have a further source of its own being that was not experienced? Of course, theologians may not see this problem at all: they equate whatever mystics experience with their theological version of the transcendent, and thus understandably jump quickly to seeing all mystical experiences as support for their full theological conceptions without seriously considering or perhaps even seeing other possible options. The issue arises for nontheists too: how could Buddhist contemplatives know on the basis of their experiences alone that they "have experientially probed the origins and evolution of the universe back to its divine source" (Wallace 2009: 195)?

In sum, the diversity of religious doctrines presents a grave problem even for those who reject naturalistic reductions of the depth-mystical experience. What exactly is the depth-mystical experience evidence of? The Christian version of a god? The Muslim version? A generic "creator"? Brahman? The true self? Of course, believers in each tradition will try to show that their interpretation is superior to that of other traditions and will be confident that they are right. But such arguments will have to be based on grounds other than merely the mystical experiences themselves, since the objective in the end is to convince others who also have had the experience that their interpretation is *wrong*. Perhaps religious theorists in some one tradition will be able to come up with a stronger argument, although convincing those who do not share the same metaphysical presuppositions will be difficult. Even coming up with a common ground upon which all groups can agree to dispute is difficult (as discussed below).

There may be arguments for preferring one religious interpretation over other, but the important point for the issue at hand is that the depth-mystical experience itself will not be evidence for one doctrine over another. The depth-mystical experience can be added to a cumulative case that incorporates revelations, natural theology, and philosophical arguments for a "best available explanation" argument for a particular religion. But the same depth-mystical experience can be incorporated into a cumulative case for any tradition, and thus it adds no weight against cumulative cases for other traditions since it itself gives the same weight to all.

The Limitation of Any Mystical Knowledge

Moreover, even if we accept the mystical experience as a genuine contact with a transcendental reality, the flexibility of interpretation limits its claim to be specific knowledge of a transcendental reality. No doctrine is given beyond being an experience of a profound reality or a general source of some or all of reality. Mystics in dualistic states of consciousness can remember that the depth-mystical experience is free of any sense of a surface-level ego and filled with another reality, but what is the *nature* of that reality? An "ineffable insight" is a contradiction in terms: the awareness of a transcendental reality may be free of conceptions, but part of any insight must be statable—how can mystics know *that* something exists without knowing at least something of *what* it is? But what is the insight? What exactly is the knowledge gained? Mystics will know that something fundamental exists that makes our ordinary world seem less real, but any characterization of what it is beyond "beingness," "real," and "one" does not appear to be experientially given but is the result of different interpretations outside the depth-mystical state of consciousness. The mystics' total understanding will come only outside the experience with elements supplied by their tradition's religious theory. A theology based only on a core of descriptions common to all major religious doctrines would be very minimal indeed and would not satisfy any classical mystics. But this greatly limits the extent of any specific "mystical knowledge."

Thus, the experience has less cognitive content than mystics realize: even if the content is not ineffable, knowledge-claims are not determined by the experience itself. Consider these basic questions. Is the reality nonpersonal, or do mystics only experience a nonpersonal aspect of a personal reality? Is God the source of an impersonal beingness, or vice versa? Does consciousness underlie matter? Is what is experienced the source of all objective and subjective phenomena, or just the ground of the self? Must there be one source to everything, or are there multiple realities as in Samkhya? Is the experience just an intense awareness of the beingness of the world or the natural ground of the self with no further ontological significance? Is the natural world a distinct reality in its own right, or, on the other extreme, is the transcendent the only reality? Does the sense of bliss in a mystical experience come from experiencing the infusion of a loving and benevolent reality, from a more neutral sense that everything is all right as is, from freedom from a sense of self, or simply from the mind being undisturbed when it is empty of all intentional content? Does the fact that mystics may become more compassionate and loving indicate that they are in contact with a loving transcendental reality, or does it only indicate that they have ended all sense of self-importance and self-centeredness and do not feel alienated from the rest of the world? Do they project a natural human feeling of love from themselves that results from the joy they feel? Have some mystics merely internalized their tradition's ethical teachings?

In the end, mystics are in no better position to answer these questions than nonmystics, even if they have been aware of a transcendental reality and thus have a broader base of experience. Even if (contra Kant and John Hick) mystics have direct and unmediated access to a noumenal reality free of the Kantian categories that make phenomena and free of our cultural concepts structuring them, the problem of conflicting interpretations and knowledge-claims once they return to "dualistic" consciousness still persists. This also raises the question of whether the mystics themselves, after the depth-mystical experience, have a memory of the transcendent "as it really is." A memory of the depth-mystical experience makes what was experienced present to the dualistic mind—i.e., it becomes an intentional object—and so the memory of the experience is different in basic nature from the experience itself. This problem is behind Dionysius the Pseudo-Areopagite's claim that God is *unknown to the mystics themselves* except in the moment of experience.

This in turn leads to the issue of whether *any* mystical theory with its theory-laden, highly-ramified concepts actually "corresponds to" or "captures" any of the reality experienced—there will always be a human-generated, nonmystical element to any knowledge-claim. One of the possible interpretations may in fact be the best that is humanly possible, but in the absence of neutral criteria for adjudication, the presence of conflicting interpretations that have stood the test of time will remain a barrier to our knowing which one it is. In our situation, all we can do is test whether each system is internally coherent and able to explain all the available phenomenological (experiential) data. Again, theorists from each religious tradition insist their position is best and offer arguments in its favor and against other options, but to those who do not share their doctrinal framework the arguments are never convincing. It also may be that no set of doctrines is any better than any other—all are our poor, human attempts to comprehend what is beyond our ken.

At a minimum, this means that "mystical knowledge" will always have a conceptual element that mystics supply outside the experiences. As noted in Chapter 2, it is only mystical experiences in the context of mystical ways of life that actually give the alleged knowledge; the experiences alone do not dictate any concrete doctrinal claim. An appeal to more than the experiences themselves will always have to be made to justify any knowledge-claim. Religious and philosophical ideas from the mystic's tradition thus will always play a necessary role in how the mystical experience is construed and claims justified. Theists normally treat revelations and other nonmystical experiences as more fundamental in interpreting the significance of the depth-mystical experience. Nontheists will offer their reasons for their positions. But in all cases, factors outside the experiences themselves are a necessary part of the picture and will need their own justifications.

Mystics may insist that only they know reality's true nature or that the proof of their claims lies within their own hearts. But the problem again is the competing answers to all the basic questions noted above—mystics cannot get around the fact that other mystics, apparently with the same experiences, support conflicting views and have the same personal conviction. A mystic cannot say "Sorry, I've had the experience and you haven't" when making claims about the *nature of what is experienced* because equally qualified mystics are making conflicting interpretations. The certitude and finality mystics feel from the experience is transferred to a version of their traditions' beliefs, but this does not mean their interpretation is necessarily true or part of the experience itself.

The Role of Doctrine in Mystical Knowledge

Mystics may share the commonality and friendly camaraderie with mystics from other traditions of having had the same experience, and thus they may not want to dispute its interpretation with friends. Or they may have less confidence in any human conceptualizations and so be less inclined to argue with others, even if they are certain that they have verified their traditions' claims. So too, being selfless may make them less confrontational in general. But this does not negate the doctrinal differences or lead mystics to believe that doctrines do not matter or that all doctrines are really the same. As noted in Chapter 7, classical mystics themselves do not see things as so irenic: they see their own view as "correct" or "best" or "least inadequate," even if they believe that there is more to the transcendent than they have experienced, and they will contest other doctrines. If the depth-mystics' claims were only about the experiential, phenomenological nature of the experience itself rather than about what is allegedly experienced, there would not be so much of a problem, but mysticism is not about these experiences but about aligning one's life with the way things really are, and this makes doctrines about the nature of what was experienced central to mystical ways of life.

The assessment of the significance of the experience remains an issue after the experience even for the mystics themselves, as does coming up with an interpretation of a tradition's doctrines that are "adequate for" and "consistent with" the experience. But mystics' claims are about the nature of the reality experienced, and no mystical experience can guarantee the insight it allegedly provides about that—there are no "self-confirming," "self-authenticating," or "self-verifying" doctrines about the nature of what is experienced, no matter how powerful the experience giving rise to them. Again, the conflicting interpretations preclude this. Experiences of internal states of the mind may be self-authenticating (e.g., the immediate, direct knowledge of having a headache or having a memory) and thus in need of no further justification or confirmation. But any *ontological claims* beyond those for the psychological state itself are in need of further justifications—certainly the depth-mystical experience does not fall into the "self-authenticating" category when its ontological significance is open to such diverse interpretations. The memory of having had a depth-mystical experience is not any more self-authenticating than the content of any other memory. In short, no claims about the nature of reality are impervious to error or immune to challenge, even when mystical experiences are involved. Unless extreme constructivists are correct, the reality experienced has a say in such metaphysical matters by adding to the pool of experiences from which mystics make their doctrines, but what is experienced nevertheless does not determine one doctrine or a more general worldview over another. The interpretation and validation of the experience remains a philosophical enterprise after the depth-mystical is over, even for the mystics themselves.

In sum, there is a gap between experience and doctrine—between any experiential claim and any ontological claim about the reality experienced. This gap cannot be bridged by mystical experiences. No experience carries its own interpretation, and this is plainly true here. These experiences radically underdetermine different mystics' metaphysics. In explaining new phenomena in science there may be an initial diversity of conflicting theories, but scientists can test the interpretations against fresh experiential input and agreed-upon criteria for selecting the better theory; thus, eventually a consensus usually arises. But in mysticism there is no empirical way to test the interpretations and no cross-cultural set of criteria for determining the best interpretation. In particular, there is no fresh experiential input. Mystics are not learning more about a transcendental reality (if one in fact exists) that could help resolve any of the disputes. There are no new, genuinely novel depth-mystical experiences to challenge or correct previous mystical conceptions or otherwise test the various interpretations—if it is truly devoid of differentiable content, the experience remains the same each time for everyone. Mystics thus do not engage the transcendent the way scientists engage the world: there are no experiments or other input from new experiences as time goes on, but simply the same "pure consciousness" event empty of "dualistic" content recurring over and over again.[3]

The Impossibility of a Neutral Resolution

If the depth-mystical experience is indeed the same for all experiencers, this would cut both ways for the cognitive issue. It may be cited for support that mystics are in contact with a transcendental reality, although naturalists will respond that it only indicates that all mystics are undergoing the same natural process and misinterpreting it. But it also removes the experience as a way of adjudicating which interpretation is best. In such circumstances, no "thick" account of the nature of what is experienced as advocated in any particular religious tradition can be said to be given in the experience itself. Even if phenomenologists can abstract some common, universal "thin" core to the depth-mystical experience, that will not solve the problem: any minimalist account of the experience itself is free of reference to what is experienced—i.e., any thin description upon which all depth-mystics could concur about the experience itself—and thus obviously cannot resolve the problem of which of the diverse interpretations of *the nature of the reality experienced* is best. Any phenomenological account simply brackets the question of the nature of what is experienced and thus could not help resolve this issue.[4]

It must also be noted that there is no simple *empiricism* in mysticism: the experience may be essential to knowing the transcendent, but it does not dictate a concrete knowledge-claim about the nature of what is experienced—knowledge-claims even here are always more than what can be justified by the experience alone. Nevertheless, in science-and-mysticism studies, mysticism is often portrayed as a form of empiricism. Buddhism is seen as a form of "radical empiricism" (Jayatilleke 1984). A more recent example is Alan Wallace who talks about a "return to empiricism" (2006: 37).[5] He decries "mystical theology" and any "leap of faith that violates reason" (ibid.: 36). But he also has no problem utilizing the Yogacara Buddhist concept of the *alayavijnana*—a substrate consciousness that precedes life and continues beyond death in which karmic seeds take root and develop; it is the ultimate ground state of consciousness, existing prior to all conceptual dichotomies, including subject/object and mind/matter (ibid.: 33-36). But it is hard to see how such a substrate could be tested empirically—as Wallace admits, the Buddhist substrate hypothesis does not easily lend itself to a third-person scientific repudiation (ibid.: 35). It appears more like a Mahayana analog to Abhidharma theorizing—it is an attempt to answer the problem of the continuity of the mental life and the fact that karmic effects can take place in the future when everything under Buddhist metaphysics is momentary. Buddhists may invoke reincarnation experiences and accept that this is an empirical basis for the claim that we survive death (rather than reincarnation experiences being merely fantasized pseudo-memories or parapsychological knowledge of other people's lives). But this would not help with a substrate like the *alayavijnana*: such experiences do not prove that there is a reality that existed prior to the dichotomy of "mind" and "matter" or is common to more of reality than oneself, or is common to all conscious beings, or that consciousness has no beginning but has existed since the beginning of the universe, or that consciousness will never end.[6] Indeed, it is hard to see how we could come up with such a concept from any experience alone, rather than from reflecting on the problems of mental continuities (e.g., dispositions) and karmic effects when there is no self and everything is momentary. Speculation would still be involved, and, indeed, this mental substrate does appear to be a metaphysical posit. Moreover, not all Buddhists accept such a posit. In fact, the permanence of such a substrate makes it very problematic in light of Buddhist metaphysics of impermanence and momentariness. In the schools influenced by the earliest Buddhist teachings, there is no permanent continuum underlying the changing configurations of the parts constituting a person that can be found in any of our experiences. In particular, an individual's constantly changing consciousness does not arise from a permanent reality. For example, the Vaibhashikas believe, in Wallace and Hodel's words, that only "brief, irreducible moments of consciousness are the absolute level of the mind" (2008: 121). In sum, positing the substrate consciousness is not the simple result of empiricism connected to meditative or other experiences. An empiricist rather would remain agnostic about claims beyond our experience.

Nor is there any philosophical or religious point of view outside the depth-experience neutral to the competing systems. There are no agreed upon non-empirical criteria as in science for adjudicating between competing interpretations, and nothing in history suggests that all theists and nontheists will ever agree upon a set of criteria. And even if such a set were agreed upon, the application of the criteria would nevertheless turn on the competing underlying metaphysics from different traditions. Indeed, even if all theory about what is experienced can be totally separated here from the experience itself (unlike in dualistic experiences), the problem still persists. The "overbeliefs" that William James thought were imposed on the experiences themselves still remain essential to the understanding that even the mystics themselves need for their own experiences and for incorporating the experiences into a way of life.

"Properly Basic Beliefs"

Recent approaches in religious epistemology toward establishing mystical experiences as evidence for a particular conception of the transcendent fare no better than the traditional argument from religious experience for the existence of God. Consider the ideas of two philosophers—Alvin Plantinga and William Alston. Both reject the classical foundationalism of Western Enlightenment, i.e., that our knowledge-claims must ultimately be based on self-evident and incorrigible premises that stand in need of no further justification. Foundationalists argue that such basic premises are necessary in order to avoid an infinite regress of premises—i.e., otherwise, we would have no genuine knowledge but only a series of reasons that need to be supported by further reasons on and on without end. In a mystical foundationalism, mystical experiences would give doctrines in a simple, straightforward manner that proves the existence of God or Brahman or whatever. However, foundationalism in general has been rejected because philosophers, influenced by Kant, agree that there is always a conceptual element supplied to sense-perception and that this makes it impossible for any claims based on experience, including those in science, to be self-evident and beyond argument. This position also led to the constructivism discussed in the last chapter. There are no concept-free sense-experiences upon which a scientific edifice could be built. Instead, our knowledge-claims are justified more holistically by considering all our experiences and beliefs—realists and postmodernists differ over how wide a circle of such experiences and beliefs we must consider. (See Jones 2009: chap. 3.) Mysticism is in no better position with regard to foundationalism: either a conceptual element is present in the experiences themselves (as constructivists argue) or some post-experiential interpretation must be supplied to understand what was experienced (as nonconstructivists argue); either way, the diversity of religious understandings of what is experienced in a depth-mystical experience indicates that there is no culture-free depiction of what is experienced that can be the foundation for all further claims. Thus, both mindfulness and depth-mystical experiences end up in the same boat with ordinary sense-perception here.

But while both Plantinga and Alston agree in rejecting classical foundationalism, they nevertheless advance their own modified forms of foundationalism in connection to religious claims. Plantinga argues that core Christian beliefs are "properly basic" (2000). For him, "basic beliefs" are those beliefs that are not derived from other beliefs or accepted on the basis of other beliefs, and "properly" basic beliefs are basic beliefs that are formed in circumstances that rationally entitle someone to hold them (i.e., they are the result of the proper functioning of our cognitive faculties in the right epistemic environment). "Basic" does not mean the beliefs cannot be supported by experiences or are immune to all criticism but only that logically they are the most fundamental beliefs in a belief-system and are not supported by other beliefs. Belief in the existence of an objective world and the typical belief based on sense-experience or memory are examples: there is no way to question the general reliability of sense-experiences or memory, since the only way to question one sense-experience or memory is with another. To defeat a properly basic belief, any potential defeater must have a *greater* warrant than the basic belief itself; without this greater warrant, we can reject a defeater without actually advancing any independent evidence against it. In such circumstances, it is reasonable to believe a properly basic belief until shown otherwise, even if one can never devise an argument that will satisfy skeptics.

Within this framework, Plantinga argues that belief in God is properly basic. Christians have an epistemic right to hold this belief without further argument, and alleged defeaters such as the problem of evil, possible naturalistic reductions, or the diversity of conflicting religious beliefs can be rejected because they do not have a greater warrant than the basic beliefs themselves. But the Christian's properly basic belief is not groundless. It is not supported by other beliefs, but it is supported by a non-propositional experience: our sense of God. The beliefs supported by this sense are basic since they are not derived from other beliefs and are properly basic since God gave us a "sense of the divine (*sensus divinitatis*)," a mental faculty similar to sense-perception that disposes human beings to accept belief in God and enables us to form properly basic beliefs about God's presence and nature. It provides a natural knowledge of God and provides grounds for the belief (but not *evidence* for the truth of one's beliefs.) Needless to say, naturalists deny there is any such proper mental functioning and offer other explanations for why we may be disposed to believe in transcendental realities. But as long as this alleged sense has not actually been discredited, Plantinga claims that it is just as rational for Christians to hold their belief in God without further argument as it is rational for them to hold their basic perceptual beliefs. In other words, it is rational for Christians to hold their belief since it is supported by an experience that has not been shown to be unreliable. Consequently, atheism is not properly basic (since there is the God-given sense of the divine). Atheists, nontheists, and those who have lost their faith are comparable to blind people with respect to sense-perception, and the burden of proof shifts to atheists to prove their position.

However, not even everyone who is sympathetic to religion agrees with this approach. It is hard to see bedrock Christian beliefs as not in need of any support by evidence or arguments from other beliefs when so many other people do not see them as true. The same holds for a more general belief in theism. Such beliefs do not seem "basic" but in need of support by reasons at least recognizable to critics. Plantinga alleges the "sense of God" is analogous to sense-perception, but most people would admit that we can disagree about the existence of God in a way that we cannot dispute the general reliability of sense-perceptions or memories. Nor does his position account for the diversity of views within various theistic traditions over fundamental issues. Nor does his posited sense seem to account for the presence of atheists and the nonreligious who simply are not interested in religious matters—the segment of society that, in Max Weber's phrase, is "religiously unmusical." Many people looking at the glory of the night sky may well think that there must be a designer/creator behind all this to whom we owe gratitude and obedience, but there are still many others who are awed by the grandeur of the universe and do not think of anything transcending it—and there are many who are impressed by science who agree with Steven Weinberg when he says "[t]he more the universe seems comprehensible, the more it also seems pointless." Claiming that a God-given "sense of the divine" is malfunctioning in these nontheistic reactions is simply question-begging and demands further argument. And invoking the Calvinist position that God has not *chosen* those who do not react theistically is only an *ad hoc* excuse. How do we know that the intuition of a designer and creator is not a purely natural anthropomorphic projection of agency and purpose where there is none rather than a divinely implanted sense? In the end, in introducing a "sense of the divine," Plantinga seems to be trying to make what is no more than any other metaphysical *belief* that needs support into something like an *experience* in order to shield it from criticism.

Plantinga's posited sense also does not explain why there are nontheistic traditions—why should a major segment of humanity be "blind"? In his characterization, the religious sense is not merely a sense of a fundamental, transcendental reality, but a sense of *God*—he may not see the difference, but others do. Why do, for example, Advaitins and Buddhists respond differently in circumstances where theists respond with theistic beliefs? Why do they not need a creator god among their deities? In addition, there is the problem of the diversity of belief among theists—there does not appear to be one "sense of God" beyond the sense of a person and the metaphysical requirement of a creator. Why do Hindus respond to faith in the Vedas with the same "spontaneity" that Plantinga claims Jews, Christians, and Muslims respond to their theistic texts? In such circumstances, why shouldn't theists question whether in fact there is a "sense of the divine" and attempt to find reasons for their beliefs? How can such beliefs be "basic"?

Plantinga thinks his epistemology allows him to speak of what Christians *know as Christians* rather than what they *believe*. He thinks the warrant that is needed to make a "true belief" into "knowledge" is a matter of *reliability*: if our belief is produced by a reliable faculty or cognitive process, then we have the necessary warrant to claim knowledge. He, of course, thinks the "sense of the divine" is an instance of a properly functioning mental belief-forming apparatus. But religious nontheists do not agree there is a personal creator behind the natural realm, and naturalists are not at all convinced that they have not shown that the brain is malfunctioning in such experiences. And lowering the standard of what can be rationally believed to what cannot actually be disproved introduces the problem of whether one is entitled to believe *anything* that has not been conclusively disproved. This opens the door to many different beliefs becoming acceptable, accompanied by the smugness of people saying "Well, at least you can't prove I'm wrong!" Even if there is some general mystical sense of a transcendental reality that is analogous to sense-perception or memory that we could not question any more than those functions, we still have competing sets of knowledge-claims—i.e., different specific interpretations of the results of this mystical sense—that are based on other beliefs and are not "basic" but need defending. Thus, even if Plantinga can get around the general objection that his epistemology allows belief in voodoo or the Great Pumpkin to be properly basic by arguing that religious beliefs are grounded in a specific mental capacity—the "sense of the divine"—still the diversity of religious traditions resulting from this alleged sense presents a major hurdle. To nontheists, the sense does not seem to present a personal being, and their beliefs seem as "basic" to them as theistic ones seems to theists.

Plantinga's attempt to deal with religious diversity (2000: 437-57) does not adequately address the problem. He defends Christian exclusivism: human beings need salvation, and God has provided a unique way through the incarnation, life, sacrificial death, and resurrection of his divine son, Jesus of Nazareth. In the absence of any proof or argument that can be counted on to convince exclusivists to reject their beliefs, he believes exclusivism is a rational position to hold. That is, it is rational to hold any position that others cannot *prove* wrong, and, since it is virtually impossible to produce a definitive disproof of anything in the matter of the relation of conflicting religious truth-claims, Plantinga believes his rationality in holding exclusivism is established. To others, this situation means precisely the opposite—that we have to defend whatever position we adopt with positive arguments. But because of his views on rationality, Plantinga feels that he does not have to offer positive support for his Christian exclusivism, nor does he actually have to argue *against* any other tradition's doctrines—he only has to show that Christian exclusivism is not logically impossible and that there are no contrary positions that can be definitively established in the field, and then his case is made.

Plantinga is, of course, aware of the difference between mere *logical consistency* and a more convincing *plausibility*. But he thinks that only the absence of both logical contradictions and proof of a contrary position is enough for an exclusivist to be rational. However, by this standard *every* theological and philosophical position in the field of religious diversity is established as "rational"—pluralism, inclusivism, and non-Christian exclusivisms are consistent and cannot be refuted by any finding on religious diversity, and so anyone can rationally hold any of these positions. The bar of rationality is lowered dramatically, and there is very little left for philosophers of religion to do. In this postmodern world, everyone can maintain their position even though they are aware than others have conflicting positions. Of course, exclusivists may assert that they in fact have no epistemic peers in other traditions: only members of their own tradition are properly inspired by the inner witness of the Holy Spirit or whatever.[7] But exclusivists in all traditions must feel the same way or they would not be exclusivists—each must feel in his or her heart that members of that tradition are in a unique position with regard to religious diversity. What exactly the "sense of the divine" that Plantinga alleges is in this situation is unclear. And one cannot help but think that if Plantinga had been born in a Muslim country, he would be writing just as enthusiastically about Islamic exclusivism; indeed, if we change only a single word in his writings—"Christ" to "Qur'an"—his writings become works of exclusivism for that religion. But this situation suggests that all exclusivists are all in the same epistemic position, and in that case they all must make a further defense of their claims to be deemed "rational."

Plantinga's response to the criticism of exclusivism is two-fold: to the charge of "moral" arbitrariness and arrogance, he replies that those who believe they are right believe they are right, and it is not arrogance but simply a matter of logic to say so; and he relies again on the idea of a *sensus divinitatis* as a special source of knowledge entitling Christians to deny that non-Christians are on an epistemic par with them.[8] Needless to say, members of other religions, both theistic and nontheistic, would disagree with the second part, and Plantinga does not have a further reply except to reassert his faith. He even concedes that his approach only works for those who find that the belief that God exists is within their own set of basic beliefs. He admits that people in other faiths will have quite different beliefs that they consider properly basic. This makes it impossible to offer an argument for the superiority of theism or any religious tradition. Theism is cut off into a postmodern intellectual ghetto, and Plantinga cannot respond to those who do not have the belief that God exists within their own set of basic beliefs.

Saying, as Plantinga does, that the sense of the divine is simply malfunctioning by sinfulness or spiritual immaturity in the case of atheists, members of nontheistic religious traditions, and those who have lost their faith does follow directly from his particular basic beliefs, but to others it seems to be arbitrarily privileging the tradition he just happened to have been raised in. Buddhists and Advaitins may respond that it is belief in a personal god that in fact is the result of a malfunctioning mystical cognitive faculty: the proper sense of the transcendent is contaminated by theists' all-too-human response of seeing personal agents behind everything, a vestige of our primitive anthropomorphism. There is no neutral way to decide the question, but only a battle of competing basic beliefs. So, are all believers *ipso facto* rational, and no further defense of any tradition is possible? Plantinga shapes the notion of an innate spiritual sense to fit the position he was already committed to, and those in other traditions would have the same right to shape the sense differently to fit their preconceived conclusions. Again, everyone ends up being "rational," whatever their religious tradition's basic doctrines. But the great diversity of religious and nonreligious views is not what one would expect if one truly "properly basic belief" were in fact involved. If there are rival sets of "properly basic beliefs," then the situation strongly suggests none are in fact so and a defense of one's beliefs is in order.

Religious diversity *per se* does not defeat exclusivism, but the apparent parity of practices behind claims from different traditions that appear to compete and conflict with each other is a *prima facie* defeater. Without some further argumentation, the awareness that believers in other traditions appear to be in the same position—making claims based on the same type and quality of sources as one's own—neutralizes exclusivism. One cannot exempt one's own beliefs from a need for reasons by calling them alone "properly basic"—since only they would reflect the properly functioning "sense of God"—once one is aware that competitors are apparently in the same position as one's own. Each competitor has as much right to claim that its beliefs are "properly basic," and we end up with a pluralism of exclusivisms, all equally rational. This pluralism would extend even to within theism: different theistic religions and even subtraditions within the same religion have different views of God. Plantinga would have to present arguments for why Christian basic beliefs of his subtradition are reliably formed while others are not and hence that other mystics are not in fact in the same epistemic situation as certain Christian mystics. Part of this would be trying to show that one's scriptural sources are epistemically superior. But this situation presents a problem for the idea that the "sense of the divine" leads to "properly basic beliefs": if only one set of religious beliefs is in fact epistemically superior, then all the other sets based on the same "sense of the divine" are in some way wrong; thus, the alleged "sense of the divine" is *not a reliable means to formulating beliefs*, unlike sense-experience, since the majority of people are in fact misled.

As things stand now, mystics of the various religious traditions of the world do appear to be relying on their own equally compelling experiences and similar sources and thus appear to be epistemic peers. Simply asserting by fiat that one set of religious beliefs is superior to all others without some independent and non-question-begging argument for this claim would be arbitrary and not grounds to claim any epistemic superiority. In short, without arguments showing that apparent competitors are not epistemic peers, we will end up in a relativism of "properly basic beliefs," and in such circumstances no one would be warranted in claiming that one set of beliefs is superior to others—when everyone can claim that their beliefs are privileged, none are. Unlike beliefs based on sense-experiences, no beliefs in religious matters are exempt from a need for argument—i.e., none are "basic," let alone "properly basic."

In addition, Plantinga's admission that other religious tradition's beliefs may also be "properly basic" conflicts with any claim to exclusivism. Exclusivism involves the claims that one tradition's beliefs are superior to the combined claims of any other tradition, and to be justified in claiming this we would actually have to compare the claims or how the claims were formed. How can we know one is better off epistemically without actually studying others' situation? Personal certitude or intuitive obviousness concerning one's own beliefs would not justify any claim to epistemic superiority or give one the right to make such a claim while ignoring others' circumstances. Falling back on faith or trust cannot justify a claim to exclusivism since all believers can do the same. One's experiences, no matter how vivid or strong, and one's conviction that no other religious beliefs could possibly be superior, no matter how well-established, do not warrant believing that one's beliefs are superior to others without such a comparison of the various practices of belief-formation. Calling these beliefs "properly basic" does not change this. Only after one has examined the epistemic situations of all competitors is one warranted in believing they are not one's peers in this regard.

In sum, not too many people who are not already committed to Christianity would be satisfied with privileging any Christian or other theistic mystical beliefs in this way, and those who do so privilege Christian beliefs would not have a response to people who either do not share the alleged theistic *sensus divinitatis*. There would be no way to judge which, if any, of the mystical systems is superior. We end up with a relativism of competing "divine senses" and allegedly "properly basic beliefs" and equally rational believers. But, if anything, this shows that the Christian commitment, and by extension any other religious commitment, is not "properly basic" but in need of further rational support: even if there is a mystical sense comparable to sense-experience, still the commitments of any specific religious tradition depend on beliefs that must be defended on other grounds.

The Analogy to Sense-Perception

William Alston also stresses an analogy to sense-perception, calling mystical experiences "mystical perceptions" (1991).[9] He focuses, not on the experiences themselves, but on the belief-forming and evaluating practices connected to them ("doxatic practices"). His basic position is that if a mystical practice as a whole can be shown to be epistemically similar to the practice of forming beliefs on the basis of sense-perceptions or memories than it is just as rational to accept the former as it is to accept the latter. There is no non-circular way to justify the latter as a whole since we must rely on other sense-perceptions or memories to confirm or disconfirm any claims based them. We must accept the general reliability of sensing and memory, and he argues that the same holds for some mystical practices. He concentrates on Christian mysticism and argues that Christian mystical practices do give Christian mystical beliefs the same epistemic status as beliefs formed from sense-experiences and memories and have nothing to disqualify their rational acceptance. But he admits that the mystical belief-forming practice does not have the *same degree* of reliability as sense-perception's since there is nothing comparable in mystical practices to third-person checking of beliefs based on sense-perception (ibid.: 211-13, 238).

According to Alston, both sense-experience and mystical experience involve a direct realism, i.e., the perceptions involve access to, and a direct awareness of, its objects. In both cases, there is also no independent way of establishing the purported objects of the experience. Alston also accepts both types of experience as reliable. Under a principle of credulity, just as we have to trust a sense-experience until it is proved unreliable, so too do we have to accept basic Christian mystical beliefs at face value until we have good reasons for rejecting them. In short, mystical perception is "innocent until proven guilty." And the Christian mystical practice is rationally engaged in because it is a socially-established belief-forming practice that is not demonstrably unreliable or otherwise disqualified for rational acceptance (1991: 194). Thus, Christian mystical perception should be accepted as a reliable cognitive access to God. Like sense-experience, this basic mode of apprehension needs no other support, and it can become the foundation for other beliefs. It is therefore rational for Christians to regard the Christian mystical practice as sufficiently reliable to be the source of *prima facie* justification for the Christian beliefs it engenders. Of course, the *rationality* of the practice does not establish the *truth* of the claims—just as sense-experiences may be hallucinatory and memories can be faulty, so too basic mystical claims can be wrong even if it is rational to accept them.

The analogy to sense-perception has not convinced many (see Gale 2005: 428-33 for standard objections). "Participatory knowledge" does not seem like a "non-sensory sense-perception" since it has no object-like content to perceive. Moreover, we cannot avoid sense-perception—we cannot help but have the world impinge on us and must rely upon sense-experience to survive—but we can avoid mystical experiences without difficulty. Indeed, spontaneous mystical experiences are comparatively rare; even for those who have one or a few such experiences, they are rare compared to a life-time of sense-experiences. In addition, the difference in the matter of public-checkability between mystical experiences and sense-perceptions remains too significant for most critics. Even if requiring third-person checking and testing for any claim about reality is "epistemic imperialism" (Alston 1991: 216), that there is a way to falsify beliefs based on sense-experiences by new experiences while the depth-mystical experience remains constant still breaks the analogy. So too, we must trust the general reliability of sense-experience and memory in a way that we do not have to with mystical experiences. This is especially so when we are aware of the conflict of established mystical doxastic practices from around the world: there is no alternative explanation for the sensory claims, as Alston admits (ibid.: 275), but there is a significant variety of religious explanations of the mystical experiences. So too, the alternative of plausible naturalistic reductions of mystical experiences must be taken into consideration; if nothing else, this limits any analogy.

The world is "religiously ambiguous" (Hick 1989: 226), both between natural and religious explanations and among competing religious explanations, but it is not "physically ambiguous" when it comes to sense-experiences. There simply are more types of choices in the case of depth-mystical experiences than for sense-experiences: religious beliefs are more diverse and even incompatible on the very nature of what is experienced in a way that beliefs about the external world are not. Cultural beliefs may well shape our sense-experiences and produce diverse catalogs of the objects populating the world, but beliefs lead to variations in the understanding of the mystical experiential input in a way that they do not in sense-experience:

identifying the experience as, say, an experience of a theistic god is not given in the experience itself in any straightforward way but depends on applying a large body of theological background beliefs. It is a difference about the *fundamental nature of what is experienced*, not merely a difference in classification as with sense-objects. Mystical experiences have a smaller role in the final determination of knowledge-claims based on the experiences than in the case of sense-experiences. And, as with Plantinga's "sense of the divine," if in the end one religious conception is correct and the rest are wrong, then most mystics are wrong, and thus mystical experience, unlike sense-perception, is an *unreliable basis for belief-formation*.

On the other side, those who think that the depth-mystical experience is unique epistemically as well as physiologically (and so requires a unique scientific explanation) also reject the analogy to sense-perceptions as misleading—just because theistic mystics use sensory terms ("seeing," "touching," "grasping," "penetrating") taken from the everyday world does not mean that the depth-mystical experience is in any substantive way like a sense-experience or that forming beliefs based on it is parallel in epistemic status. Even advocates of the analogy to sense-experience admit that the analogy is only very loose (see Gale 2005: 432-33), and Alston in the end concedes the analogy amounts to no more than that sense-experiences and mystical experiences are both "*socially embedded.*"

But even if there is a parallel between sense-experience and the depth-mystical experience, there is still a problem: it will not help to establish the claims of any specific mystical practice. At most, all that is established is that mystics have contact with a transcendental reality, not the superiority of any particular interpretation or theism in general. The diversity of established religious traditions with conflicting characterizations again raises its head. Even if Alston is correct about the rationality of Christian mystical practices, he admits that Buddhists and Hindus are just as rational in engaging in their own socially-established doxastic practices, even though these three traditions are incompatible in their claims (1991: 274-75).[10] The doxastic justification makes the claim to the equal rationality of all mystics fairly easy to establish—in fact, it is hard *not* to be rational by Alston's criterion of an established social practice that we do not have sufficient reason for regarding as unreliable (ibid.: 6) since each tradition has survived a long time and has responded extensively to the scrutiny and criticism of opponents. Each tradition would thus be rational to engage in by this standard. But Alston's approach does not provide any way to prefer one tradition over another or any way to adjudicate the conflicting truth-claims. With no independent, non-question-begging way to establish that one's own doxastic practices are more reliable for getting at the truth than its competitors, other established practices appear to be epistemic peers. The result is an unresolvable relativism. And Alston also has to admit that this diversity does *lessen the rationality* of all mystical practices (ibid.: 275): if we stick to the belief-output of any one religious tradition, it is not internally incoherent in a major way, but if we look at the output of all mystical traditions, major inconsistencies between traditions do prevail.

The bottom line is that Alston's argument, if successful, may be grounds to accept beliefs based on accepting the depth-mystical experience as an awareness of a transcendental reality comparable in an epistemic way to sense-experience of natural objects, but the diversity of competing and equally "rational" established ways of life and interpretations of what is experienced eviscerates the idea that these experiences can uniquely support the concrete knowledge-claims of any particular mystical tradition. That is, they cannot support the knowledge-claims that mystics actually make in the different traditions over other interpretations. Thus, we cannot create a foundation of actual knowledge-claims in mysticism this way. Support will have to come for each tradition's knowledge-claims from sources outside the mystical experiences themselves.

Ultimate Decisions

Thus, both Plantinga's and Alston's arguments falter against the hard case of religious diversity. But in the end, the depth-mystical experience—even if it is the basis for properly basic beliefs or is analogous to sense-experience—does not do what the advocates here hope. The metaphysical and epistemological problems connected to it remain unresolved. Are we left then with simply a conflict of metaphysics? There may be systems-neutral reasons for why one metaphysical system is better than another, i.e., reasons that disputants on all sides can agree upon to show what seems more plausible in light of all we know. But this would be doubtful in any metaphysical dispute—e.g., in the mind/body field today, many disputants do not believe that their opponents really believe what they are saying.

And here too the conflict appears to remain stubbornly unresolvable. We have reached the level of bedrock beliefs—the conflict will come down to our intuitions and judgments about what is the fundamental nature of reality, what we consider ultimately valuable, and what types of experiences we accept as cognitive. No fundamental choice among competing basic belief-systems can ever be fully justified on rational grounds, since there is no further mutually agreed-upon level of beliefs or values to appeal to. As Ludwig Wittgenstein said: "If I have exhausted the justifications, I have reached bedrock and my spade is turned. Then I am inclined to say 'This is simply what I do'(*Philosophical Investigations,* para. 217)." The situation is much shakier than the foundationalisms proposed by Plantinga and Alston would suggest. This is not to say that the final decision is irrational or cannot be well-informed and carefully considered, including examining possible alternatives and criticisms, but only that ultimately we have to make a choice that we cannot further justify.

The most important point to note for the issues at hand is that neither the scientific study of meditators (as discussed in Chapter 13) nor the mystical experiences themselves can help to resolve the disputes between naturalism and religion or among the various religious traditions. We have a conflict of starting points for any argument or justification; it becomes a matter of worldviews and metaphysics, and philosophy will not be able to resolve the dispute. In a "religiously ambiguous" universe, we are forced to choose. Thus, we are not in a position to resolve the issue of this chapter. But whether any mystics are correct or not, it is hard to argue by the standards of today's religious epistemology that mystics are *irrational* in believing that they have been aware of a transcendental reality, even if the nature of that reality remains a mystery. This is enough to make it reasonable for the rest of us to accept, at least for the sake of argument, both that a transcendental reality exists and that the depth-mystical experience is an awareness of that reality. Thus, it is reasonable to proceed to see if it is possible to accommodate both science and mysticism as ways of knowing.

Notes

1. Many philosophers and theologians today have given up the idea that the existence of God can be proved or disproved. Rather, the attempt today is not to convince a nonbeliever to become a believer, but to show that participation in one's own religious way of life is rational and that holding particular religious beliefs is rational. Moving from *proving* the existence of a transcendental reality to showing merely the *rationality* of believing a given religious belief significantly lowers the bar of what has to be accomplished: one can be shown to be rational without proving that the beliefs are true—e.g., based on the evidence available at the time, it was rational two thousand years ago to believe the earth was flat. In practice, showing that it is rational to believe something becomes merely showing that it is *not irrational*, i.e., contrary to reason and evidence. An intermediate position is to argue that theism is "more reasonable" to hold than naturalism or vice versa, and thus that it is "less rational" to be a naturalist or a theist. (Note that Plantinga and Alston argue that it is *rational* for Christians to participate in their way of life, but not that non-Christians and the non-religious are *irrational* in rejecting it even while accepting that sense-experience leads to epistemically justified beliefs.) This at least requires more positive support for a position. But in the end each party ends up defining what is "reasonable" from their own point of view. Merely showing that participation in a given religion is not irrational in the sense of not being contrary to the canons of logic or to the best available empirical evidence is much easier than having to prove that its doctrines are true—in fact, it is hard to show that, for example, the general idea of a creator god involves a logical inconsistency or defies empirical experiences, especially after thinkers have spent so much time reflecting on all sides of the issues involved and at least liberals can always adjust their religious beliefs to be compatible with the scientific and other beliefs of the day. That is, if opponents cannot show that one's position involves a logical contradiction or must deny what everyone admits is the best available evidence, then it is at least not irrational to hold one's beliefs, even though they are not confirmable. To be rational, we do not need compelling evidence or prove that our opponents are wrong. And if it is rational to accept *unexplainable mysteries* (e.g., why God or the world exists), the argument for being rational becomes almost trivially easy. Thus, if it is rational, for example, to respond to the problem of natural suffering by saying "It's not irrational to believe that a creator god has his reasons for permitting suffering that we mortals cannot be expected to know," then showing that theists are rational is not a problem at all. But shifting the problem to only being rational also introduces the problem

of religious diversity: participants in other religions are just as likely to be rational. Virtually everyone, naturalist and religious alike, is rational by these standards (at least if they have considered the issues), and no positions can be eliminated. But the most important point for the issues at hand is that the depth-mystical experience is neutral to all such assessments.

2. Philosophers who rely on a principle of credulity often downplay the importance of any third-person checking since such checking is ultimately circular (e.g., Gellman 2001): the reliability of any third-person checking depends on other third-person checking of that checking. But just because we do have to make assumptions here does not mean that anything goes and that we should accept mystical claims simply because many mystics over the centuries have made them.

3. The Abrahamic theists' views of the nature of God have evolved over the last three thousand years from a warrior tribal chieftain to a universal being, from a wrathful authority to a loving being. Arguably, depth-mystical experiences contributed to this process in the past. But these experiences can no longer offer fresh input for any future theological revisions since the depth-mystical experience does not offer any fresh experiential insights but remains the same "pure consciousness" event for everyone every time.

4. Ralph Hood (2002) argues from phenomenology alone that the depth-mystical experience involves a transcendental self. But again, the diversity of interpretations in the various theistic and nontheistic traditions precludes making an argument about the nature of what is experienced based on the experience's phenomenological features alone.

5. Wallace may mean by "empiricism" simply "empirical" by which he means "experiential" (2006: 146). However, as pointed out in Chapter 5, note 10, "empiricism" is a philosophical position about what we can know. It contrasts with rationalism, but it involves more than simply being "experiential." Some scientists may like the positivist position that there should be no unobservables in a scientific theory, but most scientists accept the need of such entities in explanations. Einstein is an example of a scientist who went from being a positivist to being a realist in this regard. In mystical studies, we cannot go from simply the fact that mysticism involves experiences to an endorsement of empiricism.

6. See Wallace 2009: 105-18 on the issue of rebirth and how to test for it. (Also see Stevenson 1987 for a case for rebirth.)

7. On the issue of whether acknowledging members of other religious traditions as one's epistemic peers would necessarily lead to rejecting one's own religious commitment or at least rejecting exclusivism, see Kraft and Basinger 2008: part 1.

8. Plantinga does not address the real moral problem with Christian exclusivism: more than three quarters of mankind who do not belong to Christian. Thus, if one must be a Christian to escape eternal punishment, then according to orthodox views in Christianity since Augustine all those people are condemned to being tortured in hell for eternity. Why would a moral god create people when so many of them will be tortured for eternity for no more fault than being born in the wrong part of the world to appreciate or even know of the "true religion"? If the creator has foreknowledge, the problem is only compounded. Indeed, what is the moral point of *eternal* punishment? Why doesn't a loving and merciful god do something about it? (Since Vatican II, Roman Catholics have modified their official position into an "inclusivism": those who through no fault of their own do not know of Christ and the church but who are otherwise Christian in their actions and beliefs may be saved by God even though they are not consciously or explicitly part of his church.)

9. Shankara too made an analogy to sense-perception for the mystical experience. However, his nondualistic metaphysics limits the analogy: sensory knowledge is dependent on causal relations, unlike awareness of the underlying Brahman. (See Phillips 2001.)

10. Alston speaks of the "*practical rationality*" of engaging in any socially-established doxastic practice that one does not have sufficient reasons for regarding as unreliable (1991: 168) since there is no non-circular way to distinguish between different reliable doxastic practices. But religious diversity once again presents a problem. As a practical matter, we all of course do have to choose how to live, but once the religious know of the variety of socially-established but conflicting mystical practices there is the issue of *arbitrariness* in their choice, and labeling adherence to the tradition one grew up in as "practical rationality" or "the most reasonable course of action" does not get around this.

— 16 —

A Reconciliation of Science and Mysticism

If we accept that we are living in a "religiously ambiguous" universe, what are those of us whose starting point is the value of science supposed to do about mysticism? A naturalistic reduction is one option (as noted below), but it can also be shown that the depth-mystical experience can be accepted as cognitive of a transcendental reality without giving up anything of science. Most of us begin with the mind-set that science and mysticism must be about the same thing (since they are both allegedly cognitive of reality) and thus are in competition—we must accept one and reject the other. But if we can get out of this mind-set and realize that science and mysticism are ways of knowing *different aspects* of reality, the solution is straight forward: science provides insights into the various natural structures ordering the natural world, and mystical experiences provide awareness of the source of beingness underlying ourselves or the entire world (depth-mystical experience) and direct awareness free of the conceptualizing mind of the beingness, impermanence, and interconnectedness of the everyday world (mindfulness).[1]

If we are willing to grant simply for the sake of argument that both endeavors are cognitive—obviously a big "if"—science and mysticism can be taken as each supplying insights into the world that the other does not. They offer alternative pictures of the same world—one in terms of its structures, the other in terms of beingness—but we need not accept one and reject the other.[2] Both endeavors are fundamentally different and serve different purposes. One does not resolve the mysteries encountered by the other. Scientists are not on the path to "mystical unity," nor are mystics supplying information on the components and structures of nature or offering support for scientific claims. At most, mystical experiences supply new data on mental states. Nor is either science or mystical enlightenment the culmination of all our cognitive development. Each enterprise does something the other does not, and thus neither is reducible to the other—mysticism deals with the warp of reality and science the woof, as it were. And because of their different subject matters, they cannot be integrated into one epistemic endeavor: each pierces the veil between us and reality, but different things are revealed behind it through the different means. In short, both endeavors are needed to supply us with a fuller view of reality. (Also see Jones 1986: 214-18, 2004: 388-95.)

A Worldview Incorporating Science and Mysticism

Unlike in Chapter 10, the objective here is not to come up with *a set of metaphysical beliefs* about the nature of the world upon which science and mysticism are allegedly converging. Rather, the objective is to sketch the metaphysics of a worldview that accepts both science and mysticism as *distinct ways of knowing reality with unrelatable theories*.

The basic metaphysical premise must be that both the natural realm and a transcendent realm are fundamentally real. This involves accepting the classical mystics' claim of experiencing transcendental realities. However, a naturalistic alternative is possible that keeps what is experienced in a depth-mystical experience firmly within the natural realm without claiming it is the result of a brain malfunction: the depth-mystical experience is merely the experience of a bare but purely natural consciousness or is awareness of a purely natural self. (See Sullivan 1995; Austin 1998, 2006; Angel 2002.) Naturalists can also differentiate the consciousness of mindfulness (the differentiation of the witnessing awareness from the stream of phenomenal content flowing through any conscious state) from that of the depth-mystical experience (after the mind is emptied of all sensory and conceptual content, the monitoring activity of the mind still continues even in the absence of any processing) (Peters 2000). In fact, all mystics could accept that consciousness is a purely natural product or even that the presence of conscious beings in the universe is merely an amazing coincidence resulting from random events—there would still be the awareness of beingness in a mystical experience, and this is all mystics could claim from their experiences. Any transcendental explanation would be untestable and hence go beyond science. For that reason naturalists would reject any classical mystical explanation. To them, what is experienced in the depth-mystical experience is only the natural mind; it only seems to be a greater reality that is conscious in nature because of the mental nature of all experiences. In mindfulness, all that happens is that attention is shifted from a figure to the encompassing background, and the area of the brain responsible for a sense of a boundary between the self and the rest of the universe receives less input and so naturally we feel more connected to the universe, which in naturalistic metaphysics we are. Thereby, the self-transcendence valued in spirituality can be achieved, even though this transcendence does not transcend the natural realm. To naturalists, there is nothing wrong in practicing this mindfulness—it is merely a Gestalt-like switch from an object to its field. But this does not mean that the objects are not real, nor is this shift in attention of any value to science since it ignores real distinctions in nature.[3]

Such a naturalistic reconciliation may be easier to maintain than the one proposed here since it keeps the depth-mystical experience within the natural universe. But it is not necessary to naturalize the depth-mystical experience for a reconciliation of mysticism with science. It is possible to accept the classical mystical position that the experience is contact with a transcendental reality. For all classical mystical traditions, consciousness is a reality of some type that transcends the natural order and thus conflicts with any form of naturalism, let alone reductive materialism. Thus, if we are to accept anything of the classical mystics' cognitive claims, the mystical experience cannot be reduced to experiences of only the natural world. For a reconciliation therefore, naturalism must be abandoned, and some transcendental dimension to both reality and a human being that is open to experience must be accepted. But as discussed in Chapter 12, science is not naturalism, and thus giving up naturalism is not giving up science.

To accept any conciliation with science, mystics must make one major concession: they must accept the full reality of the natural world in order to give science its due. The natural world is fully real in the sense that, although it may be dependent in some way on a transcendental source, it is now part of the ultimate makeup of reality and must be treated as such. No matter how powerful the depth-mystical experience feels, any mystical metaphysics that dismisses the natural universe as less than fully real must be rejected. So too, we cannot make our ultimate goal our escape from this world. Even Buddhist Bodhisattvas who forego a final nirvana and choose to remain in the realm of rebirth in order to help others still have the objective of helping all sentient beings to escape this realm. Instead, we all must treat the natural realm as an end in itself. But the depth-mystical experience can in fact be accepted as an insight into the nature of reality without denigrating the world of time at all: it can be accepted as an experience of another dimension to the world—a transcendental source of the self or the being of all of the natural universe. Science is neutral to the possible reality of a transcendental realm, and so its theories do not intersect claims about such a realm.

Classical mystics, however, would reject this concession. To them, we are in the world but not of it. Any acceptance of a this-worldly dimension to what is ultimately real is in effect an endorsement of naturalism and a denial of transcendental realities. The knowledge connected to our bodies and our ego is ultimately insignificant at best or not knowledge at all at worst. Instead, we need to get in touch with the source of our being. What the scientifically-minded count as knowledge is only the illusion of wisdom: we need to break free of the tyranny of the senses to attain true wisdom—we need to break free of the chains of Plato's cave and see the source of the shadows on the cave walls. To such mystics, we in the modern world are so thoroughly secularized today that we have totally lost sight of the source of our being and do not even realize that we live in a cave and are responding to mere shadows on the walls.

That is, classical mystics typically conclude from the powerful depth-mystical experience that there is a conflict of interests between this-worldly knowledge and mystical knowledge, and that we cannot serve two masters—we have to be focused with our entire being exclusively the transcendental realm or we are really serving the natural world. They see things solely in terms of accepting either one or the other realm as real and end up devaluing the latter completely. Classical depth-mystics are so overwhelmed by the transcendent that they reject the natural realm as either unreal (in the sense being dependent upon the transcendent for its existence and so having no ontological reality of its own) or as not significant enough to care about when compared to the transcendental realm. Either way, the natural world is seen as an enemy to be overcome. Not that, for example, Advaita Vedanta has any explanation for why the "unreal" realm exists at all—both for why the invisible *brahman/atman* was refracted into visible colors by the limiting conditions (*upadis*) of the root ignorance, and for where this ignorance (*avidya*) came from. Indeed, all mystical traditions, both theistic and nontheistic, have the problem of why both the natural and the transcendental realities exist, and why there would need to be two types of knowledge.

The response to the classical mystics' position begins by accepting that no experience carries its own interpretation. As discussed in Chapter 14, the distinction between "experience" and "interpretation" exists for depth-mystical experiences, if not all experiences. The depth-mystical experience radically underdetermines its interpretation—it is open to various nondualisms and dualisms. As discussed, after the depth-mystical experience, mystics return to a state of consciousness where they have to understand what has occurred and where the transcendental reality becomes an object of intentional consciousness. If mystics are correct, the basic ontological implication of the depth-mystical state of consciousness is that mystics have indeed been aware of a reality having profound significance for the nature of their individual being or for the whole natural world. At a minimum, it is an infusion of a reality that blows away any sense that the everyday ego is an irreducible reality. It can overwhelm all other types of experiences in its cognitive importance, leading to the dismissal of everything else experienced as unreal (as with Advaita). But it is also open to other interpretations. For example, Samkhya-Yogins take it to be the experience of our true self (*purusha*) distinct from matter—thereby, the material realm (*prakriti*) remains equally fully real, even though the goal for this way of life is to separate the true self from the material, and thus to leave the material world.

No one mystical interpretation needs to be endorsed for a basic conciliation with science as ways of knowing—only a transcendental dimension to reality that is open to mystical experiences needs to be affirmed. Whatever interpretation of the content of the depth-mystical experience that a particular person finally adopts depends on considerations other than the depth-mystical experience itself. But whatever interpretation is finally applied, mystical experiences still must be understood outside the depth-mystical state of consciousness and must be weighed against our other experiences—mystical experiences themselves do not entail the judgment that the world must be rejected or that what is revealed by ordinary states of consciousness is unreal. Advaitins cannot simply say that the depth-mystical experience reveals the diversity of the sense-experience realm to be an illusion in the way that sense-experience exposes some perceptions to be optical illusions; this must be seen as a judgment since the world of diversity remains intact. It is one thing to claim "There is a transcendental source to this world" and something quite different to claim "Nothing is real but the source." The Advaita interpretation is not given in the experience itself; it is merely one possible interpretation that must be supported by reasons encompassing more than the consideration of what is experienced in the depth-mystical experience alone. That Shankara appealed to revealed scripture—interpreted with a hammer to fit his metaphysics—for the correct understanding of experiences is an admission that the correct understanding is not given in the depth-mystical experience itself. While mystical experiences are an element in the decision, any such decision is ultimately based also on factors outside mystical experiences themselves. In the end, we all must choose how to weigh our various experiences, based on values and considerations outside any one type of experience, and this choice will be made outside of the depth-mystical experience in a "dualistic" state of mind. Indeed, the very fact that we have to make such choices by itself points to the reality of our situation and thus this world.

The relation of the realm of ceaseless becoming to the root of changeless being—how a source gives rise to the natural world—remains a mystery. Neither science nor a mystical experience offers help on this issue. But if a mysticism is to accept the reality of the natural world, anything like the Advaita interpretation must be rejected. (It should also be noted that Shankara's own practices contradicted his theory: he did not treat the world as a dream in which actions do not matter. He did not simply stop moving—an act in itself—but wrote treatises and founded meditation centers. Nor did he adopt the antinomian values of simply letting his body do whatever it desired.) Advaitins are no doubt correct in arguing that what is permanent, changeless, and eternal must be real, but they are wrong in thinking this entails that other things cannot also be real. A changeless beingness may be experienced in the depth-mystical experience, but our other experiences are not negated by the depth-mystical experience—as Shankara realized, in the enlightened state experiences still occur just as they did before enlightenment, and he could not explain why the "optical illusion" of the natural realm remains after the enlightened have corrected their knowledge. There may be an overwhelming sense of reality to the experience, but no experience, no matter how powerful, can disprove the existence of things continue to exist outside that experience; thus, Advaita's ontological claim must be defended on more grounds than just one type of experience. Within our world, there may not be anything "real" in the Advaita sense (as Buddhists argue), but at least those things in our world that have causal power are not "illusory" or "nonexistent" in any meaningful sense: even if their being is supplied by a transcendental source and underlying structuring supplies their order, they cannot be dismissed but must be dealt with, and thus they are *real* in any legitimate sense of the word.

In short, the phenomena of our world may be dependent on a transcendental source, but their reality cannot be denied.[4] The analogy of the dream is helpful for our understanding how the natural world may be dependent upon another reality, but the fact remains that the "dream" is now part of reality—it may have a derivative reality (and hence be "less real" in that sense), but the mental event of dreaming is itself also part of what now exists in the universe even though the content of the dream is not part of the objective world. Thus, even if it has no reality apart from its source, the world is "real enough" that we must take it with complete seriousness. Why there is a natural world at all—for theists, why God chose to create the world; for Shankara, why the world of diversity exists at all—may remain a mystery, but it is here now and must be treated as part of all that is deemed real. When even Shankara admitted that the "dream" world of multiplicity does not disappear for the enlightened (*Brahma-sutra-bhashya* IV.1.15), it is hard to maintain that ultimately the natural realm is not real, and labeling its status "indescribable (*anirvacaniya*)" does not change this.

Mindfulness exposes the common being behind the cultural conceptual differentiations we apply to the natural realm and also the impermanence, interconnectedness, and dependency of the parts of this realm. The individual parts within the natural world must also be accepted as real in one sense. The parts are not unique in their being (all being is one, and if there is a source of the universe, this being is supplied by that source), nor in the causal structures that operate in everything in nature, but each is real and unique in its particular configuration of structures and contingent circumstances. Most importantly, each thing makes a causal contribution to the whole. Thus, it is causally real, even though it is not real in the sense of being a separate and self-existing entity. Nothing is a monad, isolated from the rest of nature. Each thing is connected, impermanent, and constantly changing, but it is still a cause. This also applies particularly to our sense of an *individual ego*: there may be one transcendental self or multiple transcendental selves or none (if no individuality continues after death), but each person in the realm of becoming is a product of natural factors and has causal power within this realm. We should attach value to our individual survival since our existence in the natural realm is part of what is real, and our actions matter. But in determining our actions and values, we must remember that no man is an island, either socially or ontologically.

The distinction between scientific and mystical approaches to reality can be seen in their relation to the realm of time: mystics are interested in the changeless beingness existing outside the category of time, while scientists are interested in understanding the causes of the changes within the world of time. For mystics only the "now" of immediate, lived experience matters. The "now" moment of experience has nothing to do with relativity (in which there is no absolute "present") or anything else within science, but is not outside of time—it is that elusive moment in time that is not part of the measurement of time but is the space on the temporal continuum within which we are aware of reality. The experience in that moment seems timeless since the experience is free of any temporal structuring. Just as mystics can experience all of being in the being of any object, so too they can experience eternity (the sum of all times) in one timeless moment. However, to scientists there is no "now" in the description of reality, only the before-and-after stream of the causally related events, as evidenced by the fact that "now" has no place in any scientific equations, including those that have time intervals as a variable. Through mysticism, we can live with full awareness in the present, but this does not mean that the experience does not also occur in a time-line of past and future or that time is not also part of reality. To dismiss time as an illusion would also be to dismiss the irreversibility of time indicated by thermodynamic processes as ultimately an illusion. Instead we can accept that both the analytical mind and the meditative mind reveal different aspects of the reality of time and the timeless, and so both are needed to give as full a view of reality as is humanly possible.

Mindfulness involves seeing the changing, differentiated world of time, but the focus is on the common beingness rather than the differentiations that normally control our thoughts, perceptions, and actions. The enlightened are freed of our habitual conceptual responses and freed of greed and other emotions associated with the sense that there is an ego within the natural world that is distinct from the rest of the universe and that must be protected and enhanced. They see the natural world "as it really is," at least with regard to its beingness and its lack of discrete objects. In the enlightened state, knowledge, memories, and language are not destroyed, but the mindful mind is free of the reification of linguistic differentiations that creates a false conceptual universe of distinct entities and thus is also free of all the accompanying attachments to our own artificial creations. Nevertheless, the structures guiding the differentiated realm are real, regardless of our knowledge or how we classify them. Mystics need not deny this—the component of reality responsible for order in the changes in the realm of becoming simply is not the aspect of reality that their experiences expose. Thus, mystics need not reject science, at least as far as the mystical experiences go (with a possible major qualification concerning the nature of human beings discussed below).

Our Metaphysical Situation in the World

Thus, if we are going to affirm both science and classical mysticism, accepting either the transcendental realm or the natural world alone as real is a mistake. We cannot reduce our situation to one dimension. Focusing only on what scientists study can easily lead to a life devoted totally to only the natural realm. But any bliss from "clinging to the Void" is as one-sided as denying a transcendental reality and living only in the world of becoming. Affirming both a transcendental mysticism and science means that we live at once in both the realm of the eternal and of time. In short, accepting both science and mysticism means that we realize that we live in two environments: the natural world through which life is evolving and a dimension of changeless beingness transcending this realm. The two cannot be reduced to one order; instead, both must be accepted and valued. As Plotinus put it, we human beings are amphibians living in two realms at once (*Enneads* IV.8.4), and how this is possible remains a mystery. But this means that we are beings at home in this world, not alien "spiritual beings" having a "human experience" while waiting to return to our true home. We cannot "avoid all concerns with the world," to cite a Christian mystics' refrain. Any sort of permanent ascetic renunciation of all things worldly cannot express the total reality that we are.

The vertical dimension of permanent being and the horizontal dimension of constant change within the natural world are both present in us—something in us is deathless and uncreated, and yet we are also active agents in the realm of the differentiated. We have no being apart from whatever is the source of our being (and thus are "nothing" in ourselves in that sense), but we still have a causal presence in the natural world (and thus are real parts of the realm of becoming). We cannot obliterate this causal "lower self" and remain in only the transcendental "higher self" of being—both are irreducible parts of reality. Indeed, the combination of structures constituting personhood may itself be a fundamental category of reality, as personalists argued. Even if the self has no permanent core among surface-phenomena or is dependent in some way on the rest of the web of the differentiated world, we still are nodes with causal force in the web: we are not exhaustively constituted by our interconnections to the web, but also contribute to the whole through our actions. We are more than a shadow on Plato's cave wall—we have reality and substance. Our personalities may be largely socially constructed, but we are also agents effecting changes—including to the society and natural environment that shape us—and this aspect of reality must be given its due.

But our connectedness to the rest of the natural realm and our lack of self-existence means that centering reality upon oneself is impossible, and thus all self-centered striving must be rejected. However, acting totally free of all self-concern and self-assertion or otherwise leading a passive life with no care for oneself would also not reflect our reality in this world—such total selflessness may free us from the fear of death, but it would also lead to an early death and also cannot reflect the fact that our thoughts and actions make real contributions to the reality of this world. Experiencing reality free of a personal point of view may reveal something that is otherwise missed about our situation in the world (the underlying common beingness, interconnectedness, and impermanence of it all), but to deny we are also real agents in the web of reality is as distortive as losing all sense of the source of our being and identifying only with our bodies, distinct from everything else. If we have to sacrifice all that is distinctive about being human to become enlightened, then enlightenment does not encompass all that is real about us.

In sum, if we accept the value of both science and mysticism, we live in a world that is one in one sense (being) and many in another (the natural structures) producing a complex realm of contingent multiple parts. Both being and structure are equally fundamental components to reality, neither reducible to the other, and thus each must be treated equally with a worldview. And whether there is one source to both is a question that neither mystics nor scientists can answer. It is one of the many mysteries surrounding why and how the world can be as it is.

Science's Contribution

The job of scientists is to identify patterns of change in the everyday world and then find the underlying structures that explain them. To realists, scientists have some genuine knowledge of these structures; to empiricists, there is something there in nature responsible for the changes, but we cannot experience those causes and thus cannot know them. These structures are a fundamental part of reality: they are as real in their own right as the beingness of the phenomena that they order. Under realism, whether our ultimate scientific picture will have only one level of physical structure or will have multiple physical, chemical, biological, and psychological structures is a debate over structural and theoretical reductionism in both scientific and philosophical circles. Currently at least, scientists still deal with a variety of levels of structure and the relations between them.

However, there can be no science of the domain of mystics: beingness. It may be that beingness has structures, but it cannot be pushed and pulled or otherwise subjected to tests or experiments or any type of analysis. Thus, mysticism by its nature cannot be a natural science—whatever the exact standards of empirical science are, mysticism cannot meet them because of its subject matter. On the other hand, scientific analysis, with its commitment to intersubjective testing, is the appropriate approach for studying the differentiated phenomena within the realm of becoming. This also means that the domain of mysticism proper (beingness) is immune to any findings in science about the structures of reality.

In Chapter 9, how classical mysticism trespasses into the domain of science through the beliefs about the world of the different world religious traditions was discussed. But whether mysticism as a way of life can be stripped of all the claims that might in principle impinge on scientific theories was also an issue. Nevertheless, to value science equally, scientists must be given a free hand since mystical insights contribute nothing about nature's structures. Of course, like any part of culture, mystical literature may offer up ideas that can be worked into scientific hypotheses, but scientific decision-making cannot be restricted by considerations of religious beliefs or any other non-scientific forms of thought. In particular, mystics may expect scientists to give up the materialistic framework eventually in biology and neuroscience, but mystical experiences are not themselves a reason to accept or reject any scientific theory. Thus, mystics must let the chips fall where they may in both scientific research and theorizing as science progresses.

In sum, science must proceed on its own terms since science alone has the authority on such matters. Even Shankara accepted that, while the Vedas may be authoritative on the issue of what is ultimately real, revelation is not authoritative on other issues—a hundred scriptural texts declaring fire to be cold or without light would not make it so (*Bhagavad-gita-bhashya* XVI.66). More generally, "knowledge of the nature of a thing does not depend on human notions or on authoritative statements—it depends only on the thing itself" (*Brahma-sutra-bhashya* I.1.13). This means that for any reconciliation to be rational, the religious beliefs of any mystical tradition concerning the realm of becoming must conform to scientists' findings on structure. Thus, for example, the belief in a beginningless cycle of rebirths would have to be given up if scientists show the universe is not eternal or establish that consciousness is a product of matter.

Currently the framework for neuroscience remains materialistic. Of course, neuroscientists may give up this framework of their own accord as they explore mental phenomena, including mystical states of consciousness. Scientists may conclude that the depth-mystical experience or some other mental phenomena cannot be explained by the materialist framework, and neuroscience would then have to adopt a nonmaterial framework with new ways of theorizing; research would then take a different direction. Depth-mystical experiences themselves would become data for any scientific theory—any alleged *insight* conveyed in the experience would still not be grounds supporting or conflicting with any scientific theory, but the experience itself would then be a mental phenomenon taken seriously by neuroscientists and not merely dismissed as the result of a malfunctioning brain or grouped with some other experiences or states that are already being studied. Again, no belief-claims from a religious tradition can legitimately try to restrict the course of science—no "control beliefs" from any source are. Of course, the materialistic framework may end up being abandoned for metaphysical reasons, and mystical concerns may be part of that picture. Nevertheless, if the current framework is abandoned, it will be because of problems within science itself, not because of extrascientific considerations alone.

However, the centrality of *consciousness* in the classical mystical systems presents a problem. If scientists persist in seeing consciousness as a material phenomenon, a conflict between classical mysticism and science cannot be avoided. Traditional religion in general also rejects metaphysical naturalism with regard to consciousness and a life after death. If science does not change concerning consciousness, the traditionally religious will have to see the range of science's authority as restricted to only part of what constitutes a human being. The religious may be able to argue successfully that neuroscience deals with only reproducible phenomena and so misses something in us that transcends the natural realm and that is not detectable by causal tests—i.e., that neuroscientists are "methodological naturalists" who must bracket the ontological question of whether there is more to our mental existence than what they study, and so they need not engage in a naturalistic reduction. So too, under this conciliation mystics will have to leave the full nature of consciousness and a human being (including whether there is life after death) as a metaphysically open question while allowing neuroscience to proceed on its own on other matters. That is, neuroscience would not be rejected, but its scope would have to be limited to less than all of our mental life. But one way or another, classical mystics and the traditionally religious will insist that consciousness is not reducible to a random or deterministic natural product, but is a transcendental reality.

Mysticism's Contribution

With this important limitation concerning consciousness in mind, mystics can accept any scientific theories of phenomena within the realm of becoming. Whatever scientists find or do not find about structures is simply irrelevant to the dimension of reality that is the focus of mystics' attention—beingness free of differentiations. More generally, there need not be anything antiscientific about the mystics' ways of life or about this attempt at a conciliation. To be a mystic, one need not be antiscientific or an anti-technology Luddite but can accept the world as fully real. Mystics can live fully in modern society, even if they do not contribute to the technological aspect. And, most importantly for the issue at hand, they can fully embrace the findings of the scientific approach to reality as indicative of one aspect of the true nature of reality.

To accept mystical experiences as cognitive, one obviously must reject scientism, i.e., that science is the only source of true knowledge of the nature of reality and all other approaches are superstition, and its accompanying notion that it is irrational to propose a way of gaining knowledge of an aspect of reality not open to scientific checking.[5] But scientism is not science any more than naturalism is. There is nothing irrational in abandoning those notions while retaining all of science. Nor is it an abandonment of reason to argue that an experience of reality unrelated to the type of experiences and reasoning needed for science can supplement science in our total view of reality. This is true whether the depth-mystical experience is naturalized or not. More broadly, mystics in fact need not be irrational in any way—nor do they "have their own unique logic," as is often alleged—even though they argue from a wider range of experiences and from different metaphysical premises than do nonmystics in the modern world. Classical mystics have produced books of quite logical arguments, implicitly or explicitly relying on the laws of noncontradiction and the excluded middle—Nagarjuna and such Buddhist logicians as Dignaga and Dharmakirti have resorted to such sophisticated arguments as *reductio ad absurdum*—even though their ultimate goal was to transcend the realm of reason. Mystics' claims simply confront a tribunal of both ordinary and mystical experiences. (See Jones 1993: 59-78 and 2010.)

As discussed, the mystics' focus is on reality's being: the underlying source of the self's being or all of the universe's being in the depth-mystical experience, and the beingness of the realm of becoming in mindfulness. Classical depth-mystics would disagree insofar as they will always have a more metaphysically-loaded understanding of what is experienced, and they would keep the focus on the transformed state of the enlightened who are now aligned with reality, not on any experience or state of consciousness or knowledge alone. Accepting mindfulness as a direct, unmediated awareness of the beingness of the phenomenal world is not difficult to reconcile with science since it need not deny any scientific or naturalistic views of consciousness but merely involves shifting one's focus to an aspect of the phenomenal world that science does not cover. That is, mindfulness simply focuses our attention on another aspect of the same realm that scientists study, and thus is neutral to scientific findings. Even materialists do not have to deny anything connected to mindfulness beyond their general metaphysical problem with consciousness. It is mindfulness mystics' broader belief-systems that impinge on science's domain, not the mindful states of consciousness *per se*.

But the depth-mystical experience, in adding a "deeper" ontological dimension to our total picture of reality—a reality both transcending and underlying the natural realm—presents a problem to naturalists. To the religious, this dimension will be sacred and an avenue through which to re-enchant the world with a transcendental purpose. The transcendental interpretations of the depth-mystical experience that assert that the transcendent is the source of the natural realm is an ontological claim that cannot in principle be inconsistent with any scientific finding on structures—the claims simply bypass each other without intersecting. Indeed, any claims about the ultimate ontological status of the natural realm as a whole cannot support or conflict with any statements about the more limited topic of nature's structure. Thus, even in principle, the two endeavors cannot conflict in their core pursuits (although, again, as discussed in Chapter 9 the beliefs about the natural realm in mystical traditions are another matter).

On the basis of mystical experiences alone, the religious—both the mystically-minded and the nonmystical—cannot attempt to offer supernatural explanations of natural phenomena as part of science itself, as advocates of "intelligent design" do. Nor do mystical experiences suggest how consciousness as a phenomenal feature of the universe fits in with the rest of the natural realm. But the religious can respect the boundaries of science in offering metaphysical explanations of the natural realm *in toto* or its most general features (e.g., its lawfulness) since such transcendental explanations do not infringe on the practice of science or any specific scientific theories. Nevertheless, mysticism remains a matter of the beingness of things, not of the structures of interest to scientists or of metaphysical interpretations of other aspects of the natural universe.

A Balanced Life

It may well be easier to live following the classical mystics' either/or choice—the world or the transcendent—than to adopt a way of life that includes both the world and the transcendent as real. But if we accept both science and mysticism, we cannot live a life rejecting either. Classical mystics see the analytical mind as only a source of delusion and the receptive/contemplative mind as the only source of insight, and thus only the latter is worth developing. To them, the meditative functions do not supplement the analytical functions to reveal another dimension of reality. Instead, there is ultimately no place in the mystics' systems for the analytical mind: any mental function only applicable within the realm of separation and diversity is obviously ultimately valueless—this is needed for survival in the "dream" realm, but it is not needed for what is ultimately valuable. Thus in the end, mystics do not accept the analytical functions of the mind as revealing part of what is in fact real and so want to replace it entirely. (But again, even enlightened mystics like Shankara and the Buddha do use the analytical function of the mind in order to teach, raising the issue of whether any mystic is truly *enlightened* in this life or what "enlightenment" actually is.[6])

However, if we accept both mysticism and science, the analytical mind must reveal something irreducibly real. Structural order remains part of the ultimate makeup of reality; thus, focusing our awareness on it in the scientific approach does not mean we are deluded. The "instrumental mind" supported by a brain that has evolved for the survival of our particular nodes in the web of life in this world reveals something finally real. We may be more than a natural being, but we are at least that, and trying to ignore it for the purpose of attaining our "higher self" is to be out of touch with our total reality. And if mysticism is in fact cognitive, the brain has also evolved for the still mind to produce an awareness of something real, and thus it is also needed to know all we are capable of knowing. (Since the receptive mental functions of mysticism are not necessary for survival, they are understandably harder to cultivate than the instrumental functions and may be engaged only fleetingly until they are fully integrated into one's mind.) In sum, the still mind and the imaginative mind that deals with differentiations each supply something valuable that the other misses.

And that is the dilemma for a balanced life: radically different functions of the mind are involved, and we cannot abide in both sets of functions at the same time. The idea of a "golden mean" and "middle way" are popular in the classical world, both East and West, but how is such a way possible when it comes down to taking the world to be real or not? Going from a mystical approach to reality to a scientific one or vice versa is something like a Gestalt-switch in perception. How can we combine a calm meditative mind with an active analytical mind when they are two distinct functions of the mind? How do we combine the intentional mind with the non-intentional? We can live mindfully in the "now," but how can we still be fully human if we live totally immersed in the "now" with no thought for the future? Indeed, if we truly live fully in the present, how can we have any concern for the consequences of our present actions for ourselves or for others? Nor could we survive long with a mind empty of the differentiations in nature and with no sense of the future causal effects. In order to survive in this world we need a conceptual "dualistic" consciousness to determine what we need and what to avoid—in a state of pure mindfulness, everything we encounter would be treated as equal, and we could not differentiate a clear liquid poison and water. So too, if we live in constant mindfulness, we would also lose the attention to particulars needed, not only to avoid danger, but to conduct scientific research and theorizing. Thus, if we accept this world as fully real, we also need the concept-driven consciousness. We would need factual beliefs and values implicitly or explicitly driving our decisions. The calming and focusing of *concentrative* meditation on the mystical path may focus attention and lessen emotion; thus, it can be valuable training for a concept-driven consciousness. But it leads ultimately to a "pure consciousness" event void of any differentiations—to be permanently in this state would obviously limit our ability to survive or even function in this world.

A balanced life integrating both sides of our existence in the world would be needed. But how can an unchanging depth to the self or the world and a constantly changing differentiated realm be balanced? How do we live Plotinus's "amphibious" life? It is not as simple as merely accepting both science and mysticism as ways of knowing or accepting some metaphysical claims about the universe. We would need both the more "passive" approach of contemplation and the more "assertive" approach of science—both silence and analysis, *yin* and *yang*.[7] We have to come up with a balanced way of life that does not forego part of what is in the final analysis real in the world and part of what it is to be fully human. If we are overwhelmed by the depth-mystical experience, we would reject this world as ultimately real; but if we affirm this world as being as real and eternal as the source (or even *identical* to the source since it shares the same being), we may reject the still vertical dimension entirely and be caught up in the realm of differentiations. It is the problem in Christian mysticism of fusing the "contemplative life" with the "active life," as exemplified in Meister Eckhart on detachment and "living without a why," rather than oscillating between the two. There is also the risk of a schizophrenic life that compartmentalizes mysticism from the rest of one's life, rather than fully integrating it with a mindfulness informing all aspects of life. Granted, our mental life may never be unified but always be a jumble of different functions. Still, how does acting while resting in the ground of being work? How do we act both with an awareness of differentiations and a sense of the identity of beingness? How do we take both transcendent realities and the differentiated world seriously? How do transformed dispositions affect our actions?[8]

Accepting the reality of the person as a causal agent also presents problems for classical mysticism. So too, the modern Western value of the worth and dignity of *the individual* is hard to reconcile with the impersonal ideals found in premodern cultures of the selfless *karma-yoga* of the *Bhagavad-gita* or the frictionless flow of the Way in actions without personal assertion (*wu wei*). When social values were only in terms of one's role within a group and not individual freedom, it was easier to think in terms of following the human being's particular *dao*. What role is there for individuality as we try to surf the Way? More importantly, is it our free will that makes us the one thing in nature that is out of step with our with the Way? Do we have to give up free will to be enlightened?

The only way around this dilemma is to limit the extent of mindfulness: we need less than a pure mindfulness to conduct science and to live in the natural realm in general. The conceptualizing function of consciousness cannot be obliterated completely if we are to survive in a world of diversity. Whether the positive and negative emotions calmed by meditation are an essential part of a human being is also an issue. So too, with the depth-mystical experiences: there may be periods of training devoted to cultivating the concentrative mind needed to tap the transcendental source in a depth-mystical experience, and periods of retreat from the world, just as there can be periods for cultivating mindfulness and periods for studying science and other analytical approaches to the differentiated realm. The issue is life outside these periods: how do we integrate *yin* and *yang* of consciousness so that each influences the other without overwhelming it? How do we maintain an awareness of the root of beingness while operating in the world of differentiations? How can we remain in a continuing state of consciousness with a permanent interior stillness while yet being engaged in thought and activity? How can we remain aware of our own awareness while simultaneously remaining conscious of thoughts, sensations, and actions (Forman 1998: 186)? We would need to learn to swim with a concern for both the waves and the ocean depth, and not be caught up in the waves alone as most people do or in the depth as classical depth-mystics do. At a minimum, this means limiting mysticism in a way that classical mystics would not accept. (See Jones 2004: 399-402.)

A World of Two Dimensions

In sum, adopting a worldview shaped by science does not require denying that mystical experiences are cognitive of a transcendental dimension to reality, even though how to lead a life fully integrating mystical and analytical states of mind remains a problem. We can interpret depth-mystical experiences as a cognitive insight into the depth of reality and still affirm the full reality of the diversity of the natural world and ordinary states of consciousness. Mystical matters can be limited to the issue of beingness; even depth-mystical experiences need not be taken as overwhelming other types of cognitive experiences. Thus, we do not have to choose between "the path of spirituality" and "the path of reason," as the biologist Edward O. Wilson and many other naturalists believe, at least when it comes to mysticism.

This conciliation, however, does not *integrate* science and mysticism into one enterprise—because of the differences in their subject matter and ways of approaching reality, any convergence or integration would be impossible. Nor does this conciliation remove any of the mysteries surrounding each endeavor. But it does show that it is possible to accept both endeavors as knowledge-giving. This position does reflect a nonmystical point of view, since it gives equal weight to a nonmystical approach to the world, but it shows one way that mysticism can be incorporated into a nonmystical point of view while retaining the traditional mystics' claim to an insight into transcendental matters. In addition, this conciliation removes one possible objection to the cognitive validity of the depth-mystical experience by showing that its claim to be aware of a transcendental reality is consistent with science's cognitive claims. But whether this accommodation of both science and mysticism is successful or not will ultimately depend, as with all basic decisions, upon our philosophical judgments transcending both endeavors.

Notes

1. If we take the simpler approach Alvin Plantinga took on the issue of religious pluralism as the model, all we have to do is show that mysticism and science are *logically compatible* and then there is no problem at all. And this is very simple since no claim in either science or about mystical experiences logically entails that there are no aspects of reality except what is available through one way of knowing or that there are no other ways to know other aspects of reality; thus, claims about different aspects must be "in harmony." The logical rejection of one endeavor follows only once other metaphysical premises are adopted. But to make a position actually seem *plausible*, more is needed than simply showing that it is not logically inconsistent and not in defiance of the best available evidence—believing in invisible elves who cannot be detected by science does not involve a logical contraction, but this does not mean the belief is rational, let alone plausible. To make any conciliation plausible, each enterprise must have a place in a plausible way of life, not merely be shown not to logically conflict with the basic approach of the other. A further step—showing why advocates of each endeavor *ought to* accept the other—is beyond the scope of this book.

2. It is whether mystical experiences are possible of sources of insight that is the issue for a possible reconciliation, not any purported benefits for focusing attention in a world of ever-increasing distractions and interruptions, calming emotions, or fostering general physical and psychological health.

3. Even while rejecting any alleged mystical claim to cognitivity, naturalists could still accept any verified physiological or psychological benefits to such practices. Naturalists may also have mystical experiences, and the phenomenology of the experience will remain the same regardless of the explanation accepted. Such experiences may have long-term beneficial effects, such as enhancing our sense of "well-being" (a sense of satisfaction with life or a purpose or meaning to life). But it is interesting to note that without a religious interpretative framework mystical experiences may not have positive effects but lead instead to less well-being. (See Byrd, Lear, and Schwenka 2000 on distinguishing the effects of mystical experiences from religious beliefs or general religiousness on well-being.) Thus, it may be that naturalists would have to work out a framework in which mystical experiences are treated positively as cognitive and fully integrated into a naturalistic worldview if mystical experiences are not to have a negative effect on their sense of well-being. Thus, if naturalists want to reject any mystical cognitive claims and look only at its effects, mystical experiences may not have the same effects as they would have in a religious framework.

4. Emergent realities can be ontologically dependent upon another reality and yet still be structurally irreducibly and causally real. Naturalists who are antireductionists in the mind/body field argue that the mind is such a reality. (See Jones 2000: 83-88, 103-10.)

5. Even if the depth-mystical experience can be naturalized, naturalists tend to reject mysticism because they consider it antiscientific and associate it with all things irrational. But cultivating mystical experiences alone is not enough to associate mysticism with any particular way of thinking or with a premodern worldview. So too, the existence of transcendental realities or seeing the natural realm as dependent on a source for its existence is consistent with the scientific study of structures. The depth-mystical experience may not seem to cohere with our other experiences since it takes us out of the ordinary realm, but this in itself is not a scientific reason to conclude that it is a delusion; at most, this can lead naturalists only to a natural explanation of it. In addition, mindfulness focuses attention on the impermanence and interconnectedness of the everyday world; this may seem irrelevant

to scientists since all it does is change our focus of attention to miss the real divisions in nature that are important to science, but such a stance is not in conflict with science. Mysticism is nonscientific but not unscientific—no experience in itself is either "scientific" or "unscientific." Still, it is only adherents to the philosophies of naturalism and scientism who should have a problem if something valuable should be developed from mystical experiences. So too, if the scientific study of meditators and their experiences shows that mystical experiences are not a product of a malfunctioning brain or a pathology, then another typical naturalistic charge against mysticism would also fall.

6. Many Hindu philosophers, especially in theistic traditions, have seen this as the reason to reject the idea of being "enlightened in life (*jivanmukti*)"—i.e., no one can be fully enlightened and yet still be living in this world, despite the usual status ascribed to figures such as Shankara. (See Fort and Mumme 1996.) To Huston Smith, enlightenment is only an ideal in this life because our "mortal coils" are too tight. But the problem for all classical mystics again is why this would be the case unless this realm is *real* in the final analysis.

7. The dot of *yin* (the shady—in general, the yielding) in the *yang* (the bright—in general, the assertive) and vice versa in the traditional *yin-yang* symbol is worth remembering. Here, the dash of *yang* in the *yin* would represent the need for some conceptualized knowledge in the mystical enlightened way of life, and the dash of *yin* in the *yang* would represent the mysteries of the natural world that cannot be captured by scientific methods—if nothing else, why the world exists and has an objective causal order.

8. To John Horgan, the greatest gift mystical experiences can bestow is not any alleged insights into another dimension of reality, but letting us finally see how truly miraculous the everyday universe is—enriching the wonder of normality—and really seeing all that is right with the world, and mysticism's greatest danger is a permanent case of derealization and depersonalization rather than returning to the normal world reborn (2002). Mary Garden would concur: after giving up a mystical quest in the 1970's, her life is "immeasurably richer" without meditation or seeing the world as something from which to escape or detach oneself (2007: 24).

References

Abe, Masao. 1985. "Religion and Science in the Global Age: Their Essential Character and Mutual Relationship." In William R. LeFleur, ed., *Zen and Western Thought*, pp. 241-48. Honolulu: Univ. of Hawai'i Press.
Albin, Rochelle and Donald D. Montagna. 1977. "Mystical Aspects of Science." *The Humanist* 37 (March/April): 44-46.
Albright, Carol Rausch. 2000. "The 'God Module' and the Complexifying Brain." *Zygon* 35 (December): 735-44.
Alston, William P. 1991. *Perceiving God: The Epistemology of Religious Experience*. Ithaca, N.Y.: Cornell Univ. Press.
Alter, Joseph S. 2004. *Yoga in Modern India: The Body Between Science and Philosophy*. Princeton: Princeton Univ. Press.
Ambjørn, Jan, Jerzy Jurkiewicz, and Renate Loll. 2008. "The Self-Organizing Quantum Universe." *Scientific American* 299 (June): 42-49.
Ames, William L. 2003. "Emptiness and Quantum Physics." In B. Alan Wallace, ed., *Buddhism and Science: Breaking New Ground*, pp. 285-302. New York: Columbia Univ. Press.
Andresen, Jensine. 2000. "Meditation Meets Behavioural Medicine: The Story of Experimental Research on Meditation." *Journal of Consciousness Studies* 7 (no. 11): 17-73.
Angel, Leonard. 2002. "Mystical Naturalism." *Religious Studies* 38 (September): 317-38.
_____. 2004. "Universal Self Consciousness Mysticism and the Physical Completeness Principle." *International Journal for Philosophy of Religion* 55 (Fall): 1-29.
Arntz, William, Betsy Chase, and Mark Vicente. 2005. *What the BLEEP Do We Know? Discovering the Endless Possibilities for Altering Your Everyday World*. Deerfield Beach, Fl.: Health Communications.
Austin, James H. 1998. *Zen and the Brain: Toward an Understanding of Meditation and Consciousness*. Cambridge: MIT Press.
_____. 2006. *Zen-Brain Reflections: Reviewing Recent Developments in Meditation and States of Consciousness*. Cambridge: MIT Press.
Bagger, Matthew C. 1999. *Religious Experience, Justification, and History*. Cambridge: Cambridge Univ. Press.
Balasubramaniam, Arun. 1992. "Explaining Strange Parallels: The Case of Quantum Mechanics and Mādhyamika Buddhism." *International Philosophical Quarterly* 32 (June): 205-23.
Barbour, Ian G. 2000. *When Science Meets Religion: Enemies, Strangers, or Partners?* New York: HarperCollins.

Barnard, G. William and Jeffrey J. Kripal, eds. 2002. *Crossing Boundaries: Essays on the Ethical Status of Mysticism*. New York: Seven Bridges Press.
Barr, Stephen M. 2007. "Faith and Quantum Theory." *First Things* 171 (March): 21-25.
Batchelor, Stephen. 1997. *Buddhism Without Belief: A Contemporary Guide to Awakening*. New York: Riverhead Books.
Batten, Alan H. 1995. "A Most Rare Vision: Eddington's Thinking on the Relation Between Science and Religion." *Journal of Scientific Exploration* 9 (no. 2): 231-55.
Beauregard, Mario and Denyse O'Leary. 2007. *The Spiritual Brain: A Neuroscientist's Case for the Existence of the Soul*. New York: HarperCollins.
Benson, Herbert. 1975. *The Relaxation Response*. New York: William Morrow.
Bernstein, Jeremy. 1979. "A Cosmic Flow." *The American Scholar* 48 (January): 6-9.
Bitbol, Michel. 2003. "A Cure for Metaphysical Illusions: Kant, Quantum Mechanics, and the Madhyamaka." In B. Alan Wallace, ed., *Buddhism and Science: Breaking New Ground*, pp. 325-61. New York: Columbia Univ. Press.
Bohm, David. 1981. *Wholeness and the Implicate Order*. Boston: Routledge & Kegan Paul.
Bohm, David and B. J. Hiley. 1993. *The Undivided Universe: An Ontological Interpretation of Quantum Mechanics*. New York: Routledge.
Boslough, John. 1985. *Stephen Hawking's Universe*. New York: Quill.
Bouyer, Louis. 1980. "Mysticism: An Essay on the History of the Word." In Richard Woods, ed., *Understanding Mysticism*, pp. 42-55. Garden City: Doubleday.
Brett, Caroline. 2002. "Psychotic and Mystical States of Being: Connections and Disconnections." *Philosophy, Psychiatry & Psychology* 9 (December): 321-41.
Brooke, John Hedley. 2008. "Can Scientific Discovery be a Religious Experience?" In Alex Bentley, ed., *The Edge of Reason? Science and Religion in Modern Society*, pp. 155-69. New York: Continuum.
Brown, C. Mackenzie. 2002. "Hindu and Christian Creationism: 'Transposed Passages' in the Geological Book of Life." *Zygon* 37 (March): 95-114.
_____. 2012. *Hindu Perspectives on Evolution: Darwin, Dharma, and Design*. New York: Routledge.
Byrd, Kevin R., Delbert Lear, and Stacy Schwenka. 2000. "Mysticism as a Predictor of Subjective Well-Being." *The International Journal for the Psychology of Religion* 10 (no. 4): 259-69.
Cabezón, José Ignacio. 2003. "Buddhism and Science: On the Nature of the Dialogue." In B. Alan Wallace, ed., *Buddhism and Science: Breaking New Ground*, pp. 35-68. New York: Columbia Univ. Press.
Cahn, B. Rael and John Polich. 1999. "Meditation States and Traits: EEG, ERP, and Neuroimaging Studies." *Psychological Bulletin* 132 (no. 2): 180-211.
Campbell, Colin. 2007. *The Easternization of the West: A Thematic Account of Cultural Change in the Modern Era*. Boulder: Paradigm Publishers.
Capra, Fritjof. 1983. *The Turning Point: Science, Society, and the Rising Culture*. New York: Bantam Books.
_____. 1996. *The Web of Life: A New Scientific Understanding of Living Systems*. New York: Random House.
_____. 2000 [1975]. *The Tao of Physics: An Exploration of the Parallels Between Modern Physics and Eastern Mysticism*. 4th ed. Boston: Shambhala Press.
Capra, Fritjof and David Steindl-Rast. 1991. *Belonging to the Universe: Explorations of Science and Spirituality*. New York: HarperCollins.
Certeau, Michel de. 1992. *The Mystic Fable, vol. 1: The Sixteenth and Seventeenth Centuries*, trans. Michael B. Smith. Chicago: Univ. of Chicago.

Chalmers, David J. 2004. "How Can We Construct a Science of Consciousness?" In Michael S. Gazzaniga, editor-in-chief, *The Cognitive Neurosciences*, 3rd ed., pp. 1111-19. Cambridge: MIT Press.
Chan, Wing-Tsit. 1957. "Neo-Confucianism and Chinese Scientific Thought." *Philosophy East & West 6* (January): 309-22.
Chari, C. T. K. 1976. "Quantum Mechanics and Concepts of Consciousness." *Indian Philosophical Annual* 11: 50-56.
Clarke, Christopher. 1981. "Comment: On Physics and Mysticism." *Theoria to Theory* 11 (February): 333-37.
_____, ed. 2005. *Ways of Knowing: Science and Mysticism Today*. Exeter: Imprint Academic.
Clarke, Christopher, Frederick Parker-Rhodes, and Jonathan Westphal. 1978. "Discussion of *The Tao of Physics*." *Theoria to Theory* 11 (February): 287-300.
Clarke, D. S., ed. 2004. *Panpsychism: Past and Recent Selected Writings*. Albany: State Univ. of New York.
Clifton, Robert K. and Marilyn G. Regehr. 1990. "Toward a Sound Perspective on Modern Physics: Capra's Popularization of Mysticism and Theological Approached Reexamined." *Zygon* 25 (March): 73-104.
Cooper, Robin. 1996. *The Evolving Mind: Buddhism, Biology, and Consciousness*. Birmingham, England: Windhorse.
Crease, Robert P. and Charles C. Mann. 1987. "Physics for Mystics." *The Sciences* 29 (July/August): 50-57.
_____. 1990. "The Yogi and the Quantum." In Patrick Grim, ed., *Philosophy of Science and the Occult*, pp. 302-14. Albany: State Univ. of New York Press.
Cremo, Michael A. and Richard L. Thompson. 1998. *Forbidden Archeology: The Hidden History of the Human Race*. Los Angeles: Bhaktivedanta Book Publishing.
His Holiness the XIVth Dalai Lama (Tenzin Gyatso). 1996. *Beyond Dogma: The Challenge of the Modern World*, ed. Marianne Dresser. London: Souvenir Press.
_____. 2003. "Understanding and Transforming the Mind." In B. Alan Wallace, ed., *Buddhism and Science: Breaking New Ground*, pp. 91-103. New York: Columbia Univ. Press.
_____. 2005. *The Universe in a Single Atom: The Convergence of Science and Spirituality*. New York: Morgan Road Books.
d'Aquili, Eugene G. and Andrew B. Newberg. 1999. *The Mystical Mind: Probing the Biology of Religious Experience*. Minneapolis: Fortress Press.
Davis, Caroline Franks. 1989. *The Evidential Force of Religious Experience*. New York: Oxford Univ. Press.
DeCharms, R. Christopher. 1997. *Two Views of Mind: Abhidharma and Brain Science*. Ithaca, N.Y.: Snow Lion Publications.
Deery, June. 1996. *Aldous Huxley and the Mysticism of Science*. New York: MacMillan.
Dorman, Eric R. 2011. "Hinduism and Science: The State of the South Asian Science and Religion Discourse." *Zygon* 46 (September): 593-619.
Du Pré, Gerald. 1984. "Buddhism and Science." In Buddhadasa P. Kirtisinghe, ed., *Buddhism and Science*, pp. 92-96. Delhi: Motital Banarsidass.
Dunn, Bruce R., Judith A. Hartigan, and William L. Mikulas. 1999. "Concentration and Mindfulness: Unique Forms of Consciousness." *Applied Psychophysiology and Biofeedback* 24 (no. 3): 147-65.
Eckhart, Meister. 2009. *The Complete Mystical Works of Meister Eckhart*. Ed. and trans. by Maurice O'C. Walshe. Revised by Bernard McGinn. New York: Crossroads.

Ecklund, Elaine Howard, Jerry Z. Park, and Phil Todd Veliz. 2008. "Secularization and Religious Change Among Elite Scientists." *Social Forces* 86 (June): 1805-39.
Eddington, Arthur. 1958. *The Nature of the Physical World*. Ann Arbor: Univ. of Michigan Press.
Edelmann, Jonathan B. 2012. "The Role of Hindu Theology in the Religion and Science Dialogue." *Zygon* 47 (September): 624-42.
Einstein, Albert. 1954. *Ideas and Opinions*, trans. Sonja Bargmann. New York: Crown Publishers.
Esbenshade, Donald H., Jr. 1982. "Relating Mystical Concepts to Those of Physics: Some Concerns." *American Journal of Physics* 50 (March): 224-28.
Fales, Evan. 1996a. "Scientific Explanations of Mystical Experiences, Part I: The Case of St. Teresa." *Religious Studies* 32 (June): 143-63.
_____. 1996b. "Scientific Explanations of Mystical Experiences, Part II: The Challenge of Theism." *Religious Studies* 32 (September): 297-313.
_____. 1999. "Do Mystics See God?" In Michael L. Peterson and Raymond J. Vanarragon, eds., *Contemporary Debates in the Philosophy of Religion*, pp. 145-57. Oxford: Blackwell.
Feynman, Richard P. 1967. *The Character of Physical Law*. Cambridge: MIT Press.
Finkelstein, David Ritz. 2003. "Emptiness and Relativity." In B. Alan Wallace, ed., *Buddhism and Science: Breaking New Ground*, pp. 365-84. New York: Columbia Univ. Press.
Flanagan, Owen. 2007. *The Really Hard Problem: Meaning in a Material World*. Cambridge: MIT Press.
Forman, Robert K. C., ed. 1990. *The Problem of Pure Consciousness: Mysticism and Philosophy*. New York: Oxford Univ. Press.
_____. 1998. "What Does Mysticism Have to Teach Us About Consciousness?" *Journal of Consciousness Studies* 5 (no. 2): 185-201.
Fort, Andrew O. and Patricia Y. Mumme, eds. 1996. *Living Liberation in Hindu Thought*. Albany: State Univ. of New York.
Gale, Richard M. 1991. *On the Nature and Existence of God*. Cambridge: Cambridge Univ. Press.
_____. 2005. "On the Cognitivity of Mystical Experiences." *Faith and Philosophy* 22 (October): 426-41.
Garden, Mary. 2007. "Can Meditation be Bad for You?" *The Humanist* 67 (September/October): 20-24.
Garfield, Jay, trans. 1995. *The Fundamental Wisdom of the Middle Way: Nāgārjuna's Mūlamadhyamakakārikā*. New York: Oxford Univ. Press.
Gellman, Jerome I. 1997. *Experience of God and the Rationality of Theistic Belief*. Ithaca, N.Y.: Cornell Univ. Press.
_____. 2001. *Mystical Experience of God: A Philosophical Enquiry*. London: Ashgate.
Goldberg, Ellen. 2005. "Cognitive Science and Hatha Yoga." *Zygon* 40 (September): 613-29.
Goldstein, Thomas. 1980. *Dawn of Modern Science: From the Arabs to Leonardo da Vinci*. Boston: Houghton Mifflin.
Goleman, Daniel and Robert A. F. Thurman, eds. 1991. *MindScience: An East-West Dialogue*. Boston: Wisdom Publications.
Gooding, David C. 1991. "Michael Faraday's Apprenticeship: Science as a Spiritual Path." In Ravi Ravindra, ed., *Science and Spirit*, pp. 389-405. New York: Paragon House.

Gosling, David. 1976. *Science and Religion in India*. Madras: Christian Literature Society.
_____. 2007. *Science and the Indian Tradition: When Einstein Met Tagore*. New York: Routledge.
_____. 2012. "Science and the Hindu Tradition: Compatibility or Conflict?" *Zygon* 47 (September): 575-88.
Goswami, Amit, with Richard E. Reed and Maggie Goswami. 1993. *The Self-Aware Universe: How Consciousness Creates the Material World*. New York: Putnam.
Goswami, Amit, with Maggie Goswami. 1997. *Science and Spirituality: A Quantum Integration*. New Delhi: Project of History of Indian Science, Philosophy and Culture.
Graham, Loren and Jean-Michel Kantor. 2009. *Naming Infinity: A True Story of Religious Mysticism and Mathematical Creativity*. Cambridge: Harvard Univ. Press.
Griffiths, Bede. 1989. *A New Vision of Reality: Western Science, Eastern Mysticism and Christian Faith*. London: Collins.
Griffiths, R. R., W. A. Richards, U. McCann, and R. Jesse. 2006. "Psilocybin Can Occasion Mystical-Type Experiences Having Substantial and Sustained Personal Meaning and Spiritual Significance." *Psychopharmacology* 187 (August): 268-83.
Grünbaum, Adolph. 1996. "Theological Misinterpretations of Current Physical Cosmology." *Foundations of Physics* 26 (no. 4): 523-43.
Gruner, Rolf. 1975. "Science, Nature, and Christianity." *Journal of Theological Studies* 26 (April): 55-81.
Haisch, Bernard. 2006. *The God Theory: Universes, Zero-point Fields and What's Behind it All*. San Francisco/Newburyport, Mass.: Weiser Books.
Hameroff, Stuart, Alfred W. Kaszniak, and Alwyn C. Scott, eds. 1996. *Toward a Science of Consciousness: The First Tucson Discussions and Debates*. Cambridge: MIT Press.
Hardy, Alister. 1983. *The Spiritual Nature of Man*. Oxford: Clarendon Press.
Harrington, Anne. 1996. *Reenchanted Science: Holism in German Culture from Wilhelm II to Hitler*. Princeton: Princeton Univ. Press.
Harrington, Anne and Arthur Zajonc, eds. 2006. *The Dalai Lama at MIT*. Cambridge: Harvard Univ. Press.
Harrison, Peter. 2006. "'Science' and 'Religion': Constructing the Boundaries." *Journal of Religion* 86 (January): 81-106.
Hayward, Jeremy W. and Francisco J. Varela, eds. 1992. *Gentle Bridges: Conversations with the Dalai Lama on the Sciences of the Mind*. Boston: Shambhala.
Heisenberg, Werner. 1958. *Physics and Philosophy*. New York: Harper & Row.
Hick, John. 1989. *An Interpretation of Religion: Human Responses to the Transcendent*. New Haven: Yale Univ. Press.
_____. 2006. *The New Frontier of Religion and Science: Religious Experience, Neuroscience, and the Transcendent*. New York: Palgrave.
Hood, Ralph W., Jr. 1997. "The Empirical Study of Mysticism." In Bernard Spika and Daniel N. McIntosh, eds., *The Psychology of Religion: Theoretical Approaches*, pp. 222-32. Boulder, Colo.: Westview Press.
_____. 2002. "The Mystical Self: Lost and Found." *The International Journal for the Psychology of Religion* 12 (no. 1): 1-14.
Horgan, John. 2002. "Between Science and Spirituality." *The Chronicle of Higher Education* 49 (November 29): B7.
_____. 2003. *Rational Mysticism: Dispatches from the Border Between Science and Spirituality*. Boston/New York: Houghton Mifflin.

Houshmand, Zara, Robert B. Livingstone, and B. Alan Wallace, eds. 1999. *Consciousness at the Crossroads: Conversations with the Dalai Lama on Brain Science and Buddhism.* Ithaca, N.Y.: Snow Lion Publications.

Huff, Toby E. 1993. *The Rise of Early Modern Science: Islam, China, and the West.* Cambridge: Cambridge Univ. Press.

Hull, David. 1992. "The God of the Galapagos." *Nature* 352 (8 August): 486.

Huston, Tom. 2004. "Taking the Quantum Leap . . . Too Far?" *What is Enlightenment?* 27 (October-December). http://www.wie.org/j27/what-the-bleep.asp.

Hutcheon, Pat Duffy. 1996/97. "Science and Mysticism: Are They Compatible?" *Humanist in Canada* 115 (Winter): 20-24.

Jacobson, Nolan Pliny. 1986. *Understanding Buddhism.* Carbondale/Edwardsville: Southern Illinois Univ. Press.

James, William. 1958. *The Varieties of Religious Experience: A Study of Human Nature.* New York: New American Library.

Jammer, Max. 1999. *Einstein and Religion: Physics and Theology.* Princeton: Princeton Univ. Press.

Jantzen, Grace M. 1989. "'Where Two Are to Become One': Mysticism and Monism." In Geoffrey Vesey, ed., *The Philosophy in Christianity*, pp. 147-66. Cambridge: Cambridge Univ. Press.

Jayatilleke, K. N. 1984. "Buddhism and the Scientific Revolution." In Buddhadasa P. Kirtisinghe, ed., *Buddhism and Science*, pp. 8-16. Delhi: Motital Banarsidass.

Jaynes, Julian. 1990. *The Origin of Consciousness in the Breakdown of the Bicameral Mind.* Boston: Houghton Mifflin.

Jinpa, Thupten. 2003. "Science as an Ally or a Rival Philosophy? Tibetan Buddhist Thinkers' Engagement with Modern Science." In B. Alan Wallace, ed., *Buddhism and Science: Breaking New Ground*, pp. 71-85. New York: Columbia Univ. Press.

_____. 2012. "Buddhism and Science: How Far Can the Dialogue Proceed?" *Zygon* 45 (*December*): 871-82.

Jones, Richard H. 1986. *Science and Mysticism: A Comparative Study of Western Natural Science, Theravāda Buddhism, and Advaita Vedānta.* Lewisburg, Pa.: Bucknell Univ. Press. (Paperback ed., BookSurge, 2008.)

_____. 1993. *Mysticism Examined: Philosophical Inquiries into Mysticism.* Albany: State Univ. of New York Press.

_____. 2000. *Reductionism: Analysis and the Fullness of Reality.* Lewisburg, Pa.: Bucknell Univ. Press.

_____. 2004. *Mysticism and Morality: A New Look at Old Questions.* Lanham, Md.: Lexington Books.

_____. 2009. *Curing The Philosopher's Disease: Reinstating Mystery in the Heart of Philosophy.* Lanham, Md.: Univ. Press of America.

_____. 2010. *Nagarjuna: Buddhism's Most Important Philosopher.* New York: Jackson Square Books/Createspace.

_____. 2011. *For the Glory of God: Positive and Negative Roles of Christian Doctrines in the Rise and Development of Modern Science, vol. 1: The Dependency Thesis and Control Beliefs.* Lanham, Md.: Univ. Press of America.

_____. 2012. *For the Glory of God: Positive and Negative Roles of Christian Doctrines in the Rise and Development of Modern Science, vol. 2: The History of Christian Ideas and Control Beliefs in Science.* Lanham, Md.: Univ. Press of America.

_____. 2013. *Analysis and the Fullness of Reality: An Introduction to Reductionism & Emergence.* New York: Jackson Square Books/Createspace.

_____. Forthcoming. *Philosophy of Mysticism: Raids on the Ineffable.*
Josephson, Brian D. 1987. "Physics and Spirituality: The Next Grand Unification." *Physics Education* 22 (January): 15-19.
Kasulis, Thomas P. 1995. "Sushi, Science, and Spirituality: Modern Japanese Philosophy and its Views of Western Science." *Philosophy East & West* 45 (April): 227-48.
Katz, Steven T., ed. 1978. *Mysticism and Philosophical Analysis.* New York: Oxford Univ. Press.
_____. 1983. *Mysticism and Religious Traditions.* New York: Oxford Univ. Press.
Kim, Yung Sik. 1985. "Some Reflections on Science and Religion in Traditional China." *Journal of the Korean History of Science Society* 7 (no. 1): 40-49.
King, Ursula. 1980. *Towards a New Mysticism: Teilhard de Chardin and Eastern Religions.* London: Collins.
_____. 1983. "Modern Cosmology and Eastern Thought, Especially Hinduism. Some Brief Bibliographical Considerations." In David Tracy and Nicholas Lash, eds., *Cosmology and Theology*, pp. 76-83. New York: Seabury Press.
Kirtisinghe, Buddhadasa P., ed. 1984. *Buddhism and Science.* Delhi: Motital Banarsidass.
_____. 1984a. "The Universe and Cosmology." In Buddhadasa P. Kirtisinghe, ed., *Buddhism and Science*, pp. 85-88. Delhi: Motital Banarsidass.
_____. 1984b. "Galaxies and Śūnyatā." In Buddhadasa P. Kirtisinghe, ed., *Buddhism and Science*, pp. 89-91. Delhi: Motital Banarsidass.
Kohl, Christian Thomas. 2007. "Buddhism and Quantum Physics: A Strange Parallelism of Two Concepts of Reality." *Contemporary Buddhism* 8 (May): 69-82.
Kraft, James and David Basinger, eds. 2008. *Religious Tolerance Through Humility: Thinking with Philip Quinn.* Burlington, Vt.: Ashgate.
Kripal, Jeffrey J. 2002. "Seeing Inside and Outside the Goddess: The Mystical and Ethical in the Teachings of Ramakrishna and Vivekananda." In Barnard, G. William and Jeffrey Kripal, eds., *Crossing Boundaries: Essays on the Ethical Status of Mysticism*, pp. 230-64. New York: Seven Bridges Press.
Lam, Harry Chi-sing. 2008. *The Zen in Modern Cosmology.* Hackensack: World Scientific.
Lancaster, Brian L. 2004. *Approaches to Consciousness: The Marriage of Science and Mysticism.* New York: Palgrave Macmillan.
Langer, Ellen J. 1989. *Mindfulness.* Reading, Mass.: Addison-Wesley.
Larson, Edward J. and Larry Witham. 1999. "Scientists and Religion in America." *Scientific America* 281 (September): 88-93.
Laszlo, Ervin. 2004. *Science and the Akashic Field: An Integral Theory of Everything.* Rochester, Vt.: Inner Traditions.
Lopez, Donald S., Jr. 2008. *Buddhism and Science: A Guide for the Perplexed.* Chicago: Univ. of Chicago.
Lorimer, David, ed. 1999. "Introduction: From Experiment to Experience." *The Spirit of Science: From Experiment to Experience*, pp. 17-29. New York: Continuum.
Lutz, Antoine, Lawrence L. Greischar, Nancy B. Rawlings, Matthieu Ricard, and Richard J. Davidson. 2004. "Long-Term Meditators Self-Induce High-Amplitude Gamma Synchrony During Mental Practice." *Proceedings of the National Academy of Sciences* 101: 16369-73.
Macy, Joanna. 1991. *Mutual Causation in Buddhism and General Systems Theory—The Dharma of Natural Systems.* Albany: State Univ. of New York.
Malin, Shimon. 2001. *Nature Loves to Hide: Quantum Physics and the Nature of Reality, A Western Perspective.* New York: Oxford Univ. Press.

Mansfield, Victor N. 1976. Review of Fritjof Capra's *The Tao of Physics*. *Physics Today* 29 (August): 56.
_____. 1989. "Mādhyamika Buddhism and Quantum Mechanics: Beginning a Dialogue." *International Philosophical Quarterly* 29 (September): 371-91.
_____. 2003. "Time and Impermanence in Middle Way Buddhism and Modern Physics." In B. Alan Wallace, ed., *Buddhism and Science: Breaking New Ground*, pp. 305-21. New York: Columbia Univ. Press.
_____. 2008. *Tibetan Buddhism & Modern Physics: Toward a Union of Love and Knowledge*. West Conshohocken, Pa.: Templeton Foundation Press.
Marshall, Paul. 2005. *Mystical Encounters with the Natural World: Experiences and Explanations*. New York: Oxford Univ. Press.
Martin, Michael. 1990. *Atheism: A Philosophical Justification*. Philadelphia: Temple Univ. Press.
Matt, Donald C. 2005. "Kabbalah and Contemporary Cosmology: Discovering the Resonances." In James D. Proctor, ed., *Science, Religion, and the Human Experience*, pp. 129-42. New York: Oxford Univ. Press.
McFarlane, Thomas J., ed. 2002. *Einstein and Buddha: The Parallel Sayings*. Berkeley: Seastone.
McGinn, Bernard, ed. 2006. *The Essential Writings of Christian Mysticism*. New York: Random House.
McMahan, David L. 2004. "Modernity and the Early Discourse of Scientific Buddhism." *Journal of the American Academy of Religion* 72 (December): 897-933.
_____. 2008. *The Making of Buddhist Modernism*. New York: Oxford Univ. Press.
McMullin, Ernan. 1981a. "How Should Cosmology Relate to Theology?" In Arthur R. Peacocke, ed., *The Sciences and Theology in the Twentieth Century*, pp. 17-57. Notre Dame, Ind.: Univ. of Notre Dame Press.
_____. 1981b. "Is Philosophy Relevant to Cosmology?" *American Philosophical Quarterly* 18 (No. 2): 177-89.
McNeill, William H. 1970. Review of Joseph Needham's *The Grand Titration*. *Science* 167 (23 January): 367.
Mungello, David E. 1977. *Leibniz and Confucianism: The Search for Accord*. Honolulu: Univ. of Hawai'i Press.
Munitz, Milton K. 1965. *The Mystery of Existence: An Essay in Philosophical Cosmology*. New York: Appleton-Century-Crofts.
_____. 1986. *Cosmic Understanding: Philosophy and Science of the Universe*. Princeton: Princeton Univ. Press.
_____. 1990. *The Question of Reality*. Princeton: Princeton Univ. Press.
Nanda, Meera. 2003. *Prophets Facing Backward: Postmodern Critiques of Science and Hindu Nationalism in India*. New Brunswick, N.J.: Rutgers Univ. Press.
_____. 2003-2004. "Postmodernism, Hindu nationalism and 'Vedic science.'" *Frontline* 20 and 21 (December 20 and January 2).
Nasr, Seyyed Hossein. 1993. *The Need for a Sacred Science*. Albany: State Univ. of New York Press.
_____. 1999. "Spirituality and Science: Convergence or Divergence." In L. L. Mehrotra, ed., *Science, Spirituality and the Future: A Vision for the Twenty-first Century*, pp. 166-79. New Delhi: Mudrit.
Needham, Joseph. 1956. *Science and Civilization in China*, vol. 2. Cambridge: Cambridge Univ. Press.

Nelson, Lance E. 1996. "Living Liberation in Śankara and Classical Advaita: Sharing the Holy Waiting of God." In Andrew O. Fort and Patricia Y. Mumme, eds., *Living Liberation in Hindu Thought*, pp. 17-62. Albany: State Univ. of New York.

———. 1998. "The Dualism of Nondualism: Advaita Vedānta and the Irrelevance of Nature." In Lance E. Nelson, ed., *Purifying the Earthly Body of God: Religion and Ecology in Hindu India*, pp. 61-88. Albany: State Univ. of New York.

Newberg, Andrew, Eugene d'Aquili, and Vince Rause. 2002. *Why God Won't God Away: Brain Science and the Biology of Belief*. New York: Ballantine Books.

Newberg, Andrew B. and Bruce Y. Lee. 2005. "The Neuroscientific Study of Religious and Spiritual Phenomena: or Why God Doesn't Use Biostatistics." *Zygon* 40 (June): 469-89.

Newberg, Andrew and Mark Robert Waldman. 2009. *How God Changes Your Brain: Breakthrough Findings from a Leading Neuroscientist*. New York: Ballantine Books.

Nisbett, Richard E. 2003. *The Geography of Thought: How Asians and Westerners Think Differently . . . and Why*. New York: Free Press.

Nisker, Wes. 1998. *Buddha's Nature: Who We Really Are and Why This Matters*. London: Rider.

———. 2002. "Introduction." In Thomas J. McFarlane, ed., *Einstein and Buddha: The Parallel Sayings*, pp. vii-x. Berkeley: Seastone.

Papineau, David. 2002. "Prospects for the Scientific Study of Phenomenal Consciousness." In his *Thinking About Consciousness*, pp. 175-231. Oxford: Clarendon Press.

Payne, Richard K. 2002. "Buddhism and the Sciences: Historical Background, Contemporary Developments." In Ted Peters and Gaymon Bennett, eds., *Bridging Science and Religion*, pp. 153-172. London: SCM Press.

Penrose, Roger. 1994. *Shadows of the Mind: A Search for the Missing Science of Consciousness*. New York: Oxford Univ. Press.

Persinger, Michael A. 1987. *Neuropsychological Bases of God Beliefs*. New York: Praeger.

Peters, Frederic H. 1998. "Lucid Consciousness in Traditional Indian Psychology and Contemporary Neuro-Psychology." *Journal of Indian Psychology* 16 (January): 1-25.

———. 2000. "Neurophenomenology." *Method & Theory in the Study of Religion* 12 (no. 3): 379-415.

Phillips, Stephen H. 2001. "Could There be Mystical Evidence for a Nondual Brahman? A Causal Objection." *Philosophy East & West* 51 (October): 492-506.

Plantinga, Alvin. 2000. *Warranted Christian Belief*. Oxford: Oxford Univ. Press.

Plotnitsky, Arkady. 2003. "Mysteries Without Mysticism and Correlations Without Correlata: On Quantum Knowledge and Knowledge in General." *Foundations of Physics* 33 (November): 1649-89.

Price, Robert M. 2008. *Top Secret: The Truth Behind Today's Pop Mysticism*. Amherst, N.Y.: Prometheus Books.

Proudfoot, Wayne. 1985. *Religious Experience*. Berkeley: Univ. of California Press.

Pyysiäinen, Ilkka. 2006. "Does Meditation Swamp Working Memory?" *Behavioral and Brain Sciences* 29 (no. 6): 626-27.

Ramachandran, V. S. and Sandra Blakeslee. 1998. *Phantoms of the Brain: Probing the Mysteries of the Mind*. New York: William Morrow.

Raman, Varadaraja V. 2002a. "Traditional Hinduism and Modern Science." In Ted Peters and Gaymon Bennett, eds., *Bridging Science and Religion*, pp. 185-95. London: SCM Press.

———. 2002b. "Science and the Spiritual Vision: A Hindu Perspective." *Zygon* 37 (March): 83-94.

_____. 2008. "Variety in Mysticism and Parallels with Science." *Theology and Science* 6 (August): 273-86.

_____. 2012. "Hinduism and Science: Some Reflections." *Zygon*: 47 (September): 549-74.

Ramanna, Raja. 1999. "Divergence and Convergence of Science and Spirituality." In L. L. Mehrotra, ed., *Science, Spirituality and the Future: A Vision for the Twenty-first Century*, pp. 159-65. New Delhi: Mudrit.

Ratanakul, Pinit. 2002. "Buddhism: Allies or Enemies?" *Zygon* 37 (March): 115-120.

Ravindra, Ravi, ed. 1991. *Science and Spirit*. New York: Paragon House.

Redmond, Geoffrey P., ed. 1995-96. "Buddhism: Medicine, Science and Technology." *The Pacific World: The Journal of the Institute of Buddhist Studies* 11-12.

_____. 2008. *Science and Asian Spiritual Traditions*. Westport, Ct.: Greenwood Press.

Restivo, Sal. 1983. *Social Relations of Physics, Mysticism, and Mathematics: Studies in Social Structure, Interests, and Ideas*. Boston: D. Reidel.

Ricard, Matthieu. 2003. "On the Relevance of a Contemplative Science." In B. Alan Wallace, ed., *Buddhism and Science: Breaking New Ground*, pp. 261-79. New York: Columbia Univ. Press.

Ricard, Matthieu and Trinh Xuan Thuan. 2001. *The Quantum and the Lotus: A Journey to the Frontiers Where Science and Buddhism Meet*. New York: Crown Publishers.

Rosenblum, Bruce and Fred Kuttner. 2006. *Quantum Enigma: Physics Encounters Consciousness*. New York: Oxford Univ. Press.

Rothman, Tony and George Sudarshan. 1998. *Doubt and Certainty*. Reading, Mass.: Perseus Books.

Roy, Raja Ram Mohan. 1999. *Vedic Physics: Scientific Origin of Hinduism*. Toronto: Golden Egg Publishing.

Sadakata, Akira. 1997. *Buddhist Cosmology: Philosophy and Origins*, trans. Gaynor Sekimori. Tokyo: Kōsei Publishing.

Samartha, Stanley J. 1988. "The Cross and the Rainbow." In John Hick and Paul F. Knittner, eds., *The Myth of Christian Uniqueness: Toward a Pluralistic Theology of Religions*, pp. 69-88. Maryknoll, N.Y.: Orbis Books.

Sattler, Rolf. 1999. "Life Science and Spirituality." In L. L. Mehrotra, ed., *Science, Spirituality and the Future: A Vision for the Twenty-first Century*, pp. 151-58. New Delhi: Mudrit.

Saver, Jeffrey L. and John Rabin. 1997. "The Neural Substrates of Religious Experience." *Journal of Neuropsychiatry and Clinical Neurosciences* 9 (no. 3): 498-510.

Scerri, Eric R. 1989. "Eastern Mysticism and the Alleged Parallels with Physics." *American Journal of Physics* 57 (August): 687-92.

Schäfer, Lothar. 2008. "Nonempirical Reality: Transcending the Physical and Spiritual in the Order of One." *Zygon* 43 (September): 329-52.

Schmidt, Leigh Eric. 2003. "The Making of Modern 'Mysticism.'" *Journal of the American Academy of Religion* 71 (June): 273-302.

Schumacher John A. and Robert M. Anderson. 1979. "In Defense of Mystical Science." *Philosophy East & West* 29 (January): 73-90.

Sharpe, Kevin J. 1984. "Mysticism in Physics." In Kevin J. Sharpe and John M. Ker, eds., *Religion and Nature—With Charles Birch and Others*, pp. 43-51. Auckland: Univ. of Auckland Chaplaincy.

_____. 1993. *David Bohm's World: New Physics and New Religion*. Lewisburg, Pa.: Bucknell Univ. Press.

Shear, Jonathan. 2004. "Mysticism and Scientific Naturalism." *Sophia* 45 (no. 1): 83-99.

_____, ed. 2006. *The Experience of Meditation: Experts Introduce Major Traditions.* New York: Paragon House.
Shear, Jonathan and Ron Jevning. 1999. "Pure Consciousness: Scientific Exploration of Meditation Techniques." *Journal of Consciousness Studies* 6 (no. 2-3): 189-209.
Shermer, Michael. 2005. "Quantum Quackery." *Scientific American* 292 (January): 34.
Sivin, Nathan. 1970. Review of Joseph Needham's *The Grand Titration. Journal of Asian Studies* 30 (no. 4): 870-73.
_____. 1978. "On the Word 'Taoist' as a Source of Complexity. With Special Reference to the Relations of Science and Religion in Ancient China." *History of Religions* 17 (no. 3): 303-30.
_____. 1995. "Taoism and Science." In his *Medicine, Philosophy and Religion in Ancient China*, Part VII. Brookfield, Vt.: Variorum.
Skrbina, David. 2005. *Panpsychism in the West.* Cambridge: MIT Press.
Sloan, Richard P. 2006. *Blind Faith: The Unholy Alliance of Religion and Medicine.* New York: St. Martin's.
Smith, Huston. 2001. *Why Religion Matters: The Fate of the Human Spirit in an Age of Disbelief.* New York: HarperCollins.
Sorrell, Tom. 1994. *Scientism: Philosophy and the Infatuation of Science.* London: Routledge.
Spector, Marshall. 1990. "Mind, Matter, and Quantum Mechanics." In Patrick Grim, ed., *Philosophy of Science and the Occult*, pp. 326-49. Albany: State Univ. of New York Press.
Spencer, Robert F. 1984. "The Relation of Buddhism to Modern Science." In Buddhadasa P. Kirtisinghe, ed., *Buddhism and Science*, pp. 17-20. Delhi: Motital Banarsidass.
Staal, Frits. 1975. *Exploring Mysticism: A Methodological Essay.* Berkeley/Los Angles: Univ. of California Press.
Stanley, Matthew. 2007. *Practical Mystic: Religion, Science, and A. S. Eddington.* Chicago: Univ. of Chicago Press.
Stenger, Victor J. 1995. *The Unconscious Quantum: Metaphysics in Modern Physics and Cosmology.* Amherst, N.Y.: Prometheus Books.
Stevenson, Ian. 1987. *Children Who Remember Previous Lives : A Question of Reincarnation.* Charlottesville : Univ. Press of Virginia.
Stoeber, Michael F. 1994. *Theo-Monistic Mysticism: A Hindu-Christian Comparison.* New York: St. Martin's Press.
Studstill, Randall. 2005. *The Unity of Mystical Traditions: The Transformation of Consciousness in Tibetan and German Mysticism.* Boston: Brill.
Sullivan, Philip R. 1995. "Contentless Consciousness and Information-Processing Theories of the Mind." *Philosophy, Psychiatry & Psychology* 2 (March): 51-59.
Swinburne, Richard. 1991. *The Existence of God*, 2nd ed. Oxford: Clarendon Press.
Tart, Charles T. 2009. *The End of Materialism: How Evidence of the Paranormal is Bringing Science and Spirit Together.* Oakland, Ca.: Noetic Books.
Thompson, Evan. 2006. "Neurophenomenology and Contemplative Experience." In Philip Clayton and Zachary Simpson, eds., *The Oxford Handbook of Religion and Science*, pp. 226-35. Oxford: Oxford Univ. Press.
Thuan, Trinh Xuan. 2006. "Science and Buddhism: At the Crossroads." In Fraser Watts and Kevin Dutton, eds., *Why the Science and Religion Dialogue Matters: Voices from the International Society for Science and Religion*, pp. 101-19. Philadelphia: Templeton Foundation.

Thurman, Robert A. F. 2004. *Infinite Life: Awakening the Bliss Within.* New York: Riverhead Books.

Thurman, Robert A. F. and Stephen Batchelor. 1997. "Reincarnation: A Debate." *Tricycle* 6 (Summer): 24-27, 109-16.

Tillich, Paul. 1951. *Systematic Theology*, vol. 1. Chicago: Univ. of Chicago.

Trusted, Jennifer. 1991. *Physics and Metaphysics: Theories of Time and Space.* New York: Routledge.

Varela, Francisco J., Evan Thompson, and Eleanor Rosch. 1991. *The Embodied Mind: Cognitive Science and Human Experience.* Cambridge: MIT Press.

Verhoeven, Martin J. 2001. "Buddhism and Science: Probing the Boundaries of Faith and Reason." *Religion East and West* 1 (June): 77-97.

———. 2003. "Western Science, Eastern Spirit: Historical Reflections on the East/West Encounter." *Religion East and West* 3 (June): 27-57.

Wainwright, William G. 2005. "Mysticism and Morality." In his *Religion and Morality*, pp. 209-39. Burlington, Vt.: Ashgate.

Wallace, B. Alan. 1989. *Choosing Reality: A Contemplative View of Physics and the Mind.* Boston: Shambhala New Science Library.

———. 2000. *The Taboo of Subjectivity: Toward a New Science of Consciousness.* New York: Oxford Univ. Press.

———, ed. 2003. *Buddhism and Science: Breaking New Ground.* New York: Columbia Univ. Press.

———. 2006. "Buddhism and Science." In Philip Clayton and Zachary Simpson, eds., *The Oxford Handbook of Religion and Science*, pp. 24-40. Oxford: Oxford Univ. Press.

———. 2007. *Contemplative Science: Where Buddhism and Neuroscience Converge.* New York: Columbia Univ. Press.

———. 2009. *Mind in the Balance: Meditation in Science, Buddhism, and Christianity.* New York: Columbia Univ. Press.

Wallace, B. Alan and Brian Hodel. 2008. *Embracing Mind: The Common Ground of Science and Spirituality.* Boston: Shambhala.

Walsh, Roger. 1992. "Can Western Philosophers Understand Asian Philosophies?" In James Ogilvy, ed., *Revisioning Philosophy*, pp. 281-302. Albany: State Univ. of New York Press.

Walter, Katya McCall. 1996. *Tao of Chaos: Merging East and West.* Rockport, Mass.: Element.

Weber, Renée. 1986. *Dialogues with Scientists and Sages: The Search for Unity.* New York: Routledge & Kegan Paul.

Weinberg, Steven. 1992. *Dreams of a Final Theory.* New York: Pantheon.

———. 1996. "Sokal's Hoax." *New York Review of Books* 43 (August 8): 11-15.

Wertheim, Margaret. 2002. "Space and Spirit." In Clifford N. Matthews, Mary Evelyn Tucker, Philip Hefner, eds., *When Worlds Converge: What Science and Religion Tell Us About the Story of the Universe and Our Place in it*, pp. 187-206. Chicago and LaSalle, Il.: Open Court.

Wessels, Linda. 1989. "The Way the World Isn't: What the Bell Theorems Force Us to Give Up." In James T. Cushing and Ernan McMullin, eds., *Philosophical Consequences of Quantum Theory: Reflections on Bell's Theorem*, pp. 80-96. Notre Dame, Ind.: Univ. of Notre Dame.

West, Michael A., ed. 1987. *The Psychology of Meditation.* New York: Oxford Univ. Press.

Weyl, Hermann. 1932. *God and the Universe.* New Haven: Yale Univ. Press.

Wheeler, John Archibald. 1983. "Law without Law." In John A. Wheeler and Wojciech H. Zurek, eds., *Quantum Theory and Measurement*, pp. 182-213. Princeton: Princeton Univ. Press.

Wilber, Ken., ed. 1982. *The Holographic Paradigm and Other Paradoxes: Exploring the Leading Edge of Science*. Boulder: Shambhala Publications.

_____, ed. 1984. *Quantum Questions: Mystical Writings of the World's Great Physicists*. Boulder: Shambhala New Science Library.

_____. 1998. *The Marriage of Sense and Soul: Integrating Science and Religion*. New York: Broadway Books.

Wilson, Edward O. 1998. *Consilience: The Unity of Knowledge*. New York: Alfred A. Knopf.

Woit, Peter. 2006. *Not Even Wrong: The Failure of String Theory and the Continuing Challenge to Unify the Laws of Physics*. London: Jonathan Cape.

Wolf, Fred Alan. 1994. *The Dreaming Universe: A Mind-Expanding Journey into the Realm Where Psyche and Physics Meet*. New York: Simon & Schuster.

_____. 1996. *The Spiritual Universe: How Quantum Physics Proves the Existence of the Soul*. New York: Simon & Schuster.

Wright, Arthur F. 1957. Review of Joseph Needham's *Science and Civilization in China*, vol. 2. *American Historical Review* 62 (no. 4): 918-920.

Wulff, David M. 2000. "Mystical Experience." In Etzel Cardeña, Steven J. Lynn, and Stanley C. Krippner, *Varieties of Anomalous Experiences: Examining the Scientific Evidence*, pp. 397-440. Washington, D.C.: American Psychological Association.

Yandell, Keith E. 1993. *The Epistemology of Religious Experience*. New York: Cambridge Univ. Press.

Zajonc, Arthur, ed. 2004. *The New Physics and Cosmology: Dialogues with the Dalai Lama*. New York: Oxford Univ. Press.

_____. 2006. "Reflections on 'Investigating the Mind,' One Year Later." In Anne Harrington and Arthur Zajonc, eds., *The Dalai Lama at MIT*, pp. 219-41. Cambridge: Harvard Univ. Press.

Zohar, Danah and Ian Marshall. 1990. *The Quantum Self: A Revolutionary View of Human Nature and Consciousness Rooted in the New Physics*. London: Bloomsbury.

_____. 1993. *The Quantum Society: Mind, Physics and a New Social Vision*. London: Bloomsbury.

Zukav, Gary. 2001 [1977]. *The Dancing Wu Li Masters: An Overview of the New Physics*. Perennial Classics ed. New York: HarperCollins.

Index

Abhidharma, 13, 58, 59, 102-105, 159, 160, 170, 175n4, 175n15, 177, 182
Alston, William, 248, 254-57, 258, 258n1, 260n10
Angel, Leonard, 201n3
antireductionism, 110-11, 115, 276n4
Augustine, 260n8
Aurobindo Ghose, 54, 128, 183
Austin, James, 203
Ayer, A. J., 204

Bacon, Francis, 53, 68
Bagger, Matthew, 195-97
Barbour, Ian, 62n8
basic beliefs, 248-54
Batchelor, Stephen, 172
Beauregard, Mario, 90, 214, 225n12
beingness, 7-8, 10, 14, 19, 30-31, 41-43, 44-45, 46, 96-98, 183-89, 243
Benson, Herbert, 208, 224n9
Bernstein, Jeremy, 154
biology, 166-68, 171
Boehme, Jacob, 24
Bohm, David, 97, 107-108, 126
Bohr, Niels, 52, 75n10, 118, 142n5
Broad, C. D., 33
Brooke, John Hedley, 76n8
Bruno, Giordano, 155n4

Cabezón, José, 81, 156
Campbell, Colin, 173
Capra, Fritjof, iii, 49, 73, 75n10, 99, 100, 113, 115, 119n5, 139-40, 147, 152-53, 166, 181
Carus, Paul, 70
causation, 21n13, 65, 136-38, 160, 171

Chalmers, David, 87
Chandogya Upanishad, 11, 55-56
Chardin, Pierre Teilhard de, 54, 120n12, 183
Chari, C. T. K., 120n9
Chew, Geoffrey, 139
Chinese philosophy, 21n9, 59, 65-66, 68, 73, 74, 75n5, 130, 148
Chopra, Deepak, 109, 121n16
Christianity, iv, 32, 33, 52, 66-67, 68, 69, 72, 126, 130, 132, 140, 170, 172, 173, 176n12, 177n16, 201n2, 240, 241, 249-252, 254-56, 268, 274
Chu Hsi, 111
Cloud of Unknowing, 6
Coleridge, Samuel, 64
complementarity, nature of, 143, 150-52
consciousness, 5-11, 14-17, 25-26, 32, 50, 52, 56, 78, 80, 82-85, 85-89, 91nn5-6, 104-107, 124, 127, 130, 132-33, 135, 146, 161-63, 165-66, 168, 170-71, 180, 182-84, 193, 208, 209-10, 226, 227, 230-33, 243-44, 247, 262-64, 270-71
constructivism, 226-36, 245, 248
control beliefs, 170-73, 270
convergence, nature of, 143, 147-150
Conze, Edward, 62n9
Copenhagen interpretation, 142n5
Copernicus, Nicolas, 74, 180, 235n2
cosmology, 62n10, 64, 70, 163-66, 170
credulity, principle of, 217-18, 255

Dalai Lama (Tenzin Gyatso), iv, 11, 54, 103, 129, 168-69, 169-73
Daoism, 15, 20n9, 34, 57, 59, 66, 73, 74,

75n5
d'Aquili, Eugene, 79, 92n12, 224n10
Darwin, Charles, 116
Davies, Brian, 225n15
Davies, Paul, 196
Davis, Caroline Franks, 241
Dawkins, Richard, 198
Deikman, Arthur, 203
deists, 196, 201n2
Democritus, 108, 149
dependent arising, 125, 137-38, 167-68, 170, 173
depth-mystical experience, nature of, 14-16, 30-32
Descartes, René, 74, 176n13
Dewey, John, 194
Dharmakirti, 271
dharmas (elements of the experienced world), 58, 59, 102-103, 160, 175n4
dialogue, 155n2
Dignaga, 271
Dionysius the Areopagite, 244
Dogen, 28

Eckhart, Meister, 6, 15, 17, 26, 34, 35, 37, 175n2, 233, 241, 274
Eddington, Arthur, 70, 114, 116-17, 119, 153-54
Einstein, Albert, 51, 52, 71, 114, 116, 119, 125, 126, 134, 184, 259n5
emanation, 22n13, 22n16, 28-29, 32, 34, 39n4, 59, 68, 100, 105, 108-109, 129, 130, 162, 164, 180, 182
emergence, 39n4, 276n4
empiricism, 68, 91n9, 127, 131, 246-47, 259n5, 269
emptiness, 101-105, 158-59, 160
energy, 44, 45, 58, 59, 60-61, 100-101
Everett, Hugh, 126
evolution, 28, 39n4, 54, 166-67
exclusivism, 251-52, 259n8

Faraday, Michael, 51, 61n5
Fishacre, Richard, 39n8
Flanagan, Owen, 172
Francis of Assisi, 67
free will, 114, 122n19, 202n8

Galileo, 134, 225n15

Garden, Mary, 277n8
Gell-Mann, Murray, 149
Gellner, Ernest, 197
Gilbert, William, 74
Gimello, Robert, 229
Gödel, Kurt, 64
Gooding, David, 61n5, 64
Goswami, Amit, 105-107, 120n9, 120n11, 121n16
Graham, Loren, 52
Gray, Asa, 116
Greek philosophy and science, 65, 66, 155n4, 175n5
Grünbaum, Adolph, 101

al-Hallaj, 34
Hardy, Alister, 225n11
Harrison, Peter, iv
Hawking, Stephen, 50, 198
Heisenberg, Werner, 52, 63, 161
Heraclitus, 126, 184
Hick, John, 90, 221, 229, 235n1, 244
Hood, Ralph, 259n4
Hook, Sidney, 38n1
Horgan, John, 277
Hull, David, 116
Hume, David, 62n9, 217-18
Huxley, Aldous, 33, 38n3, 119n1

idealism, 72, 105, 106, 107, 120n11, 204, 216
Indra's net, 140
ineffability, 15, 28, 78, 233, 236n5, 243
Inge, Dean William, 153
intuitions, 51, 100
Islam, 27, 33, 65, 73, 75n9, 250

James, William, 4, 33, 211
Jayatilleke, K. N., 129
Jaynes, Julian, 225n14
Jeans, James, 33
Jinpa, Thupten, 90n4
John of the Cross, 21n12, 33, 36
Josephson, Brian, 50

Kabbala, 68, 118
Kantian philosophy, 21n11, 27-28, 62n9, 126-27, 228, 230, 232, 236n6, 244, 248

Kantor, Jean-Michel, 52
karma, 22n16, 43, 55, 58-59, 119n6, 125, 137, 160, 163, 165, 170, 177n17
Katz, Steven, 235n4
Kekelé, Friedrich August, 51
Kepler, Johannes, 68
Kim, Yung Sik, 64
King, Winston, 57
Kipling, Rudyard, 187
Krishnamurti, Jiddu, 107
Kuttner, Fred, 161, 175n7

Lam, Harry, 101
language, 9, 12, 18, 25, 44, 146, 267
Laszlo, Ervin, 135, 142n7
Law, William, 69
Leibniz, Gottfried, 38n3, 74, 76n12
levels of reality, 29, 96, 97, 97, 109-11, 113-14, 122n18
Lodge, Oliver, 62n10
Lopez, Donald, 169

Madhva, 27
Malin, Shimon, 129
Mansfield, Victor, 49, 96, 122nn20-21, 129, 138, 151, 154, 160, 166
Marshall, Ian, 175n2
Marshall, Paul, 20n10
mathematics, 52, 54, 64-65, 125, 127, 142n5, 150, 175n5, 220, 225n15
matter, 28, 32, 100, 102-105, 196, 108, 159, 162-63, 168, 170-71, 175n4
McFarlane, Thomas, 123
McMahan, David, 177n18
methodological naturalism, 198-99, 270
mindfulness, nature of, 9-13, 20n7
miracles, 199, 201n2, 202n8, 206, 218
More, Henry, 68
Mungello, David, 76n12
Munitz, Milton, 25, 44-45
mystical enlightenment, 16-19
mystical experiences, nature of, 5-7, 20n2, 98-99
mystical experiences, types of, 7-9
mystical knowledge, 5-7, 19, 22n16, 23-27, 33, 37, 44, 46, 49, 226-36, 237-48
mysticism, 4, 19n1, 20nn3-4, 41, 42-43, 63, 75nn3-4

Nagarjuna, 102, 103, 119n7, 137, 138, 158-59, 271
Nasr, Seyyed, 27, 28, 29
naturalism, 29, 60, 91n6, 117, 119n3, 122n22, 147, 162, 172, 173, 184, 191-200, 201n1, 202-31, 239, 249, 272, 275, 276n2, 277n5
near-death experiences, 90n8
Needham, Joseph, 66, 76n12
Nelson, Lance, 167
Neoplatonism, 27, 32, 34, 52, 59, 68, 129
Neumann, John von, 123
Newberg, Andrew, 79, 92n12, 224n10
Newton, Isaac, 68, 125, 142n4
Nicholas of Cusa, 73, 142n9
Nietzsche, Friedrich, 194
Nisbett, Richard, 174

objectivity, 14, 15, 53, 61n5, 84, 86, 88, 91n9, 127, 133
Occam's razor, 215-17, 225n13
Oppenheimer, J. Robert, 118
Owen, Richard, 75n4

panpsychism, 163, 176n8
pantheism, 32
paradox, 121n17, 146
parallels, nature of, 143, 144-47
Parfit, Derek, 184
Parmenides, 44, 149, 155n4
Payne, Richard, iv
perennial philosophy, 27-29, 140, 157, 173, 174, 182, 194
Persinger, Michael, 90
Plantinga, Alvin, 248-54, 258, 258n1, 259n8, 276n1
Plato's cave, 263, 268
Plotinus, 37, 129, 267
Poincaré, Henri, 51, 153
positive naturalistic explanations of mystical experiences, 193-94, 262
Prigogine, Ilya, 111
Ptolemy, 235n2

quantum mysticism, 112-15, 119n1

Rabi'a of Basra, 65
Rahula, Walpola, 48, 154
Ramachandra, V. S., 79

Ramakrishna, 202n4
Raman, Varadaraja, 54, 155n4
Ramanuja, 27
Ratanakul, Pinit, 131
rationality, 258n1, 260n10, 271
Ravindra, Ravi, 50
realism and antirealism, 12, 41, 91n6, 175n6, 199, 248, 255, 269
rebirth, 24, 59, 62n6, 163, 167, 172, 177n17, 247
Redmond, Geoffrey, 63
reductionism, 96, 110, 111-15, 117, 126, 198, 205-207, 227, 269
Rees, Martin, 71, 121n13
Reid, Thomas, 217-18
relativism, 196, 254, 257
religious diversity, 238-43, 251-54
religious naturalists, 201n2
Restivo, Sal, iii
Rosak, Theodore, 127
Rosenbaum, Bruce, 161, 175n7
Rothman, Tony, 70
Roy, Raja Ram Mohan, 155n3
Ryle, Gilbert, 114

Sadakata, Akira, 129, 177n15
Salam, Abdus, 76n9
Samkhya-Yoga, 32, 34, 35, 39n7, 56, 130, 162, 163, 182, 177n14, 264
Santayana, George, 63
Sattler, Rolf, 50
Schopenhauer, Arthur, 71
Schrödinger, Erwin, 51, 70, 113, 114, 118
Schuon, Fritjof, 38n3
science, nature of, 40, 41, 42-43, 68-69, 124-25, 197-200, 269-70
scientific explanations of mystical experiences, 205-214, 222nn1-3, 223n6, 238
scientific studies of meditators, 77-92
scientific worldview, 185n3, 198
scientism, 29, 140, 198, 202n7, 271
Searle, John, 134
Sellars, Wilfrid, 228
Sloan, Richard, 78
Smart, Ninian, 101, 241
Smith, Huston, 27, 29, 277n6
Smoot, George, 108-109
social implications, 115-18

sociocultural explanations, 222n1
space and space-time, 58, 68, 98-99,101-102, 107-109, 113, 120n11, 135, 137, 139, 141n3, 146, 159, 160, 181, 182, 193
Spinoza, Benedict, 126
spirituality, 38n1
Stenger, Victor, 117
structures, nature of, 40, 45-47
Sudarshan, George, 70
Sufi, 33, 48, 57, 65
Suzuki, D. T., 140, 141
systems theory, 179, 185n2

Tagore, Rabindranath, 52
Tart, Charles, 224n8
Teresa of Ávila, 232
Theologia Germanica, 67
thought experiments, 134
Thuan, Trinh Xuan, 133
Thurman, Robert, 75n6
Tillich, Paul, 68
time, 47, 99, 123, 163-66, 266-67, 141n3, 149, 155n4, 184
Transcendental Meditation, 8, 91n10
truth, levels of, 56, 62n7
Tsongkhapa, 99
Tu, Wei-ming, 115

union, mystical, 32-35
unknowing, 6, 20n6, 20n7, 25, 42, 47

Vedic science, 72-73, 76n11, 155n3, 176n12, 176n14
Vivekananda, 128, 141n2, 201n4

Wallace, B. Alan, iii, 21n8, 88, 91n9, 120n10, 146-47, 156, 168, 175n6, 247, 259n5
ways of life, 6, 23, 36-38, 38n1, 156-57
Weinberg, Steven, 71, 73, 118
Wells, H. G., 149
Wessels, Linda, 113
Weyl, Hermann, 64
Wheeler, John, 106, 121n13
Wigner, Eugene, 124, 225n15
Wilber, Ken, 70, 98, 112, 119n4
William of Occam, 215
Wilson, Edward O., 192, 198, 275

Wittgenstein, Ludwig, 44, 180, 257
Wolf, Fred Alan, 121n15
Wordsworth, William, 64
worldview, New Age, 178-84

yin/yang, 29, 151, 277n7
Yoga-sutras, 61n1

zero, 175n5
Zohar, 68
Zohar, Danah, 175n2
Zukav, Gary, iii, 141n1

Printed in Great Britain
by Amazon